Fandom and the Beatles

T0355268

Fandom and the Beatles

The Act You've Known for All These Years

Edited by

KENNETH WOMACK AND KIT O'TOOLE

OXFORD
UNIVERSITY PRESS

OXFORD
UNIVERSITY PRESS

Oxford University Press is a department of the University of Oxford. It furthers
the University's objective of excellence in research, scholarship, and education
by publishing worldwide. Oxford is a registered trade mark of Oxford University
Press in the UK and certain other countries.

Published in the United States of America by Oxford University Press
198 Madison Avenue, New York, NY 10016, United States of America.

Library of Congress Control Number: 2021930032

ISBN 978-0-19-091786-9 (pbk.)
ISBN 978-0-19-091785-2 (hbk.)

DOI: 10.1093/oso/9780190917852.001.0001

1 3 5 7 9 8 6 4 2

Paperback printed by Marquis, Canada
Hardback printed by Bridgeport National Bindery, Inc., United States of America

For Astrid Kirchherr (1938–2020),
Beatles Fan and Visionary

Contents

PART III. TOMORROW

Preface

Mark Lapidos

Believe it or not, the idea behind the longest-running Beatles festival began in, of all places, an ice cream parlor. It was a Saturday night, mid-November 1973, on the Upper East Side of New York City. Realizing that it was only a few short months until the tenth anniversary of the Beatles' legendary performance on the *Ed Sullivan Show* in February 1964, I felt that somebody ought to do something about it. As I contemplated a dish of vanilla ice cream, the word *Beatlefest* popped into my head. I knew that an event of that kind should be in a big Midtown hotel, with scads of Beatles-related events and fan-based activities.

The idea seemed so all-consuming that I didn't breathe a word about it for six weeks, when I finally broke down and shared the concept for a Beatlefest with a few friends and family members. Shortly after New Year's Day, I decided that it was time to proceed. Unfazed, I booked the weekend of September 7–8, 1974. While I knew that the time was right for a Beatles convention, I didn't feel it was right to make the festival a reality without the band members' support. In those days, the Fabs had gone solo—that is, when they weren't suing each other to dissolve their partnership. Unfazed, I booked the first weekend of September 1974 at the old Commodore Hotel on East 42nd Street. I was so confident that I paid a nonrefundable deposit with my own money.

But that turned out to be the easy part. At that point, I painstakingly sent a letter with an accompanying cassette recording to each Beatle, in which I shared with them my idea and asked for permission to hold the festival. Not surprisingly, I didn't receive a response back from any of them. But still, I wasn't discouraged. After all, I was young and determined to bring my dream to fruition. Undaunted, I placed an ad in a February issue of the *Village Voice*. The two-line, $14 notice read, "BEATLEFEST—Anyone interested?" along with my address. Within a few days, I received some 400 letters from fans in all walks of life. But they all had one thing in common: they were excited to be a part of a Beatles-themed celebration.

My biggest break yet came on Friday, April 26, when I heard a commercial on WABC radio. Legendary deejay Cousin Brucie announced that John Lennon and Harry Nilsson were going to be appearing at a March of Dimes event in the city on that very weekend. The Fifth Dimension was the musical headliner, and with the likes of Lennon in town, the event was sure to be packed. That Sunday was an unusually warm late April day, so I wore my brand new Beatles tenth-anniversary T-shirt, courtesy of Capitol Records. At the time, I worked as a manager for Sam Goody, the largest record chain in the country, and I outfitted my entire staff at the chain's Radio City location with the commemorative shirts that were exclusive to only my store, to mark the occasion.

When I arrived at Central Park that day, the lawn was already teeming with more than 100,000 fans, many of whom were there to catch a glimpse of Lennon. As I scanned the crowd, I noticed a guy wearing the same tenth-anniversary shirt that I had on. Making my way through the throng, I asked him how he'd gotten his hands on such a hot new item. He told me that he had been driving his pickup truck through Times Square the night before, when he happened upon two inebriated fellows sitting on the curb on 42nd Street. When he got out of his truck, he discovered that they were none other than John Lennon and Harry Nilsson. He offered to give them a lift, and they directed him to the Pierre Hotel over on Fifth Avenue, just across the street from Central Park. When he dropped the musicians off, Lennon invited him up to their suite, where he rewarded the guy with an autograph and one of the commemorative shirts. Without missing a beat, the guy volunteered Lennon's room number. I simply couldn't believe it: 100,000 fans overrunning the park, and I happened upon the one person who knew where Lennon was staying that weekend, and all because of that shirt!

My mission was suddenly clear. Biding my time, I caught Lennon, Nilsson, and Cousin Brucie's stage banter that afternoon, listening intently as they shared the good news about the March of Dimes and answered questions. With that, they left the stage and made their way out of the park. And so did I. Nonchalantly strolling over to the Pierre, I sat on a bench in the lobby just long enough to gather my nerves and confidence. After taking the elevator up to their floor, I took a deep breath and knocked on the door. Nilsson answered a few moments later, and I told him, "I'm Mark Lapidos, and I would like to speak to John about Beatlefest." Nilsson showed me into the parlor, and in short order, Lennon came out, and we shook hands. Sitting down in the hotel suite, I told him about my idea for a convention for Beatles fans. To mark the tenth anniversary, we would watch the Fabs' films, enjoy presentations by special guests and music experts, listen to live music, and buy and sell Beatles items. It would be something for everyone. Lennon gushed with excitement about the idea, exclaiming, "I'm all for it. I'm a Beatles fan, too!" I simply could not believe my good fortune. Not missing a beat, I asked Lennon to choose a charity for a raffle of special Beatles items. He picked the Phoenix House Foundation, a New York City drug-rehabilitation center. He even offered up an old guitar that he would sign and donate for the raffle. Before I left, he signed a piece of paper to mark his support for the festival and asked me to return a few days later to work out the details.

Etched in my mind to this very day, the entire visit had taken no more than twenty minutes. But the repercussions from that afternoon at the Pierre proved to be a seismic moment. Suddenly—with Lennon's explicit encouragement—everything had changed. More than 7,000 fans attended the inaugural Fest that September. The convention made the cover of *Rolling Stone* on October 24, 1974, and 46 years and 135 national Fests later, it is still going strong.

When I look back on the Fest now, I realize that we've created something lasting and special—an event that celebrates the Beatles' timeless music and, year after year, draws new folks into their incredible, affirmative, and life-changing story. As no less than Paul McCartney once said, the Beatles' songs aspire to a greater good, daring the world to embrace love, peace, and understanding. "It's all very 'All You Need Is Love' or John's 'Give Peace a Chance,'" McCartney said. "There was a good spirit behind it all, which I'm very proud of."

But just as important, I have come to understand the Fest's vital role in celebrating the idea of being a fan. After all, the Fest—from its humble beginnings—was created *by* fans *for* fans. Over the years, we've not only elevated the fan experience, but the Fest has acted as the birthplace for an evolving knowledge base associated with the Beatles. From that very first event back in September 1974, we have featured a parade of musicians and insiders that has included the likes of Mal Evans, Klaus Voormann, Mike McCartney, Cynthia Lennon, Pattie Boyd, Billy Preston, Donovan, Gerry Marsden, Billy J. Kramer, Astrid Kirchherr, Ronnie Spector, and Peter and Gordon, to name just a few. And the result has been, conservatively, the publication of several thousand works devoted to understanding the Beatles' indelible impact on musical culture and history. I am especially proud that the Fest has provided Beatles scholars with an ongoing event, held in different cities around the country, devoted to in-depth discussion about the Fabs and their unforgettable music.

The Fest has provided myself and my family with a front-row seat as we've watched successive generations of fans share their love for the Beatles. The book that you're holding in your hands documents fan culture as it relates to the Act You've Known for All These Years. And I'm humbled to think that my dream, hatched over a bowl of ice cream nearly 50 years ago, has played a part in making this kind of work possible.

Introduction

The Act You've Known for All These Years

Kit O'Toole and Kenneth Womack

One of John Lennon's most beloved compositions, "In My Life," both reflects and projects, visiting nostalgia but looking to the future. The narrator states that he will "never lose affection" for events and loved ones from his past, but their connotations change "when I think of love as something new."[1] Here nostalgia transforms meaning when applied to present events; the person's memories are not erased but are altered and perhaps given new meaning depending on the person's current position in life. The same can be said for fandom of any type, be it film, television, or music. Nostalgia is largely malleable, changing with future generations' experience and ever-evolving technology. The Beatles fan community is no exception. First-generation fans to millennials and beyond have expressed their devotion to their favorite band in different ways, contributing new knowledge and even creating new products that translate the band's lasting impact to the present.

Fandom and the Beatles: The Act You've Known for All These Years defines and explores fan response and the band's enduring appeal. The chapters in this volume study these unique qualities and the key ways in which this particular pop fusion has inspired such loyalty and multigenerational popularity. *Fandom and the Beatles* also explores the ways in which technology has shaped the band's legacy, introducing new listeners to its music through streaming services such as Spotify, Apple Music, and Tidal, and documentaries such as 2016's hugely successful Ron Howard film *The Beatles: Eight Days a Week—The Touring Years*. The band's enduring images and style, its musical skills and songwriting craftsmanship, the proliferation of Beatles lookalike and tribute bands, and the ways in which the group continues to impact our thinking about gender and sexuality all contribute to answering one question: why does this band inspire such particular devotion? Before

Kit O'Toole and Kenneth Womack, *Introduction* In: *Fandom and the Beatles.* Edited by: Kenneth Womack and Kit O'Toole, Oxford University Press (2021). © Oxford University Press. DOI: 10.1093/oso/9780190917852.003.0001 exploring the topic, a brief overview of fan studies places this text in the context of previous work.

Fan Studies Overview

Fan studies has grown along with fandom itself, particularly in defining the term *fandom*. The term eludes easy categorization, as it encapsulates several behaviors. Mark Duffett argues that key elements of music fandom have remained consistent: "a fascination with music, various romantic and folk ideologies, an emphasis on the star system, a tendency of fans to form social communities, to pursue shared concerns, and to follow characteristic practices."[2] Daniel Cavicchi proposes a description that may best summarize the various qualities one engages in to be considered a "fan." "Fandom is ... more of a process of distinction in which a fan must constantly question and monitor his or her experience, background, attitudes, and behaviors, relative to all the other people involved in any rock audience."[3] Ultimately, he concludes, the definition resides in "the *tension between* all of those relationships at any given moment. That is why fandom is so difficult to grasp. It is also why fandom is so central to understanding popular music."[4]

As Henry Jenkins notes in his article "Fan Studies," the history of fandom research has transformed from general to specific, defining fandom as its own culture. Jenkins defines fans as "individuals who maintain a passionate connection to popular media, assert their identity through their engagement with and mastery over its contents, and experience social affiliation around shared tastes and preferences."[5] Thus, fan cultures provide "social and cultural infrastructures that support fan activities and interests."[6] In Jenkins's *Textual Poachers*, he described the activities of *Star Trek* fans (primarily female), analyzing how they continued the show's legacy through writing their own stories.[7] Previous methods, such as the Birmingham cultural tradition, looked at larger effects on audiences, but today research further explores fans who have self-identified as fans of a particular television show, film, musician, game, or other media.

In addition, studies have transformed fan research from fan reception to what Jenkins terms "fan cultural production," a particularly important subject considering the emergence of digital technologies. Fans are no longer passive receptacles of an artist's product; rather, they create their own product inspired by the original source, whether it be art, fan fiction, podcasting, or other forms. Richard Mills addresses these issues in *The Beatles and Fandom: Sex, Death, and Progressive Nostalgia*.[8] The term *progressive nostalgia* summarizes the organization of this book, as it encompasses past, present, and future expressions of fandom.

It can be argued that rock music itself demands more participation than previous genres. According to Steven D. Stark, due to the post–World War II baby boom, "the percentage of young people in the culture was near a historical high. In turn, youth had formed their own subculture, and at the heart of that rebellious enclave was rock and roll music. In sum, rock music defined what it meant to be a teenager."[9] Fandom is, of course, nothing new; before the Beatles, other idols inciting hysteria included Benny Goodman, Frank Sinatra, and Elvis Presley.

Previous Fan "Manias": Goodman, Sinatra, and Presley

On March 3, 1937, Goodman played what he and his band assumed would be a typical gig at New York's Paramount Theater. To their surprise, more than 12,000 fans crammed into the venue. By the time they concluded the set with "Sing, Sing, Sing," the young audience had spilled into the aisles, onto the stage, anywhere they could find to dance and express their joy. The clapping, whistling, and stomping astounded Goodman, with the ecstatic audience reaction signaling two changes: the rise in swing music and the then-unprecedented uninhibited fan response. Instead of being "just another gig," the concert transitioned into "a kind of celebration of the spirit, a love feast of communal frenzy."[10]

Seven years later, a similar event occurred in, coincidentally, the Paramount Theater. Beginning at 3 a.m., teenage girls lined up at the box office to see their idol, Sinatra. More than 30,000 people gathered outside the theater, hoping to score tickets. Women swooned, overwhelming police officers and shocking adults with their seemingly insane behavior. "Who could have predicted that a throng of girls would smash windows, trample passersby, and even, according to one report, overturn a car?"[11] These young female fans, often called "bobby soxers," previewed fan hysteria to come.

In 1956, a new idol with considerable sex appeal emerged: Presley. His swagger and slightly dangerous image both enthralled teenagers and shocked older generations, although his first appearance on the *Ed Sullivan Show* on

September 6 attracted more than 60 million viewers. In later appearances, Sullivan famously only showed Presley from the waist up due to the singer's supposedly lewd gyrations. Despite these efforts, the screaming of excited teenage girls could not be drowned out. By the early 1960s, Presley had shifted his focus to film, unintentionally creating an opportunity for another act to capture fans' excitement and devotion.

First in Britain and then in Canada, the United States, and numerous other countries, the Beatles inspired unprecedented hysteria wherever they went. Unlike the fan adulation experienced by Presley, Sinatra, and Goodman, the "Beatlemania" phenomenon signaled a larger cultural shift. As Barbara Ehrenreich, Elizabeth Hess, and Gloria Jacobs state in their seminal work "Beatlemania: Girls Just Want to Have Fun," "Beatlemania was the first mass outburst of the sixties to feature women—in this case girls, who would not reach full adulthood until the seventies and the emergence of a genuinely political movement for women's liberation."[12]

Beatles Fandom History: First Generation

What distinguished Presley and the Beatles from previous idols was not only musical genre but also attitude. As Ehrenreich argues in her essay "Thawing Out" in Penelope Rowlands's *The Beatles Are Here! 50 Years after the Band Arrived in America, Writers, Musicians, and Other Fans Remember*, one word personified pre-rock teenage culture: *cool*, meaning "a kind of aloofness, emotional affectlessness, and a sense of superiority."[13] In contrast, rock music demanded "immediate and unguarded physical participation, thawed out the coolness, summoned the body into action, and blasted the mind out of the isolation and guardedness that had come to define the Western personality."[14] Indeed, this new participation immediately surfaced upon the Beatles' arrival in both the United Kingdom and the United States.

When the Beatles first landed on American shores in February 1964, teenagers across the country instantly reacted with great emotion and unprecedented hysteria. While this behavior may have bewildered parents in the States, British families had already been affected by this new phenomenon: Beatlemania. The Beatles would go on to become one of the most critically and commercially successful bands of all time, a symbol of the 1960s and its rapidly changing cultural and political landscape. John Muncie posits that the Beatles' greatest contribution to youth culture may have been Beatlemania itself, as "of all the social movements and cultural symbols of the 1960s, it was, at least, something that they could genuinely claim to be their own."[15]

Screaming fans not only reacted to the music—they became part of it, participants, particularly during concerts. As critic Geoffrey O'Brien writes in his memoir *Sonata for Jukebox: Pop Music, Memory, and the Imagined Life*, "to become involved with the Beatles, even as a fan among millions of others, carried with it the possibility of meddling with ferocious energies. Spectatorship here became participation. There were no longer to be any bystanders, only sharers."[16] Mark Kirkup posits that "the Beatles created the first modern pop mass fanbase, with the full power of the press, the record industry, television and radio. Even non-fans knew them, their story and their music, and the force of that fandom even had a name ('Beatlemania') that likened it to a disorder."[17] In the 1960s, not all critics found this new fandom beneficial; in the February 28, 1964, edition of *New Statesman*, Paul Johnson laments the chaotic experience of a Beatles concert: "The teenager comes not to hear but to participate in a ritual, a collective groveling to gods who are themselves blind and empty. . . . Here, indeed, is 'a new cultural movement': music which not only cannot be heard but does not need to be heard."[18]

In "Beatlemania," Ehrenreich, Hess, and Jacobs argue that the band also introduced a new era not only for teenage girls but for teenagers in general. Departing from the conservative 1950s, the 1960s ushered in new mores concerning sexuality and gender roles. The Beatles helped define this era, encouraging women to express their sexual selves more openly. However, their notion of marketing applies to both sexes, in that rock music has recognized how adolescent fans identify themselves as teenagers. Rather than just being a phase on the journey to adulthood, "it was a status to be proud of—emotionally and sexually complete unto itself. Rock 'n' roll was the most potent commodity to enter the teen consumer subculture."[19]

As *Beatlefan* executive editor Al Sussman recalls in his essay "The Communal Sgt. Pepper," 1967 teenage fans did not possess the tools present today for instant communication. The rock press was just emerging, and only small local fan clubs (consisting chiefly of women) existed. The release of *Sgt. Pepper's Lonely Hearts Club Band*, however, bonded Beatles fans in a new way. "That weekend became a very communal experience for Beatles fans of all ages throughout the world. Getting to know this monumental, ground-breaking record and the package around it was somehow different than the introductory process for any previous Beatles album. And I, like millions of others, knew I was not alone," Sussman writes.[20]

Another way first-generation fans networked was through *Beatles Monthly*, the official fan-club publication. While it began as a channel for the group to communicate with fans as an informational service, readers ultimately played a greater part in the magazine. As Kirkup explains, it soon transformed into "the voice of the fans themselves. Fans' opinions are the dominant feature of the original *Beatles Monthly*, with their delight, their fears, their humour, their obsessions and their fanaticism."[21] Overall, Kirkup concludes, in the current mass-media landscape, "audiences are saturated by every latest popular group/sound/dance routine/TV show/film franchise not only by the traditional media channels, but through media actually produced and distributed by fans themselves."[22]

Even after the Beatles' 1970 breakup, fans clearly feel a special connection to the group. As fan Art Murray told Garry Berman for Berman's book *"We're Going to See the Beatles!" An Oral History of Beatlemania as Told by Fans Who Were There*, "For me . . . the Beatles represented the true vanguard. What they did was more than just a musical statement. It had a lot to do with how you visualized how you were going to look, what you were going to do, what you're gonna think. For me, and for a lot of people like me, the Beatles represented models of a sort."[23]

Fandom Legacy

While enduring acts such as Bob Dylan, Bruce Springsteen, and the Rolling Stones have retained fans, they have not inspired the same fan expression. Their concerts continue to sell out, and dedicated Facebook groups allow fellow enthusiasts to network. Yet the Beatles' popularity has endured through international fan conventions, numerous tribute bands, and theatrical productions. Beatles courses have proliferated on college campuses, and new products such as box sets and even Beatles-themed movies such as *Yesterday* have racked up impressive sales. An April 2020 YouTube singalong screening of *Yellow Submarine* drew more than 70,000 viewers from around the world.

In *We're Going to See the Beatles!* Berman interviewed first-generation fans about how the Beatles impact their lives up to the present day. One interviewee, Paul Chasman, explained how the Beatles' influence extended beyond music.

"What I think maybe was the most significant to me about the Beatles was how much they grew and how much they always challenged the boundaries, and never seemed to be satisfied with where they were. They were always trying to grow and do something interesting and creative and exciting. To me, that was one of the most important models I had for how I wanted to live my life."[24]

Fan Carol Cox adds that in the 1960s, "the Beatles influenced every single thing that was going on at that point, especially if you were young. They influenced our way of thinking, the clothing they were wearing, guys grew their hair—you couldn't live through that era without being influenced by the Beatles. And whether you realized it or not, you were influenced by the Beatles. The Beatles are a part of me, and that's something that will always be."[25]

Through her study of first-generation fans, *Beatleness*, Candy Leonard concluded that they continue to find meaning in the Beatles' music. "Fans continue . . . approaching it with more life experience, wisdom, and maturity as they've grown older. . . . But because the Beatles have been so internalized, bringing them to mind or listening to their music doesn't necessarily recall the past. Rather, fans have carried the Beatles with them into the present."[26]

More than 50 years later, the Beatles are still attracting fans from various generations, all while retaining their original fan base from the 1960s. Why have those first-generation fans continued following the Beatles, and why are they now introducing their grandchildren to the group? Why are current teens affected by the band's music? And perhaps most important, how and why do the Beatles continue to resonate with successive generations? The Beatles continue to inspire fan conventions, fanzines, and academic conferences around the world. In addition, Beatles products consistently perform well in the marketplace, with releases such as the 2009 CD catalog remasters and box sets such as *Live at the BBC* and *The Beatles in Mono*. Surviving band members Paul McCartney and Ringo Starr continue playing sold-out concerts and releasing new albums. Even Cirque du Soleil has capitalized on the Beatles' enduring popularity with their hit Las Vegas production *Love*.

Another way the Beatles were introduced to younger generations was through the 2009 *The Beatles: Rock Band* video game. As Jaigris Hodson writes in "When I'm Sixty-Four: Beatles Rock Band and the Commodification of Nostalgia," "The Beatles are much more than just a musical group. They are Apple Corps. Ltd.'s only brand, and arguably one of the most well-known brands in the history of popular music."[27] The game not only presents a digitized representation of the band; it is what Hodson calls a "remediation of many different well-known multi-media interpretations of that group. It is based on several tropes that were developed and refined through albums, motion pictures, television shows, action figures, graphic novels, fan clubs, and of course the musicians themselves."[28]

Unlike other bands of their era, the Beatles have never descended into "nostalgia act" territory. Instead, even after the announcement of the band's breakup in 1970, the group has maintained its cultural and musical relevance. In her study of first-generation Beatles fans, Leonard disputes Lennon's assertion in tracks such as "God" that fans wanted the band to remain frozen in time. Instead, "watching and learning from their evolution was a key part of what made growing up with them so enriching and nurturing. But as fans grew with the Beatles, they came to cherish them and developed genuine feelings of protection toward them, as one would with family."[29]

In the decades since the Beatles' breakup, their image has undergone several transformations. In *Dreaming the Beatles*, Rob Sheffield describes how the Beatles' image and influence changed according to decades. The 1970s brought a sense of deprivation, a type of mourning concerning their breakup. By the 1980s, the Beatles were bound by a nostalgia surrounding psychedelia and hippie culture, represented in magazines such as *Rolling Stone*. It was the 1990s that brought a new relevance to the band's music, with the *Beatles Anthology* documentary (and accompanying CDs) attracting renewed attention to the group. The decade culminated in the surprise success of the *1* compilation, a collection that reintroduced the music to second-generation fans and their children. Sheffield argues that during this decade, the Beatles were untethered from 1960s symbolism. During the 1990s, "if for you rock and roll is about nostalgia, the Beatles are your best weapon. If for you rock and roll is the long, hard fight against nostalgia, the Beatles are also your best weapon."[30]

Their timeless quality appeals to younger generations while maintaining the loyalty of older fans. While the Beatles indeed represent a specific time period, their music and words address issues as meaningful today as they were during the Summer of Love: politics, war, sex, drugs, art, and creative liberation. As Richard Mills posits in chapter 9 of this volume, younger generations have engaged in what he terms "progressive nostalgia," or looking far back to look forward. These younger fans take a more active role in their shared passion by creating original art, re-editing YouTube videos, creating podcasts, and writing fan fiction. In other words, Mills states, millennial fans transform "the Beatles' songs, lyrics, and image and make them relevant to their own lives; they appropriate 1960s Beatles culture and refashion it into the web and weft of their own lives—recasting Beatles texts to give them a 21st-century spin."

Put another way, Stephanie Fremaux's notion of "DIY heritage" resembles progressive nostalgia, in that it involves creating a new cultural form and transmitting it to others using available resources.[31] In turn, this participatory culture has forever altered the dynamics between artist and audience. These developments have changed "the relationship between fans and artists as challenging previous theories of youth and music culture, in opening up forms of empowerment for the audience in relation to music stars."[32]

In "Revolution 2.0: Beatles Fan Scholarship in the Digital Age," Jeffrey Roessner states that progressive nostalgia also exists in what he terms "fan scholarship." Instead of simply recounting history, these researchers further the notion that "nostalgia also bridges gaps in time by hauling the past into the present."[33] He cites Peter Doggett's *You Never Give Me Your Money* as an example, explaining that the author's biography of the Beatles' post-breakup careers entices readers with the possibility of a reunion that will never happen. By illuminating a series of missed chance and writing in present tense, Doggett teases readers with an ending that they already know. Yet this technique retells this chapter in the Beatles story with a sense of urgency not present in traditional biographies.

Joli Jensen suggests that fans play an even bigger role in knowledge creation. "Online gathering, sharing, evaluating and displaying of individual and collective affection offers new evidence to support my . . . claim that fans can be understood as uncredentialed scholars."[34] Technology has further enabled fans to participate in creating knowledge; as David Beer and Roger Burrows explain, Web 2.0 (denoting a shift toward user-generated content) has enabled four interrelated types of activities: wikis (communal projects such as Wikipedia), folksonomies (archives searchable through keywords), mash-ups (combining two free-to-access data sources), and social networking sites (such as Facebook).[35] Applying these activities to Beatles fandom, enthusiasts have created sites such as the Beatles Bible, a repository for historical information, and social networking groups for every interest such as the "Beatles Book Collectors" Facebook group.

Book Organization

In studying the evolution of the Beatles fan community, *Fandom and the Beatles* is organized in three thematic sections: "Yesterday" (focusing on first-generation fans), "Today" (examining how gender, technology, and fan expressions such as fan fiction and tribute band concerts have further united multigenerational fans), and "Tomorrow" (exploring how millennial fans have continued transforming the band's legacy).

Part I. Yesterday

Candy Leonard's "Beatles Fandom: A De Facto Religion" (chapter 1) explores how fandom can resemble aspects of religion in terms of influences on people's lives and examines how cultural, social, and psychological processes inspire such devotion to the band. She further argues that fan studies should enhance understanding of how the fan experience can enrich lives, eliminating the stigma surrounding the stereotype of the "obsessive fan."

How has the Beatles' music stood the test of time and continued to attract new fans? Image plays a great part in marketing bands, and the Beatles' initial "moptop" label appealed to teenage fans in particular. Michael Frontani explains in "The Beatles and Their Fans: Image and the Media, October 1963–February 1964" (chapter 2) how the group was presented to British fans as "young, funny, smart, carefree, fun-loving, handsome (or cute), and hardworking." Their Liverpudlian roots and class ranking were also stressed; in contrast, these elements were de-emphasized for American audiences, their wild days in Hamburg largely scrubbed in favor of the witty, fashionable, fun-loving group presented when they arrived in New York in 1964.

Punch Shaw also describes how one's image transitions through time in "John Lennon as Pop-Cultural and Political Icon: Giving Peace a Chance" (chapter 3). He traces Lennon's evolution as a cultural and political symbol, his shortcomings as a person fading from public view as his position as a truth-teller endures. As Shaw points out, the artist's consistent message—peace—reverberates through multiple generations and remains one of his major contributions to culture.

Part II. Today

Through technology, fans have found new ways to connect and create their own expressions of their Beatles devotion. Kit O'Toole's "Magic Circles: The Fan Sites, Fanzines, and Festivals at the Heart of Beatles Fandom" (chapter 4) explores the revealing intersections among websites, magazines, and conventions as means for stimulating fandom and for activating fans in successive generations. First-generation and millennial fans are interviewed to determine how much social media, streaming, and sites such as YouTube have both maintained the interest of original fans and attracted newcomers. Jenkins's theory of participatory culture is applied specifically to how technology has impacted Beatles fandom in two forms: affiliation and expression.

Katie Kapurch's "The Beatles, Gender, and Sexuality: I Am He as You Are He as You Are Me" (chapter 5) reveals the complex gendered and sexual dynamics involved in the Beatles' continuing popularity. For example, when the Beatles' lyrics involve first-person narratives addressing longing and desire, they present what Kapurch terms "a range of gendered sexual subject-object positions with which both boys and girls could (and still can) identify."

From the stage show *Beatlemania* to groups such as the Fab Faux and American English, tribute shows ensure that the music will endure. Audiences indulge in two forms of nostalgia: remembering the music and experiencing a simulated version of a Beatles concert. Aviv Kammay explores the intricacies of this fan expression in "How Does It Feel to Be: Beatles Tribute Bands and the Fans Who Dream Them" (chapter 6). A member of the Wisconsin-based tribute band Madison Mystery Tour, Kammay discusses how the Beatles' images are frequently represented in such shows, how fan fantasies figure into performances, and how bands handle issues of musical accuracy.

Finally, another aspect of fan expression, fan fiction, is discussed in Mark Duffett's "A Hard Day's Write: Beatles Fanfic and the Quantum of Creativity" (chapter 7). Duffett studies the role of Beatles fan fiction as a means for expressing central aspects of fan identity, as well as a vital way by which Beatles fans establish a shared sense of community.

Part III. Tomorrow

How will future generations experience the Beatles? Kenneth L. Campbell explores that question in "The Beatles Today . . . and Tomorrow" (chapter 8), drawing from his experience teaching a Beatles course to first-year students. While teaching the class for more than a decade at Monmouth University, he has discovered that "the Beatles are not just part of the past to the students who take my course; the Beatles are part of *their* past." Indeed, millennials and future generations are as capable of experiencing nostalgia as first-generation fans are, but their nostalgia emanates from the ways they were introduced to the group—through their parents, films, video games, CDs, and streaming media.

As previously mentioned, Richard Mills's "Anthems of Whose Generation? The Beatles and the Millennials" (chapter 9) addresses the concept of progressive nostalgia and how younger generations have reinterpreted the Beatles' messages and music to fit their worldview, whether through forming tribute bands, writing fan fiction, creating fan videos, or participating in fan conventions. In general, he states, "millennial Beatles fans are a generation who want to appropriate the Beatles into their lives and make the band relevant to the here and now."

Finally, Michael Brocken's "Beatles Heritage Tourism in Liverpool: Standing at the Crossroads?" (chapter 10) discusses a lesser-known aspect of image and fandom: heritage tourism. Liverpool tourism has acted as a key entry point for fans to venerate the Beatles and to walk in their footsteps at sites that are central to their legend. The Beatles have been presented to visitors through museums and walking tours, but do these same methods appeal to younger fans? What changes can be made to ensure that interest in Beatles tourism will remain? In turn, Brocken addresses the ways in which such tourist practices contribute to fan practices and fan identity.

In an April 16, 1969, interview, a UK reporter asked George Harrison how he felt about Beatles fans at that time. "Their part in the play is equally important as ours," he replied. "We're acting out our scene as they are doing theirs. They're just as important as anyone."[36] Fans play an important part in a band's legacy: not only do they purchase the albums and attend concerts, but they help ensure that the group remains a presence in popular culture. Through networking and creating original works, multigenerational fans have kept the Beatles visible 50 years after the group's breakup. David Gauntlett in *Making Is Connecting* declares that technology has transformed culture from "sit back and be told" to "making and doing."[37]

As Mills states in chapter 9, this "unnostalgizing" or progressive nostalgia removes the Beatles from their 1960s contexts and remixes them for a contemporary cultural setting. Returning to "In My Life," the lyrics celebrate the past but welcome the present; in turn, the narrator reflects on how his present circumstances color his memories. He may fondly remember past places, friends, and lovers, but he concludes, "in my life, I love you more."[38] While he may not have realized it, Lennon explained progressive nostalgia perfectly and further provides a framework for this volume.

Notes

1. John Lennon and Paul McCartney, "In My Life," *Rubber Soul* (1965), EMI/Parlophone.
2. Mark Duffett, "Introduction," in *Popular Music Fandom: Identities, Roles and Practices*, ed. Mark Duffett (London: Routledge, 2014), 4.
3. Daniel Cavicchi, *Tramps Like Us: Music and Meaning among Springsteen Fans* (New York: Oxford University Press, 1998), 107.
4. Cavicchi, *Tramps Like Us*, 107.
5. Henry Jenkins, "Fan Studies," *Oxford Bibliographies* (2012), https://www.oxfordbibliographies.com/view/document/obo-9780199791286/obo-9780199791286-0027.xml.
6. Jenkins, "Fan Studies."
7. Henry Jenkins, *Textual Poachers: Television Fans and Participatory Culture* (New York: Routledge, 2013).
8. Richard Mills, *The Beatles and Fandom: Sex, Death, and Progressive Nostalgia* (New York: Bloomsbury Academic, 2019).
9. Steven D. Stark, *Meet the Beatles: A Cultural History of the Band That Shook Youth, Gender, and the World* (New York: HarperCollins, 2005).
10. Ross Firestone, *Swing, Swing, Swing: The Life and Times of Benny Goodman* (New York: W. W. Norton, 1993), 199.
11. "What Girls Want: Seventy Years of Pop Idols and Audiences," Perspectives on Media from the Paley Center for Media (updated 2009), https://www.paleycenter.org/what-girls-want-seventy-years-of-pop-idols-audiences.
12. Barbara Ehrenreich, Elizabeth Hess, and Gloria Jacobs, "Beatlemania: Girls Just Want to Have Fun," in *The Adoring Audience: Fan Culture and Popular Media*, ed. Lisa A. Lewis (New York: Routledge, 1992), 183.
13. Ehrenreich, "Thawing Out," in *The Beatles Are Here: 50 Years after the Band Arrived in America, Writers, Musicians, and Other Fans Remember*, ed. Penelope Rowlands (New York: Workman, 2014), 183.
14. Ehrenreich, "*Thawing Out*," 183.
15. John Muncie, "The Beatles and the Spectacle of Youth," in *The Beatles, Popular Music and Society: A Thousand Voices*, ed. Ian Inglis (London: Palgrave, 2000), 52.
16. Geoffrey O'Brien, *Sonata for Jukebox: Pop Music, Memory, and the Imagined Life* (New York: Counterpoint, 2004), 149.
17. Mike Kirkup, "'Some Kind of Innocence': The Beatles Monthly and the Fan Community," *Popular Music History* 9, no. 1 (2015): 77.

18. Paul Johnson, "The Menace of Beatleism," in *The Beatles Paperback Writer: 40 Years of Classic Writing*, ed. Mike Evans (London: Plexus, 2009), 105.
19. Ehrenreich, Hess, and Jacobs, "Beatlemania," 98.
20. Al Sussman, "The Communal Sgt. Pepper," in *The Beatles and Sgt. Pepper: A Fans' Perspective*, ed. Bruce Spizer (New Orleans: 498 Productions, 2017), 58.
21. Kirkup, " 'Some Kind of Innocence,' " 77.
22. Kirkup, " 'Some Kind of Innocence,' " 77.
23. Garry Berman, *"We're Going to See the Beatles!" An Oral History of Beatlemania as Told by the Fans Who Were There* (Santa Monica, CA: Santa Monica Press, 2008), 274.
24. Berman, *We're Going to See the Beatles*, 279.
25. Berman, *We're Going to See the Beatles*, 282.
26. Candy Leonard, *Beatleness: How the Beatles and Their Fans Remade the World* (New York: Arcade, 2014), 265.
27. Jaigris Hodson, "When I'm Sixty-Four: Beatles Rock Band and the Commodification of Nostalgia," *Journal of the Canadian Game Studies Association* 6, no. 10 (2012): 79.
28. Hodson, "When I'm Sixty-Four," 79.
29. Leonard, *Beatleness*, 209.
30. Rob Sheffield, *Dreaming the Beatles* (New York: HarperCollins, 2017), 302.
31. Stephanie Fremaux, "Coming Together: DIY Heritage and the Beatles," in *Preserving Popular Music Heritage: Do-It-Yourself, Do-It-Together*, ed. Sarah Baker (New York: Routledge, 2015).
32. Sofia Johansson, "Music as Part of Connectivity Culture," in *Streaming Music: Practices, Media, Cultures*, ed. Sofia Johansson, Ann Werner, Patrik Aker, and Gregory Goldenzwaig (New York: Routledge, 2018), 45.
33. Jeffrey Roessner, "Revolution 2.0: Beatles Fan Scholarship in the Digital Age," in *New Critical Perspectives on the Beatles: Things We Said Today*, ed. Kenneth Womack and Katie Kapurch (London: Palgrave Macmillan, 2016), 234.
34. Joli Jensen, "Afterword: Fans and Scholars: A Reassessment," in *Popular Music Fandom: Identities, Roles and Practices*, ed. Mark Duffett (London: Routledge, 2014), 208–209.
35. David Beer and Roger Burrows, "Sociology and, of and in Web 2.0: Some Initial Considerations," *Sociological Research Online* 12, no. 5 (2007), http://www.socresonline.org.uk/12/5/17.html.
36. Keith Badman, *The Beatles off the Record* (London: Omnibus, 2008).
37. David Gauntlett, *Making Is Connecting* (Malden, MA: Polity, 2011), 8.
38. Lennon and McCartney, "In My Life."

Bibliography

Badman, Keith. *The Beatles off the Record*. London: Omnibus, 2008.
Beer, David, and Roger Burrows. "Sociology and, of and in Web 2.0: Some Initial Considerations." *Sociological Research Online* 12, no. 5 (2007). http://www.socresonline.org.uk/12/5/17.html.

Berman, Garry. *"We're Going to See the Beatles!" An Oral History of Beatlemania as Told by the Fans Who Were There*. Santa Monica, CA: Santa Monica Press, 2008.

Cavicchi, Daniel. *Tramps Like Us: Music and Meaning among Springsteen Fans*. New York: Oxford University Press, 1998.

Duffett, Mark. "Introduction." In *Popular Music Fandom: Identities, Roles and Practices*, edited by Mark Duffett, 1–15. London: Routledge, 2014.

Ehrenreich, Barbara. "Thawing Out." In *The Beatles Are Here: 50 Years after the Band Arrived in America, Writers, Musicians, and Other Fans Remember*, edited by Penelope Rowlands, 183. New York: Workman, 2014.

Ehrenreich, Barbara, Elizabeth Hess, and Gloria Jacobs. "Beatlemania: Girls Just Want to Have Fun." In *The Adoring Audience: Fan Culture and Popular Media*, edited by Lisa A. Lewis, 83–106. New York: Routledge, 1992.

Firestone, Ross. *Swing, Swing, Swing: The Life and Times of Benny Goodman*. New York: W. W. Norton, 1993.

Fremaux, Stephanie. "Coming Together: DIY Heritage and the Beatles." In *Preserving Popular Music Heritage: Do-It-Yourself, Do-It-Together*, edited by Sarah Baker, 139–150. New York: Routledge, 2015.

Gauntlett, David. *Making Is Connecting*. Malden, MA: Polity, 2011.

Hodson, Jaigris. "When I'm Sixty-Four: Beatles Rock Band and the Commodification of Nostalgia." *Journal of the Canadian Game Studies Association* 6, no. 10 (2012): 71–90.

Jenkins, Henry. "Fan Studies." *Oxford Bibliographies*. 2012. https://www.oxfordbibliographies.com/view/document/obo-9780199791286/obo-9780199791286-0027.xml.

Jenkins, Henry. *Textual Poachers: Television Fans and Participatory Culture*. New York: Routledge, 2013.

Jensen, Joli. "Afterword: Fans and Scholars: A Reassessment." In *Popular Music Fandom: Identities, Roles and Practices*, edited by Mark Duffett, 207–234. London: Routledge, 2014.

Johansson, Sofia. "Music as Part of Connectivity Culture." In *Streaming Music: Practices, Media, Cultures*, edited by Sofia Johansson, Ann Werner, Patrick Åker, and Greg Goldenzwaig, 44–61. New York: Routledge, 2018.

Johnson, Paul. "The Menace of Beatlism." In *The Beatles Paperback Writer: 40 Years of Classic Writing*, edited by Mike Evans, 103–106. London: Plexus, 2009.

Kirkup, Mike. "'Some Kind of Innocence': The Beatles Monthly and the Fan Community." *Popular Music History* 9, no. 1 (2015): 64–78.

Lennon, John, and Paul McCartney. "In My Life." *Rubber Soul*, 1965, EMI/Parlophone.

Leonard, Candy. *Beatleness: How the Beatles and Their Fans Remade the World*. New York: Arcade, 2014.

Mills, Richard. *The Beatles and Fandom: Sex, Death, and Progressive Nostalgia*. New York: Bloomsbury Academic, 2019.

Muncie, John. "The Beatles and the Spectacle of Youth." In *The Beatles, Popular Music and Society: A Thousand Voices*, edited by Ian Inglis, 35–52. London: Palgrave, 2000.

O'Brien, Geoffrey. *Sonata for Jukebox: Pop Music, Memory, and the Imagined Life*. New York: Counterpoint, 2004.

Roessner, Jeffrey. "Revolution 2.0: Beatles Fan Scholarship in the Digital Age." In *New Critical Perspectives on the Beatles: Things We Said Today*, edited by Kenneth Womack and Katie Kapurch, 221–240. London: Palgrave Macmillan, 2016.

Sheffield, Rob. *Dreaming the Beatles*. New York: HarperCollins, 2017.

Stark, Steven D. *Meet the Beatles: A Cultural History of the Band That Shook Youth, Gender, and the World*. New York: HarperCollins, 2005.

Sussman, Al. "The Communal Sgt. Pepper." In *The Beatles and Sgt. Pepper: A Fans' Perspective*, edited by Bruce Spizer, 57–59. New Orleans: 498 Productions, 2017.

"What Girls Want: Seventy Years of Pop Idols and Audiences." Perspectives on Media from the Paley Center for Media. Updated 2009. https://web.archive.org/web/20100117010414/ https://www.paleycenter.org/what-girls-want-seventy-years-of-pop-idols-audiences.

PART I

YESTERDAY

1

Beatles Fandom

A De Facto Religion

Candy Leonard

The Beatles came from Liverpool. They did not descend from heaven with
a roll of thunder in a chariot of fire. But they did create an experience that
cannot be adequately described if we are afraid to think of the miraculous
or the divine. Words like "divine" are just metaphors in any case. They point
to something that can be experienced but not named.

—Nick Bromell, *Tomorrow Never Knows*

Introduction: Incredible Weirdness

The Beatles' emergence on the world stage was a grand cultural disrup-
tion, a joyful, epochal event. They captured the imaginations of millions of
young people across a 15-year age range—a huge swath of the population in
the West.

For seven years, they were a constant presence, dazzling fans with their
ever-changing sound, appearance, attitude, and nonstop deluge of new.
Several fans I interviewed for *Beatleness: How the Beatles and Their Fans
Remade the World* describe this experience as a "journey";[1] some say it was
"like a virus" or "brain rewiring."[2] The global siblinghood of Beatle fans, the
majority still in single digits in the early years of Beatlemania, paid very close
attention to what soon became a kind of other curriculum, parallel to what
they were learning in school.

Many first-generation fans say they feel blessed to have experienced the
Beatles in real time; some say they witnessed "a miracle."[3] The Beatles' ability
to elicit joy and elevate people of all ages, across cultures, for a half century
makes fans feel they are part of something larger than themselves.

The unlikely story of the four lads from Liverpool and their impact on
the world is especially ripe for myth-making. In his 1968 review of Hunter

Candy Leonard, *Beatles Fandom* In: *Fandom and the Beatles.* Edited by: Kenneth Womack and Kit O'Toole, Oxford
University Press (2021). © Oxford University Press. DOI: 10.1093/oso/9780190917852.003.0002

Davies's authorized biography of the Beatles, *Rolling Stone* founder and superfan Jann Wenner mused that no one talked about "the incredible weirdness of it."[4]

Early press coverage of Beatlemania didn't call it "weird" but routinely used religion-tinged language to describe the never-before-seen scale of pop-music fandom the world was witnessing. In the decades since, similar language has been used, reinforcing the perception, for three generations, that there is something about the very existence of the Beatles that requires further explanation—or defies explanation.

The uniqueness of the phenomenon and fans' feelings of joy and gratitude lead many to ascribe a spiritual component to the Beatles, and it's not uncommon to hear fans say, "The Beatles are like a religion to me."[5] While most don't mean this literally, this chapter will show how Beatles fandom serves a function in fans' lives similar to the function that religion serves in the lives of believers. Using a framework that synthesizes sociocultural and phenomenological analyses, I identify the processes that gave rise to this de facto religion.

This chapter is divided into five parts. The first part briefly reviews the arguments for and against comparing fandom to religion. The second part looks at the significance of the religionish thread that runs through the Beatles' historiography. The third part looks at the religion-like affordances of the first-generation fan experience, and the fourth part examines Beatle fan practices today. The final part discusses how Beatles fandom can be leveraged to enhance health and well-being.

A Broader Understanding of Religion

Many observers of pop culture phenomena have compared fandom to religion, and the practice is not without controversy. According to Mark Duffett, the comparison perpetuates an "ongoing joke . . . locating fans as misguided, irrational and servile zealots."[6] In this view, even sympathetic comparisons are "derogatory" and have been, in Duffett's view, used to "attack fandom."[7] This analysis is not intended as an attack on fandom or religion or on people who participate in either. Those who are discomfited by the comparison may be holding to the traditional Western model of organized, patriarchal, monotheistic religions. A broader understanding of religion and the religious impulse is required.

The comparison doesn't denigrate religion; to the contrary, it reveals religion's ongoing cultural presence and vital functions, albeit not in its traditional forms. As the West has become more secular and media consumption has become the primary leisure activity, media texts and popular culture have become the raw material for identity formation and the search for meaning. The human desire for the sacred and for transcendent experience has become disconnected from religious tradition and is "relocated" in media texts.[8]

The media have become the realm where important projects of "the self" take place, projects that include spiritual, transcendent, and deeply meaningful "work."[9] Thus, "there is now a substantial convergence between religion and popular culture."[10]

In 1967, sociologist Thomas Luckmann predicted the rise of "individual religiosity"—invisible or neo-religions—based on family and consumption experiences in the private sphere. Luckmann assumed these new forms would have no backing from public institutions.[11] (Interestingly, the de facto religion of Beatles fandom has always been, more or less, backed by public institutions.)

With regard to music, Rupert Till discusses the decline of institutional religion in the postmodern world and seeks to reclaim the term *cult* and the "glorious transgression" implied by its pejorative connotation. In a passage especially relevant to Beatles fandom, Till explains how popular music cultures fill needs once met by religion:

> Popular music cults and culture have enormously enriched our lives. . . . They have impacted upon the way we sustain relationships with one another, our spirituality, offering popular philosophy through its lyrics, and facilitating social interaction through dancing, concerts and mood and scene setting. Pop cults help disconnected postmodern individuals connect to one another and to their inner selves. They offer opportunities for self-loss, transcendental and mystical experiences.[12]

Similarly, in her study of Jimmy Buffett fans, known as Parrotheads, Julie J. Ingersoll writes, "Essential human needs for meaning, purpose, ritual, community, and 'transcendent experience' have been met in different ways in different societies" and that people will always find ways to fulfill those needs. She continues: "The Parrotheads who live in the secular world in which institutional religion has lost its cultural clout, and is imbued with skeptical cynicism about institutions generally, will create a sense of community where they find the necessary tools to do so"[13] (and Ingersoll's observation about the decline of church clout, that is, moral leadership, predates public knowledge that the Catholic church had been systematically protecting sexual predators for decades).

In *Traces of the Spirit: The Religious Dimensions of Popular Music*, Robin Sylvan writes that music subcultures provide everything that a traditional religion would, including "an encounter with the numinous."[14] About the Beatles, Sylvan said they had "a huge impact on planetary culture"[15] and that fan practices had "powerful but unconscious religious dimensions" due to the traces of West African spirituality in their music and because fans "deified" them and "engaged in what could be described as a form of worship."[16]

In *Tramps Like Us*, a study of Bruce Springsteen fandom, author Daniel Cavicchi says it's not that fandom is a religion but that both fandom and religion are addressing similar concerns in similar ways. He offers numerous examples, including this one, in which "The Beatles" could easily replace the word "Springsteen":

> Christianity and fandom . . . share a particular kind of moral orientation in which people derive meaning and value not from direct communication with the other but rather by signs and representations. Rather than devotion to God and interpretation of the Bible, its devotion is to the music of Springsteen and puzzling over how the music addresses their experience.[17]

Cavicchi shows that just as religion "stands aside from the rest of life and represents an alternative society based on the kingdom of God, fandom represents for fans a refuge from the turmoil of everyday life, an institution that exists above the ordinary and provides a steady and continual source of values, identity, and belonging."[18]

Fandom exists on a continuum, and based on my research with Beatle fans, it seems that any fans, anywhere on the continuum, can point to other fans they consider more "obsessed" than themselves and say, with humor and not in an unkind way, that some "make it a religion." But as Elvis Presley fandom researcher Erika Doss points out, "Humor, jokes, and derision are all forms of participation, ways of mocking and celebrating at the same time. Whether straight-faced or sarcastic about it being a religion, there lurks a real contemporary yearning for spiritual intensity and belonging."[19]

Doss defines religion as "those practices and attitudes that imbue a person's life with meaning by linking him or her to a transcendent reality: that which is beyond purely immanent, or secular experience and understanding."[20] As for defining fandom, Cavicchi suggests we think about it as "the creation of much-needed meaning in the daily lives of otherwise ordinary people, a way in which members of this modern media-driven society make sense of themselves and their relation to others."[21] Both of these definitions accurately describe Beatles fandom; a synthesis of these definitions provides a working definition of religion for this discussion.

In *The Gospel According to the Beatles*, Steve Turner writes, "The human instinct for fellowship, ritual, and worship hadn't disappeared. It merely sought a new focus, and the Beatles found themselves as the object of an unusual level of devotion. People expected from them the sort of guidance that had once come from the pulpits."[22]

Beatlemania was compared to earlier fan reaction to Franz Liszt, Rudolph Valentino, Frank Sinatra, and Elvis Presley, yet the grander scale of the frenzy was immediately apparent and utterly novel. Commentary about the Beatles included religious language from the beginning and continues to do so into the present.

Numinous Language

A religious thread runs through Beatles historiography, continually brought forth in widely read histories, of which there are hundreds. Cultural transmission to subsequent generations is a defining feature of religion, and the vast body of writings about the Beatles, read by fans of all ages and all degrees of fandom, is just one of the ways the religious meaning of the Beatles is culturally transmitted.

Reports in 1964 that parents brought sick and disabled children to Beatles concerts hoping the band could heal them were an early example of this religious thread. No entity had ever elicited this simultaneous, extreme reaction in so many people, and no one had ever witnessed anything like the worldwide, joyful frisson the Beatles caused. Bringing children to be healed was, in some way, a rational response to the fervor and power they were witnessing. Reporting on the presence of children who came to be healed amplified that perception, and "children were brought to the Beatles to be healed" became part of their story, part of their meaning.

Religionish language surrounded the Beatles even before the disabled children came on the scene. In March 1964, *Photoplay* editor Ken Ferguson's headline asked, "Are the Beatles a Religion?" Asked if he thought worship of the Beatles was unhealthy, Rev. Brian Bird replied, "In a sense they have become a religion." He observed that most young people no longer go to church and that Beatlemania was not merely mass hysteria but rather "a feeling of solidarity, of belonging, of security," and that they were providing what religion ought to provide: "an object of worship and a feeling of identity."[23]

In *Can't Buy Me Love*, Jonathan Gould notes that "the zeal of Beatlemaniacs" was compared to "that of religious devotees" and offers several examples of the religion-infused language surrounding early Beatlemania. In 1964, *Newsweek* said the Beatles were "a band of evangelists, whose gospel is fun." *Variety* wrote, "Lo! Beatles Descend from the Sky for Apotheosis in Frisco." Writing in the *Partisan Review*, albeit somewhat tongue-in-cheek, Jonathan Miller said that the Beatles "have become a religion in fact."[24]

Al Aronowitz, writing in the widely read *Saturday Evening Post*, quoted press agent Derek Taylor's reaction to the Beatles' reception in Australia, saying, "it was as if some savior had arrived and all these people were happy and relieved."[25] Observing the fervor, Rev. David Noebel, a Baptist minister, authored a pamphlet called *Communism, Hypnotism, and the Beatles*, warning of the need to protect children and the nation from the "four mop-headed anti-Christ beatniks."[26]

Three years later, former Harvard professor and early LSD evangelist Timothy Leary described the Beatles as "prototypes of evolutionary agents sent by God with a mysterious power to create a new species—a young race of laughing freemen. . . . They are the wisest, holiest, most effective avatars the human race has ever produced."[27] Leary may not have been the most authoritative commentator, but his remarks affirmed fans' perception that the Beatles were "heralding a whole new mode of style, thought, and action"[28] and affirmed fans' sense that they were witnessing and participating in an extraordinary historical event.

Turner makes the case that the Beatles were, in effect, shamans, and aspects of the relationship between the Beatles and their fans "were similar to those between shaman and ritual participant, or between guru and disciple. They were the enlightened ones that passed on their insights in three minute sermons."[29] The notion of musicians as spiritual leaders was unheard of in the West, though such figures could be found in other cultures. Turner notes that after the band's breakup, Lennon said, "The Beatles were a kind of religion," and Lennon saw music festivals of the late '60s as the formation of a new church.[30]

If there was a new church, the Beatles were recognized as its leaders. In *The Beatles: Image and the Media*, Michael Frontani shows how both emerging underground newspapers and mainstream media routinely described the Beatles as the leaders of the youth culture, from 1966 on.[31]

Further, the notion that the Beatles were ushering in a new era in the development of music *and* culture was both explicit and implicit in the pages of *Rolling Stone*, from the magazine's inception in November 1967.[32] This anointment of the Beatles affirmed fans' own feelings about them and the role they played in their lives.

The Beatles' trip to India for meditation study was widely covered at the time and continues to inform their religious aura. Philip Goldberg writes in *American Veda: How Indian Spirituality Changed the West, and* that the Maharishi Mahesh Yogi and meditation were broadly featured in the mainstream media upon the Beatles' return.[33] In addition, *Newsweek*'s year in review for 1968 included an article titled "What the Beatles Gave Science."[34] Goldberg credits the Beatles, especially Harrison, with bringing Eastern spiritual practices and music to the West.[35] The lasting impact of the Beatles' journey to India is also discussed in Wade Clark Roof's *A Generation of Seekers: The Spiritual Journeys of the Baby Boom Generation.*[36]

Religionish language and allusions to transcendence continue to be woven into more recent writings about the Beatles, perpetuating the perception of them as a religion-like phenomenon for new generations of readers. In *Magic Circles: The Beatles in Dream and History*, Devin McKinney writes:

> More than anything that has reached us through the medium of popular art . . . the Beatles became a religion. Kids, American kids especially, laded the Beatles with aspirations, the psychic fears and physical intensities which religion had traditionally sought to absorb. Kids knelt in prayer to the Beatles, erected shrines to them. At Beatles concerts these kids found a community of worship, in which many white teenagers experienced the nearest thing they would ever know to the mass ecstasy of the revival meeting.[37]

McKinney, born in 1966, writes with breezy authority that fans were described as "followers" by the late '60s and that "records were played in churchly environments," with "candles, incense, mystical chants" and "even sacramental wafers of LSD."[38] This caricature of how hippie fans engaged with the Beatles for the purpose of transcendence becomes part of the story and the Beatles' meaning.

According to McKinney, what made the Beatles "different from any other religion before or since" is that instead of trying to repress young people's anxieties and energies or direct them "in the service of a doctrine, they gave the fan free reign to explore them, intensify them, take them anywhere."[39] McKinney says the Beatles were from "the church of Do Your Own Thing"—another bit of '60s caricature—and that they "preached a faith of complete and open possibility that was by its very innocent nature a transcendent vision."[40]

Writing in 2014 about the momentum of Beatlemania and the band's "ecstatic affect" in *How Does It Feel? Elvis Presley, the Beatles, Bob Dylan, and the Philosophy of Rock and Roll*, Grant Maxwell says of the Beatles, "there was increasingly a sense that they possessed the kind of spiritual force usually attributed to prophets, saints, and shamans," and, quoting Bob Spitz's 2005 biography, he adds, "as if they gave off some special juju, as if they would make everything all right, which, in a sense, they actually did."[41] Among other examples of the religious discourse around the Beatles, Maxwell offers Spitz's observation that McCartney's talent "was at the service of some hidden energy."[42]

Commenting on Spitz, Gould, and others who wrote about the Beatles in numinous language, Maxwell contends these authors write with the "ironic distance" and "slight condescension" often used by "cultural elites," because the "plain truth" that "the Beatles were essentially a religious phenomenon" is "slightly distasteful to admit."[43] McKinney also employs ironic distance, for the same reason.

According to Maxwell, the Beatles were a "postmodern Trojan Horse for the return of affective knowledge," and the band knew that to be the case.[44] Consistent with Maxwell's observation, Turner writes that rock and roll was "about rediscovering primal urges and chipping away at the encrusted values of Western civilization" and communicated these values "through its spirit."[45]

In *Yeah! Yeah! Yeah! The Story of Pop Music from Bill Haley to Beyoncé*, a 2014 book that could be used as an academic text, author Bob Stanley says the Beatles gave the impression of "being in on some cosmic pop secret."[46] He devotes a chapter to them, ending with a question: "So why them?" Stanley concludes: "The only answer is that the Beatles were, literally, miraculous. They seemed to have some force protecting them."[47]

In 2017's *Into the Mystic: The Visionary and Ecstatic Roots of 1960s Rock and Roll*, Christopher Hill writes that the Beatles' music "sounded like good news" and that the band offered a "new-thing otherliness when they first emerged into the common consciousness."[48] This optimism explains much of the music's appeal for subsequent generations as well. Hill continues, "There was a pattern, from Romeo and Juliet to the Shangri-Las, that when love met the world it was doomed, but the Beatles' love didn't sound doomed. The whole unexpectedness of the Beatles made it feel as though this time we could start over and get it right."[49]

Frye Gaillard, in 2018's *A Hard Rain: America in the 1960s, Our Decade of Hope, Possibility, and Innocence Lost* quotes Gould's observations about the Beatles: "Like princes in a fairy tale, they seemed to awaken some great, slumbering need."[50] Talking about the Beatles' encounter with Cassius Clay (not yet Muhammad Ali) in 1964, Gaillard writes that they all seemed to have "a similar freshness of spirit, as if together they were part of something new that was essentially beyond their power to explain," and calls the Beatles "apostles of joy."[51]

Lennon's death, often referred to as an "assassination" rather than a "murder," shifts him from the "realm of stardom and aligns him with Christ, Gandhi, Martin Luther King Jr., and other heroes who had died for their principles,"[52] thus contributing to his ongoing iconic status. His mission to bring world peace through the possibilities of modern media had religious overtones, and many have observed that his death adds weight to ideas around the quasi-religious nature of the Beatles phenomenon.[53]

The numinous language permeating the Beatles' historiography is a cultural record reflecting fans' trust and devotion and the Beatles' ever-rising status throughout the '60s. Taking the fan perspective, the next section looks at selected moments from those years, offering a granular analysis of the cultural, social, and psychological processes that transformed young people into engaged, lifelong fans who would go on to share their reverence for the Beatles with others throughout their lives, sustaining the phenomenon.

Born at the Right Time

In *Tomorrow Never Knows*, Nick Bromell correctly observes that the significance of Beatlemania has been overlooked by a half century of (predominantly male) analysis, which "marvels" at its "orphic force" yet "condescends" to the girls who created it.[54] It was, after all, fan experiences and perceptions that created Beatlemania and established the foundation for everything that came later.

In this analysis, the "Beatlemania years" (1964–1966) were the period of *accruing* authority and fan trust; the "studio years" (late 1966–1970) were the period of *acting* on that authority as the acknowledged leaders of the counterculture. The transition between these periods occurred in the spring of 1966 with the release of "Nowhere Man" and the Jesus kerfuffle.

Two months after their appearance on the *Ed Sullivan Show*, the Beatles occupied the top five slots on the *Billboard* Hot 100 chart, creating an echo chamber. Often dismissed as insignificant relative to the Beatles' overall body of work, concentrated doses of these infectious songs had a profound effect on the intensity and trajectory of Beatles fandom.

Engaging with these five songs ("Can't Buy Me Love," "Twist and Shout," She Loves You," "I Want to Hold Your Hand," and "Please Please Me") within the context of the Beatles' wall-to-wall press coverage not only brought the pleasure of the music but, equally important, brought the pleasure of empowerment that came with being a knowledgeable participant in the larger cultural conversation about the Beatles. Hearing the recordings in German added global consciousness to nascent fan identity. From these earliest days of Beatlemania, baby boomers knew they were part of something bigger than themselves—and they were. They were part of a global siblinghood of Beatle celebrants.

Immersed in that April 1964 echo chamber and inseparable from their transistor radios, fans dialed between two or three local AM stations, seeking, finding, and engaging with Beatles music *constantly*. These early hits—high-energy explosions with compelling melodies and novel harmonies—became instantly familiar, activating the reward circuitry in the brains of preschoolers, college students, and everyone in between.

In addition to being heard repeatedly, these five songs—the longest barely more two and a half minutes long—include highly repetitive chunks of both musical syntax and lyrics, elements that make the songs especially engaging, to the point where listeners feel as if they are inhabiting the music.[55] One female fan, a child of 6 in 1964, said she was "hardwired for joy with the Beatles."[56]

Repetitive music invites physical participation, and fans danced and sang along, activating every part of their being. Sometimes alone but more often with friends and siblings in mixed age groups, the more fans listened and moved, the more they wanted to listen and move. These early hits became vital necessities, and fans came to trust the Beatles to provide them with satisfying, immersive experiences. Once trust was established, fans continued paying attention, even as the band's output required more work.

The process described above affirms Theodor Adorno's critique of pop music—that listeners are "manipulated into a system of response mechanisms wholly antagonistic to the ideal of individuality in a free, liberal society."[57] But over time, a complex system of fan responses emerged that was oppositional to the system from which it arose. In addition, as Henry Jenkins observed, songs don't lose meaning with repeated consumption but assume increased significance as listeners rework them according to their own interests.[58]

The Beatles' first film, A Hard Day's Night, was a key event in the band's accrual of authority and trust. Fans sat in rapt attention, watching the cooler-than-cool, larger-than-life Beatles cavort like living superheroes through a world of inept adults and dysfunctional systems. As a male fan age 12 at the time put it, the film "suggested a different way of being."[59]

A Hard Day's Night exceeded the expectations of film critics and thereby created delight, just as the Beatles had exceeded expectations and created delight at the Kennedy Airport press conference six months before. This recurring pattern—creating delight by exceeding expectations—fueled fans' ever-deepening gratitude and devotion. Critical response to A Hard Day's Night elevated the Beatles' cultural authority generally, including in the eyes of fans, who started paying even closer attention.

Discussions of rock music and religion often call on Émile Durkheim's notion of "effervescence," the energy that flows in both directions between a totem and participants in early religious rituals.[60] Every Beatles concert since 1962 could be described in this way, but the Beatles' power to assemble 55,000 people at Shea Stadium on August 15, 1965, and the resulting frenzy were on an entirely new scale.

The unprecedentedness of the Shea concert gives it a prominent place in the Beatles' story. The image of four bemused figures in tan jackets and black pants, looking up at the historic crowd as they dash across the field with their instruments, is an artifact that embodies the Beatles' power to elicit joy and bring people together on the grandest scale.

One of the arguments against equating fandom and religion is that fandom lacks "a central theology."[61] Thinking about "theology" a bit more broadly, this critique is easily dismissed in the case of the Beatles. Though the Beatles said they never intended to tell people how to live, a coherent philosophy can be found within their body of work. Based on my fan research and analysis of lyrical content, I've identified a core group of 12 songs from which a Beatles philosophy may be gleaned. Each will be discussed briefly below within the context in which fans encountered it.

The earliest song in this group, "We Can Work It Out," was released in December 1965, the same day as *Rubber Soul*, in the United States. Ostensibly about a romantic relationship, the song can also be heard as a plea for "we" humans to use our capacity for communication to move beyond discord and bring about a more loving world. With a sense of urgency, it suggests that we focus on that ultimate goal and not waste time on petty conflict. The song is a statement of optimism.

Rubber Soul's "The Word," another in the group of 12, is the first time the Beatles remove love from the pop song context entirely and advocate for love as a universal principle; it's also the first song Lennon and McCartney wrote together while high. Turner describes it as their first gospel song.[62]

In "The Word," Lennon invites fans to "say the word and be like me." The Beatles, with Lennon out front, announce they are "here to show everybody the light," explicitly positioning themselves as the spiritual leaders of the emerging youth movement and counterculture—a position the press would soon acknowledge. Every religious tradition espouses love, and now fans heard this familiar message proffered by their beloved Beatles, who were, as one fan put it, "starting to illuminate every part of our life."[63]

Another song in my group of 12, also on *Rubber Soul*, is Harrison's "Think for Yourself." There is irony, perhaps intended, in a song advocating independent thought coming right before a song asking the listener to "be like me." As with "We Can Work It Out," the song fits the heteronormative relationship schema that fans brought to pop music yet suggests a broader frame. The most repeated and salient element is a strong statement of principle: do what you want, go where you want, and think for yourself. Despite Harrison's miffed tone and the aggressive fuzz bass, the song is optimistic: the future is open with possibility, and mistakes of the past can be overcome.

"Nowhere Man," also in the core group, was a major departure from the band's previous 45s, and fans as young as ten at the time recall "trying to find meaning in the lyrics."[64] The song is preachy like "The Word," further defining the Beatles as, well, preachers. Turner points out that the song is "built like a sermon, with rhetorical flourishes similar to those used by vicars, reticent to cast the first stone at sinners, and that the nowhere man's root problem, blindness, also has "a biblical ring."[65]

The takeaway message from "Nowhere Man," according to a fan who was 18 at the time, was "you shouldn't miss out; you need to pay attention."[66] American philosopher Kenneth Burke called literature "equipment for living," because it offers wisdom and common sense that people use to guide their lives.[67] The same can be said about young people's relationship with pop music in general, but the Beatles were offering deluxe equipment.

Another song in this core group, "Rain," invited fans to reflect on reality and their ability to see it differently. Often considered the band's first psychedelic song, "Rain" has a simple, almost nursery rhyme quality, but even the youngest fans could feel the weight of other meanings as they were introduced to the concept of "state of mind." Lennon's emphatic "Can you hear me?" builds on the Beatles' claim, first made in "The Word," that they have special knowledge to share, and it goes further than "Nowhere Man" in setting up an "us versus them," with fans and the Beatles on one side and conventional thinkers or straight society on the other.

In the summer of '66, the Beatles entered what Ian Inglis calls their "men of ideas" stage, when interviewers spent increasingly more time asking about the band's views on issues of the day, such as the war in Vietnam, the decriminalization of marijuana, and the possibilities of religious exploration, and less time talking about their music.[68] This progression demonstrates the band's increasing cultural authority. In addition, the opinions they expressed would be embraced, or at least considered, by millions of young people around the world.

In July, less than a month before the start of their '66 tour, Lennon's casual observation about the declining popularity of the church—made during an interview with the *London Evening Standard* that March—was taken out of context and reprinted in *Datebook*, an American fan magazine. The takeaway, then and since, was that Lennon said the band was "more popular than Jesus." Conservative media in the Bible Belt seized on the opportunity to, as one fan put it, "knock Lennon and the Beatles down a peg."[69]

A fan in her late teens at the time recalls her minister talking about it: "He said the Beatles were a bad influence." As she saw it, "They were just free spirits who made you feel free and more like yourself."[70] Another remembers visiting family in Arkansas that summer who called Lennon "lowlife scum," but she thought he was right: "If you asked young people, 'would you rather go to church or a musical event,' what would they say? Come on. There's no question."[71] Another fan had a similar reaction: "Some of my friends didn't like it, but what he said was true. Would you stand in line for two days to take Communion? Of course not; but you'd stand in line for three days to see them."[72]

Whether or not fans liked or agreed with what they thought he said, or even if they were too young to grasp its significance, Lennon's ability to rile the establishment around a matter as weighty as religion made him a more powerful figure in fans' eyes.

Broader themes in their music, the Jesus kerfuffle, and the band explicitly expressing opposition to the war in Vietnam during interviews in the United Kingdom and the United States marked the end of Beatlemania. They had been accruing authority and trust for more than two years; now they would start acting on that authority. Sociologist Max Weber's notion of charismatic authority provides a good description of the Beatles from 1966 on:

> A certain quality of an individual personality by virtue of which he is set apart from ordinary men and treated as endowed with supernatural, su-perhuman, or at least specifically exceptional powers or qualities . . . not accessible to the ordinary person, but regarded as of divine origin or as ex-emplary, and on the basis of them the individual concerned is treated as a leader.[73]

The Beatles were charismatic authorities, leaders whose personalities, ap-pearance, words, music, and attitude elicited a range of emotions in fans. As the whole Beatles package became a more complex stimulus, or text, if you prefer, the emotions elicited also became more complex.

Recent research in psychology suggests that "interest" itself may be an emotion, and it seems especially useful for understanding fans' response to the Beatles as they evolved. Without getting too technical, interest comes from two appraisals: first, evaluating novelty, which is the degree to which a stimulus is perceived as new, surprising, mysterious, or obscure; second, evaluating complexity or comprehensibility. If people appraise an event as both new and comprehensible, they will find it interesting.[74]

Bromell's description of fans' response to *Revolver*, the band's clear foray into psychedelia released in the midst of the Jesus kerfuffle, offers a good ex-ample of interest as an emotion and how it intertwined with fans' feelings of trust:

As they gazed at Klaus Voormann's cover art—in which small photos and drawings of the Beatles emerge from the tangled, spaghetti-like hair of four larger renderings of the Beatles' heads—they heard music that required them to learn a new way of listening, to develop a new kind of taste. (Only the fact that the Beatles had already proven themselves could persuade their fans to make an effort so contradictory to pop culture's customary work of creating a familiar, frictionless world.) *Revolver* seemed to draw them out of the home of rock and take them somewhere else.[75]

Harrison's sonically novel "Love You To," on *Revolver*, another song in the core group, celebrates love and sex and cautions against allowing oneself to be defined by others (i.e., the establishment, straight society) and wasting time with needless drama. Consistent with the emerging Beatles philosophy, the song celebrates love at the micro and macro levels. It advocates thinking for yourself and the challenging task of figuring out who you are in a thoughtful, deliberate manner. These were big ideas for the teens who were listening and even bigger ideas for the huge proportion of the fan base who were children.

Most fans were not parsing lyrics, but what came through were cool (in the Marshall McLuhan, "low-def" sense of the word) ideas that invited play and tickled young brains. Fans found the Beatles endlessly fascinating. They became a presence in fans' homes, a presence at the dinner table, a focal point of daily existence. As one fan recalled, "You brushed your teeth, you went to the bathroom, you went to school, you listened to the Beatles."[76]

"Tomorrow Never Knows," also in the core group, celebrates alternative states of consciousness and other ways of knowing—more new, big ideas for most Beatle fans. The song is about the quest for transcendence—and you're invited. Songs such as this were too challenging for some fans; they didn't trigger their "interest emotion."

Six months after *Revolver*'s release, fans saw and heard the Beatles in full psychedelic splendor and facial hair for the first time in promotional films for "Strawberry Fields Forever" and "Penny Lane." Some younger fans were put off by the Beatles' new appearance, but a college-age fan at the time saw their look as "a statement that they were part of and sympathetic to the movement and hippie culture."[77]

These early '67 promo films were also the first time most fans saw what would become Lennon's signature glasses, a style often associated with literary interests, thinking professions, and intellectualism.[78] Thus, the viewer's overall impression was of older and wiser Beatles.

Sgt. Pepper's Lonely Hearts Club Band, released at the beginning of 1967's "Summer of Love," differed in many important ways from pop albums that came before, but for purposes of this discussion, the words on the back cover may be the most significant. Printed on a tangible, designed object, the lyrics took on the stable, fixed status of sacred text. Fans assumed the Beatles wanted them to follow along and think about the meaning. A fan, age 12 at the time, recalled, "By this point, everything they did was like it was handed down on golden tablets from on high." Another, then 17, remembered, "We trusted them; they seemed like good people, and they had an angelic quality."[79]

Radio DJs instructed fans to listen to the album in its entirety, which made it seem even more momentous and mysterious. One fan recalled, "no one on the cover was smiling and it suggested something vaguely negative and strange."[80] Another fan, age 10 at the time, expressed his trust in the Beatles, putting it this way: "It was like approaching something forbidden that I wasn't prepared for; something leading me into forbidden territory. But it was the Beatles and I knew that ultimately it would be a good place, based on my history with them."[81]

Fans had strong reactions to Harrison's "Within You Without You," another song in my group of 12. Drawing on principles from several religious traditions and picking up where "The Word" left off, Harrison preaches the transformative power of love and connectedness and shares his LSD-inspired realization that getting beyond your ego will bring peace of mind and a better world. Like "Nowhere Man" and "Rain," it asks fans to take a side: "Are you one of them," or are you with us?—that is, the Beatles and all they represented. Fans may not have caught all the Vedantic and Christian references, but the song made a strong impression. A male fan, not yet a teenager at the time, recalled, "It was like being in church and so you had to pay attention because it was important."[82]

Fans had been emulating the Beatles since the beginning, and many emulated their drug use as well. McCartney's LSD evangelism in *Life* magazine[83] gave fans something to consider: if the wise, talented, successful Beatles used drugs, maybe drugs weren't so bad. One fan, who was 17 at the time, recalled, "We saw drugs as assistance for spiritual enlightenment; we thought they were something good; cooler than alcohol; more peaceful."[84]

Three weeks after the release of *Sgt. Pepper*, the Beatles presented the world with "All You Need Is Love." Another song in the group of 12, it is inextricably associated with the Beatles' role as leaders of the counterculture and central to the band's meaning today. The song was written to be performed on the BBC's *Our World*, the first live international satellite broadcast, which was watched by an estimated 400 million people. With simple lyrics, a touch of humor, and a powerful message, the song is often a gateway into the Beatles for second- and third-generation fans.

When fans learned the Beatles had renounced drugs and were planning to travel to India to study mediation with the Maharishi, they looked at their Beatles and saw four young men, with all the money and fame they could ever want, searching for something more. Many younger fans remember thinking "it was all very exotic; part of their mystique."[85] Some fans, college-age at the time, knew people who meditated and understood more about it.

The Beatles' interest in meditation was a catalyst for decades of research into the practice and its widespread acceptance. But more pertinent to this discussion is that the Beatles were seekers, and they modeled seeking behavior for millions of young people around the world.

Fans, then and now, associate the Beatles with transcendent experiences and the search for them. As one fan, a teenager in '67, put it, "The Beatles made everyone think about aspiring to spiritual enlightenment,"[86] and this association remains for subsequent generations of fans.

The Beatles (White Album) was a sprawling collection that one fan described as "the Beatles challenging us with their weirdness."[87] One of the least weird tracks, "Blackbird," is among the 12 that convey a Beatles philosophy. It gently offers a powerful suggestion: seize the day, and find a way forward. It's about remaining hopeful and optimistic, and it's about faith in one's own agency. One of the most successful advertising campaigns in history, from Nike, said, "Just Do It"; the Beatles, decades earlier, had said, "You were only waiting for this moment to arise."

Another song in the group of 12 is the children's sing-along "All Together Now," written by McCartney during the latter part of the psychedelic period and heard twice in the film *Yellow Submarine*. The chorus promotes love and unity, and the verses reflect the hippie valorization of pure, childlike perceptions, which, like the LSD experience, are free of constraints imposed by society. Shortly after the film's release, several "Submarine Churches" appeared in the United States, preaching love, understanding, and social justice.[88]

In the fall of '69, a college radio station started a hoax that McCartney had been killed in a car crash three years earlier and had been replaced. The story, refuted by the Beatles' inner circle, persisted for two months and was discussed on the pages of the *New York Times, Life, Rolling Stone*, and other publications. Fans from 10 to 25, in grade school and grad school, in mixed age groups, scrutinized album covers and listened to songs, sometimes backward, searching for clues.

That the hoax was a significant moment in fans' Beatle journey is apparent in their still vivid memories. One fan, who was 8 at the time, recalled, "I was at a friend's house and her older brothers and sisters were talking about the rumor that Paul was dead, and playing the records backwards. They were having lunch; grilled cheese and chicken soup." And another fan, a 22-year-old college student at the time, said, "We played some songs backwards. We followed the clues. We didn't think he was dead, but it was fun."[89]

The Beatles provided rich, dense text; fans with good imaginations used that text to create meaning to fit an absurd narrative. Most didn't believe McCartney was dead, but the hoax provided an opportunity to engage communally with the Beatles' most enigmatic qualities—perhaps not a transcendent experience but deep engagement with something inexplicable. Each new generation of fans learns about the hoax and explores the clues. At its core, the hoax was, and is, consistent with fans' perceptions of the Beatles as mysterious and powerful—and playful.

Fans followed John Lennon and Yoko Ono's peace campaign with great interest—a compelling spin-off that tickled fans' Beatles-cultivated appreciation for spectacle. Lennon's appearance was Christlike and larger than life, as he towered over Ono by nine inches. Lennon understood that modern media and demographics had given him the largest platform any communicator ever had in the history of the world, and his identification with Jesus may have fueled his responsibility to use it for good. This identification was also expressed in the chorus of "The Ballad of John and Yoko," which once again asks fans to consider Lennon in a religionish, even if humorous, context. A male fan, 13 at the time, said, "Only Lennon would have the balls to sing about being Jesus and getting crucified."[90]

Fans "appreciated that they were using their position to call attention to something, rather than just being celebrities," and thought it was "brilliant." As one fan put it, "Anytime any Beatle breathed the world stopped and listened."[91] "Give Peace a Chance"—associated with Lennon but technically a Beatles song—is the final song in the group of 12.

Many fans said they were "devastated" by the April 1970 news of the Beatles' breakup. Their feelings of distress weren't about the music that would never be heard but were about losing a comforting presence that provided rich intellectual, emotional, aesthetic, and spiritual experiences that fans had come to rely on, which had nurtured them in a unique way for as long as they could remember. A male fan, 16 when they broke up, said, "We took comfort in knowing the Beatles were in the world."[92]

The Beatles philosophy contained in these 12 songs is a spiritual humanism that celebrates the ability of human beings to solve the problems of living and embraces the universal, transcendent principles of love and connectedness.[93] The Beatles were perfect Maslovians, exemplifying the principles of humanistic psychology as developed by Abraham Maslow, one of the founders of the Human Potential Movement that came to prominence in the early '60s.

Humanistic psychology emphasizes rationality, consciousness, and the realization of individual potential, or self-actualization. It's also concerned with experiences often ignored by mainstream psychology such as love, empathy, creativity, intuition, mystical experiences, and compassion. Self-actualized people (such as the Beatles) seek transcendent experiences and the actualization of universal human values.[94]

A key tenet of the Human Potential Movement was self-development: one cannot change the world but can change oneself.[95] This was the political philosophy Lennon expressed in "Revolution" that so angered the New Left in 1968.

Fans invested the Beatles with three kinds of authority: moral, spiritual, and aesthetic. As Bromell says in *Tomorrow Never Knows*: "They were musicians who were also prophets and healers. Their fans started to listen to them as if their music carried answers, pathways, wisdom."[96] This is still true, as one fan expressed on Facebook: "We listen to the boys pretty much every day in some shape or form and try to live out their messages of love, peace, togetherness, acceptance, humor, etc. I'm not sure that even the most religious/spiritual people could have as much devotion in their daily lives as a Beatle fan."[97]

Inside the Beatles Fan Community

The Beatles' continued global popularity and ubiquity rest on the historically unique relationship between the Beatles and first-generation fans, whose ongoing interest has sustained and solidified the fandom in several ways.

As children, teenagers, and young adults, they exposed younger siblings, neighbors, cousins, and friends to the Beatles, and they, too, became fans. As baby boomer fans began their working lives, many became writers, designers, musicians, educators, and therapists and found ways to reference the Beatles in their work. Also, fans talk about the Beatles often, thus "reminding" friends, family, and co-workers about the Beatles, often sparking new or dormant interest.

First-generation fans made a point of introducing the Beatles to their children, and now to grandchildren and great-grandchildren, much as a religious tradition is passed down through generations. The cultural authority the Beatles enjoyed throughout the '60s has morphed into reverence in the decades since. The *Beatles Anthology* series in the mid-'90s rekindled boomers' interest and created a new cohort of fans.

The psychedelic animation and Beatles music in *Yellow Submarine* appeal to children as young as 2, and the film, depicting the Beatles as superheroes, is often children's first encounter with them. *Yellow Submarine* merchandise reinforces interest in the film. The animated cartoon series *Beat Bugs* opens and closes with "All You Need Is Love" and offers preschoolers basic life lessons and two Beatles songs in each episode.[98] There is a growing number of books about the Beatles for children of all ages.

In fan families, children hear Beatles music and see Beatle items in their homes. They start to notice Beatles references in the media, or pictures of them hanging, randomly, at a local restaurant, or they notice someone at the grocery store in a Beatles T-shirt—and they realize the Beatles are important not only to their parents and grandparents but, apparently, to lots of people.

The story of the Beatles' rise to unprecedented fame from their humble Liverpool origins is well known, even by casual fans. Ripe for myth-making, their creation story includes lucky coincidence, lots of hard work, and persistence in the face of setbacks. Somehow, against all odds, the pieces fell into place. They emerged to enchant the multitudes, reach the "toppermost of the poppermost," and change the world.

The story is filled with supporting characters—Allan Williams, Bob Wooler, Bill Harry, Stu Sutcliffe, Brian Epstein, Neil Aspinall, Mal Evans, Pete Best, Mona Best, George Martin, and many others. Special places in Beatles lore are reserved for Ivan Vaughan, who is said to have introduced Lennon and McCartney, and Raymond Jones, who some say requested an early Beatles disc at Epstein's store. Epstein and Martin are also given greater importance, of course. Beatles parents, aunts, uncles, friends, girlfriends, and wives are also part of the story.

Certain action taken by these characters—such as Lennon's aunt, Mimi Smith, asking the headmaster at Quarry Bank High School to write the letter that got him into art school, or the Beatles winning Bill Harry's Mersey Beat music poll—are recalled as highly consequential. Fans never tire of engaging with the Beatles' creation story, offering commentary and exploring hypotheticals.

Every new Beatles history or biography, longer and more minutiae-filled than those that came before, holds the promise of new insights into how the Beatles came to be and new details about their personal and professional lives. Widely read books are discussed, and the facts therein become part of the mix for further discussion and trivia contests.

There are numerous Beatles-related Facebook groups with active participants from all over the world, where fans of all ages can discuss the Beatles 24/7. Fans share pictures of their Beatle rooms or tattoos to publicly express personal devotion and commitment. Some fans refer to their Beatle rooms as "shrines"––sacred spaces where fans find refuge from the stressors of daily life, surrounded by comforting images and objects imbued with private and shared meaning.

Posting Beatles content to social media expresses fans' love for and fascination with the Beatles, but, more important, it connects them with other fans. Posts that ask an engaging question or offer an interesting observation can elicit hundreds of comments in minutes.

Although most of these fans have never met or see one another once or twice a year at Beatles events, their shared love for the Beatles often becomes a basis for genuine friendship among people who might have little else in common. When someone becomes ill or shares the loss of a parent or a pet, fans in the group post heartfelt responses. The posters, appreciative of the support, thank their "Beatles family." One fan, a child of 7 when Beatlemania erupted, put it this way: "The Beatles have made my life joyous. My children listen to the Beatles, my home is filled with Beatles memorabilia as well as music. They taught me about love and kindness and how music can touch my heart. The internet has connected me to other fans and a world of new friends."[99]

Fans keep up with daily Beatles news in a variety of formats, including items such as planned releases of remastered material, new awards, chart positions, set lists from McCartney's and Starr's tours, and new books.

Beatles podcasts, hosted by fans of all ages, with varying degrees and kinds of Beatles knowledge, offer in-depth discussion and opinions. These activities keep the Beatles alive, confirm their importance, and thus affirm fan identity and energize the community.

Fans never tire of looking at their favorite Beatle images; never-before-seen images are especially appreciated. Their fresh, young faces reflect possibility and hope for the future, while providing continuity with the past and grounding in the present. The nonstop flow of images on social media from fans all over the world is a highly interactive celebration that never ends.

Fans display Beatle images in their homes for the same reasons people display family photos: the images elicit feelings of love, belonging, and gratitude and represent relationships that have been and continue to be profoundly meaningful. The images are comforting; a chance glance provides a momentary interlude. One fan talked about her Beatles decor as her "personal Feng Shui" and arranges her house so that she can see Beatles in any direction she looks.[100]

A 2016 report commissioned by Liverpool's mayor found that Beatles tourism generates £82 million annually for the city and is linked to 2,300 jobs. It's estimated that the Beatles-related economy grows between 5% and 15% each year, and it's assumed that the city will attract Beatles tourists long into the future.[101]

To actually see the shelter in the middle of the roundabout at Penny Lane or peek through the red gates at Strawberry Field is to revisit a mythic place seen countless times in the mind's eye. In that moment, while one stands where Lennon and McCartney stood, these mythic places become real yet even more mythic.

Seeing the Beatles' childhood homes is a similarly awe-inspiring experience, making fans feel both special and humbled. That these homes, some rather ordinary, are recognized as historic "blue plaque" sites further affirms the righteousness of fan devotion and rewards their journey. Fans come away with the sense that they know something they didn't know before and feel closer to the Beatles and to others who made the same trip. After reading about Lennon and McCartney listening to the radio in their bedrooms as teenagers, standing in those bedrooms is a profoundly moving experience.

There are numerous Beatles tourism sites in London, including the Asher home where McCartney had a room, the gardens where the "Rain" and "Paperback Writer" films were made, and Marylebone Station from the opening scenes of A Hard Day's Night. But the most important site is the zebra crosswalk where the *Abbey Road* album photo was taken. There's an EarthCam set up at the intersection, allowing fans to look at it anytime they want. Beatles tourism also extends to the Reeperbahn area of Hamburg, where the Beatles honed their craft.

Traveling to these sites, often at great expense, makes these familiar yet abstract places real; they become concrete—part of the built environment that can be touched. Crossing Abbey Road is thrilling because fans walk in the Beatles' footsteps and feel closer to them, their music, and everything they represent. As Jennifer Otter Bickerdike says in her study of pop-culture pilgrimages, it "creates a feeling of communion with the mediated figure."[102] Seeing other tourists from all over the world performing the same ritual adds to the sense of being part of something larger, even as it remains a very personal experience. The site's power to draw people from all over the world makes it sacred.

There are Beatles tourist sites in New York, the most famous of which is the Dakota building, in front of which Lennon was shot on December 8, 1980. Fans gather at the memorial Imagine mosaic in the Strawberry Fields area of Central Park on that day and on October 9, Lennon's birthday, to make music together, celebrate his life, feel his absence, and collectively express sadness about his senseless murder. These rituals are attended by fans of all ages from all over the world and will likely continue long into the future.

Other important dates on the Beatles fan calendar are the other Beatles' birthdays, their appearance on the *Ed Sullivan Show* (perhaps more for US fans), and the day Lennon and McCartney met at the Woolton fête—an event that was reenacted, complete with surviving members of the Quarry Men, on its 60th anniversary on July 6, 2017. Fans post pictures of albums or links to songs on the anniversaries of their release dates, prompting others to share memories and express gratitude.

Beatles tribute bands, with musicians of all ages and cultural backgrounds, perform at venues all over the world. Whether or not they attempt to look like the Beatles, these bands are, indeed, paying tribute to the Beatles, and good tribute bands communicate reverence for the music. Faithful renditions, complete with splendid flourishes where needed, are expected. Because the Beatles stopped touring in 1966, only a very small proportion of their fan base has seen them live. In fact, it's estimated that fewer than 2.5 million people worldwide saw the Beatles perform live between 1963 and 1966.[103]

Tribute bands give fans of all ages an opportunity to listen and dance to Beatles music with other fans, a joyful ritual that celebrates the band's artistry, longevity, and positivity. Tribute bands are one of the mechanisms through which the de facto religion of Beatles fandom is culturally transmitted.

Fans create artful variations on album covers and other images, which are then widely shared on social media. The Beatles are painted, drawn, sketched, collaged, decoupaged, and rendered in everything from coffee beans to feathers, by fans with enormous talent in the visual arts. These devotional works, some very labor-intensive or with painstaking detail, are shared with great pride.

A small number of fans create and share images that depict Lennon and Harrison in celestial scenes or insert them as "ghosts" in scenes with McCartney and Starr, sometimes as angels, sometimes reuniting them. Renderings of how Harrion and especially Lennon might look today are also shared. These images express deep sadness. Writer fans, especially second- and third-generation fans, create Beatles fan fiction.

Fans are excited to hear remastered music, and many buy it as soon as it's available, even if they've purchased it many times before in previous formats. Fans are enthralled by outtakes and demos because they reveal the Beatles' creative processes and offer glimpses into the mysteries of their craft. The between-song banter reveals new bits of personality.

Beatle fans are a cross-section of the population, with diverse backgrounds and lifestyles, but they identify as members of a community and enjoy getting together in celebration. Fan gatherings welcome all fans, from newbie to geek.

Since 1974, Mark Lapidos has been convening fans for three days at the Fest for Beatles Fans, which takes place annually in New York and Chicago. The Fest draws fans of all ages from all over the United States and beyond. Fest attendees describe it as "three of the best days of the year"; many say they "can't ask for a better vacation."[104]

Abbey Road on the River, an annual festival that began in 2002, draws fans from great distances to Indiana to celebrate the Beatles. Another widely attended annual festival is Beatles at the Ridge, in Arkansas. These festivals include live Beatles music, expert panel discussions, presentations by authors and people who had or have personal or professional ties to the four Beatles, films, vendors with new and vintage Beatles merchandise, art shows, and trivia contests.

Fans say the main appeal of these events is sharing their love of the Beatles with other fans. Some have met future spouses at these events and have made other important long-term social and professional connections—the kinds of connections once made in traditional faith-based communities. These festivals provide a great opportunity for further research into some of the issues addressed in this chapter and to learn more about how the Beatles' meaning differs for fans of different ages.

McCartney continued to be part of the cultural conversation in 2018, touring in support of a new album and doing a "pop-up concert" in New York's Grand Central Station. At this show, he gave advice to young fans dealing with bullies and encouraged the audience to "dance and feel free." In a recent interview with comedian Marc Maron, McCartney humbly described the Beatles as "kind of magical" and said he was moved by the "real sense of community" at his shows. He said that when he does "Hey Jude" or "Let It Be," he realizes that "people are despairing and the song reminds them it gets better," and, he said, "I get to be the MC of that; I feel proud."[105]

Beatles Fandom and Enhanced Well-Being

Every known human culture has had both music and religion of some kind, and the two have always been intertwined. Some anthropologists and ethnomusicologists believe that both serve survival functions. Human beings who sing together feel connected; doing this routinely creates a community. When the music elicits transcendence from the whole group, even for fleeting moments, the bonds of community are reinforced, and members have had a "religious" experience. This happens routinely at the events described above.

A huge body of research shows that religious belief and practice—being part of a community with a shared belief system and shared transcendent moments—confer health benefits.[106] Fandom confers these same benefits, for the same reasons.

Traditionally, fandom has been associated with childhood and adolescence and is seen as inappropriate in adults, suggestive of some sort of psychological deficit, or a way to resist "social aging."[107] Perhaps because music fandom has long been associated with out-of-control young women, adult female fans are judged more harshly. One fan said her feelings about the Beatles have "a kind of clandestine quality" because her husband doesn't approve; one said her husband finds her Beatles fandom "exasperating."[108] Another said, "My fascination with the Beatles has waxed and waned over the years. In fact, my recent reentry into the Beatle world, which came about three years ago, felt as strong as it did when I was a teenager. My husband doesn't even know the extent of it. It embarrasses me to talk about them with him."[109]

It's unfortunate that these women feel they have to hide the simple fact that the Beatles still bring joy to their lives. Many first-generation fans stopped engaging with the Beatles as they got older, often because work and parenting responsibilities left little time for fan activity. But it's clear that the social, emotional, and intellectual experiences of fandom can enhance quality of life throughout the life span.

Baby boomers have been challenging cultural norms throughout their lives (with inspiration from the Beatles) and were the first generation whose identities were so extremely informed by the popular culture of their youth. Thus, identifying as a fan in adulthood is almost a logical progression; it's certainly not a far reach. Rekindling a 70-year-old's dormant Beatles passion, for example, could have a variety of positive impacts on health and quality of life, consistent with the conceptualization of fandom as a "personal resource."[110]

The Beatles have been a constant, grounding presence in fans' lives for more than half a century, providing familiar input as fans "narrate a version of individual identity across time."[111] As I write this, Beatle fans are eagerly awaiting the 50th anniversary box set of the *White Album*, just as they looked forward to—and were delighted by—the 50th anniversary remaster of *Sgt. Pepper*. These objects are "a condensed form of personal biography."[112]

Recent studies in psychology show a positive relationship between fandom and well-being, with social connection as the link. Research psychologists studying fandom—a new area of research—see further efforts in this area as very important, given the growing prominence of fan communities on the internet and elsewhere.[113]

The health benefits of fandom could be leveraged to address the epidemic of social isolation in the United States and the United Kingdom, across all age groups.[114] First-generation Beatle fans—baby boomers—face more chronic health problems than previous generations,[115] and these health problems are often exacerbated by social isolation. Recognizing the health benefits of fandom requires that it lose its stigma, and there is evidence that this is happening—with younger populations.

Teen Vogue recently ran an article on the health benefits of fandom,[116] as did an online science, tech, and culture magazine.[117] But fandom should also be legitimized and celebrated by people in their 60s and 70s and those who care for them. Suggestions for baby boomers on how to alleviate social isolation seem to ignore fan-based activities.[118]

Fans engage with their records and memorabilia in ways that stimulate memories and facilitate reflection and insight, suggesting that fan practices may play a role in staving off or managing cognitive decline or Alzheimer's disease. Activities that were important prior to a senior's diagnosis of dementia can continue to be meaningful and provide enjoyment. The playful aspects of fandom, health-promoting at any age, may also be useful for managing any form of cognitive decline.[119]

Fandom may also provide relief from depression, at any age. British writer and journalist Johann Hari traveled the world interviewing researchers, looking for the causes of depression. Among his key findings, many of which have relevance to fandom—and highlight the similarities to religion—is that not only do people need social connection, but escape from loneliness comes from sharing things that one finds meaningful and important, things that bring joy and make life worth living.[120]

There is a great deal of promising research being done on the benefits of music therapy in aging populations. According to music and memory expert Rory Silvia, "There have been studies that show our brains are hard-wired to connect music with long-term memory. Music or songs that have an association with a personal event can linger in a person's mind and reconnect them with that moment if they hear the song again."[121]

Tia DeNora's research on music's role as a medium of consciousness and health promotion shows that people suffering from forms of chronic illness use music on a daily basis for pain management and to experience periods of time spent in sleep and relaxation. According to DeNora, music is a "health technology" when coupled with personal narrative, and it can "instill courage" and a different attitude toward pain.[122]

The Beatles and the experience of growing up with them are seared deeply into the synapses of aging first-generation fans. But Beatles music can function as a health technology for all baby boomers, because the band was omnipresent in the culture during their most formative years. Family members and healthcare professionals should encourage boomers' engagement with Beatles music, images, and artifacts. The Beatles had an exceptionally strong developmental impact on those born between 1952 and 1958, and this group may be especially responsive to Beatles stimuli.[123]

Research efforts in fandom should further our understanding of the fan experience and fandom's potential to enhance people's lives. Like religion, fandom is a rich, motivating, social process, laden with meanings that are deeply personal yet bigger than ourselves, and could be leveraged to solve pressing problems at the individual and societal level. Finally, fandom is like religion in that, through moral suasion, it can be a political force. Many Beatle fans have been active in gun control and animal rights efforts, and there is potential for further political action. The siblinghood of first-generation Beatle fans helped bring about liberalizing change in government policies throughout the West. As I write these words, democracy is weakening across the globe. Repressive, right-wing nationalism is mounting a resurgence. More than ever, the world needs to hear and heed the Beatles' call for love, peace, unity, freedom, and maximizing human potential.

Notes

1. Candy Leonard, *Beatleness: How the Beatles and Their Fans Remade the World* (New York: Arcade, 2014), 209.
2. Leonard, *Beatleness*, 267.
3. Leonard, *Beatleness*, 272.
4. Jann S. Wenner, "Review: 'The Beatles: The Authorized Biography,'" *Rolling Stone*, October 26, 1968, https://www.rollingstone.com/music/music-news/review-the-beatles-the-authorized-biography-188671/.
5. Leonard, *Beatleness*, 272.
6. Mark Duffett, *Understanding Fandom* (London: Bloomsbury, 2013), 143.
7. Duffett, *Understanding Fandom*, 150.
8. Chris Rojek, *Celebrity* (London: Reaktion, 2001), 57.
9. Stewart M. Hoover, "The Cultural Construction of Religion in the Media Age," in *Practicing Religion in the Age of the Media*, ed. Stewart M. Hoover and Lynn Schofield Clark (New York: Columbia University Press, 2002), 2.
10. Rojek, *Celebrity*, 57.
11. See Matthew Hills, "Media Fandom, Neoreligiosity, and Cult(ural) Studies," *Velvet Light Trap*, no. 46 (Fall 2000): 76.
12. Rupert Till, *Pop Cult: Religion and Popular Music* (London: Continuum, 2010), 189.
13. Julie J. Ingersoll, "The Thin Line between Saturday Night and Sunday Morning," in *God in the Details: American Religion in Popular Culture*, ed. Eric Michael Mazur and Kate McCarthy (Routledge, 2010), 264.
14. Robin Sylvan, *Traces of the Spirit: The Religious Dimensions of Popular Music* (New York: New York University Press, 2002), 4.
15. Sylvan, *Traces of the Spirit*, 12.
16. Sylvan, *Traces of the Spirit*, 72.
17. Daniel Cavicchi, *Tramps Like Us: Music and Meaning among Springsteen Fans* (New York: Oxford University Press, 1998), 186.
18. Cavicchi, *Tramps Like Us*, 188.

19. Erika Doss, "Believing in Elvis: Popular Piety in Material Culture," in *Practicing Religion in the Age of the Media*, ed. Stewart M. Hoover and Lynn Schofield Clark (New York: Columbia University Press, 2002), 76.

20. Doss, "Believing in Elvis," 76.

21. Cavicchi, *Tramps Like Us*, 8–9.

22. Steve Turner, *The Gospel according to the Beatles* (London: Westminster John Knox, 2006), 13.

23. Ken Ferguson, "The Beatles as a Religious Cult," *Photoplay*, March 1964, http://jot101. com/2015/10/the-beatles-as-religious-cult/.

24. Quotes in Jonathan Gould, *Can't Buy Me Love: The Beatles, Britain, and America* (New York: Harmony, 2007), 341.

25. Quoted in Gould, *Can't Buy Me Love*, 341.

26. David A Noebel, *Communism, Hypnotism and the Beatles* (Tulsa: Christian Crusade, 1965), 15.

27. Quoted in Philip Norman, *Shout* (New York: MJF, 1981), 293.

28. Devin McKinney, *Magic Circles: The Beatles in Dream and History* (Cambridge, MA: Harvard University Press, 2003), 322.

29. Turner, *The Gospel according to the Beatles*, 11.

30. Turner, *The Gospel according to the Beatles*, 11.

31. Michael R. Frontani, *The Beatles: Image and the Media* (Jackson: University Press of Mississippi, 2007), Kindle loc. 356.

32. Frontani, *The Beatles*, loc 304.

33. Philip Goldberg, *American Veda: How Indian Spirituality Changed the West* (New York: Harmony, 2010), 153.

34. Goldberg, *American Veda*, 289.

35. Goldberg, *American Veda*, 266.

36. Wade Clark Roof, *A Generation of Seekers: The Spiritual Journeys of the Baby Boom Generation* (San Francisco: Harper, 1973), 70.

37. McKinney, *Magic Circles*, 143.

38. McKinney, *Magic Circles*, 143.

39. McKinney, *Magic Circles*, 150.

40. McKinney, *Magic Circles*, 150.

41. Grant Maxwell, *How Does It Feel? Elvis Presley, the Beatles, Bob Dylan, and the Philosophy of Rock and Roll* (Nashville: Persistent, 2014), Kindle loc. 4356.

42. Maxwell, *How Does It Feel?* loc. 4175.

43. Maxwell, *How Does It Feel?* loc 4071.

44. Maxwell, *How Does It Feel?* loc 4164.

45. Turner, *The Gospel according to the Beatles*, 58.

46. Bob Stanley, *Yeah! Yeah! Yeah! The Story of Pop Music from Bill Haley to Beyoncé* (New York: W. W. Norton, 2014), 80.

47. Stanley, *Yeah! Yeah! Yeah!* 8.

48. Christopher Hill, *The Visionary and Ecstatic Roots of 1960s Rock and Roll* (New York: Park Street, 2017), 152.

49. Hill, *The Visionary and Ecstatic Roots*, 154.

50. Frye Gaillard, *A Hard Rain: America in the 1960s, Our Decade of Hope, Possibility, and Innocence Lost* (Montgomery, AL: NewSouth, 2018), 192–193.

51. Gaillard, *A Hard Rain*, 193.

52. Janne Mäkelä, *John Lennon Imagined: Cultural History of a Rock Star* (New York: Peter Lang, 2004), 215.

53. Martin King, *Men, Masculinity and the Beatles* (Surrey, UK: Ashgate, 2013), 147.

54. Nick Bromell, *Tomorrow Never Knows: Rock and Psychedelics in the Sixties* (Chicago: University of Chicago Press, 2000), 24.

55. Elizabeth Hellmuth Margulis, *On Repeat: How Music Plays the Mind* (New York: Oxford University Press, 2014), Kindle loc. 18.

56. Leonard, *Beatleness*, 264.

57. Theodore Adorno, "On Popular Music," in *On Record: Rock, Pop, and the Written Word*, ed. Simon Frith and Andrew Goodwin (London: Routledge, 1990), 305.

58. Henry Jenkins, "How Texts Become Real," in *Textual Poachers*, ed. Henry Jenkins (London: Routledge, 1992), 51.

59. Leonard, *Beatleness*, 67.

60. Duffett, *Understanding Fandom*, 150.

61. Duffett, *Understanding Fandom*, 145.

62. Turner, *The Gospel according to the Beatles*, 5.

63. Leonard, *Beatleness*, 101.

64. Leonard, *Beatleness*, 106.

65. Turner, *The Gospel according to the Beatles*, 109.

66. Leonard, *Beatleness*, 107.

67. Kenneth Burke, "Literature as Equipment for Living," in *Philosophy of the Literary Form: Studies in Symbolic Action*, ed. Kenneth Burke (Berkeley: University of California Press, 1973), 297.

68. Ian Inglis, "Men of Ideas: Popular Music, Anti-Intellectualism and the Beatles," in *The Beatles, Popular Music and Society: A Thousand Voices*, ed. Ian Inglis (New York: St. Martin's Press, 2000), 9.

69. Leonard, *Beatleness*, 115.

70. Leonard, *Beatleness*, 115.

71. Leonard, *Beatleness*, 115.

72. Leonard, *Beatleness*, 115.

73. Max Weber, *The Theory of Social and Economic Organization*, trans. A. M. Henderson and Talcott Parsons (New York: Free Press, 1924), 328.

74. Paul J. Silvia, "Interest: The Curious Emotion," *Current Directions in Psychological Science* 17, no. 1 (2008): 57–60.

75. Bromell, *Tomorrow Never Knows*, 89.

76. Leonard, *Beatleness*, 139.

77. Candy Leonard, "When the Beatles Brought Psychedelia to Prime Time," *Huffington Post*, February 22, 2017, https://www.huffingtonpost.com/entry/when-the-beatles-brought-psychedelia-to-prime-time_us_58adbc3ae4b0598627a55f2c.

78. Mäkelä, *John Lennon Imagined*, 119.

79. Leonard, *Beatleness*, 150.

80. Leonard, *Beatleness*, 141.

81. Leonard, *Beatleness*, 141.

82. Leonard, *Beatleness*, 145.

83. Thomas Thompson, "The New Far-Out Beatles," *Life,* June 16, 1967, 100.

84. Leonard, *Beatleness*, 151.

85. Leonard, *Beatleness*, 158.

86. Leonard, *Beatleness*, 159.

87. Leonard, *Beatleness*, 207.

88. Corey Barnett, "How the Beatles' 'Yellow Submarine' Changed Christianity in America," *World Religion News*, July 15, 2018, https://www.worldreligionnews.com/entertainment/beatles-yellow-submarine-changed-christianity-america.

89. Leonard, *Beatleness*, 234.

90. Leonard, *Beatleness*, 220.

91. Leonard, *Beatleness*, 215.

92. Leonard, *Beatleness*, 255.

93. Of course, not every Beatles song expresses positive, uplifting themes. But this group of songs reflects a coherent value system that defines the Beatles' cultural meaning.

94. Christopher Partridge, "Modern Western Cultures," in *New Religions: A Guide*, ed. Christopher Partridge (New York: Oxford University Press, 2004), 367.

95. Partridge, "Modern Western Cultures," 400.

96. Bromell, *Tomorrow Never Knows*, 31.

97. "Do you think Beatles fandom is a religion, or like a religion?" Beatles Fans Around the World (group), Facebook post, Sept. 4, 2018, https://www.facebook.com/groups/2204708817/permalink/10156534266918818.

98. Scott Porch, "How 'Beat Bugs' Sells the Beatles to a New Generation," *Rolling Stone*, August 3, 2016, https://www.rollingstone.com/tv/tv-features/how-beat-bugs-sells-the-beatles-to-a-new-generation-252062/amp/.

99. Leonard, *Beatleness*, 271.

100. Leonard, *Beatleness*, 265.

101. Catherine Jones, "The £82M Beatles Boost to Liverpool's Economy," *Liverpool Echo*, February 8, 2016, https://www.liverpoolecho.co.uk/news/82m-beatles-boost-liverpools-economy-10847567.amp.

102. Jennifer Otter Bickerdike, *The Secular Religion of Fandom* (Los Angeles: Sage, 2016.), 95.

103. Personal communication in October 2018 from Chuck Gunderson, author of *Some Fun Tonight: The Backstage Story of How the Beatles Rocked America*, 2 vols. (Milwaukee, WI: Backbeat, 2013).

104. Leonard, *Beatleness*, 272.

105. Paul McCartney, interviewed by Marc Maron, *WTF* podcast, episode 948, September 6, 2018, http://www.wtfpod.com/podcast/episode-948-paul-mccartney.

106. Laura Greenstein, "The Mental Health Benefits of Religion and Spirituality," *National Alliance of Mental Illness Blog*, December 21, 2016, https://www.nami.org/Blogs/NAMI-Blog/December-2016/The-Mental-Health-Benefits-of-Religion-Spiritual; Kevin S. Seybold and Peter C. Hill, "The Role of Religion and Spirituality

in Mental and Physical Health," *Current Directions in Psychological Science* 10, no. 1 (2001): 21–24, https://doi.org/10.1111/1467-8721.00106; W. J. Strawbridge et al., "Frequent Attendance at Religious Services and Mortality over 28 Years," *American Journal of Public Health* 87, no. 6 (1997): 957–961, https://www.ncbi.nlm.nih.gov/pmc/articles/PMC1380930/.

107. Laura Vroomen, "Kate Bush: Teen Pop and Older Female Fans," in *Music Scenes: Local, Translocal and Virtual*, ed. Andy Bennett and Richard Peterson (Nashville: Vanderbilt University Press, 2004), 243.

108. Leonard, *Beatleness*, 270.

109. Leonard, *Beatleness*, 270.

110. Duffett, *Understanding Fandom*, 279.

111. Duffett, *Understanding Fandom*, 280.

112. Duffett, *Understanding Fandom*, 280.

113. Stephen Reysen, Courtney Plante, and Daniel Chadborn, "Better Together: Social Connections Mediate the Relationship between Fandom and Well-Being," *AASCIT Journal of Health* 4, no. 6 (2017): 68–73.

114. Emily Gurnon, "Loneliness: A Growing Health Threat for Older Adults," *Forbes*, December 25, 2016, https://www.forbes.com/sites/nextavenue/2016/12/25/loneliness-a-growing-health-threat-for-older-adults/#57291979407e; Barbara Sadick, "The Loneliness Effect," *US News and World Report*, September 6, 2018, https://www.usnews.com/news/healthiest-communities/articles/2018-09-06/loneliness-the-next-great-public-health-hazard; Zahid Mahmood, "UK Tackles Social Isolation with Minister for Loneliness," *CNN.com*, January 17, 2018, https://www.cnn.com/2018/01/17/health/uk-minister-loneliness-intl/index.html.

115. Alison Kodjak, "Baby Boomers Will Become Sicker Seniors Than Earlier Generations," *NPR*, May 25, 2016, https://www.npr.org/sections/health-shots/2016/05/25/479359856/baby-boomers-will-become-sicker-seniors-than-earlier-generations.

116. Brianna Wiest, "Psychologists Say That Belonging to a Fandom Is Amazing for Your Mental Health," *Teen Vogue*, July 20, 2017, https://www.teenvogue.com/story/psychologists-say-fandoms-are-amazing-for-your-mental-health.

117. Sarah Sloat, "Science Explains Why Being a Fan Is Good for You," *Inverse*, October 16, 2015, https://www.inverse.com/article/7120-science-explains-why-being-a-fan-is-good-for-you.

118. Casey Dowd, "Tips for Baby Boomers on How to Deal with Loneliness," *Fox Business*, September 3, 2017, https://www.foxbusiness.com/features/tips-for-baby-boomers-on-how-to-deal-with-loneliness.

119. Hester Anderiesen et al., "Play Experiences for People with Alzheimer's Disease," *International Journal of Design* 9, no. 2 (2015): 155–165, http://www.ijdesign.org/index.php/IJDesign/article/view/1865/699.

120. Johann Hari, *Lost Connections: Uncovering the Real Causes of Depression and the Unexpected Solutions* (New York: Bloomsbury, 2018), 83.

121. Quoted in Nathan Lamb, "Aging Well Explores Music Therapy and Dementia," *Somerville-Cambridge Elder Services Blog*, August 15, 2017, https://eldercare.org/aging-well-explores-music-therapy-and-dementia/.

122. Tia DeNora, *Music Asylums: Wellbeing through Music in Everyday Life* (London: Routledge, 2015), 112.

123. Candy Leonard, "7 Ways the Beatles Changed Boomer Childhood Overnight," *Huffington Post*, January 26, 2015, https://www.huffingtonpost.com/candy-leonard/beatles-changed-boomer-childhood_b_6494786.html.

Bibliography

Adorno, Theodor. "On Popular Music." In *On Record: Rock, Pop, and the Written Word*, edited by Simon Frith and Andrew Goodwin, 301–314. London: Routledge, 1990.

Anderiesen, Hester, Erik Scherder, Richard Goossens, Valentijn Visch, and Laura Eggermont. "Play Experiences for People with Alzheimer's Disease." *International Journal of Design* 9, no. 2 (2015): 155–165. http://www.ijdesign.org/index.php/IJDesign/article/view/1865/699.

Barnett, Corey. "How the Beatles' 'Yellow Submarine' Changed Christianity in America." *World Religion News*, July 15, 2018. https://www.worldreligionnews.com/entertainment/beatles-yellow-submarine-changed-christianity-america.

Bickerdike, Jennifer Otter. *The Secular Religion of Fandom*. Los Angeles: Sage, 2016.

Bromell, Nick. *Tomorrow Never Knows: Rock and Psychedelics in the Sixties*. Chicago: University of Chicago Press, 2000.

Burke, Kenneth. "Literature as Equipment for Living." In *Philosophy of the Literary Form: Studies in Symbolic Action*, edited by Kenneth Burke, 293–304. Berkeley: University of California Press, 1973.

Cavicchi, Daniel. *Tramps Like Us: Music and Meaning among Springsteen Fans*. New York: Oxford University Press, 1998.

DeNora, Tia. *Music Asylums: Wellbeing through Music in Everyday Life*. London: Routledge, 2015.

Doss, Erika. "Believing in Elvis: Popular Piety in Material Culture." In *Practicing Religion in the Age of the Media*, edited by Stewart M. Hoover and Lynn Schofield Clark, 63–85. New York: Columbia University Press, 2002.

Dowd, Casey. "Tips for Baby Boomers on How to Deal with Loneliness." *Fox Business*, September 3, 2017. https://www.foxbusiness.com/features/tips-for-baby-boomers-on-how-to-deal-with-loneliness.

Duffett, Mark. *Understanding Fandom*. London: Bloomsbury, 2013.

Ferguson, Ken. "The Beatles as a Religious Cult." *Photoplay*, March 1964. http://jot101.com/2015/10/the-beatles-as-religious-cult/.

Frontani, Michael R. *The Beatles: Image and the Media*. Jackson: University Press of Mississippi, 2007.

Gaillard, Frye. *A Hard Rain: America in the 1960s, Our Decade of Hope, Possibility, and Innocence Lost*. Montgomery, AL: NewSouth, 2018.

Goldberg, Philip. *American Veda: How Indian Spirituality Changed the West*. New York: Harmony, 2010.

Gould, Jonathan. *Can't Buy Me Love: The Beatles, Britain, and America*. New York: Harmony, 2007.

Greenstein, Laura. "The Mental Health Benefits of Religion and Spirituality." *National Alliance of Mental Illness Blog*, December 21, 2016. https://www.nami.org/Blogs/NAMI-Blog/December-2016/The-Mental-Health-Benefits-of-Religion-Spiritual.

Gurnon, Emily. "Loneliness: A Growing Health Threat for Older Adults." *Forbes*, December 25, 2016. https://www.forbes.com/sites/nextavenue/2016/12/25/loneliness-a-growing-health-threat-for-older-adults/#57291979407e.

Hari, Johann. *Lost Connections: Uncovering the Real Causes of Depression and the Unexpected Solutions*. New York: Bloomsbury, 2018.

Hill, Christopher. *The Visionary and Ecstatic Roots of 1960s Rock and Roll*. New York: Park Street, 2017.

Hills, Matthew. "Media Fandom, Neoreligiosity, and Cult(ural) Studies." *Velvet Light Trap*, no. 46 (Fall 2000): 73–84.

Hoover, Stewart M. "The Cultural Construction of Religion in the Media Age." In *Practicing Religion in the Age of the Media*, edited by Stewart M. Hoover and Lynn Schofield Clark, 1–6. New York: Columbia University Press, 2002.

Ingersoll, Julie J. "The Thin Line between Saturday Night and Sunday Morning." In *God in the Details: American Religion in Popular Culture*, edited by Eric Michael Mazur and Kate McCarthy, 253–266. London: Routledge, 2010.

Inglis, Ian. "Men of Ideas: Popular Music, Anti-Intellectualism and the Beatles." In *The Beatles, Popular Music and Society: A Thousand Voices*, edited by Ian Inglis, 1–22. New York: St. Martin's Press, 2000.

Jenkins, Henry. "How Texts Become Real." In *Textual Poachers*, edited by Henry Jenkins, 50–84. London: Routledge, 1992.

Jones, Catherine. "The £82M Beatles Boost to Liverpool's Economy." *Liverpool Echo*, February 8, 2016. https://www.liverpoolecho.co.uk/news/82m-beatles-boost-liverpools-economy-10847567.amp.

Kodjak, Alison. "Baby Boomers Will Become Sicker Seniors Than Earlier Generations." *NPR*, May 25, 2016. https://www.npr.org/sections/health-shots/2016/05/25/479359856/baby-boomers-will-become-sicker-seniors-than-earlier-generations.

King, Martin. *Men, Masculinity and the Beatles*. Surrey, UK: Ashgate, 2013.

Lamb, Nathan. "Aging Well Explores Music Therapy and Dementia." *Somerville-Cambridge Elder Services Blog*, August 15, 2017. https://eldercare.org/aging-well-explores-music-therapy-and-dementia/.

Leonard, Candy. *Beatleness: How the Beatles and Their Fans Remade the World*. New York: Arcade, 2014.

Leonard, Candy. "7 Ways the Beatles Changed Boomer Childhood Overnight." *Huffington Post*, January 26, 2015. https://www.huffingtonpost.com/candy-leonard/beatles-changed-boomer-childhood_b_6494786.html.

Leonard, Candy. "When the Beatles Brought Psychedelia to Prime Time." *Huffington Post*, February 22, 2017. https://www.huffingtonpost.com/entry/when-the-beatles-brought-psychedelia-to-prime-time_us_58adbc3ae4b0598627a55f2c.

Mahmood, Zahid. "UK Tackles Social Isolation with Minister for Loneliness." *CNN.com*, January 17, 2018. https://www.cnn.com/2018/01/17/health/uk-minister-loneliness-intl/index.html.

Mäkelä, Janne. *John Lennon Imagined: Cultural History of a Rock Star*. New York: Peter Lang, 2004.

Margulis, Elizabeth Hellmuth. *On Repeat: How Music Plays the Mind*. New York: Oxford University Press, 2014.

Maxwell, Grant. *How Does It Feel? Elvis Presley, the Beatles, Bob Dylan, and the Philosophy of Rock and Roll*. Nashville: Persistent, 2014.

McCartney, Paul. Interviewed by Marc Maron. *WTF* podcast, episode 948, September 6, 2018. http://www.wtfpod.com/podcast/episode-948-paul-mccartney.

McKinney, Devin. *Magic Circles: The Beatles in Dream and History*. Cambridge, MA: Harvard University Press, 2003.

Noebel, David A. *Communism, Hypnotism and the Beatles*. Tulsa,: Christian Crusade, 1965.

Norman, Philip. *Shout*. New York: MJF, 1981.

Partridge, Christopher. "Modern Western Cultures." In *New Religions: A Guide*, edited by Christopher Partridge, 358–416. New York: Oxford University Press, 2004.

Porch, Scott. "How 'Beat Bugs' Sells the Beatles to a New Generation." *Rolling Stone*, August 3, 2016. https://www.rollingstone.com/tv/tv-features/how-beat-bugs-sells-the-beatles-to-a-new-generation-252062/amp/.

Reysen, Stephen, Courtney Plante, and Daniel Chadborn. "Better Together: Social Connections Mediate the Relationship between Fandom and Well-Being." *AASCIT Journal of Health* 4, no. 6 (2017): 68–73.

Rojek, Chris. *Celebrity*. London: Reaktion, 2001.

Roof, Wade Clark. *A Generation of Seekers: The Spiritual Journeys of the Baby Boom Generation*. San Francisco: Harper, 1973.

Sadick, Barbara. "The Loneliness Effect." *US News and World Report*, September 6, 2018. https://www.usnews.com/news/healthiest-communities/articles/2018-09-06/loneliness-the-next-great-public-health-hazard.

Seybold, Kevin S., and Peter C. Hill. "The Role of Religion and Spirituality in Mental and Physical Health." *Current Directions in Psychological Science* 10, no. 1 (2001): 21–24.

Silvia, Paul J. "Interest: The Curious Emotion." *Current Directions in Psychological Science* 17, no. 1 (2008): 57–60.

Sloat, Sarah. "Science Explains Why Being a Fan Is Good for You." *Inverse*, October 16, 2015. https://www.inverse.com/article/7120-science-explains-why-being-a-fan-is-good-for-you.

Stanley, Bob. *Yeah! Yeah! Yeah! The Story of Pop Music from Bill Haley to Beyoncé*. New York: W. W. Norton, 2014.

Strawbridge, W. J., R. D. Cohen, S. J. Shema, and G. A. Kaplan. "Frequent Attendance at Religious Services and Mortality over 28 Years." *American Journal of Public Health* 87, no. 6 (1997): 957–961. https://www.ncbi.nlm.nih.gov/pmc/articles/PMC1380930/.

Sylvan, Robin. *Traces of the Spirit: The Religious Dimensions of Popular Music*. New York: New York University Press, 2002.

Thompson, Thomas. "The New Far-Out Beatles." *Life*, June 16, 1967, 100.

Till, Rupert. *Pop Cult: Religion and Popular Music*. London: Continuum, 2010.

Turner, Steve. *The Gospel according to the Beatles*. London: Westminster John Knox, 2006.

Vroomen, Laura. "Kate Bush: Teen Pop and Older Female Fans." In *Music Scenes: Local, Translocal and Virtual*, edited by Andy Bennett and Richard Peterson, 238–254. Nashville: Vanderbilt University Press, 2004.

Weber, Max. *The Theory of Social and Economic Organization*. Translated by A. M. Henderson and Talcott Parsons. New York: Free Press, 1924.

Wenner, Jann S. "Review: 'The Beatles: The Authorized Biography." *Rolling Stone,* October 26, 1968. https://www.rollingstone.com/music/music-news/review-the-beatles-the-authorized-biography-188671/.

Wiest, Brianna. "Psychologists Say That Belonging to a Fandom Is Amazing for Your Mental Health." *Teen Vogue*, July 20, 2017. https://www.teenvogue.com/story/psychologists-say-fandoms-are-amazing-for-your-mental-health.

2

The Beatles and Their Fans

Image and the Media, October 1963–February 1964

Michael Frontani

By the time the Beatles arrived at John F. Kennedy International Airport for their first US visit, they were already stars—"Beatlemania," as the press and media had come to call the frenzied reaction of young female fans to any appearance by their idols, had already taken root. Urged on by New York City's rock-and-roll disc jockeys, themselves in a "genial conspiracy to promote the Beatles, so that Beatlemania would in turn promote them,"[1] 3,000 screaming fans greeted the band as it exited Pan Am flight 101 from London's Heathrow Airport. In addition, 200 reporters and photographers from newspapers, magazines, foreign publications, and radio and television stations were all looking to exploit the band's visit. Two days later, on February 9, 1964, between 8 and 9 p.m. EST, the Beatles appeared on CBS's popular variety program the *Ed Sullivan Show*, and Beatlemania was introduced to a record-breaking television audience of 73 million people.[2]

In the days following the historic broadcast, the Beatles played their first US concert before a packed Washington Coliseum audience of more than 8,000 screaming teenagers; 10,000 greeted them at Penn Station upon their return to New York; two successful, raucous shows at Carnegie Hall followed; the day after that, 7,000 teenagers welcomed them as they deplaned in Miami; and the Beatles' second appearance on the *Sullivan* show, a special broadcast from Miami Beach's Deauville Hotel, drew 70 million television viewers.[3] The Beatles were, in the words of the *New York Times*'s McCandish Phillips, the "undisputed titans of American popular music."[4] Phillips, like many observers, wondered how this had come to be. Specifically, he asked, "What brought the Beatles to their present station in Britain, and how was it transferred here whole?"[5] More than half of a century later, these questions continue to reverberate and, broadly speaking, provide us with our starting point.

Michael Frontani, *The Beatles and Their Fans* In: *Fandom and the Beatles*. Edited by: Kenneth Womack and Kit O'Toole,
Oxford University Press (2021). © Oxford University Press. DOI: 10.1093/oso/9780190917852.003.0003

This chapter focuses on the Beatles' transition from an English sensation to an international phenomenon during fall and winter 1963–1964, with particular attention to the Beatles' image and their evolving fan base. For our purposes, this is a period marked by two inflection points in the Beatles' progress. The Beatles' historic performance on *Val Parnell's Sunday Night at the London Palladium* on October 13, 1963, is the first. As Brian Epstein, the Beatles' manager, indicated to a reporter during the Beatles' first visit to the United States, it was at the Palladium that the Beatles "became national."[6] Overnight, the British national press was infected with "Beatlemania," and a national phenomenon was born.

The second inflection point is the Beatles' historic performance on the *Ed Sullivan Show* on February 9, 1964. In one fell swoop, the Beatles "conquered America" and became an international phenomenon, well on the way to becoming a global one. On its surface, the Beatles' "present station in Britain," as it was called by the *Times* reporter, appeared to have been "transferred here whole." Capitol Records had invested heavily in recreating the Beatlemania phenomenon in the United States, and to that end, its promotion of the Beatles in early 1964 closely resembled the band's promotion in the United Kingdom. Further, early coverage of the Beatles phenomenon in the American national media largely mirrored the British national media's focus on the mania of the fans. Hence, British and American promotion and publicity were similar on most counts and identical in more than a few. Yet there are important distinctions to be made between them. Some aspects of the Beatles' image were radically altered in transition to something more suited to the American experience and marketplace, notably the Beatles' northern English identity and the more adult themes at play within the British media as a result of the Beatles' experience playing in clubs and ballrooms prior to their establishment as teen idols. These elements of the image were left in England that February day in 1964 when the Beatles boarded Pan Am flight 101 for the journey to America.

When the Beatles stepped off the airplane and onto the tarmac at New York's Kennedy Airport, Beatlemania had already arrived, and so had a Beatles image that was less adult and less purely a British teenage fantasy, one honed to best serve the band's commercial interests and that of the various American media recording its progress—not only during that first visit to the United States but also over the following months and years, as the Beatles' image navigated an international media environment dominated by American commerce and culture.

Stars, Image, Media, and Materials

Before considering the specific elements of the Beatles' image and the function of fandom within, it is important to define "image," its relationship to the star, and the materials from which it is constructed. Richard Dyer notes that the media construction of stars "encourages us to think in terms of 'really.' What is [the star] really like?"[7] Simon Frith and Andrew Goodwin, referring to the star's function in the music industry, lament that songs "work on us and records sell to us because of our identity with or response to them— an identity and response almost invariably mediated through a performer, a person who stands for what we possess, how we are possessed."[8] The star is the necessary vehicle of identification for the audience and a spur to consumption. A star's "image" emerges from all that is "known" of the star and coalesces out of all information that is publicly available. It is a product of its time and place. It is self-reflexive, and it evolves. Individual traits may predominate at certain points and recede at others. An image outlasts the star it represents and may evolve yet further.

Throughout 1962 and much of 1963, while the London-based and London-centric national press paid scant attention to the Beatles beyond mention in the weekly record charts and daily television and radio schedules, the specialized music publications, including *New Musical Express*, the *Record Mirror*, *Disc*, *Melody Maker*, and Liverpool's own *Mersey Beat*, provided extensive coverage of the Beatles and put on display many elements of the Beatles' image that were later echoed in the national media. These elements were also presented through newsreels, mass-market magazines, teen periodicals, the Beatles' own magazine, the *Beatles Monthly Book*. While space does not allow for a full accounting of all of the aforementioned media, even a casual review reveals recurring themes and elements contributing to a well-defined and widely recognized image by the time of the Beatles' appearance on *Val Parnell's Sunday Night at the London Palladium* program.

The focus here is on the coverage of the Beatles and their fans in the British press and the implications of and for that image as the Beatles chased success in America. Publications under review include national newspapers, among them the weekly, the *Observer*, and the dailies, the *Daily Mirror* and the *Guardian* (formerly the *Manchester Guardian*). British coverage and analysis of the Beatles phenomenon and its causes were an essential source for American media as they first took note in late 1963 and early 1964.

The Beatles' brief first tour of the United States brought them to Miami, Washington, DC, and, first and foremost, New York City, the hub of American image making and mass media, including music, publishing, film, mass-market magazines, advertising, and national radio and television networks. Over the brief time under consideration, the framing and coverage of the Beatles and Beatlemania by the nationally distributed mass-market publications, among them *Time*, *Life*, *Newsweek*, and *Look*, were determinative elements in Americans' experience of the Beatles phenomenon, as was that of the *New York Times*, which was among the most influential news and media organizations in the country. The Associated Press (AP) and United Press International (UPI) also published syndicated stories that were published nationally, and so they are considered.

Image, Beatles, and "Beatlemania" in Britain, 1963

On October 9, 1963, BBC TV broadcast the documentary *The Mersey Sound*[9] in London and the northern England regions.[10] It profiled the band and included, among other things, footage of the Beatles performing before and interacting with their young, primarily female, fans. The television critic for the Sunday *Observer*, writing in the October 13 edition, noted that the Beatles made a "distinctly agreeable impression"[11] and, in one of the earliest uses in print of a term that would soon explode into the public consciousness, opined that the "degree of *Beatlemania*, with fans sleeping under Beatles' windows and sending them jellybabies by the ton, seemed to be fairly acute."[12] That night, the acuity of that response was on full display as the Beatles made their historic first appearance on ITV's popular television program *Val Parnell's Sunday Night at the Palladium*, broadcast live across the United Kingdom. The spectacle of screaming fans inside the theater was watched by 15 million television viewers in nearly 10 million British homes, while frenzied fans outside closed down the street in front of the venue and provided fodder for journalists and photographers documenting the event for the following day's newspapers and broadcasts, when the term "Beatlemania" was fully and forever adopted into the lexicon.[13]

The mania that caught the national press's attention following the London Palladium appearance had, in fact, been breaking out for some time over much of the British Isles. Unruly fans were nothing new and had prompted countless news articles in local and regional newspapers. A short sampling provides a sense of the reporting and its constructions of the Beatles and, even more so, the fans. As early as February, the *Record Mirror* reported that Beatles fans in Manchester had refused to leave a theater until "the boys" returned to the stage for an encore and that afterward, the band's taxi had been mobbed by fans who broke off the vehicle's antenna and mirrors and smashed a window.[14] In early July, a headline in the *Liverpool Echo* declared, "Norwich Crowd of 6,000 Mobs Beatles—Women and Girls Hurt."[15] Members of the Norwich Council linked arms with police in an attempt to maintain the barrier, as did the queen's father, but to no avail. The response of the chairman of the council was unintentionally humorous: "I have never seen anything so ridiculous in all my life. It was mainly the dancing troupes who were responsible."[16]

A consistent narrative arose in which mobs of teenage girls were held in check and kept safe only through the intervention of the local police and emergency services. The headline of a brief item in the *Birmingham Post* in early September declared, "500 Girls Force Gates to See Beatles."[17] Days later, as the Beatles performed at the Great Pop Prom at the Royal Albert Hall, girls, in what the *Daily Mirror* called "the siege of the Beatle-crushers," rushed the stage, only to be repelled by "a solid block of forty commissionaires."[18] A week before the Beatles' performance on *Val Parnell's Sunday Night at the London Palladium*, the daily newspaper the *Guardian* (formerly the *Manchester Guardian*) reported that a planned concert by Gerry and the Pacemakers in Glasgow's new concert hall had been canceled due to, in the words of one member of the responsible committee, the "semi-savage" conduct of "some of the thousands of teenagers" who attended two shows given by the Beatles.[19] According to the *Stage*, a weekly London entertainment newspaper, "several thousand fans, jumping up and down in time to the music, loosened plaster in the ceiling of the Concert Hall, damaged 100 seats and caused the balcony to sway."[20]

Following the London Palladium show, the coverage by the national media intensified, as did the frenzied reaction of the fans to any appearance by the band or, often, to any competitive activity related to the band, such as buying tickets for a future show. In fact, as far as much of the mainstream national press was concerned, the mania of the fans was the most newsworthy aspect of the Beatles phenomenon and so generated the most stories, as it would in the United States. A week after the Palladium appearance, the Beatles were greeted by 2,000 screaming fans as they made their way to Birmingham's Alpha Television Studios, to record performances for ABC Television's *Thank*

Your Lucky Stars. The fans swarmed the Beatles' car, bringing traffic to a halt. According to the *Liverpool Echo*,[21] 50 police officers struggled against a surging mob of 3,500 teenagers. The newspaper also noted the riotous scene in Leicester, where extra police were called out to deal with 3,000 screaming teenagers, mostly girls, lining up to buy tickets for an upcoming Beatles show. Teenagers had been lining up since early Saturday evening without incident, but as dawn broke, "they became restive and seventy policemen and two police dogs were brought in."[22] The story noted that ambulances shuttled fainting girls to hospital and that "[a]bout fifty were treated."[23]

An account of the "Beatlecrush" at Leicester appeared a couple of weeks later in the *Guardian*. Space does not allow a full accounting of this fascinating letter from a self-described "fairly normal 15-year-old" girl, but it is well worth a look for interested readers. Let her recollection of the magic hour suffice. Suddenly, at 7 a.m., "only screams, groans, flashes of caustic wit and blaspheming were heard, for the pushing had started."[24] The author recalled "the unnerving experience of realizing my feet were not on the ground" and the smell of "hot bodies and cheap hair lacquer—it was not surprising that people were fainting at the rate of one every five minutes. . . . Some people were being crushed against the stone wall and shop windows, others, suffering from . . . claustrophobia, broke down completely." Nevertheless, our hero persevered and, finally, "staggered up to the grille and asked for two of the best tickets they had, as near to the front as possible. . . . Minutes later I came out clutching in my hand two little pink slips of paper and feeling rather like someone who has just conquered Everest." "Was it all worth it?" she asks herself. "Yes," she declares, "even if it was just for the smug satisfaction of seeing the incredulous and rather admiring looks of my friends as I recounted my frightful saga in full gory detail."[25]

Our chronicler spoke for many that fall and early winter. In an article entitled "Police Battle with Screaming Beatles Fans,"[26] the *Liverpool Echo* reported mayhem across northern England. In Hull, early Saturday morning, 2,000 teenage fans in a ticket line toppled police barriers in a mad rush toward the box office. A police spokesman said it was "just like hell let loose. It is a wonder no one was trampled on."[27] In Carlisle, more than 600 fans arrived the night before tickets were to go on sale for a show the following month. Police were on hand to keep things in good order, but "as midnight approached, a rustle went along the queue, girls screamed and patient fans turned impatient," and the mass surged forward, injuring nine girls who were treated by ambulance personnel.[28] In Newcastle upon Tyne, police and ambulance crews equipped with gallons of smelling salts toiled to control 7,000 fans lined up at the city hall, barreling over the girls who had camped out in the street for nearly two days. One 13-year-old girl who had been trampled at the front of the line told the *Newcastle Journal* that the ordeal was "terrifying" and a 9-year-old girl "huddled alone in a blanket against a wall, shivering with cold," said, "My Mummy is in the queue somewhere. We have been here since Saturday night."[29]

On November 4, the Beatles made another historic appearance, the Royal Variety Performance, which was taped for broadcast the following week. Lennon famously addressed the audience: "Will the people in the cheaper seats clap your hands? And the rest of you, if you'll just rattle your jewelry," which the queen mother graciously acknowledged, and the band set into a raucous "Twist and Shout."[30] The *Guardian* reported, "The Queen Mother . . . came face to face with Beatlemania, that disease prevalent mainly among young girls and brought on by the appearance of four young Liverpool entertainers."[31]

Later that month, 100 police officers were mobilized to control a crowd of 2,600 fans for both performances of the Beatles at the ABC Cinema in Ardwick, Manchester, and there were "at least thirty casualties, mainly fainting cases."[32] Days later, in Liverpool, a reported 12,000 fans, "mostly teenage girls." lined up for tickets to two upcoming Beatles shows at the Odeon Cinema. According to the *Guardian*'s reporting, police ranks swelled to "more than a hundred mounted, foot, and women police" as three ambulances stood ready and crews tended more than 100 casualties, mostly from exposure and from a predawn stampede down a side street.[33] In the aftermath, the streets were littered with "discarded cushions, blankets, eiderdowns, and waste paper."[34] It was reported that on the day of the shows, more than 100 extra police, including some on horseback, reinforced the constabulary.[35] Despite "30 teenage girl casualties, most of whom had fainted," the chief constable of Liverpool expressed relief that "It all passed off much more quietly than we had dared hope."[36]

In the midst of the mania, the Beatles persona was explicitly drawn for the young fans at the heart of the growing national phenomenon. No single text captures the promoted Beatles image as fully as the magazine *Meet the Beatles* (World Distributors, 1963), written and compiled by the Beatles' press secretary, Tony Barrow. Hitting British magazine racks in late October, this "Special Collector's Edition" was a bestseller with British teenagers[37] and later, with a different cover, with American teenagers. Its jacket promises "an informal date in words & personal album pictures." An introduction by "THEMSELVES," penned by Barrow, writing as "George, John, Paul and Ringo," is addressed to "Beatle People," the journalese phrase Barrow used for Beatles fans and which was thereafter picked up by the press. In true teen-idol fashion, the Beatles assure their fans that they have not let success and all the "fab things" change them:

> We're just as nutty, just as happy and just as handsome (*Ringo wrote that last bit so we won't give him his sticks until he rubs it out*) as we've always been. . . . Luckily there are three other Beatles ready to sit on any one of us who may show signs of swelling about the bonce, so we don't think it will happen![38]

These "Beatles" are witty, charming, and humble and, in closing, gush, "Thanks a million all you Beatle People—you're the gear!" Beatleisms and slang abound.

In the following pages,[39] each Beatle is given a two-page spread, with a biography on the left and a headshot on the right-hand page. At the bottom of each biography is a section presenting "Beatletistics" for each Beatle, containing vitals such as birthdates and locations, heights and weights, hair and eye colors, and likes and dislikes. Each Beatle is clearly differentiated so that their young female fans can pick a favorite or favorites. For instance, "George's personality mixes a deeply ingrained desire to be artistically ingenious. . . . By nature he is kind, fairly quiet, invariably helpful, noticeably considerate of other folks' feeling . . . and loath to end any friendship of long or short standing," and his "Beatletistics" section notes that he likes "smallish blondes" and "[h]ates haircuts." John, "the most 'way out' member," has "the courage of his convictions and will leap into the most heated argument if he feels strongly about any subject under discussion." He "makes a bee-line for blondes who are intelligent." Neither Cynthia, his wife since October 1962, nor Julian, his newborn son, is mentioned. Paul, the "uncomplicated" and "brainy Beatle," "laps up life, has a ball when he's singing to a 'live' audience and has no fear of the hard work which any successful entertainers have to put in on rehearsal," and he likes "long-haired girls who are witty conversationalists." Ringo "thinks a lot but says very little until someone makes a point of involving him in conversation," and he likes "neatly-dressed girls." Liverpool, "where the Beatles were born and where their big beat was bred," is incorporated into Barrow's Beatles narrative: "Big chimney stacks blowing clouds of darkening smoke into a low, grey sky. . . . This is the colourless, joyless side of Liverpool, the sea-port city. . . . Everyone who has or has not visited Liverpool claims to know the colourless, joyless side of the city."[40]

Other sections contain photo essays with the unwaveringly smiling Beatles "Beatling Beside the Seaside," racing go-carts, riding donkeys, and horsing around on the beach in their striped Victorian bathing suits. The publication concludes with "A London Day in the Life of the Beatles," a photo diary showing happy Beatles enjoying a day packed with teatime, visits to numerous shops, photo shoots, and visits to the tailor.[41] The *Meet the Beatles* publication presents the Beatles as being like a long line of previous and contemporary teen idols, from Johnnie Ray to Cliff Richard, fellow Liverpudlian Billy Fury, and Adam Faith—young, funny, smart, carefree, fun-loving, handsome (or cute), and hardworking. Barrow presents a standardized model of enticement, with the Beatles proposed as appropriate objects of desire for teen and preteen female fans.

While the teenage audience was the band's core concern, it is worth noting that the Beatles actively cultivated a much broader audience. In the week preceding the publication of the teen-directed *Meet the Beatles* magazine, the *Liverpool Echo* ran the six-part series "It's the Beatles!"[42] also written by Barrow (who was the regular music columnist of the newspaper, writing under the name "Disker"). Free of the breathless hyperbole of the magazine, the series was intended for a broader but decidedly more mature audience. Together, the *Meet the Beatles* magazine and the newspaper series encapsulate the Beatles' promotion at the outbreak of Beatlemania as a national phenomenon.

By summer 1963, the Beatles' northern English identity was so well established among the British public that the *Guardian*'s Stanley Reynolds could observe, "as everyone with any pretension towards mass culture should know the Beatles are from Liverpool."[43] As with the mania of the fans, the importance of the association of the Beatles with Liverpool cannot be overstated. Reynolds describes the connection between the Beatles and their hometown as "deep in the well of English, and especially Northern working-class, sentimentality" and notes that "[w]hen Liverpool and the North in general, was a forgotten second class citizen, this rock group suddenly made Liverpool fashionable in the entertainment world."[44] In an *Observer* article appearing in November, a week after the release of his *Meet the Beatles* magazine, Barrow attributed much of the Beatles' good fortunes to their background and believed the Beatles were "a success with the adult world in particular because they epitomize Northern Man—his naturalness, directness, the 'truthfulness' behind those hard and nobby faces."[45]

The Beatles' northern English and Liverpudlian identity was demonstrated most distinctly and obviously in their speech, for, as reported in the *Guardian* in June 1963, "[u]nlike earlier Liverpool entertainers, who seemed to either Londonise themselves or specialize in being Scouser yokels, the Beatles have come up with a different, and heavily Northern flavoured, sound of their own. It is amusing without becoming a joke."[46] Months later, the *Observer* noted that the Beatles' "working-class accent is exaggerated, not refined away but made to sound as crude as it can be."[47] The Beatles' unrepentant retention of their native accent and dialect, a small but not insignificant blow against the cultural hegemony of London and the south, was emblematic of a major cultural shift in British culture. From the "angry young men" of the stage to the rise to prominence of a new generation of authors, artists, filmmakers, actors, and pop stars, the working class was instrumental in defining British culture in the 1960s. Looking back on the period from a distance of 30 years, actor Michael Caine, the cockney son of a fish-market porter and a charwoman, recalled defiantly, "For the first time in British history, the young working class stood up for themselves and said, . . . 'Join us, stay away, like us, hate us—do as you like. We don't care about your opinion any more.'"[48] The Beatles carried forth the banner of the northern working class and planted it in the heart of English teen culture. Kenneth Allsop described middle-class teenage girls who "talk the Lancashire and Yorkshire of their disc idols all the time among themselves, and change with polyglot dexterity into orthodox county only within earshot of their parents."[49] Suddenly, to be working-class and from the north of England carried with it a certain cultural capital, even—perhaps especially—among the young.

The Beatles' identification with northern England and Liverpool, in particular, held important implications for the Beatles' image that went beyond its appeal for modestly rebellious teenagers. In the London-centered mass media, postwar Liverpool, characterized by Dominic Sandbrook as an "imperial port in terminal decline,"[50] was virtually interchangeable with working-class malaise. Prone to stereotyping, caricature, and hyperbole, the British national media frequently depicted the city as a desolate, dangerous, economically blighted, urban jungle. This tendency is readily apparent in the reporting of the British national press as it scrambled to provide information on the band following the outbreak of Beatlemania as a national phenomenon and press preoccupation after the London Palladium broadcast. For instance, the *Observer*, opining that the Beatles were "broadcasting the true and unique voice of Liverpool's working class and this is what most people admire," referenced the *Daily Worker*, the daily newspaper of the Communist Party of Great Britain, which characterized the Mersey Sound as the "voice of 80,000 crumbling houses and 30,000 people on the dole."[51] With economic turmoil comes violence, and the *Observer* article distills much of Liverpool's reputation as a "tough, violent city" and a "wild place" with a "ganging-up tradition."[52] The *Observer*'s correspondents noted of the Beatles: "Someone asked them to say what it was about Liverpool that excited people so much. 'It's exciting trying to keep alive,' one of them said."[53] As described in the *Observer*, Liverpool is a "'crude' place and the Sound is crude, with an emphatic beat," said one "young man in a black leather jacket," and another agreed: "'There's realism in this city. It's a city of mixtures, but it's also grubby and very crude. Fundamentally, the music is like that.'"[54]

Obviously, the world described by the *Observer* is well removed from that described by Barrow in the *Meet the Beatles* magazine and indicates an alternative narrative. There were a number of elements at play within the Beatles' image that derived from the band's earlier days as a club and ballroom band and that speak to the Beatles' earlier, more mature fan base. In mid-January 1963, shortly after the release of "Please Please Me"/"Ask Me Why" (Parlophone), a *Guardian* article[55] described Manchester's thriving coffee dance clubs—"most of which have twist or jazz groups, the Beatles for instance"[56]—where patrons were "an almost metropolitan mixture of artists, Continental girls who could be students, but may just be au pair, and young manual workers having a fairly inexpensive night on the town."[57] Observing the age of the clubs' patrons, the *Guardian* continued, "These clubs are said to be for teenagers, but a manageress explained that nobody over 20 is turned away. At one with a particularly strong Continental element the manager said the men averaged 23. And the girls? 'You just can't tell with the girls.'"[58] Such clubs were "warm, classless havens in which one may defy any climatic or emotional bleakness there may be outside," where "a foreigner, of whatever nationality, can feel immediately at home, or Oxford graduates twist naturally with computer girls, or Ghanaians find that the colour of their skin is immaterial."[59]

Barely a fortnight later, as "Please Please Me" closed in on the top position in the singles charts, the *Evening Standard*'s Maureen Cleave profiled the "darlings of Merseyside," of whom "the little girls are so fiercely possessive,"[60] and described an aspect of the band that was all but absent from the later teen-idol image but quite familiar to the band's fans in the clubs. Observing that Lennon "has an upper lip which is brutal in a devastating way," she honed in on a more primal appeal. "You can dance to The Beatles," writes Cleave, but her "Liverpool housewife" friend says that most people like to listen. " 'They like to sit and throb,' she said, 'or stand and throb, and the walls stream with sweat. It's lovely.'"[61]

Similarly indicative of an older—and more working-class—fan base than that most actively sought in fall 1963 is an item appearing in the *Stage*: "It is said that fans of the Beatles are having the insect tattooed on their arms so they can join clubs named after the group."[62] Published in July, months after the first incidents of what would later be called Beatlemania were reported in the media, the article reflects a period of transition for the Beatles and their fans and, for a time, in spring and summer 1963, tattooed cosmopolitans and frenzied teenage females inhabited together the United Kingdom's mass-mediated environment. Still, the trajectory was clear. In August, Epstein decided that the band would no longer play in clubs and ballrooms and would accept only theater bookings, which offered prestige and catered to a broader swath of the record-buying audience and were also safer venues for the Beatles and fans.[63]

During the closing months of the year, the media construction of Beatles fandom focused almost exclusively on frenzied teenage girls—almost but not quite. Even as the Beatles' status as teen idols reached new heights and sparked a cultural phenomenon of unprecedented sweep and depth, a more mature depiction of a somewhat debased teen and young-adult culture briefly reared its head as a kind of riposte to the frenzy of Beatlemania that was the focus of most Beatles-related news stories. There were earlier hints of this. In early June, the *Daily Mirror*, which, prior to the Palladium show and the ensuing frenzy of the fans, scarcely mentioned the Beatles outside of the paper's weekly "Pop 30" of Britain's top-selling records or its radio and television schedules, nevertheless reported an altercation in which Lennon beat up the Cavern Club host and big supporter of the Beatles, Bob Wooler. "Why did I have to go and punch my best friend?" lamented Lennon before admitting, "I was so high I didn't realize what I was doing."[64] Interestingly, next to this item (which included a picture of Lennon) was one entitled "Big Deal," which reported that the nation's police forces were investigating a drug ring that procured drugs through seamen who smuggled them through ports to couriers who "deliver them to railway station left-luggage offices to be picked up by agents."[65] These two items reverberate in another, published on October 8 in the *Guardian*, just days before the Beatles' appearance on *Val Parnell's Sunday Night at the London Palladium*.

The profile of the Liverpool music scene seems intent on providing an autopsy of it, with its stars, including "the Beatles, Gerry, the Searchers, and Billy J.," destined to "fade away from the charts, to the Helen Shapiro hinterland of the twelve-month-wonders."[66] The article, "Ravers' Requiem," was based largely on an interview with Wooler, Lennon's aforementioned victim. The *Guardian* article described the "new look" epitomized by the Beatles' fashion and "ravolutionaries," as Wooler had christened the girls frequenting the clubs:

> Polo-neck sweaters, button-to-the-neck collarless jackets, bell-bottom jeans, Cuban-heeled boots, black leather everything—a complete break with the Italian-Ivy League, a kind of a rush into everything prewar German, ultra-kooky and slightly kinky even to the long Brecht-brushed hairstyles. And the girls assert their self-assured sexuality with extravagantly coloured and back-combed hair, heavily kohled eyes, and corpse-pale mouths.[67]

Far from the frenzied preteen and teenage fans fueling the Beatles phenomenon, these fans, claimed Wooler, had "a profound knowledge of sex."[68] They liked to go to "Raves," where they "rave it up," which, according to Wooler, meant, "You get as high as a steeple, one way or another," with the pills of choice including Drynamil, Preludin tablets, and "Bennies."[69] Though not overtly linking the Beatles with these activities, he explicitly brings the narcotics investigation in the news story noted earlier to the docks of Liverpool in his description of a music scene and a youth culture bowing under the influence of drugs:

> A young lad with a boyish grin, who said he had just spent the night in gaol, explained that he sent his girl friend down to the ship to collect the Purple Hearts, £500 worth, because girls weren't searched. He said the pills were left in the left luggage and then picked up by someone, he didn't know who. He got 100 pills for his part, but the police were on to him.
> "There is this connection between Germany," Mr. Wooler said. "Unfortunately I've never been there. I'm going to go, at the end of November. I'm going over to see if I can trace this thing. These groups come back from Hamburg and they tell me about the riotous things they see there. What intrigues me about it is that they are such a short time in Germany. It's sinister in a way, all this black leather. I'm not saying they should go all 1939

and remember the Huns, but sometimes it seems a little too much like an Isherwood novel."[70]

The *Guardian* wrote, "The Raves, the Purple Hearts, the set faces, and the undercurrent of cruelty is disturbing," and, lamented Wooler, "They are afraid of sentiment. They are cruel to each other because they are trying to prove they have no hearts. They try to show that they are not affected by anything."[71]

Thus, as we have seen, the Beatles' image in the United Kingdom evolved and, inescapably, bore the marks of that evolution. These darker aspects of the Beatles' past were themselves a thing of the past, however. As it turned out, British Beatlemania was about to make the jump to something much, much greater. Across the Atlantic Ocean, the image was being tuned and tightened, scoured and scrubbed, and honed to commercial perfection for American teenagers. In the process, there emerged an image of youth that reverberated around the world.

The Beatles and Beatles Fans in America, 1964

Certainly among the earliest, if not the first, mention of the Beatles in the US press came in a short UPI story containing 11 lines of text (two paragraphs of one sentence, each) and describing the rescue of "the Beatles rock 'n' roll quartet" from "500 stampeding teen-age girls" by police and added reinforcements following the band's performance at the London Palladium.[72] In the following weeks, the British national press's fascination with Beatlemania prompted more attention from the American press. In late October, an AP story, "New Ailment—Beatlemania Hits British Teen-Agers," described the phenomenon as a "mass hysteria generated by 'The Beatles'— four young musicians from seamy Liverpool with something called the Liverpool Sound," and "one of the wildest teen-age phenomenon yet."[73] The story listed a number of recent incidents: "In London . . . screaming teenagers rioted when tickets for a Beatle concert during Christmas week went on sale"; "Seven thousand teen-agers went wild in Newcastle-upon-Tyne yesterday in front of a box office selling tickets for a future appearance of the Beatles"; and one girl, who "had her jeans torn off" in the fracas, "reached the box office wrapped in a blanket." In Carlisle, "there were nine injured when a crowd of 600 rioted in front of a box office"; and in Hull, "50 police battled 2,000 teen-agers trying to buy tickets for a performance next month."[74]

Here, then, we see American media coverage of the Beatles phenomenon that mirrors that of the British national press, with a similar narrative focus on the fans' frenzied behavior and the response of authorities.

Over a matter of weeks, the American mass-market magazines and national press pulled together a constellation of ideas that circled around the behavior of British Beatles fans and that were the basis for the emergent image of the band. In mid-November, *Newsweek*, in an article entitled "Beatlemania," called attention to the Beatles' success and instances of Beatlemania previously described in the British press:

> Their theater appearances drew 5,000 screaming fans and a police riot squad in Manchester; 4,000 began queuing up at 3 a.m. in Newcastle-upon-Tyne; and 2,000 teen-age girls squealed their hearts out as they besieged bobbies outside the sold-out London Palladium. "This is Beatlemania," said the *Daily Mail*, and added plaintively: "Where will it all lead?"[75]

Time magazine, though dismissive of a phenomenon that it deemed "achingly familiar" to American audiences, nevertheless acknowledged that the Beatles were "irresistible" to the English.[76]

Network news coverage was similarly focused on the behavior of the fans. NBC, ABC, and CBS sent crews to the Winter Gardens Theatre in Bournemouth, Hampshire, to film a Beatles' performance and their frenzied young fans. Footage from the November 16 show at the Winter Gardens was used in reports running from mid-November through the first week of December. CBS's Alexander Kendrick, in a report that was essentially a summary of recent press coverage in the United Kingdom, repeated the views of sociologists looking for the "deeper meaning" of the Beatles phenomenon, who found that the Beatles represented "the authentic voice of the Proletariat" or "the authentic heart of Britain, in revolt against the American cult of pop singers," or "the authentic British youth or British youth as it would like to be—self confident, natural, direct, decent, vital, and throbbing."[77]

On the first Sunday of December, a *New York Times Magazine* article filed by the newspaper's London desk, "Britons Succumb to 'Beatlemania,'"[78] described the ardor of the young female Beatles fans, for whom, it observed, "[t]o see a Beatle is joy, to touch one paradise on earth."[79] The "shattering of the English peace" by frenzied Beatles fans was detailed in a "sample of the battle reports" from the previous month:

in Carlisle, 400 schoolgirls fought the police for four hours while attempting to get tickets for a Beatles show; that in Dublin, young limbs snapped like twigs in a tremendous free-for-all during the Beatles' first visit to the city (the police chief, with characteristic Irishness, said: "It was alright until the mania degenerated into barbarism"), that at London Airport, a woman news reporter had her left hand kissed repeatedly, simply because the hand had accidentally brushed the sleeve of a Beatle; that during rehearsals for the Royal Variety Show, the Beatles were marooned inside the London Palladium for 13 hours because the authorities considered it unsafe for them to leave; and that in Birmingham, the only way the boys could evade the mob was to disguise themselves as police, complete with capes and helmets.[80]

The article reflected the framing of the Beatles phenomenon in the British press. Noting that the band's appeal was "strongest to females between 10 and 30, but Beatlemania, as it is called, affects all social classes and all levels of intelligence," the author, Frederick Lewis, offered a summary of the "basic factors in the extraordinary success of the Beatles":

They are working class, and their roots and attitudes are firmly of the North of England. Because of their success they can act as spokesmen for the new, noisy, anti-Establishment generation which is becoming a force in British life. In their uncompromising Northernness, they are linked with actors like Albert Finney in the theater and films and novelists like Alan Sillitoe and John Braine. The Beatles are part of a strong-flowing reaction against the soft, middle-class South of England, which has controlled popular culture for so long. The most important thing about the Beatles is that they come from Liverpool. In this city, where the Catholics and Protestants still fight every Saturday night after the pubs have closed, there are close to 300 beat groups performing in converted cinemas, cellar clubs—anywhere where an amplifier can be plugged in. The combined din they make has come to be known as the Liverpool Sound. The significance of the Sound is that it is a raspberry blown in the direction of London.[81]

The same week as Lewis's piece appeared in the New York Times Magazine, a nationally syndicated article, also filed from London, described the Beatles as the "voice of that postwar generation which is known here as the Bulge, the million war babies for whom there are not enough schools and not enough jobs," and waxed poetic that the Beatles "sing for the jobless youths who stand in front of the Liverpool Labor Exchange, their hands in their pockets, while the wind from the River Mersey bites into their bones."[82]

The article, "Beware—The Beatles Are Coming," obviously draws heavily upon British press sources, yet it also demonstrates the degree to which the Beatles' image was already being scrubbed of its more mature elements. Compare the following passage to the *Guardian*'s "Ravers' Requiem" article described earlier:

> As for the German influence, this is most evident in their clothes. The Beatles have rejected the Ivy League-Italian look in favor of the ultra-kooky and slightly kinky look of Germany of the 1920s. Their jackets are tight-fitting and collarless, their boots have elastic sides, and sometimes have Cuban heels.
>
> The German vogue among the British pop singers like the Beatles puzzles some observers. "These groups come back from Hamburg," says Bob Wooler. who first discovered the Beatles, "and they tell me about the riotous things they see there. It's sinister in a way all this black leather."[83]

Though much here is borrowed from the British article published in early October, information is altered, garbled, even removed. All mention of drugs or sex has been excised. Gone are Wooler's "ravolutionaries," who attend "Raves" fueled by drugs smuggled through the Liverpool port by the "young lad with a boyish grin."[84] Suddenly, the German connection is solely one of fashion rather than vice.

On January 3, 1964, a month before the Beatles' appearance on the *Ed Sullivan Show*, NBC aired footage of the band on the *Jack Paar Program*. The *Paar* segment opened with footage from the Beatles' appearance at Bournemouth's Winter Gardens Theatre. Paar's interest, as he told his audience that Friday night, was "in showing a more adult audience that usually follows my work what's going on in England."[85] His introduction is emblematic of American media's construction of Liverpool: "They're from the toughest part of England. It's Merseyside, near Liverpool in the dock area, and it's a very tough area where these four nice kids come from."[86] Paar continued, clearly drawing from the previously published *Observer* (London) article, "The Roots of Beatlemania," described earlier: "They're kind of witty—one said, . . . 'What's so exciting about living on the docks at Liverpool?' He says, 'Just staying alive is exciting.' But they're nice kids."[87]

For American audiences standing outside the British experience and reared on Hollywood cinema, Liverpool emerges as something akin not to the on-location docks of *On the Waterfront* (Columbia Pictures, 1954) but, rather, to a studio contrivance for a "Dead End Kids" movie, with the Beatles as British "Bowery Boys."

American mass-market magazines, at this point less concerned with explaining the Beatles phenomenon than were the newspapers, tended to focus on more entertaining and broadly appealing stories. For instance, in November 1963, in characterizing the "boys" as "the very spirit of good clean fun," *Time* was impressed by neither the band's talent nor the reaction of its fans but nevertheless noted the Beatles' unique appearance: "They look like shaggy Peter Pans, with their mushroom-haircuts and high white shirt collars."[88] In December, *Look* magazine published a two-page photo spread showing the Beatles' effect on hair length in England.[89] Very quickly, in antic-ipation of the Beatles' arrival in the United States, the mass-market magazines turned their attention to the mania of the young female British fans. The January 31, 1964, issue of *Life* contained a description of Beatlemania and eight pages of pictures of teenage girls screaming, crying, and fainting: " 'If those girls caught those ruddy lads,' commented one officer, 'they'd tear them to pieces.' At one theater a hundred girls battled police for four hours outside when they couldn't buy tickets."[90] The trials of the constabulary were fur-ther detailed: " 'I nearly got my ruddy shoulder dislocated trying to stop three girls dashing under a bus,' grumbled one London police sergeant. 'These girls are like eels—through your legs and after the Beatles before you know where you are.' "[91] It is important to note that the Liverpool and working-class narratives of the earliest American press have all but disappeared. Certainly, this was a function of Americans' lack of knowledge of—and interest in—the British context for the Beatles' success. Just as important, though, by late January, Capitol Records' promotional campaign was in full swing.

Initially doubtful of its commercial potential, Capitol had been slow to promote the band, but once it made the commitment in November 1963, its sales force was tasked with making 1964 the "Year of the Beatles."[92] No expense was spared in a promotional campaign rolled out in January for the forthcoming Capitol album *Meet the Beatles!* (released on January 20, 1964) and, to a lesser extent, the Beatles' current American single, "I Want to Hold Your Hand" (released on December 26, 1963, with "I Saw Her Standing There" as the B-side), which reached number one on *Cashbox*'s singles chart in mid-January, just as the Capitol campaign was being implemented. The promotion incorporated, among other things, radio contests and giveaways, mass distribution of Beatles wigs for stores and disc jockeys to promote the "Beatle Hair-Do Craze that should be sweeping the country soon," motion displays, and store posters and counter stands.[93] A seven-inch record disc was distributed that included Beatles music and an open-ended interview format (which included recorded Beatles dialogue interspersed with gaps provided to allow disc jockeys to "interact" with the group, according to the scripted content).

The centerpiece of the campaign, which *Billboard* declared to be "one of the most efficient and effective . . . in recent memory,"[94] was a four-page tabloid newspaper, the *National Record News*, a document that Capitol's national merchandising manager found "deceptively legitimate" and a "simply marvelous vehicle for spreading the Beatles story."[95] The Capitol sales force was called on to "get as many copies of this tabloid as possible into the hands of potential Beatle buyers," specifically high school students.[96] The tabloid's headline leaves no doubt about the focus of the campaign, however, and equal to or perhaps even more important than defining the Beatles' image was defining the Beatles' fan. In big, bold, letters sprayed across the top of a five-column front page dedicated to the phenomenon, the *National Record News* declared, " 'Beatlemania' SWEEPS the U.S."[97] The importance of reports of the ecstatic reaction of young Beatles fans to the early image of the Beatles and Capitol's promotion of the band is impossible to overstate. Even the sleeve notes written by Barrow for the first Capitol album *Meet the Beatles!* focused on the mania of British fans, with the album containing "twelve of their most sensational songs in their wildest Beatlemanic style!"

Thus, by the time of the Beatles' arrival at New York's Kennedy Airport, the American public was primed to welcome the Beatles phenomenon on terms promoted by the Beatles. Beatlemania had already arrived.

Conclusion

Capitol Records wanted to make 1964 the "Year of the Beatles"[98] in America and so promoted the Beatles in much the same way as they had been promoted in Great Britain, to as wide an audience as possible but with a clear focus on record-buying teenagers. Capitol's promotion of the Beatles focused on their unprecedented success: their talent, particularly that of the songwriters, Lennon and McCartney; their wit and cheekiness; their unique sound and appearance, particularly their hairstyle; the individuality of each Beatle; their wide appeal; and, above all else, the frenzied ardor of young, primarily female fans. Yet, while much of the Beatles' British image was retained, some elements were altered or removed as the Beatles' image was scrubbed and sanitized for the American market. In the United Kingdom, the Beatles' northern English and Liverpool origins carried meanings and associations that were beyond the experience of most American teenagers and so were irrelevant to Capitol's promotional campaign. "Liverpool" remained an important part of the Beatles' image, but now, instead of resonating with working-class and northern English identity, as it did in the United Kingdom, it became a marker for the Beatles' Englishness and foreignness, on one hand, and their ordinariness, on the other. As such, the Beatles' image was touted in ways familiar to American audiences socialized to believe in an American myth of success in which social mobility was a matter of effort rather than one's station at birth—in other words, the Beatles' image was stripped of much of the class-based resonance so important in the British context. Capitol also extricated the image from the more mature elements of Liverpool's rave culture, including intimations of sex, drugs, and violence.

In a sense, the image was removed from the context of its creation. Wrenched from space and time, much of the Beatles' biography, and all that implied for British observers, was removed in favor of an almost exclusive focus on the fans and their mania. Now, then, is the image in its most controlled and pristine state—an ebullient ideal, a celebration of youth, of possibility. It is an image that carried the Beatles through the touring years and beyond. It continues to resonate in promotion of the band. And what resonates most strongly is, perhaps, a sense of pure, boundless, blissful innocence, of something forever lost to us but somehow forever available, if only for an instant, in considering a Beatles phenomenon that is as much "us" as it is "them"—or, better, it is somehow "we."

Notes

1. McCandish Phillips, "4 Beatles and How They Grew: Publicitywise," *New York Times*, February 17, 1964, 1, 20.
2. The AP reported that in the all-important New York area market, Nielsen sampling found that 72.7% of television sets were tuned in to the Beatles' first performance on the *Ed Sullivan Show*, and the Arbitron rating service found that the *Sullivan* show had nearly doubled its audience (Associated Press, "Television: Sponsors Eye Ratings," 8).

3. Barry Miles, *The Beatles Diary*, Volume 1, *The Beatle Years* (London: Omnibus, 2001), 133.

4. Phillips, "4 Beatles," 1.

5. Phillips, "4 Beatles," 1.

6. Phillips, "4 Beatles," 1.

7. Richard Dyer, *Heavenly Bodies: Film Stars and Society*, 2nd ed. (New York: Routledge, 2004), 2.

8. Simon Frith and Andrew Goodwin, eds., *On Record: Rock, Pop and the Written Word* (New York: Pantheon, 1990), 425.

9. Footage from *The Mersey Sound* was used in the *Anthology* series and is also readily available on YouTube. See, for instance, "The Beatles Mersey Sound 1963," https://www.youtube.com/watch?v=pyXO5p74pEI. It should be noted that the band had earlier appeared on numerous regional broadcasts. Its first television appearance was on Granada TV's *People and Places*, broadcast throughout north and northwest England on October 17, 1962. The first of many appearances on the popular music program *Thank Your Lucky Stars*, broadcast throughout the north of England and the Midlands, followed three months later, on January 13, 1963.

10. The program was broadcast to a national audience the following month, on November 13. "Television: The Mersey Sound," *The Beatles Bible*, https://www.beatlesbible.com/1963/08/30/television-the-mersey-sound-4/.

11. Maurice Richardson, "TV as I Saw It," *Observer* (London), October 13, 1963, 23.

12. Richardson, "TV as I Saw It."

13. See Hunter Davies, *The Beatle Book* (London: Penguin/Ebury Press, 2016), 561–562; and Mark Lewisohn, *The Complete Beatles Chronicles* (London: Hamlyn, 2003), 125.

14. Wesley Laine, "Beatles Beatles," *Record Mirror*, February 2, 1963, *Rock's Backpages*, http://www.rocksbackpages.com/Library/Article/beatles-beatles.

15. "Northwich Crowd of 6,000 Mobs Beatles—Women and Girls Hurt," *Liverpool Echo*, July 8, 1963, 13, British Newspaper Archive.

16. "Northwich Crowd."

17. "500 Girls Force Gates to See Beatles," *Birmingham Post* (Birmingham, UK), September 9, 1963, 5, British Newspaper Archive.

18. Don Short, "6,000 Fans—The Beatles Just Fled," *Daily Mirror* (London), September 16, 1963, 3, *British Newspaper Archive*.

19. "Show Cancelled," *Guardian* (London), October 8, 1963, 1, *Newspapers.com*.

20. "Beatles Barred!" *Stage* (London), October 31, 1963, 3, *British Newspaper Archive*.

21. "Battle of the Beatles Goes On," *Liverpool Echo*, October 21, 1963, 3, *British Newspaper Archive*.

22. "Battle of the Beatles."

23. "Battle of the Beatles."

24. "Beatlecrush," *Guardian* (London), November 6, 1963, 7, *Newspapers.com*.

25. "Beatlecrush."

26. "Police Battle with Screaming Beatle Fans," *Liverpool Echo*, October 26, 1963, 1, *British Newspaper Archive*.

27. "Police Battle."

28. "Police Battle."
29. "130 Beatles Fans Injured in Ticket Stampede," *Newcastle Journal*, October 28, 1963, 1, *British Newspaper Archive*.
30. "John Lennon: '. . . Just Rattle Your Jewelry' + 'Twist and Shout,'" *YouTube*, https://www.youtube.com/watch?v=rvBCmY7wAAU.
31. "Royal Beatles," *Guardian* (London), November 5, 1963 8, *Newspapers.com*.
32. "30 Faint at Beatle Shows," *Guardian* (London), November 21, 1963, 6, *Newspapers.com*.
33. "12,000 in Queue for Tickets to See the Beatles," *Guardian* (London), November 25, 1963, 4, *Newspapers.com*.
34. "12,000 in Queue."
35. "Street Closed for the Beatles," *Guardian* (London), December 7, 1963, 12, *Newspapers.com*.
36. "Northern News in Brief: 7,000 Greet the Beatles," *Guardian* (London), December 9, 1963, 16, *Newspapers.com*.
37. The Amazon.com description of a hardcover collector's edition of the publication notes that the original 1963 publication sold more than 1 million copies. https://www.amazon.com/Meet-Beatles-Informal-Personal-Pictures/dp/0285642898.
38. Tony Barrow, *Meet the Beatles: An Informal Date in Words & Album Pictures* (Manchester, UK: World Distributors, 1963), 1.
39. Barrow, *Meet the Beatles*, 2–9.
40. Barrow, *Meet the Beatles*, 10.
41. Barrow, *Meet the Beatles*, 20, 36.
42. "It's the Beatles! The Fabulous Story of Liverpool's Famous Four" ran over six consecutive days, October 21–26, 1963. See, for instance, Tony Barrow, "It's the Beatles!" *Liverpool Echo*, October 21, 1963, 5, *British Newspaper Archive*.
43. Stanley Reynolds, "Big Time," *Guardian* (Manchester, UK), June 3, 1963, 10, *Newspapers.com*.
44. Reynolds, "Big Time."
45. Cyril Dunn and Peter Dunn, "The Roots of Beatlemania," *Observer* (London), November 10, 1963, 29, *Newspapers.com*.
46. Reynolds, "Big Time."
47. Dunn and Dunn, "The Roots of Beatlemania."
48. Michael Caine, *What's It All About? An Autobiography* (New York: Ballantine, 1994), 159.
49. Kenneth Allsop, "Pop Goes Young Woodley," in *Class*, ed. Richard Mabey (London: Anthony Blond, 1967), 130.
50. Dominic Sandbrook, *Never Had It So Good: A History of Britain from Suez to the Beatles* (London: Abacus, 2006), 485.
51. Dunn and Dunn, "The Roots of Beatlemania."
52. Dunn and Dunn, "The Roots of Beatlemania."
53. Dunn and Dunn, "The Roots of Beatlemania."
54. Dunn and Dunn, "The Roots of Beatlemania."

55. "Not Everybody's Cup, but These Clubs Are Here to Stay," *Guardian* (Manchester, UK), January 17, 1963, 17.

56. The Beatles made the first of four visits to Manchester's Oasis Club in February 1962, for Epstein's first professionally arranged engagement for the band and its first excursion outside of Liverpool. The Beatles' last appearance there was in February 1963. See Lewisohn, *The Complete Beatles Chronicle*, 360.

57. "Not Everybody's Cup."

58. "Not Everybody's Cup."

59. "Not Everybody's Cup."

60. Maureen Cleave, "Why the Beatles Create All That Frenzy," *Evening Standard*, February 2, 1963, *Rock's Backpages*, http://www.rocksbackpages.com/Library/Article/why-the-beatles-create-all-that-frenzy.

61. Cleave, "Why the Beatles Create All That Frenzy."

62. "Club Corner," *Stage* (London), July 11, 1963, 4, *British Newspaper Archive*, https://www.britishnewspaperarchive.co.uk/viewer/bl/0001180/19630711/034/0004.

63. Lewisohn, *The Complete Beatles Chronicle*, 92.

64. Don Short, "Beatle in Brawl—'Sorry I Socked You,'" *Daily Mirror*, June 21, 1963, 28, *British Newspaper Archive*, https://www.britishnewspaperarchive.co.uk/viewer/bl/0000560/19630621/225/0028.

65. Tom Tullet, "A Big Deal," *Daily Mirror*, June 21, 1963, 28, *British Newspaper Archive*, https://www.britishnewspaperarchive.co.uk/viewer/bl/0000560/19630621/225/0028.

66. Stanley Reynolds, "Ravers' Requiem," 9.

67. Reynolds, "Ravers' Requiem."

68. Reynolds, "Ravers' Requiem."

69. Reynolds, "Ravers' Requiem."

70. Reynolds, "Ravers' Requiem."

71. Reynolds, "Ravers' Requiem."

72. United Press International, "500 Teen-Age Girls Mob British Quartet," *Tucson Daily Citizen*, October 14, 1963, 24, *Newspaper Archive*, https://newspaperarchive.com/tucson-daily-citizen-oct-14-1963-p-23/.

73. Eddie Gilmore, "New Ailment—Beatlemania Hits British Teen-Agers," AP, *Post-Star* (Glens Falls, NY), October 29, 1963, 1, *Newspaper Archive*, https://newspaperarchive.com/glens-falls-post-star-oct-29-1963-p-1/.

74. Gilmore, "New Ailment."

75. "Beatlemania," *Newsweek*, November 18, 1963, 104.

76. "The New Madness," *Time*, November 15, 1963, 64.

77. *CBS Evening News*, November 21, 1963, *YouTube*, https://www.youtube.com/watch?v=UeolhjIWPYs&t=128s.

78. Frederick Lewis, "Britons Succumb to 'Beatlemania,'" *New York Times Magazine*, December 1, 1963, 124–126.

79. Lewis, "Britons Succumb," 124.

80. Lewis, "Britons Succumb," 126.

81. Lewis, "Britons Succumb," 126.

82. Thomas A. Cullen, "Beware—The Beatles Are Coming," London/NEA, *Burlington* (N.C.) *Daily Times-News*, December 5, 1963, 8A, *Newspaper Archive*, https://newspaperarchive.com/burlington-daily-times-news-dec-05-1963-p-16/.

83. Cullen, "Beware."

84. Reynolds, "Ravers' Requiem."

85. *Jack Paar Program*, NBC, January 3, 1964, 10–11 p.m., video at Museum of Television and Radio, New York.

86. *Jack Paar Program*.

87. *Jack Paar Program*.

88. "The New Madness."

89. "What the Beatles Have Done to Hair," *Look*, December 29, 1964, 58–59.

90. Timothy Green, "Here Come Those Beatles: Four Screaming Mopheads Break Up England," with photography by Terence Spencer, *Life*, January 31, 1964, 24–31, 27.

91. Green, "Here Come Those Beatles," 30.

92. "Capital Records Memo," in Lewisohn, *The Complete Beatles Chronicle*, 94.

93. Lewisohn, *The Complete Beatles Chronicle*, 94.

94. Barry Kittleson, "Beatles Giving Trade a Solid Bite," *Billboard*, January 25, 1964, 4.

95. Lewisohn, *The Complete Beatles Chronicle*, 94.

96. Lewisohn, *The Complete Beatles Chronicle*, 94.

97. *National Record News: Special Beatles Issue*, Capitol Records Publicity Department, New York, December 1963.

98. Lewisohn, *The Complete Beatles Chronicle*, 94.

Bibliography

Allsop, Kenneth. "Pop Goes Young Woodley." In *Class*, edited by Richard Mabey, 127–171. London: Anthony Blond, 1967.

Associated Press. "Television: Sponsors Eye Ratings." *Ithaca Journal* (Ithaca, NY), February 11, 1964. Newspaper Archive.

Barrow, Tony. "It's the Beatles!" *Liverpool Echo*, October 21, 1963. *British Newspaper Archive*.

Barrow, Tony. *Meet the Beatles: An Informal Date in Words & Album Pictures*. Manchester, UK: World Distributors, 1963.

"Battle of the Beatles Goes On." *Liverpool Echo*, October 21, 1963. *British Newspaper Archive*.

"Beatlecrush." *Guardian* (London), November 6, 1963. *Newspapers.com*.

"Beatlemania." *Newsweek*, November 18, 1963.

"Beatles Barred!" *Stage* (London), October 31, 1963. *British Newspaper Archive*.

The Beatles Bible. "Television: The Mersey Sound." https://www.beatlesbible.com/1963/08/30/television-the-mersey-sound-4/.

"The Beatles Mersey Sound 1963." YouTube. https://www.youtube.com/watch?v=pyXO5p74pEI.

Caine, Michael, *What's It All About? An Autobiography*. New York: Ballantine, 1994.

CBS Evening News. November 21, 1963. *YouTube*.

Cleave, Maureen. "Why the Beatles Create All That Frenzy." *Evening Standard*, February 2, 1963. *Rock's Backpages*. http://www.rocksbackpages.com/Library/Article/ why-the-beatles-create-all-that-frenzy.

"Club Corner." *Stage* (London), July 11, 1963. *British Newspaper Archive*.

Cullen, Thomas A. "Beware—The Beatles Are Coming," London/NEA. *Burlington* (N.C.) *Daily Times-News*, December 5, 1963. *Newspaper Archive*.

Davies, Hunter. *The Beatle Book*. London: Penguin/Ebury Press, 2016.

Dunn, Cyril, and Peter Dunn. "The Roots of Beatlemania." *Observer* (London). November 10, 1963. *Newspapers.com*.

Dyer, Richard. *Heavenly Bodies: Film Stars and Society*, 2nd ed. New York: Routledge, 2004.

"500 Girls Force Gates to See Beatles." *Birmingham Post* (Birmingham, UK), September 9, 1963. *British Newspaper Archive*,

Frith, Simon, and Andrew Goodwin, eds. *On Record: Rock, Pop and the Written Word*. New York: Pantheon, 1990.

Gilmore, Eddie. "New Ailment—Beatlemania Hits British Teen-Agers," AP. *Post-Star* (Glens Falls, NY), October 29, 1963. *Newspaper Archive*.

Green, Timothy. "Here Come Those Beatles: Four Screaming Mopheads Break Up England." Photography by Terence Spencer. *Life*, January 31, 1964.

Jack Paar Program. NBC, January 3, 1964, 10–11 p.m. Video at Museum of Television and Radio, New York.

"John Lennon: '. . . Just Rattle Your Jewelry' + 'Twist and Shout.'" *YouTube*. https://www. youtube.com/watch?v=rvBCmY7wAAU.

Kittleson, Barry. "Beatles Giving Trade a Solid Bite." *Billboard*, January 25, 1964.

Laine, Wesley. "Beatles Beatles." *Record Mirror*, February 2, 1963. *Rock's Backpages*. http:// www.rocksbackpages.com/Library/Article/beatles-beatles.

Lewis, Frederick. "Britons Succumb to 'Beatlemania.'" *New York Times Magazine*, December 1, 1963.

Lewisohn, Mark. *The Complete Beatles Chronicles*. London: Hamlyn, 2003.

Miles, Barry. *The Beatles Diary*, Volume 1, *The Beatle Years*. London: Omnibus, 2001.

National Record News: Special Beatles Issue. Capitol Records Publicity Department, New York, December 1963.

"The New Madness." *Time*, November 15, 1963.

"Northern News in Brief: 7,000 Greet the Beatles." *Guardian* (London), December 9, 1963. *Newspapers.com*.

"Norwich Crowd of 6,000 Mobs Beatles—Women and Girls Hurt." *Liverpool Echo*, July 8, 1963. British Newspaper Archive,

"Not Everybody's Cup, but These Clubs Are Here to Stay." *Guardian* (Manchester, UK), January 17, 1963. *Newspapers.com*.

"130 Beatles Fans Injured in Ticket Stampede." *Newcastle Journal*, October 28, 1963. *British Newspaper Archive*.

Phillips, McCandish. "4 Beatles and How They Grew: Publicitywise." *New York Times*, February 17, 1964.

"Police Battle with Screaming Beatle Fans." *Liverpool Echo*, October 26, 1963. *British Newspaper Archive*.

Reynolds, Stanley. "Big Time." *Guardian* (Manchester, UK), June 3, 1963. *Newspapers. com*.

Richardson, Maurice. "TV as I Saw It." *Observer* (London), October 13, 1963. Newspaper. com.

"Royal Beatles." *Guardian* (London), November 5, 1963. *Newspapers.com*.

Sandbrook, Dominic. *Never Had It So Good: A History of Britain from Suez to the Beatles*. London: Abacus, 2006.

Short, Don. "Beatle in Brawl—'Sorry I Socked You.'" *Daily Mirror*, June 21, 1963. *British Newspaper Archive*.

Short, Don. "600 Fans—The Beatles Just Fled." *Daily Mirror* (London), September 16, 1963. *British Newspaper Archive*.

"Show Cancelled." *Guardian* (London), October 8, 1963. *Newspapers.com*.

"Street Closed for the Beatles." *Guardian* (London), December 7, 1963. *Newspapers.com*.

"30 Faint at Beatle Shows." *Guardian* (London), November 21, 1963. *Newspapers.com*.

Tullet, Tom. "A Big Deal." *Daily Mirror*, June 21, 1963. *British Newspaper Archive*.

"12,000 in Queue for Tickets to See the Beatles." *Guardian* (London), November 25, 1963, 4. *Newspapers.com*.

United Press International. "500 Teen-Age Girls Mob British Quartet." *Tucson Daily Citizen*, October 14, 1963. *Newspaper Archive*.

"What the Beatles Have Done to Hair." *Look*, December 29, 1964.

3

John Lennon as Pop-Cultural and Political Icon

Giving Peace a Chance

Punch Shaw

Legends are made in moments. And few notable figures in popular culture have given us more of those legacy-defining moments than John Lennon, the founder and, for many, the brain and face of the Beatles.

In sorting through Lennon's life, a kaleidoscopic array of triumphs, missteps, and turbulent battles emerges. Was he, as one author put it, "a hippie messiah," or was he a troubled and insecure artist whom we revere for what we wanted him to be rather than who he was?[1]

The following is the short summation that *Rolling Stone* columnist Rob Sheffield offered about Lennon in his delightfully scattershot analysis of the Fab Four, *Dreaming the Beatles*, which succinctly hits some of the high points that continue to define Lennon for us today:

> John Lennon: The Smart One. Born in 1940, raised by his Aunt Mimi after his parents split. Mother Julia died in 1958. Married Cynthia Powell in 1962, son Julian born in 1963. Wrote two books of poetry. Explored LSD, primal scream therapy, mantra, gita, yoga, etc. Married Yoko Ono in 1969, moved to New York City. Imagined. Son Sean born in 1975. Left music for a few years in the Seventies to be a house-husband. Murdered with a handgun, December 1980, in front of home.[2]

While intentionally incomplete, this mini-bio (which concludes with the author's list of "best" and "worst" songs) does point us toward some of the most important components of Lennon's enduring image. This chapter seeks to identify the most significant of these moments and personality traits—the events, songs, accomplishments, and challenges of Lennon's unique life that

Punch Shaw, *John Lennon as Pop-Cultural and Political Icon* In: *Fandom and the Beatles*. Edited by: Kenneth Womack and Kit O'Toole, Oxford University Press (2021). © Oxford University Press.
DOI: 10.1093/oso/9780190917852.003.0004

are most often chronicled and cited as defining examples of who he was as a person and an artist—to understand how he is viewed by American fans today and if his vaunted status as a cultural and political icon (as well as a paragon of peace) is built on sand or stone.

Lennon as a Political and Cultural Icon: The Early Days

There can be little debate about the significance of Lennon as a cultural icon. His impact on popular music, and all things connected with it, as an individual artist and a band member, was enormous, obvious, and widely understood and accepted. But he also influenced other aspects of the cultural landscape of his times, from rapidly shifting clothing fashions (the collarless suits and clean-shaven faces of the 1964 *Ed Sullivan* appearance were separated from the retro uniforms and facial hair of *Sgt. Pepper* by a mere three years) to striking the appropriate antiestablishment pose of the era. Anthony Elliott argues that "Lennon's work directly engages with dominant political antagonisms" and that his "anti-institutional aesthetic, often marginalized in rememberings of Lennon, is a politics in itself."[3]

Lennon was a Renaissance man who dipped his toe in other aspects of popular culture by dabbling in writing an offbeat sort of poetry and prose in *In His Own Write* (1964) and *A Spaniard in the Works* (1965) and maintained his interest in the visual arts as both a practitioner (primarily drawings) and a supporter of the more adventurous elements of the 1960s art world, as personified by his wife, Yoko Ono. It was these extracurricular activities, as much as or more than his work with the Beatles, that earned Lennon his tag of "the smart one."

It is, therefore, almost impossible to separate the cultural and the political when discussing Lennon's life and legacy. It is easy to forget that something seemingly as innocent as male hair length (something that was previously only a cultural issue of fashion) took on political connotations in America when young people used it as a sociopolitical statement. It was one of the many visual representations of the "generation gap," courtesy of Lennon and the Beatles.

America got its first taste of the wit and wisdom of Lennon within minutes of his arrival at New York's JFK Airport on Feb. 7, 1964. Lennon and the Beatles were sharp and funny during their initial press conference. When the group was asked to sing, all responded with a loud "no," with Lennon adding, "You'll have to pay us first."[4]

The biting sense of humor and "cheeky" personality of Lennon were further solidified in those early days by his depiction in the group's first film *A Hard Day's Night* (1964). He was characterized as a troublemaker who delighted in thumbing his nose at his overmatched road managers, Norm (Norman Rossington) and Shake (John Junkin). But while Lennon was depicted as problematic in the film, even his cinematic nemesis seemed to have trouble mustering any real animosity.

"I've only one thing to say to you, John Lennon," Norm barks at his charge in the film's closing lines. "You're a swine." But the line is delivered with a laugh.[5] In later, real life, many of those around Lennon would respond to him in a similar fashion.

The other grand "first impression" moment of 1964 was, of course, the Beatles' appearance on the *Ed Sullivan Show* on February 9, 1964. The band stuck almost entirely to singing. McCartney added a few words of introduction for the songs, but there was little else to reveal what was going on with the young men behind the guitars and drums.

Still, there was one tiny detail in that legendary broadcast that is rarely mentioned but might have been a small, early step in building Lennon's legend. As the television cameras went in for close-ups of each band member, graphics came up to tell us their first names. But when it was Lennon's turn to be visually introduced, his graphic had something extra after "John." Viewers were advised, "Sorry Girls, He's Married."[6]

It seems to be just a frivolous footnote to an earth-shattering event. But in retrospect, this was one of the first, tangential biographical points that separated Lennon from his mates for American fans. Lennon was a married man, while the other three Beatles were single boys. Being a husband (and a father, although few *Ed Sullivan* viewers were aware of that) suggested that he was more mature and of-the-world than his partners. It was certainly not something that was much noted at the time. But it may have been the beginning of American fans looking at Lennon in a slightly different light without really knowing why. This matters because Lennon would go on to separate himself from the Beatles in various ways until reaching a full break in late 1969, allowing him to evolve into an iconic individual in the eyes of fans, not just a member of the band he founded.[7]

After having such a profound cultural impact, it did not take long for Lennon and the Beatles to make one of their first real political statements on these shores: they refused to perform before segregated audiences (a practice that was commonplace in the southern United States in the 1960s) at their Jacksonville, Florida, concert on September 11, 1964, forcing the concert's promoters to change their policy.[8]

The Middle Years, 1965–1967: From Cheeky to Dangerous

In the years immediately after taking America by storm in 1964, Lennon and the Beatles continued to influence almost every aspect of popular culture. Television appearances, films, concert tours, books (both about and, in Lennon's case, written by), and press of all types made them omnipresent. But obviously, the way the Beatles reached most of their fans was via their recordings.

It could be argued that Lennon's greatest contribution to musical culture in the 1960s was his role in creating the fresh and exciting sound that made the Beatles stand out in the crowded world of rock bands in their era. Or that his entire body of work, as a member of the Beatles and as a solo artist, should be regarded as a whole and appreciated for its overall influence. Both are valid arguments. But I feel that Lennon's most profound contributions to popular music were made especially in some of his works from the period of *Rubber Soul* (1965) through *Sgt. Pepper's Lonely Hearts Club Band* (1967). The following are the songs composed primarily or entirely by Lennon that I would offer as being among the most important in influencing the music of his era and determining how fans look at him today.

"In My Life" (1965): This song was something of an outlier when it first appeared on *Rubber Soul*. It was unusual to hear a 25-year-old pop singer-songwriter nostalgically reminiscing about bygone days. It showed Lennon to be perhaps more introspective and thoughtful than other songwriters of his era. And producer George Martin's Bach-like piano solo, which was achieved with a bit of studio trickery, gave the song an air of sophistication and seriousness not commonly heard on rock records of the era.[9]

"Norwegian Wood (This Bird Has Flown)" (1965): Also from *Rubber Soul*, this dark and internalized number was a far cry from the sunny, extroverted pop-rock for which the band was known. Accompanied by an instrument not previously heard on a Beatles record, a sitar, the song dealt with an extramarital affair.[10] It reflected a new level of maturity for Lennon as a man and as a musician and took music of the era to a place it had rarely been before. Like "In My Life," it showed that the rock-and-roll idiom had possibilities yet untapped and made the statement that there was an air of gravitas about Lennon that was exceptional for his time and situation. It was one of the songs on *Rubber Soul* that led Matthew Schneider to praise the LP as "the album in which Lennon arrived at the ground floor of his artistic maturity, expressing with bracing directness the sorrow and anger sublimated beneath the boy-loses-girl conventions of his melancholy earlier songs."[11]

"Rain" (1966): This B-side of the single that also featured McCartney's "Paperback Writer" hinted at a musical style that would later emerge in full bloom in some of the Beatles' more psychedelic tracks heard on *Revolver* and *Sgt. Pepper*, including the first use of a backward recording which was the product of a stoned accident by Lennon.[12]

"Tomorrow Never Knows" (1966): The first track recorded for the *Revolver* album invited listeners to "relax, turn off your mind and float downstream." Its strange effects, psychedelic personality, and quirky structure were worlds removed from the more traditionally mainstream hits by the Beatles and presaged where the band would go so effectively in *Sgt. Pepper*. Sheffield praises the track as being "like nothing they [the Beatles] or any other band had ever come up with" and cited it as the beginning of the band's "acid phase."[13]

"Strawberry Fields Forever" (1967): Another first track, this was from the beginning of the sessions for *Sgt. Pepper*. It set the tone for the landmark album that would follow, although it did not appear on it. Instead, the song was paired with McCartney's similarly nostalgic "Penny Lane" on a double-A-side, 45-rpm gem that still stands as one of the most eloquent examples of the differences between the songwriting styles of the Beatles' primary composers.

"A Day in the Life" (1967): At first glance, this song makes little sense—a recitation of random, unrelated headlines sprinkled with a few drug references ("had a smoke and somebody spoke and I went into a dream" from McCartney, and "I'd love to turn you on" from Lennon), delivered in a three-part form with the sections bridged by orchestral crescendos. Yet the thoughtful, slightly melancholy tone and almost out-of-body character of the tune struck a chord with listeners, and it remains one of the most stunning tracks on the Beatles' most impactful record. The song further reveals the magic of Lennon and McCartney as composers. Lennon had a beginning and an end, and McCartney had a middle. There was no initial relationship between the parts, but somehow, when they were woven together, they worked.

While it must be acknowledged that "Imagine" (to be discussed later), a portrait of compositional and production simplicity, is probably Lennon's most iconic track, the compositions just identified redefined the possibilities of popular song structure and content in ways that "Imagine" did not. All were groundbreaking in one way or another. The radical architecture and often abstract lyrics of these works and other Lennon compositions made the statement that a pop record could be anything the composer wanted it to be. He opened doors that have not been closed since.

But there is also a certain irony about these tracks, because most of them were aggrandized by the creative studio wizardry of Martin. "Strawberry Fields Forever," in particular, was something of a Frankenstein monster created from two differing versions of the song (mismatched keys and tempos, among other things) that were welded together by Martin to create the version of the song we know.[14]

This runs against the grain, because Lennon often made it clear that he did not like his songs to be embellished. "I keep saying that I always preferred the double album, because my music is better on the double album; I don't care about the whole concept of *Pepper*, it might be better, but the music was better for me on the double album, because I'm being myself on it. . . . I felt more at ease with that than the production. I don't like production so much."[15] *Rolling Stone* later noted, "In the studio, Lennon tended to favor impulse over craft, sometimes with mixed results."[16]

So this is one of the cases where the legend does not exactly match the man. Lennon is known for often trippy, elaborately structured and produced numbers—tracks that made listeners rethink what a rock song could be. But while they were fine examples of Lennon's creativity and ability to musically think outside the box, the end results often ran counter to Lennon's minimalist sensibilities regarding recording.

More Popular Than Jesus

In addition to producing a great deal of fabulous music in the mid-1960s, Lennon also ran afoul of some cultural sensibilities in America. One of the defining moments of Lennon's Beatles years was the well-documented "more popular than Jesus" kerfuffle.

The whole thing started quietly enough with an interview Lennon did with journalist Maureen Cleave for the March 4, 1966, issue of London's *Evening*

Standard. In that piece, Lennon was quoted as saying, "Christianity will go. It will vanish and shrink. I needn't argue about that; I'm right and I will be proved right. We're more popular than Jesus now; I don't know which will go first—rock 'n' roll or Christianity."[17]

In England, the comment drew little public response. Nor did Lennon's words appear to ruffle any feathers when the interview later appeared in the *New York Times.*[18]

But when the interview was published in the August 1966 issue of *Datebook* magazine, a firestorm erupted in America. Lennon was vilified by Christian organizations and right-wing groups that included the Ku Klux Klan. Some radio stations stopped playing the band's songs, and Beatles record burnings were held, often in cities where the Beatles were making stops on their tour of America that summer.[19]

Lennon, who was obviously blindsided by the American reaction to his comments, reluctantly offered an apology. He began a press conference in Chicago on August 11, 1966, by saying, "If I had said television is more popular than Jesus, I might have got away with it," before attempting a clarification of his remarks. "Well, originally I was pointing out that fact in reference to England—that we meant more to kids than Jesus did, or religion, at that time. I wasn't knocking it or putting it down, I was just saying it as a fact. . . . I'm not saying that we're better, or greater, or comparing us with Jesus Christ as a person or God as a thing or whatever it is, you know. I just said what I said and it was wrong, or was taken the wrong way. And now all this."[20] He later added, "I still don't know quite what I've done wrong."[21]

The "more popular than Jesus" controversy was one of the first real tests of the loyalty of Lennon's fan base. But while some damage was done to the band in terms of making them fear for their safety, it should be remembered that most of the vitriol aimed at Lennon and the Beatles in that period came from sources such as Ku Klux Klansmen, not Beatles fans. And burning records may have been primarily an attention-getting image.

"One church-going female fan (b. '45) recalls her minister talking about it: 'He said the Beatles were a bad influence.' As she saw it, 'They were just free spirits who made you feel free and more like yourself' "; this was from an unidentified fan in Candy Leonard's fan-centric *Beatleness.* Leonard further noted, "Though the reactionary record burnings may have been more about publicity for the radio stations than genuine outrage at what Lennon said, reaction to the comment speaks to its truth."[22]

It is also perhaps telling that on August 19, 1966, the Beatles made a tour stop for two shows at the Mid-South Coliseum in Memphis. A Christian rally was held in opposition to Lennon and his views in an auditorium just a few miles away on that same date. That rally drew about 8,000, while the Beatles' concerts combined to draw more than 20,000.[23]

Moreover, *Revolver*, an album released into the teeth of the "more popular than Jesus" flap in early August 1966, and the single "Yellow Submarine," released on the same day, were both highly successful. The album reached number one, while the single peaked at number two on US charts.[24] Obviously, Beatles fans did not stop buying concert tickets and records when Lennon's comments were made public.

All of this jibes with my own memories of the controversy as an adolescent growing up in a small town about 40 miles from the Beatles' Memphis venue. All the noise seemed to be coming from adults. And even in that conservative part of the country, I remember fans of Lennon and the Beatles being mostly amused by the whole affair.

Despite the anger and anguish created by the reaction to Lennon's comments, the controversy quietly died away after the Beatles ended their American tour—and all touring—10 days later with their San Francisco concert on August 29, 1966. Ultimately, even the Vatican forgave Lennon,[25] and today the whole affair is dismissed as a "storm in a teacup."[26] In fact, Lennon and the Beatles may have benefited from the brouhaha. According to Leonard, "One of the ironies of the incident is that it transformed the Beatles, especially Lennon, into people—pop stars—whose opinions mattered."[27]

So in the wake of the controversy, Lennon went from being "cheeky" to being a little dangerous.

From Ono through the End of the Beatles, 1968–1970

The third phase of Lennon's development as an enduring cultural and political icon encompasses the period between 1968 and 1970, when he became involved with his second wife, Yoko Ono, and said goodbye to the Beatles—a period that would test his fan base in a number of ways.

When Lennon met Ono in London in 1966, she was already a prominent figure in the avant-garde art movement of the 1960s.[28] Her circle of friends and rival artists included the likes of Andy Warhol.[29] So when she and

Lennon became almost inseparable, it was clear that Lennon, a failed student at the Liverpool College of Art, wanted to be involved with an edgier and (arguably) more significant realm of artistic endeavor than the widely loved and commercially successful band he helmed.[30] To that end, Lennon collaborated with Ono on a number of projects, both musical and conceptual.

On August 30, 1968, the Beatles released their most successful single, "Hey Jude," a McCartney composition that topped the US charts for nine weeks. The flip side was the Lennon rocker "Revolution." The slower original version of the song, "Revolution 1," would later appear on *The Beatles* (the *White Album*) (1968). "Revolution" is one of Lennon's most significant songs because it was one of the few Beatles numbers in which he stated an overtly political viewpoint. "The song marked John's decision that he had political responsibilities, and that he ought to fulfill them in his music. That was a momentous decision, much more significant than the lyrics of the song," wrote Jon Wiener.[31]

But many on the political left felt the song was a rejection of their efforts and goals.[32] "Already John was revealing some ambivalence about his relationship to the New Left—and on precisely the issue that separated the radicals most sharply from the 'all you need is love' world view the Beatles had done so much to promote," wrote Wiener.[33]

Regardless of the interpretation or reaction, the song is highly significant because it reflects the complicated nature of Lennon's relationship with the political movements of his time. "Revolution" showed he was in line with the general goals of the counterculture, but he was also steadfastly opposed to hate and totalitarian regimes. In the era of the slogan "If you are not part of the solution, you are part of the problem," Lennon's nuanced response did not fly. The song once again underscored the independence of Lennon's thinking. He refused to play party politics, even when it was fashionable to do so.

In late 1969, Lennon returned the Member of the Most Honorable Order of the British Empire (MBE) award he had received from Queen Elizabeth in 1965.[34] This act of defiance, of course, had a great deal more impact in England than in America.[35] But Lennon's act did speak directly to American fans in one way, because in his note accompanying the returned medal, Lennon cited his opposition to the Vietnam War.

While it was generally understood that the Beatles opposed the war ("All our songs are anti-war," Lennon said in 1966),[36] the Beatles had rarely directly addressed the issue, probably because it was an American war.[37] But the political statement accompanying his returned MBE placed Lennon firmly in the camp of the legions of American youth who were protesting the war in Vietnam.

In the waning days of the Beatles, Lennon and Ono staged some events that would have a profound impact on how he is viewed today. In spring 1969, the couple crawled into the sack for two "Bed-Ins for Peace," the first in Amsterdam and the second in Montreal, where they recorded the single "Give Peace a Chance."[38] That hard-rhyming anthem to coexistence featured a supporting cast that included Timothy Leary, Petula Clark, Allen Ginsberg, and Tommy Smothers, among many others.[39]

With these bed-ins, it was almost as if Lennon and Ono were, in modern parlance, making peace their brand. "I'm selling peace at whatever the cost. Yoko and I are just one big advertising campaign," said Lennon.[40] In a later interview, he further reinforced that point. "Marching was fine and dandy for the Thirties. Today you need different methods—it's sell, sell, sell. If you want peace you have to sell it like soap. . . . For reasons known only to themselves, people do print what I say. And I'm saying 'Peace.' "[41]

The Post-Beatles Years, 1970–1980

In the years immediately following the announced breakup of the Beatles in 1970, Lennon went through a dizzying series of phases and periods that make for a thoroughly confused picture of who he was. Between 1970 and his death in 1980, he released several albums but few that resembled one another. They ranged from the pared-down and angst-ridden *John Lennon/ Plastic Ono Band* (1970) to the Beatles-esque *Walls and Bridges* (1974). He also pushed the envelope with Ono on the highly experimental *Unfinished Music No. 2: Life with the Lions* (1969), made a visit to his roots in *Rock 'n' Roll* (1975), and then ceased to record for almost five years between 1975 and 1980, the year he and Ono released *Double Fantasy*. The singles from this era ranged from the strident "Woman Is the Nigger of the World" (1972), which demonstrated Lennon's early endorsement of feminist causes, to the joyously mindless "Whatever Gets You Thru the Night" (1975), the only single from Lennon's post-Beatles years to reach number one on US charts.[42]

But by far the most defining song by Lennon in his post-Beatles years was "Imagine," which also served as the title track of his 1971 solo album. In this simple, piano-driven ballad wrapped in a warm, lush string arrangement, Lennon invites us to Utopia, a world in which we can "all live as one." And

Lennon seemed to know from the start that he had created something special. "There was no question that this was going to be a statement and it was going to be very commercial," he said.[43] Lennon was proven right when the album reached number one and the single peaked at number three on the *Billboard* charts.

That song, on which Ono was added as cowriter in 2017,[44] is now as much a part of Lennon's legacy as anything he did with the Beatles and has become his eternal calling card to the world. The title is the single word that marks the heavily visited memorial disc honoring Lennon in the Strawberry Fields section of New York's Central Park.[45] Its prime position in Lennon's oeuvre has been made apparent in a number of major and minor ways over the years. *Rolling Stone* noted in 2002, "Yet since 9/11, 'Imagine' has emerged as a new national hymn, a strong, quiet counterweight to the institutional psalms and fight songs—'The Star-Spangled Banner,' 'God Bless America,' 'America the Beautiful'—that have filled the air since the terrorist attacks."[46]

Lennon's personal life in this late period (spent mostly in New York) was as messy and as hard to pin down as his musical output. It included an 18-month period stretching from 1973 to 1975 known as "the lost weekend," during which he engaged in heavy drinking and drug use and had a relationship with May Pang, a personal assistant to Lennon and Ono.[47]

Ultimately, Lennon returned to Ono and settled into his house-husband period from 1975 to 1980, leaving music and recording behind in favor of childrearing (his only child with Ono, Sean, was born in 1975 on the same month and day as his father's birth) and other domestic chores. "Yoko became the breadwinner, taking care of the bankers and deals. And I became the housewife. It was like one of those role reversal comedies," said Lennon.[48]

During the post-Beatles era, Lennon also made an attempt to become more involved with radical politics. He began meeting the leaders of the American protest movement, including Jerry Rubin, one of the famed "Chicago Seven" defendants tried in the aftermath of the bloody protests at the Democratic National Convention in Chicago in 1968. "I want to do something political, and radicalize people and all that jazz," he said.[49]

Aside from a concert featuring Lennon and Ono in Michigan in 1971 that was credited with freeing an activist who had been jailed on a drug bust,[50] little came of Lennon's flirtation with politicized action, and he eventually became disillusioned with Rubin and the American left. "That radicalism was phony, really. What the hell was I doing fighting the American government just because Jerry Rubin couldn't get what he always wanted—a nice, cushy job?" Lennon asked in a *Newsweek* magazine interview in 1980.[51]

One of the few other tangible results of Lennon's failed efforts to become more politically visible was, surprisingly, "Come Together." That song, which opened the *Abbey Road* album, grew out of a campaign song Lennon wrote in 1969 for LSD guru Timothy Leary's unsuccessful run for governor of California in 1970.[52]

During much of the 1970s, Lennon was being watched by the FBI and was under a near-constant threat of deportation by the Nixon administration, which used a 1968 drug bust in England as potential justification.[53] The FBI in the Lennon case, however, was sometimes comically inept. Among its misguided efforts was getting Lennon confused with another musician who merely looked like him.[54] Wiener opined that in the pursuit of Lennon, the FBI looked "more like the Keystone Kops than the Gestapo."[55] But by the time Lennon was granted permanent residency status in 1976, thus getting the smoldering ruins of the Nixon-Ford administration off his back, his minimal ties to the upper echelons of the America left were long broken.

In the end, this unwarranted harassment of Lennon by the Nixon administration may have been a blessing for his legacy. Had Lennon become deeply involved with the more radical edge of the American protest movement, it could have been off-putting for his most peace-loving fans. As it turned out, this brief brush with the radical fringe gave Lennon cred for those who wanted him to be part of the movement, but since he never established himself as a fully radicalized firebrand, he was not permanently tainted in the eyes of those who were put off by the tactics employed by Rubin and others. As a result, the final word on Lennon as a political force is that while he may have been politically dangerous, he never became *too* dangerous.

John Lennon and Fandom

Through all of this—from the hysteria of early Beatlemania, through the "more popular than Jesus" kerfuffle, and into the complicated and often contradictory Lennon who emerged in the years after the Beatles breakup—he always had a strong fan base. However, the members of that base did occasionally change.

No band has ever enjoyed the level and scope of fan adoration showered upon the Beatles. But while most Beatles fans loved the band as a whole, many also chose favorites within the band. And from the earliest days, being a Lennon fan was a bit different. Guitarist Andy Timmons said:

> Back then, you had to make these decisions: Beatles or Stones? John, Paul, George, or Ringo? While each Beatle radiated endless charm, charisma, street smarts and good looks, John had an extra level of cool. He also had that wonderful, acerbic Liverpudlian wit, and he wasn't afraid to speak his mind—certainly not the norm for pop stars in the '60s.[56]

An unidentified female fan expressed a similar view: "He was different. He looked intelligent. He looked like someone who might sing 'We Shall Overcome,' or at least appreciate it. He looked very cool, interesting, alienated; almost fifties tough look."[57]

This view of Lennon as the free-thinking, adventurous experimenter of the band was widely held and enduring. And within the band, this rankled "the cute one," who seemed to take little solace in often being singled out in fan polls as the most popular Beatle.[58] "I was called 'The cute one.' Well I can tell you when I went home I wasn't cute at all. So without wanting to put John down, or to look as if I was justifying myself I did want to put the record straight: don't just put me down as an idiot who didn't know any of it and John taught me it all," said McCartney, further citing his appreciation of the music of John Cage as evidence that he, too, understood and embraced the avant-garde art movements of the 1960s.[59]

There were, no doubt, some fans who turned away from Lennon and the Beatles during the controversies caused by Lennon's views and paradigm-shifting musical excursions. Writing about the challenge the 1967 single "Strawberry Fields Forever" proved to be for many Beatles fans, Leonard noted, "Some were neutral about the Beatles evolution, some embraced it, and others took a break. Those who were neutral or embraced the 'weirdness' were, perhaps, a bit more open-minded and curious by nature—they found 'weird' appealing, or were willing to give it a chance."[60] Much the same thing might be said about the reaction to almost every political controversy or musical course correction of Lennon's career.

Lennon's attitude toward his fan base was as complicated and contradictory as the man himself. In the early days of Beatlemania, he was frustrated by the fans' screaming, which turned concerts into shriek-fests where little music was heard by the crowd or the band.[61] According to Elliott, Lennon "was in equal measures attracted and repelled by the cult of celebrity," and the "thrills of Beatlemania soon turned to boredom."[62] But Larry Kane contends that Lennon had great affection for his fans: "A common thread that runs through the story of Lennon on tour is his sense of caring about the fans and the average person," he wrote.[63] "The desire to reach out to fans would develop into a theme that would continue into John's solo career. It was an interesting conflict: the member of the band who feared the risks of touring the most, demanding that fans have greater access.[64]

Lennon also made it clear that he had always wanted to have fans and was sensitive to how they thought of him. In his 1980 *Playboy* magazine interview, he said:

> I made the decision at sixteen or seventeen that what I did, I wanted everybody to see. I wasn't going after the aestheticism or the monastery or the lone artist who supposedly doesn't care what people think about his work. I care a lot whether people hate it or love it, because it's part of me and it hurts me when they hate it, or hate me, and it's pleasing when they like it. But, as many public figures have said, "The praise is never enough, and the criticism always bites deep."[65]

Although Lennon avowed to be sensitive to criticism, he was also steadfastly an independent force who followed his own muse and no one else's. "I don't write for the Beatles, I write for myself," he said in 1969.[66]

It has to be inferred that if Lennon cared so little for the reactions of his fellow Beatles when he composed, he was probably even less limited by audience expectations. He certainly never shied away from throwing his faithful musical curveballs such as "Tomorrow Never Knows," "Strawberry Fields Forever," "I Am the Walrus," "Revolution 9," and the *Two Virgins* album, as well as often being shocking and outspoken on social and political issues.

Posthumous Lennon: 1980 to Present

Given Lennon's stated affection for his fans, it is tragically ironic that he was senselessly gunned down just outside his New York apartment on December 8, 1980, by a madman who may have loved his idol too much.[67] The tears of grieving fans flooded the world. Elliott enumerated just a few of the tributes that brought fans together:

In the immediate days after Lennon's shooting, people joined together in mourning throughout the world. A gathering of some 30,000 people joined in prayer and sang "Give Peace a Chance" outside St. George's Hall on Lime Street in Liverpool. In cities across America, vigils were held to commemorate the life and work of Lennon. In New York's Central Park, a crowd of more than 100,000 joined together in a minute of silence to remember Lennon. In Toronto, 35,000 people gathered in the snow for a candlelight vigil. Radio stations everywhere played the Beatles and Lennon. The buying of Lennon's records, from his late 1960s and early 1970s solo records to *Double Fantasy*, skyrocketed.[68]

And, sadly, the fan devotion to Lennon also went to extremes. "Several suicides" were linked to Lennon's assassination.[69] If Lennon's fans had fallen into a sort of dormancy during the five years that he eschewed recording, they were certainly shocked back into action by his passing.

Tributes to Lennon of various types have been continuous from his death to the present. They have ranged from large-scale gatherings of fans on anniversary dates to heartwarming honors, such as the US Postal Service honoring Lennon, an avid stamp collector, with his own stamp in 2018.[70]

And also along the way, Lennon's image received something of a makeover. Ian Inglis wrote: "After his death, John Lennon the Beatle was re-invented— as a spiritual leader, as political activist, as avant-garde artist, as religious messiah, as contemporary philosopher, as intellectual guide."[71] Writing on the 30th anniversary of Lennon's death, music journalist Ray Connolly noted that "for the past three decades the man I have been reading about has grown less and less like the John Lennon I knew and, generally, more and more like some character out of Butler's *Lives of the Saints*" and that Lennon's flaws have been "air-brushed from public memory by misty-eyed fans, and the efforts of his widow Yoko Ono."[72]

This sort of rock-and-roll sainthood that enveloped Lennon after his death was also questioned by the less-than-flattering biography *The Lives of John Lennon* by Albert Goldman in 1988, which painted a dark picture of his later years in particular. But rather than causing a public rethinking of who Lennon was, Goldman's biography was attacked. "This tawdry expose of a megalomaniacal, drug-addled, bulimic recluse was too much for his fans, and defenders of the 1960s youth legacy, and led to a public pillorying of its author across a wide swath of the mainstream media," wrote Michael Frontani, adding that *Rolling*

Stone magazine had dismissed Goldman's book as "mean scandalousness."[73] Idols have their defenders.

Conclusion

Looking back at the evolution of Lennon from moptop to revolutionary through these particular recordings, events, controversies, and actions paints a portrait of Lennon that is often difficult to rationalize and interpret. He was "the smart one" and was frequently referred to as an intellectual. But while Lennon was obviously quick-witted and thoughtful, he was not an intellectual by the traditional measures usually accompanying that term. He was not well educated (he did not make it through art college),[74] and although he claimed to be "an avid reader," that may not have always been the case.[75] When a journalist mentioned a phrase from T. S. Eliot's *The Wasteland* during a 1968 interview, Lennon was flummoxed: "I don't know that. I'm not very hip on me culture, you know."[76] He was also accused by someone close to him of being unable to channel his intellect: "John had complex ideas which he could never organize," said George Martin. "He couldn't change a lightbulb."[77]

He was a darling of the counterculture and seen as a political icon who championed the goals of the American protest movements of the 1960s.[78] Yet he rejected the methods of many radicals of his day. "The underground is as straight as the overground, and they don't like change," he once said.[79]

He was a tireless proponent of peace for the world, but he seemed to struggle to find inner peace his entire life. Lennon also lacked a peaceful, nonviolent personality. He admitted to being abusive with his first wife, Cynthia, who said she "was quite terrified of him for about 75% of the time" during their marriage.[80] "I used to be cruel to my woman, and physically— any woman. I was a hitter. I couldn't express myself and I hit. I fought men and I hit women," Lennon said in 1980, while emphasizing that those violent days were behind him.[81]

Nor did his desire to bring peace, love, and harmony to all the world always translate into presenting a pleasant demeanor in his dealings with individuals. "I have to say that, from my point of view, I felt he was a hypocrite," said son Julian Lennon in 1998. "Dad could talk about peace and love out loud to the world but he could never show it to the people who supposedly meant the most to him: his wife and son."[82] Beatles biographer Hunter Davies also wore no rose-colored glasses when gazing upon Lennon: "He could be a maneuvering swine, which no one ever realized. Now since the death he's become like Martin Luther Lennon. But that wasn't him either. He wasn't some holy saint."[83]

As a recording artist, he preferred a pared-down sound to the brilliant busy-ness of Martin's elaborations of Beatles songs. But many of his most iconic tracks owe their success, at least in part, to Martin's genius for production.

Lennon expressed his love for his fans but also made it clear that he was the only person he cared about satisfying when he composed. And he turned his back on those fans when he took a five-year hiatus from recording between 1975 and 1980.

So there are many ways in which Lennon the man and Lennon the legend are not perfect matches. This is hardly new or unusual. Americans have often seen their perspectives on revered heroes altered with the passage of time and the revelations of misdeeds, from John Kennedy to Bill Cosby. Sometimes the past missteps of these heroes are forgiven, sometimes not.

But it is important to remember that there was a vital, constant thread in all of Lennon's music and actions: truth. Above all else, Lennon was honest. The song "Gimme Some Truth," from the *Imagine* album, was not his biggest hit. But that title comes up frequently in books about Lennon (often as a title or chapter heading) and also served as the overall title of a boxed-set reissue of several of his albums in 2010. It was aptly chosen, in that it is such a pithy and accurate statement of Lennon's philosophy of life.

"To me, Lennon's legacy is honesty," said the late American rock legend, and Traveling Wilbury, Tom Petty. "When I was young and saw the Beatles performing on TV, they were the first ones who weren't up there just giving you pat showbiz banter. They'd actually say something. He was a great role model for my whole generation, because you knew when John suffered and you knew when John was happy, but it all somehow came out OK."[84]

Clearly, Beatles fans have long since decided that there is no cause to withhold their love of Lennon and the concepts for which he stands. They overlook Lennon's shortcomings as a person and concentrate instead on his colossal achievements as an artist and his ability to have stayed doggedly "on topic" in his promotion of truth and peace.

As a result, those are the concepts most closely associated with his memory. Wiener contends that Lennon's "star hovers far above the fray" and that "John Lennon the man died in 1980, but John Lennon the symbol continues to inspire idealism, promote causes, and generate revenue—in other words, to do cultural work."[85]

Almost everything Lennon did, from songwriting to bed-ins, was a quest for some type of peace and some element of truth. And in the hearts of his fans, his steadfast adherence to those ideals has trumped any human failings he may have had. That is the enduring legacy Lennon's life and death have earned.

Notes

1. James Mitchell, *The Walrus and the Elephants: John Lennon's Years of Revolution* (New York: Seven Stories), 2013, 11.
2. Rob Sheffield, *Dreaming the Beatles: The Love Story of One Band and the Whole World* (New York: HarperCollins, 2017), xi.
3. Anthony Elliott, *The Mourning of John Lennon* (Berkeley: University of California Press, 1999), 98.
4. Albert Maysles and David Maysles, dirs., *The Beatles: The First U.S. Visit* (Apple Films, 1964; DVD 2003).
5. J. Philip Di Franco, ed. *The Beatles in Richard Lester's A Hard Day's Night: A Complete Pictorial Record of the Movie*, screenplay by Alun Owen (New York: Penguin, 1977), 293.
6. *The Four Complete Historic Ed Sullivan Shows Featuring the Beatles*, presented by Ed Sullivan (1964–1965), Goodtimes Entertainment, 2003, DVD.
7. Jann Wenner, *Lennon Remembers* (New York: Verso, 2000), 31.
8. Steven Morris, "The Beatles Refused to Play to Segregated Audiences," *Guardian*, September 15, 2011, .
9. Kenneth Womack, *The Beatles Encyclopedia: Everything Fab Four* (Santa Barbara, CA: Greenwood, 2017), 251.
10. Womack, *The Beatles Encyclopedia*, 361.
11. Matthew Schneider, "Getting Better: The Beatles and the Angry Young Men," in *New Critical Perspectives on the Beatles: Things We Said Today*, ed. Kenneth Womack and Katie Kapurch (London: Palgrave Macmillan, 2016), 21.
12. Womack, *The Beatles Encyclopedia*, 405.
13. Sheffield, *Dreaming the Beatles*, 118–119.
14. Kenneth Womack, *Sound Pictures: The Life of Beatles Producer George Martin* (Chicago: Chicago Review Press, 2018), 159–161.
15. Jann Wenner, "John Lennon: The Rolling Stone Interview (Part Two)," *Rolling Stone*, February 4, 1971, www.rollingstone.com/music/music-news/john-lennon-the-rolling-stone-interview-part-two-160932/.
16. David Fricke, "The Making of 'Imagine,'" in *John Lennon: The Ultimate Guide to His Life, Music & Legend*, ed. Christian Hoard, *Rolling Stone* Special Edition, Fall 2018, 63.

17. Maureen Cleave, "How Does a Beatle Live? John Lennon Lives Like This," in *Read the Beatles,* ed. June Skinner Sawyers (New York: Penguin, 2006), 88.

18. Philip Norman, *John Lennon: The Life* (New York: Harper, 2008), 448; and Tim Riley, *Lennon: The Man, the Myth, the Music—The Definitive Life* (New York: Hyperion, 2011), 292.

19. Cleave, "How Does a Beatle Live?" 85.

20. Cleave, "How Does a Beatle Live?" 85–86.

21. Bob Spitz, *The Beatles: The Biography* (New York: Little, Brown, 2005), 633.

22. Candy Leonard, *Beatleness: How the Beatles and Their Fans Remade the World* (New York: Arcade, 2014), 115.

23. Robert Williams, "Yeah, Yeah, Yeah," *Memphis Commercial Appeal,* August 20, 1966, http://www.175moments.com/moments/beatles-perform-two-shows-at-memphis-mid-south-coliseum.php?r=2.

24. For Beatles US chart history in *Billboard,* see https://www.billboard.com/music/the-beatles/chart-history/billboard-200 and https://www.billboard.com/music/the-beatles/chart-history.

25. Tom Heneghan, "Vatican Forgives John Lennon for 'More Popular Than Jesus' Quip," *Reuters,* November 23, 2008, http://blogs.reuters.com/faithworld/2008/11/23/vatican-forgives-john-lennon-for-more-popular-than-jesus-quip/.

26. Spitz, *The Beatles,* 627.

27. Leonard, *Beatleness,* 127.

28. Womack, *The Beatles Encyclopedia,* 379.

29. Grace Glueck, "Warhol Remembered by 2,000 at St. Patrick's," *New York Times,* April 7, 1987, .

30. Spitz, *The Beatles,* 204.

31. Jon Wiener, *Come Together: John Lennon in His Time* (New York: Random House, 1984), 61.

32. Wiener, *Come Together,* 60.

33. Wiener, *Come Together,* 61.

34. Geoff Giles, "John Lennon Returns His MBE to the Queen," *Ultimate Classic Rock,* November 25, 2015, http://ultimateclassicrock.com/john-lennon-returns-mbe/.

35. Wiener, *Come Together,* 106.

36. Nakita Ramkissoon, "All You Need Is the Beatles," *Trespass Magazine,* February 12, 2010, http://www.trespassmag.com/all-you-need-is-the-beatles/.

37. Richard White, *Come Together: Lennon & McCartney in the Seventies* (New York: Omnibus, 2016) 67.

38. Norman, *John Lennon,* 595–597.

39. Spitz, *The Beatles,* 607.

40. Ian Inglis, "The Continuing Story of John Lennon," *Critical Studies in Media Communication* 22, no. 5 (August 2005): 453, https//www.tandfonline/doi/abs/10.1080/07393180500497276.

41. Norman, *John Lennon,* 596.

42. For John Lennon's US chart history in *Billboard,* see https://www.billboard.com/music/john-lennon/chart-history/billboard-200 and https://www.billboard.com/music/john-lennon/chart-history.

43. Fricke, "The Making of 'Imagine,'" 59.

44. Neda Ulab, "Yoko Ono Joins John Lennon with Credit Line for Writing 'Imagine,'" *National Public Radio*, June 17, 2017, www.npr.org/2017/06/17/533368546/yoko-ono-joins-john-lennon-with-credit-line-for-writing-imagine.

45. "Strawberry Fields," *Central Park Conservancy*, n.d., https://www.centralparknyc.org/locations/strawberry-fields.

46. Fricke, "The Making of 'Imagine,'" 59.

47. Spitz, *The Beatles*, 715–717.

48. Barbara Graustark, "The Real John Lennon," *Newsweek*, September 9, 1980, from *The Beatles Ultimate Experience*, www.beatlesinterviews.org/db1980.0929.beatles.html.

49. Mitchell, *The Walrus and the Elephants*, 21.

50. Riley, *Lennon*, 48.

51. Wiener, *Come Together*, 303.

52. Kenneth Womack, *Solid State: The Story of Abbey Road and the End of the Beatles* (Ithaca, NY: Cornell University Press, 2019), 125–126.

53. Wiener, *Come Together*, 251.

54. Wiener, *Come Together*, 251.

55. Wiener, *Come Together*, 251.

56. Andy Timmons, "Riff," *Guitar Player*, May 2016, http://web.a. ebscohost.com.ezproxy.tcu.edu/ehost/detail/detail?vid=0&sid=b2deed0e-fded-48b2-9373-1549eb1fa16e%40sdc-v-sessmgr02&bdata=JkF1dGhdGhUeXB1PWNdGhUeXB1PWNvb2tpZSxpcCx1aWQmc210ZT1laG9zdC1saXZl#AN=114976495&db=asn.

57. Leonard, *Beatleness*, 41.

58. "CBS News Poll: Who Is America's Favorite Beatle?" *CBSnews.com*, February 2, 2014, https://www.cbsnews.com/news/cbs-news-poll-who-is-americas-favorite-beatle/.

59. Steve Richards, "Beatles Fans Thought Him 'Cute'; He Saw Himself as Avant-Garde, Showing Lennon the Way," *New Statesman*, November 29, 1997, https://www.the-paulmccartney-project.com/interview/interview-paul-mccartney/.

60. Leonard, *Beatleness*, 135.

61. Ray Coleman, *John Winston Lennon* (London: Sidgwick & Jackson, 1984), 288.

62. Elliott, *The Mourning of John Lennon*, 141.

63. Larry Kane, *Lennon Revealed* (Philadelphia: Running Press, 2005), 161.

64. Kane, *Lennon Revealed*, 162.

65. David Sheff, *All We Are Saying: The Last Major Interview with John Lennon and Yoko Ono* (New York: St. Martin's, 2000), 210.

66. Steve Marinucci, "Remembering John Lennon: His Words Say It All," *Beatles News Insider*, December 8, 2015, https://beatlesheadlines.blogspot.com/2015/12/remembering-john-lennon-his-words-say.html.

67. Wiener, *Come Together*, 308.

68. Anthony Elliott, "Celebrity and Political Psychology: Remembering Lennon," *Political Psychology* 19, no. 4 (December 1998): 840.

69. Elliott, "Celebrity and Political Psychology," 841.

70. Daniel Kreps, "John Lennon Receives Commemorative U.S. Postage Stamp," *Rolling Stone*, September 7, 2018, https://www.rollingstone.com/music/music-news/john-lennon-postage-stamp-720890/.

71. Inglis, "The Continuing Story," 452.
72. Ray Connolly, "I Remember the Real John Lennon, Not the One Airbrushed by History," *Telegraph*, December 4, 2010.
73. Michael Frontani, "The Solo Years," in *The Cambridge Companion to the Beatles*, ed. Kenneth Womack (Cambridge: Cambridge University Press, 2009), 177.
74. Spitz, *The Beatles*, 204.
75. Graustark, "The Real John Lennon."
76. Jonathan Cott, "Lennon Reborn," in *John Lennon: The Ultimate Guide to His Life, Music & Legend*, ed. Christian Hoard, *Rolling Stone* Special Edition, Fall 2018, 15.
77. Sheffield, *Dreaming the Beatles*, 118.
78. Riley, *Lennon*, 292.
79. Elliott, *The Mourning of John Lennon*, 97.
80. Mark Lewisohn, *Tune In* (New York: Crown, 2013), 229.
81. Sheff, *All We Are Saying*, 182.
82. Elizabeth Grice, "Dad Was a Hypocrite," *Telegraph*, April 1, 2015, .
83. Frontani, "The Solo Years," 177.
84. Tom Petty, "Tom Petty," in *John Lennon: The Ultimate Guide to His Life, Music & Legend*, ed. Christian Hoard, *Rolling Stone* Special Edition, Fall 2018, 85.
85. Wiener, *Come Together*, 243.

Bibliography

"CBS News Poll: Who Is America's Favorite Beatle?" *CBSnews.com*, February 2, 2014. Accessed September 25, 2018. https://www.cbsnews.com/news/cbs-news-poll-who-is-americas-favorite-beatle/.

Cleave, Maureen. "How Does a Beatle Live? John Lennon Lives Like This." In *Read the Beatles*, edited by June Skinner Sawyers, 85–91. New York: Penguin, 2006.

Coleman, Ray. *John Winston Lennon*. London: Sidgwick & Jackson, 1984.

Connolly, Ray. "I Remember the Real John Lennon, Not the One Airbrushed by History." *Telegraph*. December 4, 2010.

Cott, Jonathan. "Lennon Reborn." In *John Lennon: The Ultimate Guide to His Life, Music & Legend*, edited by Christian Hoard, 10–21. *Rolling Stone* Special Edition, Fall 2018.

Di Franco, J. Philip, ed. 1977. *The Beatles in Richard Lester's A Hard Day's Night: A Complete Pictorial Record of the Movie*. Screenplay by Alun Owen. New York: Penguin, 1977.

Elliott, Anthony. "Celebrity and Political Psychology: Remembering Lennon." *Political Psychology* 19, no. 4 (December 1998): 833–852.

Elliott, Anthony. *The Mourning of John Lennon*. Berkeley: University of California Press, 1999.

The Four Complete Historic Ed Sullivan Shows Featuring the Beatles. Presented by Ed Sullivan (1964–1965). Goodtimes Entertainment, 2003, DVD.

Fricke, David. "The Making of 'Imagine.'" In *John Lennon: The Ultimate Guide to His Life, Music & Legend*, edited by Christian Hoard, 56–63. *Rolling Stone* Special Edition, Fall 2018.

Frontani, Michael. "The Solo Years." In *The Cambridge Companion to the Beatles*, edited by Kenneth Womack, 153–182. Cambridge: Cambridge University Press, 2009.

Giles, Geoff. "John Lennon Returns His MBE to the Queen." *Ultimate Classic Rock*, November 25, 2015. http://ultimateclassicrock.com/john-lennon-returns-mbe/.

Glueck, Grace. "Warhol Remembered by 2,000 at St. Patrick's." *New York Times*, April 7, 1987.

Graustark, Barbara. "The Real John Lennon." *Newsweek*, September 9, 1980, from *The Beatles Ultimate Experience*. www.beatlesinterviews.org/db1980.0929.beatles.html.

Grice, Elizabeth. "Dad Was a Hypocrite." *Telegraph*, April 1, 2015.

Heneghan, Tom. 2008. "Vatican Forgives John Lennon for 'More Popular Than Jesus' Quip." *Reuters*, November 23, 2008. http://blogs.reuters.com/faith world/2008/11/23/vatican-forgives-john-lennon-for-more-popular-than-jesus-quip/.

Inglis, Ian. "The Continuing Story of John Lennon." *Critical Studies in Media Communication* 22, no. 5 (August 2005): 451–455. https//www.tandfonline /doi/abs/10.1080/07393180500497276.

Kane, Larry. *Lennon Revealed*. Philadelphia: Running Press, 2005.

Kreps, Daniel. "John Lennon Receives Commemorative U.S. Postage Stamp." *Rolling Stone*, September 7, 2018. https://www.rollingstone.com/music/music-news/john-lennon-postage-stamp-720890/.

Leonard, Candy. *Beatleness: How the Beatles and Their Fans Remade the World*. New York: Arcade, 2014.

Lewisohn, Mark. *Tune In*. New York: Crown, 2013.

Marinucci, Steve. "Remembering John Lennon: His Words Say It All." *Beatles News Insider*, December 8, 2015. https://beatlesheadlines.blogspot.com /2015/12/remembering-john-lennon-his-words-say.html.

Maysles, Albert, and David Maysles, dirs. *The Beatles: The First U.S. Visit* (1964). Apple Films, DVD, 2003.

Morris, Steven. "The Beatles Refused to Play to Segregated Audiences." *Guardian*, September 15, 2011.

Mitchell, James. *The Walrus and the Elephants: John Lennon's Years of Revolution*. New York: Seven Stories, 2013.

Norman, Philip. *John Lennon: The Life*. New York: Harper, 2008.

Petty, Tom. "Tom Petty." In *John Lennon: The Ultimate Guide to His Life, Music & Legend*, edited by Christian Hoard, 85. *Rolling Stone* Special Edition, Fall 2018.

Ramkissoon, Nikita. "All You Need Is the Beatles." *Trespass Magazine*, February 12, 2010. http://www.trespassmag.com/all-you-need-is-the-beatles/.

Richards, Steve. "Beatles Fans Thought Him "Cute"; He Saw Himself as Avant-Garde, Showing Lennon the Way." *New Statesman*, November 29, 1997. https://www.the-paulmccartney-project.com/interview/interview-paul-mccartney/.

Riley, Tim. *Lennon: The Man, the Myth, the Music—The Definitive Life*. New York: Hyperion, 2011.

Schneider, Matthew. "Getting Better: The Beatles and the Angry Young Men." In *New Critical Perspectives on the Beatles: Things We Said Today*, edited by Kenneth Womack and Katie Kapurch, 13–30. London: Macmillan, 2016.

Sheff, David. *All We Are Saying: The Last Major Interview with John Lennon and Yoko Ono*. New York: St. Martin's, 2000.

Sheffield, Rob. *Dreaming the Beatles: The Love Story of One Band and the Whole World*. New York: HarperCollins, 2017.

Spitz, Bob. *The Beatles: The Biography*. New York: Little, Brown, 2005.

"Strawberry Fields." *Central Park Conservancy*, n.d. https://www.centralparknyc.org/locations/strawberry-fields.

Timmons, Andy. "Riff." *Guitar Player*, May 2016. http://web.a.ebscohost.com.ezproxy.tcu.edu/ehost/detail/detail?vid=0&sidb2deed)e-fded-48b2-9372-1549eb1fa16e%40sdc-v-sessmgr02&bdata=JkF1dGhUeXBIPWNvb2tpZSSxpc CxlaWQ mc2I0ZT11;aG[zdC1saXZO.

Ulab, Neda. "Yoko Ono Joins John Lennon with Credit Line for Writing 'Imagine.'" *National Public Radio*, June 17, 2017. www.npr.org/2017/06/17/533368546/yoko-ono-joins-john-lennon-with-credit-line-for-writing-imagine.

Wenner, Jann. "John Lennon: The Rolling Stone Interview (Part Two)." *Rolling Stone*, February 4, 1971. www.rollingstone.com/music/music-news/john-lennon-the-rolling-stone-interview-part-two-160932/.

Wenner, Jann. *Lennon Remembers*. New York: Verso, 2000.

White, Richard. *Come Together: Lennon & McCartney in the Seventies*. New York: Omnibus, 2016.

Wiener, Jon. *Come Together: John Lennon in His Time*. New York: Random House, 1984.

Williams, Robert. "Yeah, Yeah, Yeah." *Memphis Commercial Appeal*, August 20, 1966. www.175moments.com/moments/beatles-perform-two-shows-at-memphis-mid-south-coliseum.php?r=2.

Womack, Kenneth. *The Beatles Encyclopedia: Everything Fab Four*. Santa Barbara, CA: Greenwood, 2017.

Womack, Kenneth. *Solid State: The Story of Abbey Road and the End of the Beatles*. Ithaca, NY: Cornell University Press, 2019.

Womack, Kenneth. *Sound Pictures: The Life of Beatles Producer George Martin*. Chicago: Chicago Review Press, 2018.

PART II
TODAY

4

Magic Circles

The Fan Sites, Fanzines, and Festivals at the Heart of Beatles Fandom

Kit O'Toole

Despite rapid technological changes since the Beatles first experienced success in 1962, two elements of the fan community have remained stable: community and artistic expression. Whether one is a devotee of sports, films, television, gaming, or music, a fan typically possesses a desire to communicate with fellow enthusiasts in their shared interest. In addition, the fan wants to contribute something to that community, whether through writing fan fiction, editing a fanzine, authoring books, maintaining an online discussion group, starting a YouTube channel, or hosting a podcast. All of these activities allow individuals not only to express their devotion to a particular band but to produce an original work to contribute to the group's history and knowledge.

Throughout the 1960s and 1970s, fans would bond primarily in person at record stores, concerts, and, later, fan conventions. By the 1980s and 1990s, desktop publishing and personal computers allowed fans to design their own fanzines at a lower cost. The internet, however, changed the way fans network with one another and how they contribute to participatory culture. This chapter examines how these trends have changed and how fans both communicate with one another and ensure the Beatles' legacy among younger generations such as millennials. A survey of multigenerational fans and an interview with a Generation Z video blogger will be analyzed to further illustrate how fans connect with one another in the present day. Two forms of Henry Jenkins's participatory culture will be applied specifically to how technology has impacted Beatles fandom: affiliation and expression.

Kit O'Toole, *Magic Circles* In: *Fandom and the Beatles*. Edited by: Kenneth Womack and Kit O'Toole, Oxford University Press (2021). © Oxford University Press. DOI: 10.1093/oso/9780190917852.003.0005

Theoretical Framework: Participatory Culture, Affiliation, and Expression

What defines an individual as a "music fan"? Mark Duffett offers this description: "fandom is a way to declare a social role in relation to popular music that is both alienated from industrial processes of music making and affectively engaged with their result—a way of permitting communality between all those interested in the music."[1] Communality is key to Jenkins's list of five action categories of fan behavior: receiving the "message" through a specific device or medium; critiquing the product (television program, movie, or book); engaging in activism (such as mounting campaigns to save a television show from cancellation); creating art based on or paying homage to the object of fan admiration; and forming social communities that celebrate the television show, movie, or artist.[2]

In addition, Jenkins states that fans engage in what he terms "participatory culture." He defines the culture as (1) having low barriers to artistic expression and engagement; (2) maintaining strong communal support for creating and sharing one's original works; (3) passing on knowledge from experts to novices; (4) believing that members feel their contributions matter; and (5) forging social connections with fellow members, particularly concerning original works that other fans have created (e.g., podcasts or videos). Jenkins further defines forms of participatory culture as *affiliation* (online communities on social media) and *expression* (creating new works based on a shared love of the band, such as fan videomaking, creating mash-ups using software, or writing fan fiction). He lists two other categories: *collaborative problem-solving*, or collaborating on a project to create new knowledge such as Wikipedia, and *circulation*, or shaping the flow of media (e.g., podcasting and blogging).[3] For the purposes of this study, collaborative problem-solving and circulation will be absorbed into the expression category, since both often result in the creation of new products.

Affiliation

Affiliation in a participatory culture involves groups of enthusiasts networking with one another in person and online. John Paul Gee calls places where these interactions occur "affinity spaces," physical or virtual places where informal learning occurs.[4] Gee defines affinity spaces as having the following characteristics:

1. Participants relate to one another in terms of common interests rather than race, gender, or class.
2. Newcomers or novices are not isolated from the space; all levels of fandom are accepted.
3. Participants may create material for others to use such as guidelines.
4. Affinity space enables members to learn and spread knowledge both intensive (e.g., experts or specialists) and extensive (broad knowledge shared with everyone).
5. Space may encourage members to gain individual knowledge (stored in one's head) and provide ways to contribute to distributed knowledge (knowledge that exists in other people's heads or on a particular site).
6. Participants are encouraged to use dispersed knowledge, or knowledge that is not in a primary affinity space but is at other sites.
7. Members of the space may participate at different rates and levels.

As Gee and Elizabeth Hayes state, affinity spaces are "well-designed spaces that resource and mentor learners, old and new, beginners and masters alike."[5]

Expression

John Fiske further delineates the expression category, calling it "textual productivity," or productions created by fans primarily for fellow fans. Fiske describes these creations as approaching "much more closely the artistic productions validated by the official culture."[6] However, these creations (podcasts, videos, fanzines, mash-ups, self-published books) are self-produced and crafted on a limited budget. Books, websites, and fanzine articles have become as respected as traditional academic work; as Joli Jensen posits, "online gathering, sharing, evaluating and displaying of individual and collective affection offers new evidence . . . that fans can be understood as uncredentialed scholars."[7]

While he is describing fan fiction, Fiske's assertion of fans "filling in . . . systemic gaps in the original narrative" fits Beatles fandom as well.[8] For example, fan and filmmaker "Oh Shari Photography" filmed her own video to accompany McCartney's "Appreciate," the fourth single off his 2013 album *New*. While McCartney did produce an official video, he posted a link to her video on his Facebook page.[9] The post read: "Have you seen Oh Shari Photography's fan video for Paul's track 'Appreciate'? We love it! Let us know who you #appreciate being in your life."[10]

Participatory culture, specifically affiliation and expression, has permeated fan communities as far back as Elvis Presley or the Frank Sinatra bobbysoxers. Technology, however, has fundamentally changed how fans network and create original art. After a brief history of how technology has impacted the Beatles community since the 1960s, I will examine statistics drawn from the Pew report "Social Media Use in 2018" to evaluate how the internet influences how fans listen to music and interact with one another.[11] A small survey follows that studies Beatles fans specifically, and a profile of a popular 20-year-old YouTube creator demonstrates how she practices both affiliation and expression in the fan community. Finally, broader implications of the internet's impact on Beatles enthusiasts and the development of new knowledge are discussed.

Pre-Internet History

One of the Beatles' most charming sing-alongs, "All Together Now," represents more than peace and harmony. It also signifies belonging to and identifying oneself with a particular group. In the 1960s, first-generation Beatles fans would express their shared love of the group by attending concerts, screaming at their films, wearing clothing and jewelry emblazoned with their favorite band's faces, listening to and discussing the group's latest releases, and perhaps writing fan fiction they would share among friends. After the Beatles' breakup, disheartened fans found ways to stay connected, mainly through fan conventions and early fanzines.

According to Jenkins's article "Star Trek Rerun, Reread, Rewritten: Fan Writing as Textual Poaching," the definition of a fan involves "translating that [television] viewing into some type of cultural activity, by sharing feelings and thoughts about the program content with friends, by joining a community of other fans who share similar interest."[12] While Jenkins applied the definition to television program devotees, music fandom still fits the description. This desire for an ongoing, continuing fan community was challenged when the Beatles split in 1970; to continue this connection, certain fans founded fanzines. Chris Atton's "Popular Music Fanzines: Genre, Aesthetics, and the 'Democratic Conversation'" defines one aspect of the fanzine: "The fanzine has a central position in establishing and developing discourses about listening, where arguments about music are assayed, and where fans organize their musical experiences."[13]

Several of these magazines had short lives and were published in the 1970s and 1980s, but they share several characteristics. They were published independently and were not officially sanctioned by the Beatles. In addition, they took a do-it-yourself (DIY) approach, meaning that the publisher was also the editor, reporter, and graphic designer. Editors and readers supplied the photos or drew original cartoons. As Lynn Van Matre wrote in her June 2, 1985, *Chicago Tribune* article "Fanzines Keep Alive the Beat of Pop Musicians from Beatles to Brown," "most are clearly home-grown efforts characterized by more enthusiasm than any sort of professional expertise, composed of photo-copied or mimeographed pages stapled together and occasionally including unintentionally humorous typographical errors."[14] Technology transformed ways to stay connected, with desktop publishing and less expensive printing contributing to the proliferation of these DIY periodicals and newsletters. Fanzines such as *Beatlefan* brought journalism to the genre, with Beatles enthusiasts publishing interviews, reviews, and opinion pieces from the perspective of someone just like the reader: an avid fan.

Other mainstream magazines such as *Rolling Stone*, *Musician*, and *Guitar Player* still served as good resources, but the writing came from a somewhat detached perspective—seasoned journalists educating the readership. Fanzines came from a different place, where knowledgeable fans from around the world could share their views without having to work for a corporate entity. In other words, it was by the fans, for the fans. For second-generation fans, author Mark Lewisohn was a primary teacher, with *The Complete Beatles Recording Sessions* and *The Beatles Day by Day* serving as textbooks.

By the 1990s, the internet proved the biggest game changer. Now fans could communicate with one another worldwide through email and discussion groups. In 1995, Beatles fan sites were just starting to emerge due to free hosting sites (GeoCities, Angelfire, and Tripod) and easier design. No longer did users have to know HTML to create a professional site. In the mid-to-late 1990s, graphics were very basic compared to today; that technology, however, would experience rapid growth. Harrison's official site fully embraced graphic design early; its revamped page dedicated to the 2001 rerelease of

All Things Must Pass incorporated then-state-of-the-art animation and encouraged user interactivity. These graphics also meant slow downloading speeds for many visitors. Today, lightning-fast connections have eliminated the problem, encouraging web designers to fully unleash their imaginations. In addition, the rise of self-publishing enabled authors to release their work without relying on major publishing companies. With more control over distribution, researchers were able to publish their work on a variety of platforms, easily reaching worldwide audiences.

By the late 2000s, many of the first free website-hosting services such as GeoCities and Tripod had folded due to competitors such as WordPress and inexpensive hosting sites such as GoDaddy. Still, the early sites, such as Steve Marinucci's *Abbeyrd's Beatles Page*, Jorie Gracen's *The Macca Report*, and Adam Forrest's *The Internet Beatles Album*, remain. Other specialties such as fan fiction also exploded in the late 1990s, again due to ease of design and low cost.

Blogging exploded in popularity; anyone could post thoughts about their hobbies, and readers could leave comments, encouraging dialogue among fans (LiveJournal proved the most popular blogging platform). When social media debuted in the mid-2000s with MySpace and the even more influential Facebook, worldwide fan communities were created, where people could share concert experiences, with live video enabling viewers to feel part of the action. Today, fans attending conventions often feel as though they already know one another due to online interaction.

These fan behaviors closely mirror the five action categories Jenkins describes in *Textual Poachers*: receiving the "message" through a specific device or medium; critiquing the product (television program, movie, or book); engaging in activism (such as mounting campaigns to save a television show from cancellation); creating art based on or paying homage to the object of fan admiration; and forming social communities that celebrate the television show, movie, or artist.[15]

With faster connections came multimedia, and YouTube remains a leading player in this area. Rare clips from the group and solo years surface daily, creating a treasure trove for Beatles collectors. Streaming music and video platforms have introduced the Beatles to younger generations, enabling them to access the group's work from virtually any device. When iPods debuted, another intriguing technology also developed: the podcast. For the first time, virtually anyone could create shows devoted to their favorite topics; all one needs is recording and editing software (which often can be found for free), a microphone, Skype for guests, and a hosting sitè. Worldwide audiences can stream or download episodes and post comments. The proliferation of podcasts continues today, with multigenerational authors and fans providing new insights into Beatles history.

The major factor in connecting multiple generations, however, is social media. From its modest beginnings on MySpace to the current dominance of Facebook, social media provides a new way for fans to network outside of fan conventions. Rare videos and photos are shared, users upload video from McCartney and Starr concerts, and Facebook Live allows anyone to broadcast directly from phones and tablets. Like never before, fans can collectively share in a particular experience, further connecting people from around the world.

Today, music listeners can access music anywhere on a vast array of devices. While listening to music can be a solitary experience, streaming services allow users to easily share music with friends, further illustrating the affiliation aspect of participatory culture. An overview of how music enthusiasts commonly buy and hear songs underscores Jenkins's theory.

Listening to and Sharing Music: An Overview of Current Trends

According to the Pew Research Center's "Social Media Use in 2018" report, streaming media has become a more powerful force. The Beatles finally debuted on streaming sites Apple Music, Spotify, Amazon Prime, Google Play, Deezer, Tidal, Slacker, and Microsoft Groove on December 24, 2015; in just two days, the Beatles became the most-streamed artist on Spotify and set a record for simultaneous streams of a single artist.[16] As of January 22, 2016, the group had been streamed more than 250 million times. According to Spotify statistics, the vast majority of the service's users (and 79% of Beatles listeners) were born after the group disbanded. The data demonstrate that the largest group of Beatles listeners (32%) fell into the 25–34 age group. Second was the 18–24 age range, with 25% listenership. About a year later, *AXS* noted, the Beatles passed the 2 billion mark in online steamed music.[17]

The year 2018 continued to see rapid growth in streaming music. *Billboard*'s Ed Christman reported that in the first half of 2018, on-demand streaming increased 41.7% to reach 403.5 billion US streams. The increase surpassed the 36.3% rise over 2017's 208.9 billion streams as of June 2017.[18] According to the Recording Industry Association of America (RIAA) in its "Mid-Year 2018 RIAA Music Revenues Report," digital downloading continued to decline; as of June 2018, revenues had declined 27% to $562 million—the lowest in a decade.[19] Digital and customized radio (satellite and internet), however, continue to grow.

Interestingly, the Beatles debuted on iTunes and online streaming platforms later than other bands; they joined iTunes in 2010, seven years after the music service launched. Protracted negotiations—along with the settlement of a lawsuit between Apple and the Beatles' holding company, Apple Corps—stalled the agreement between Apple, Apple Corps, and EMI for years. A similar issue arose concerning selecting streaming services, but the Beatles ended up debuting on several major platforms at once in 2010. "In terms of digital the Beatles have always been quite late to the party," said Chris Cooke, cofounder of the music industry news site CMU.[20] Expressing some surprise that the group decided to debut on several streaming services at once, he concluded, "so, I suppose that is them accepting that streaming is now a very serious, significant part of the record industry."[21]

As with the iTunes deal, the negotiations came down to finances. "There's a really simple reason why the Beatles catalogue took so long to join streaming services—their publishers didn't want to do anything to damage potential sales of reissues and retrospectives—it's a very lucrative catalogue," said Mark Mulligan from the media research firm Midia. "But they've waited until the market has got some scale and they could get the best deal."[22]

In addition to streaming platforms, YouTube has been transformed into a prominent source for music listening and sharing. According to the International Federation of the Phonographic Industry (IFPI) in its *Music Consumer Insight Report* for 2018, 47% of listening to on-demand music was on YouTube. Some 35% of users refused to subscribe to paid streaming services because of the free music available on YouTube.[23]

Fans can also listen to music on demand on a dizzying variety of devices. According to IFPI, in 2018, 94% of consumers ages 16 to 24 accessed music via smartphones; 75% of consumers used phones to listen to music.[24] In a rising market, smart speakers (Amazon Echo, Google Home, Apple Home Pod) were increasingly being used to play music as well. Likely smart-speaker users ranged from ages 25 to 34, and 15% planned to purchase a smart speaker in the next year.[25]

Social media has infiltrated everyday life, and the Pew Research Center 2018 survey of US adults demonstrated just how pervasive sites such as

Facebook and YouTube have become. Since Pew began researching social media usage in 2012, Facebook remained the primary platform for most Americans. Roughly two-thirds of US adults (68%) reported in 2018 that they were Facebook users, and roughly three-quarters of those users visited Facebook daily. With the exception of those 65 and older, a majority of Americans across a wide range of demographic groups now used Facebook. Although not typically labeled as social media, the video-sharing site YouTube was used in 2018 by nearly three-quarters of US adults and 94% of 18- to 24-year-olds. And the typical (median) American reported using three of the eight major platforms that Pew measured in this survey. Not surprisingly, younger generations virtually raised on social media used Facebook, Instagram, Snapchat, YouTube, and Twitter more frequently.[26]

According to the March 2018 survey, 88% of 18- to 29-year-olds indicated that they used any or all of the five major social media platforms mentioned. That number fell to 78% among those ages 30 to 49, to 64% among those ages 50 to 64, and to 37% among Americans 65 and older. The 18–29 age group was also more likely to use multiple platforms at once.

Indeed, social media plays a major part in the music fan experience. According to the IFPI report, globally, 35% shared music links on WhatsApp, while 23% used Instagram to post links to songs. Using the Facebook app, other fans shared music with friends. Even more tellingly, 30% followed their favorite artists on social media.[27] Indeed, the Beatles' official YouTube channel maintains 2,304,600 subscribers, while their Facebook page boasts 40,832,612 "likes." Streaming sites such as Spotify allow consumers to easily share music links through sites such as Skype, Facebook, Tumblr, and Twitter (or a link for easy sharing via email). When Spotify opens, the right-hand column displays songs that one's Spotify and Facebook friends recently played (and links directly to those tracks). Similar to making mix tapes in the 1980s, consumers can create their own playlists organized by artist, mood, or any other desired theme. Those playlists can then be made "public" for sharing on social media with friends.

Through Sofia Johansson's conversations with focus groups of young adults in Stockholm and Moscow, she determined that "offline contexts continue to matter for musical guidance," but "online curators"—bloggers, music websites (Something Else Reviews, Pitchfork), and "experts"—serve as heavy influencers on musical taste.[28] Yet online curators such as bloggers, music websites, and certain features of streaming services such as the "radio" function, artist biographies, and artist recommendations on Spotify were also cited as inspirations for music suggestions.

As Duffett states in his introduction to *Popular Music Fandom: Identities, Roles, and Practices*, fandom can be both personal and collective. As he explains:

> an individual's understanding of their own identity can shift depending upon whether they are speaking before, during or after their time as a fan. It can also change depending upon the theoretical and discursive resources immediately available to them. The mass culture critique enabled fans to express their passion in certain ways ("Yes, I am obsessed! It's a religion!").[29]

In other words, listening to music can be an intensively personal experience, made even more so by the omnipresent earbuds. However, social media has also transformed it into a collective activity, one that involves sharing music with friends and fellow fans, thereby asserting identity through personal taste but wanting to share one's discoveries with others.

The aforementioned statistics compiled by Pew and IFPI provide overviews of worldwide consumer habits. A closer look at the behavior of multigenerational Beatles fans, however, yields more complicated results.

Beatles Fan Survey

Jenkins's and Fiske's notions of participatory culture are frequently applied to television program fans and gamers. Do these theories apply to Beatles fandom? To determine this, an online survey was distributed to Beatles fans to determine their attitudes on technology and how it affects their interaction with music and fellow devotees. The online survey essentially asked about participatory culture, specifically the affiliation category. In general, the questions addressed how respondents currently purchase and listen to music, their familiarity with online technology in general, and how they participate in the online community, particularly through social media.

The survey consisted of 10 questions: 7 multiple-choice and 3 open-ended questions (see the chapter appendix). Using the SurveyMonkey platform, invitations to take the survey were posted on Facebook, mostly to Beatles-specific groups and pages. In addition to the author's personal and professional Facebook pages, links to the survey were posted to the following pages and groups:

Talk More Talk: A Solo Beatles Videocast
Beatles Roundtable
Paperback Writer
Students of Beatles Music
Meeting the Beatles
Beatles at the Ridge Fans
Beatlefest Chicago
Screw It, We're Just Gonna Talk about the Beatles
Official Beatle Geeks Fan Club
When They Was Fab
Beatles Universe
The Fab Beatlemaniacs
Beatles/seltaeB (Worldwide Beatles Collectors)
Band on the Run: Paul McCartney and Wings Fans
Paul McCartney
Beatles Online Radio Shows
Beatles-A-Rama Fan Club
Paul McCartney's Little Rock and Rollers

The survey collected 293 responses over a week-long period, and the respondents (who submitted answers anonymously) were divided into the following age groups:

Under 18
18–24
25–34
35–44
45–54
55–64
65+

Of all the age groups, those ranging from 55 to 64 filled out the survey most, with 35.96% of all responses. The second-largest group was in the 45–54 age range, at 24.32%. The 65-and-over group came in third, with 21.58% of the responses. The remaining groups made up 8.22% and less. While the survey ended up not including as many millennials as expected, it does demonstrate how technology has significantly impacted first- and second-generation fans in how they connect with others in the Beatles community and the ways in which they contribute to community knowledge. Due to the response rate, the three age groups with the largest number of respondents will be examined.

Age 65-and-Over

Questions 2–4

In the 65-and-over group, the most respondents indicated that they maintained a website of some kind (not necessarily just Beatles-related), at 65.38%. A YouTube channel came in a close second, at 53.85%, indicating that they produce original content or created a channel for saving and viewing clips.

The average respondent reported regularly following at least one Beatles-specific podcast; the most popular ones cited included *Something about the Beatles, Fab 4 Free 4 All, Take It Away, When They Was Fab, I've Got a Beatles Podcast, 2Legs, Things We Said Today, Yesterday & Today, Beatles News Briefs YouTube: The Beatles, Talk More Talk: A Solo Beatles Videocast* (also available in podcast form), *BC the Beatles,* and *She Said, She Said.* Thirty-three responded to the question, with 14 respondents saying they either listened only to YouTube or the Beatles Sirius XM channel or watched videos on Facebook. One responded not listening to podcasts due to being "not that tech savvy."

Respondents indicated buying music predominantly at physical stores and Amazon (54.10% each). At a distant third was iTunes, at 24.59%. A few respondents also mentioned purchasing music on eBay.

Questions 5–6

An overwhelming majority in this age group reported preferring CDs (87.10%), with vinyl coming in second (61.29%). Satellite radio came in a somewhat distant third, with 35.48%, but streaming services scored well, at 29.03%. Others reported listening to internet radio (25.81%), with listening to MP3s on the computer followed closely, at 24.19%. Interestingly, the least popular option proved to be terrestrial radio.

How they listened to music proved fairly traditional, with 65.57% preferring home stereo systems; 32.79% reported listening through their computers and laptops, 29.51% marked "other" and listed listening in their car or through a tablet, 26.23% selected the MP3 player option, and the fewest (21.31%) used a smartphone.

Questions 7–8
Social media makes the greatest impact on how fans receive the latest news. Of the 65-and-over respondents, an overwhelming majority (93.55%) learned news primarily through Facebook or Twitter. Beatles-specific websites such as Beatles News came in second, at 67.74%, with print sources such as *Rolling Stone* coming in third (37.10%). Television followed closely, at 35.48%, and blogs proved to be the least popular option. Those who selected "other" indicated sources such as friends, emails, Sirius XM, and online forums such as the Steve Hoffmann forum.

Social media ruled again when respondents were asked how they communicated with follow fans, with 85.96% indicating Facebook as the chief platform. The other choices scored significantly lower, with concerts (29.82%) and fan conventions (28.07%) ranking a distant second and third.

Questions 9–10
The final questions concerned how fans believed technology has impacted them personally. Question 9—"How do you think technology has impacted how you interact with fans or express your interest in the band (or solo artists)?"—received mostly positive comments in this age group, stating that Facebook had enabled them to better connect with fellow fans. Many cited receiving responses from friends immediately as a plus. One said, "It is instant now. And able to talk to fans around the world. When I was a teenager we talked to our friends locally only." Others noted being able to learn news concerning the Beatles instantaneously. One respondent wrote, "We know what is going on with Paul & Ringo almost immediately. Years ago we wouldn't know what they were doing sometimes for weeks." Finally, others mentioned the internet increasing their knowledge, with one comment reading, "The internet and social media have connected me with Beatles fans and experts literally all over the world—and I'm sure I'm not the only one who can say that. Sharing posts and news with like-minded people is one of the best ways to increase knowledge of The Greatest Rock Band, Ever."

Question 10—"How do you think technological advancements have helped or hurt Beatles and solo fandom (e.g., connecting with fans, personal expression)?"—received a number of positive responses, much like question 9. However, others in this age group expressed frustration at the sometimes uncivil tone of the internet. One lamented, "I think technology has helped fans to connect, form friendships, exchange ideas, and debate ideas. This very same technology's inherent anonymity unfortunately has not always been good experiences, with people being rude, vulgar, trolling the fan sites. Rec.music.beatles began as a wonderful forum to Beatle information and exchanging of information, but the trolling has all but destroyed that site." Another mentioned that the nature of social media means that "everything is usually reduced to only a sentence or less, it's hard to carry on a conversation of any depth. There's always been different levels of how fans relate to the Beatles, so it tends to be useful for the more, shall we say, 'lighter' aspects of fandom; posting photos, agreeing with others with similar tastes, etc." Another wrote, "For social media often creates a false intimacy between people. So is it actually changing the conversation and what we mainly talk about? Just like the internet will hopefully never replace the need for books, etc., and reflective thought either, as well as trivia. The Beatles offered us all these levels, which different fans can relate to and express." Finally, one person speculated about how technology could have better preserved the careers of other figures such as Mozart, Bach, or Beethoven: "Imagine if the classical music giants . . . would have access to the current social media to provide greater penetration and spread of their music, and the likely increase in their core support—even more so than today. This suggests that the Beatles and their music—through advanced spread and penetration via social media and technology—could be greater and last longer than the 'classics.' "

Ages 55–64

Questions 2–4

In the 55–64 age group, responses were similar to those of the 65-and-over group, in that they maintained websites (61.54%) or YouTube channels (42.31%). Here, 25% reported maintaining a blog, substantially more than in the 65-and-over group (7.69%).

Fifty-five of the respondents reported regularly listening to podcasts, many of them the same programs the older group listed, in addition to *Fabcast*.

Similarly to the 65-and-over group, they reported buying music predominantly on Amazon (60.58%), followed by physical stores (50.96%).
Coming in third again here was iTunes, at 24.04%; in the "other" category,
21 respondents listed other sources such as eBay and Google Play; two mentioned relying on YouTube and not purchasing music.

Questions 5–6

The question regarding how respondents prefer to listen to music resulted
in physical CDs ranking first (75.00%) followed by vinyl (41.35%) and
streaming services (32.69%). Listening to MP3s on the computer (32.69%)
and satellite radio (25.96%) followed closely. Once again, terrestrial radio
scored lowest, at 17.31%. In the "other" category, respondents noted iPods,
cassettes, Google Play, and YouTube. They reported listening to music mostly
on home stereo systems (50.49%), followed by PC or laptop (33.01%) and,
in a departure from the 65-and-over group, smartphone (28.16%). The iPod
still scored a surprising 22.33%. The "other" category scored 33.01%, with
respondents citing even more ways to listen: car, TV, tablet, and Alexa.

Questions 7–8

Similarly to the 65-and-over group, the 55–64 age group obtained Beatles
news primarily from Facebook (92.16%), followed by Beatles-specific
websites (53.92%). Coming in third, however, was podcasts (27.45%),
followed by magazines (22.55%). Unlike the older group, however, these
respondents listed television last (11.76%).

In networking with fans, social media dominated, at 87.25%, with
Facebook Live and other streaming services coming in a distant second, at
24.51%. Fan connections followed, at 18.63%, with concerts ranking last, at
10.78%.

Questions 9–10

The final two questions scored similar responses to those of the older group.
For question 9, many cited convenience and low cost as key reasons they
believe technology has impacted how they interact with other fans. Others
cited how they have learned from fellow fans. One person wrote, "I am able
to actually interact with a lot of really interesting and knowledgeable people.
More is known now about the 'Fabs' than it was coming through it all in
my youth." Some, however, felt there were drawbacks. One answered, "It's
easier than before the internet, but not always satisfying. Deep-level core fans

sometimes feel entitled, making conversation with them about new and archival releases nearly impossible." Another wrote of "more interaction but less true connections." Despite these issues, one respondent mentioned not only the international aspect but also the multigenerational facet of social media. Another answered, "Social media has allowed me to join lots of sites showing photos, links to blogs and seeing interesting commentary on many Beatles related themes posted by a variety of fans of all ages." Still another said, "Well, there are a lot of ppl in the Beatles crew. It's nice to share fandom w/strangers over the internet that one wouldn't have normally had the op to interact with (e.g., Europeans, Asians, and non-Californian Americans & Canadians)."

The final question concerning the pros and cons of technology and Beatles fandom also garnered mostly positive responses. Some listed specific issues but stated they believed the convenience of the technology was worth the drawbacks. One wrote, "Sometimes social media can be a bear when reading through off-topic and whiny comments to get to the meat, but it is generally worth it." Another added, "It's helped by posting music that promotes their legacy. It hurts when people spread false information." One person described a specific mechanism to cope with some negative aspects: "for me if I see a post that is negative or very personal on any of the Beatles, or their family, I will ignore the post, I try not to get involved, I do not want to get into any arguments online." Overall, people cited the immediacy of receiving breaking news as a major benefit of technology for fandom.

Ages 45–54

Questions 2–4

In the 45–54 category, some major differences appeared. Here, 46.34% reported having YouTube channels, followed by websites (41.46%). Blogs came in third, at 29.27%, followed by podcasts, at 19.51%.

Forty-seven people responded to the podcast question, with eight stating they listened to either no podcasts or only YouTube shows. Most answered that they listened to at least one podcast regularly, with a few responding "at least 10" and "too many to list."

Interestingly, the respondents in this age group cited buying music mostly at physical stores (59.42%), followed by Amazon (56.52%), with iTunes came coming in a distant third, at 26.09%, and Spotify ranking last, at 13.04%. In the "other" category, 11 people mentioned eBay; others mentioned buying music less frequently due to YouTube, Pandora, and Sirius XM allowing them to listen to music for no or low cost.

Questions 5–6

Like the previous age groups, the 45–54 group still prefers listening to CDs (63.38%) versus vinyl (40.85%) or a streaming service (38.03%). Listening to MP3s on the computer proved popular (36.62%), followed by satellite radio (25.35%) and internet radio (21.13%). Terrestrial radio came in last; in the "other" category, 13 people listed YouTube, iPods, and car radios.

Question 6 marked the sharpest departure from the other age groups. The smartphone and home stereo tied for most frequent use (40.85%), followed by PC or laptop (38.03%) and iPod (18.31%).

Questions 7–8

Similarly to the older groups, this age group overwhelmingly cited social media as the first place they receive Beatles news (98.59%), followed by Beatles-specific websites (56.34%) and podcasts (36.62%). Music magazines (29.58%), blogs (21.13%), and newspapers (14.08%) rounded out the results.

For networking with fans, social media dominated (94.37%), with fan conventions coming in a distant second (23.94%), followed by Facebook Live (14.08%) and concerts (8.45%).

Questions 9–10

For question 9, respondents again cited the ability to communicate with like-minded fans around the world as a major benefit of technology. One person mentioned podcasts specifically: "podcasts offer a fantastic opportunity to explore specific areas of the band's careers." As for the 55–64 group, the ability to network with multigenerational fans proved appealing. One respondent stated, "I think it's offered a tighter bond and has reached even younger fans. For instance, there are countless Beatles fan blogs on Tumblr run by people who weren't born until the late '90s early 2000s. Those kids create great gifs and edits of old photos/clips and have given me a new way to look at the past." Another cited a negative: "there's also less fact and more ranting." Overall, one person stated, "it has created a sense of community that once could have only been found through fanzines or the occasional convention. It's been a pleasure to enjoy day-to-day communications with other fans, particularly since I grew up in a community in the late 1970s and early 1980s where there were no other hardcore Beatles fans and communication from fanzines happened only every couple of months."

Finally, those in the 45–54 category cited many positives for self-expression, mainly the ability to share knowledge with like-minded fans. "Way back it was monthly or three-monthly fanzines—now it is daily or hourly," one said. Another described the challenges technology presents to Beatles research: "No one seems to take scholarship seriously anymore. Someone like Mark Lewisohn can spend decades establishing impeccable credentials as a scholar, and someone blows him off because they read something on Wikipedia." One respondent wrote, "The amount of bad information floating around the internet is very disheartening. Everyone's an 'expert,' but nobody does any research." Another mentioned that technology has negatively impacted fan conventions: "While they are fun to attend for social purposes, there is no longer a need to attend if you are looking for memorabilia, or if you want to see rare films, since that is now all at our fingertips online." Others mentioned online bullying as a concern, while one individual weighed the pros and cons: "The online availability of media (music/video) has been instrumental in keeping the Beatles in the public eye and relevant. Unfortunately, social media has given a voice to the unseemly side of human nature, reinforcing stereotypes and bizarre conspiracy theories (Paul is dead, etc.)." However, many fans stated that the benefits outweighed the negatives. A respondent explained: "I think technology has helped the fans become more like a large family, as it has helped enable people to 'meet' one another. Via the familiarity of social media, fan gatherings and concerts can be more like family reunions."

These three age groups' experiences with technology largely mirror statistics published in the Pew and IFPI reports. However, the survey could not obtain meaningful statistics for younger age groups due to low numbers of respondents. An interview with Kristine Summer, a blogger in her 20s and creator of an eponymous YouTube channel, reveals how technology has transformed the ways younger generations discover the Beatles and express their fandom. In turn, Apple Corps has taken notice: the official Beatles YouTube channel posted an interview with her on December 15, 2019.[30]

Case Study: Kristine Summer, YouTube Creator

One example of how a younger Beatles fan uses technology to engage in a participatory culture is Kristine Summer, a blogger and YouTube channel creator in her 20s. In a recent interview, she discussed how her interest in the group was piqued when she was 12 or 13, thanks in part to YouTube and iTunes. Summer recalled watching the evening news in November 2010, when it was announced that the Beatles catalog would finally debut on iTunes. "I had always heard about them and knew they were a very famous band. And already being a fan of music, I decided to go to YouTube and check them out. YouTube was always my go-to for listening to music," she said. After listening to their music, she visited iTunes and downloaded a few tracks. "I just became more and more interested in the music, and then I discovered the internet fandom, which changed my life forever," she said.[31]

Summer's transition to internet fandom turned out to be a fairly logical one. She said she "grew up on social media," such as MySpace and Facebook, and decided to enter the fan community by beginning a blog on the popular micro-blogging site Tumblr. As she blogged frequently about the Beatles in late 2010, she connected with fans worldwide. "I found tons of other girls my age who felt the same way about the band, and it was amazing because I had no friends who were interested at school," she said.

Next, she returned to YouTube. She explained that she had always enjoyed watching videos on the site but felt there were not enough shows devoted to the Beatles. Thus, she decided to create her own channel in 2014; she "wanted to join that community" of Beatles fandom. Broadcasting from home using an iPhone, Summer would post clips where she would display her music collection or create "unboxing" videos featuring the newest box sets. Today she posts other kinds of videos, occasionally vlogs, and boasts 3.63K subscribers. Using Facebook and YouTube itself, she promotes the channel. "According to my YouTube analytics, a lot of my views come from people playing around on the site just like I was years ago," she said. The Universal Music Group took notice and began sending her Beatles-related products to unbox and review on her channel.

Starting a channel changed Summer's life in many ways, she explained. It expanded her social circle beyond her school. "Literally every Beatles fan I've met is someone I first connected with on social media," she said. She described meeting with some online fans in person at a concert or a fan convention: "I finally see them in person for the first time, and it's like we already know each other! We know each other's favorite Beatle and favorite albums, so we can just go straight to fangirling together." She also described meeting an Instagram friend at a McCartney concert merchandise stand. "We were both in line at the merch stand and just ran up and hugged each other. I went to my first Beatles convention, and it was the same feeling. Meeting all these people you've known for years. It was an amazing experience."

When asked how technology has impacted her fan experience, Summer replied, "Oh, it's a whole new world now compared to the previous generations. We're all connecting on Facebook or FaceTime. Keeping up with each other is so much easier, even with fans on the other side of the earth." She particularly enjoys watching events on television while live-tweeting with fellow fans. "I remember in detail the Grammys salute to the Beatles," she said. "Me and so many of my Twitter friends were all 'live-tweeting' the event, and we all pretty much had the same thoughts and reactions. We might not all be in a room together watching, but it sure feels like it."

Finally, Summer believes YouTube, websites, and social media allow fans to express themselves "more easily, and they're not so ashamed of their feelings." For example, she said, if one is a fan of a particular Beatles album, a Facebook group dedicated just to that LP most likely exists. "It's like no opinion is unpopular anymore, and you can always find someone to agree with. If you like YouTube, there are Beatles fans there; if you like reading, there are plenty of blogs and books. Beatles people are some of the most creative people."

Analysis: Come Together

The three age groups 65 and over, 55–64, and 45–54 represent the majority of those who responded to the survey. While not enough millennials and younger fans responded to allow conclusions to be drawn, Summer's experience proves useful for further understanding how technology transformed affiliation and expression. From the survey results, it can be determined that technology has impacted fandom most in affiliation, particularly in fans' communicating with one another through Facebook and Twitter. YouTube has emerged as a particularly powerful tool, as people reported listening to music through the platform and watching Beatles-specific channels. Podcasts have become a popular mode of communication, letting passionate fans share their knowledge easily with other enthusiasts.

As Johansson states, young adults in her focus group often mentioned being introduced to new music genres though friends' recommendations on Facebook and other social media sites. They discovered music through friends' suggestions on social networking sites or got "recommendations for new music on Spotify or . . . YouTube and, for some, tips from music bloggers or 'expert' sites such as *Pitchfork*. Such encounters could be understood as having led to a broader taste in music and to the appreciation of a wider range of genres."[32]

Technology has made it simple for fans to receive information quickly, cheaply, and easily anywhere they happen to be, on demand. In turn, as Beatles survey participants stated, they have been able to learn more from fellow fans, gain different perspectives (particularly from different generations), and easily participate in conversations. Their knowledge and music collections have expanded, as have their connections with fans throughout the world.

Social media and streaming enable instant connections with fans and on-demand listening. They bring multigenerational fans together, with multiple voices adding to communal knowledge. As Jeffrey Roessner writes, "third-and-fourth generation fans have emerged in the digital age, listening with new ears, asking fresh questions, voicing original opinions."[33] Fans have always been crucial in maintaining a band's legacy—a fact that remains unchanged since the 1960s. However, as Roessner states, "digital culture has fundamentally altered the relationship between the Beatles and their audiences, who now forge previously unimaginable connections to the music and the musicians."[34] Roessner discusses how instant access to songs, lyrics, videos, and bootlegs allows fans to "construct a new, popular scholarship of the band that alters what we know about the Beatles and how we know it."[35] In other words, fans form a participatory culture through affiliation and expression.

While general conclusions can be drawn about fan behavior characteristics, Duffett warns against easy categorization: " 'Music fandom' is one term for a wide range of phenomena and identifications occurring in a variety of different times and places, a term that encompasses a range of tastes, roles, identities and practices."[36] He dubs it a "cultural conviction" that involves emotional engagement with any or all of the following actions: musical appreciation, music practice, celebrity following, social networking, dancing, collecting, and self-expression.[37] Music fandom entails many or all of these activities, but technology has undoubtedly forever altered them, particularly those involving affiliation and expression.

Some respondents in the Beatles survey expressed reservations about certain aspects of social media, namely, the potential for bullying or, at the very least, having superficial relationships with Facebook "friends." Many respondents, however, stated that they coped with these drawbacks due to the positives of technology, namely, convenience and the ability to connect with fans worldwide. "Fans are, at best, communicative, imaginative, communal, expert, interesting and intelligent," Duffett writes. "Online social media platforms demonstrate this in a more public and visible way . . . they have operated as a forthright challenge to the idea that electronic mediation is an alienating and impersonal process."[38] As the survey participants demonstrated, online groupings of fans form Gee's notion of an affinity space: creating largely supportive communities bonding over a shared interest, with novices and experts exchanging information.

As Summer demonstrates, some fans represent the expression aspect of a participatory culture. Creating original content such as a website and a YouTube channel contributes to the community by sharing knowledge and providing original perspectives. Both elements have benefited greatly from online technology; as Duffett states, "in an age of 'geek chic,' fandom seems to be at the forefront of an astute, techno-savvy consumer culture."[39]

Conclusion

Fans from the 1960s passing around handwritten fan fiction, editors creating their own fanzines in the 1970s and 1980s, fans creating some of the first Beatles fan websites in the 1990s, and those now broadcasting from their homes to a worldwide audience—technology has evolved, but basic characteristics of fandom have remained the same. Duffett posits that these elements include "a fascination with music, various romantic and folk ideologies, an emphasis on the star system, a tendency of fans to form social communities, to pursue shared concerns, and to follow characteristic practices."[40] Computers and the internet enable more conversation, building of knowledge, and creation of original contributions to the community. In other words, as Duffett concludes, "the net has offered new and better ways to more easily do what we previously did before."[41] In the case of Beatles fandom, technology enables worldwide networking and the creation of books, websites, podcasts, and internet radio shows, all important elements of a thriving participatory culture.

Appendix: Technology and Beatles Fandom Survey

Technology and Beatles Fandom Survey 2   SurveyMonkey

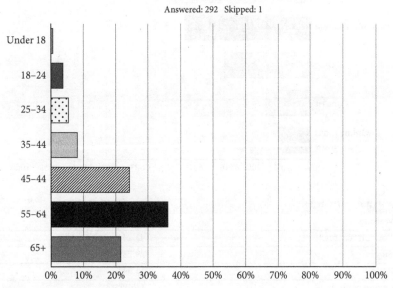

Q1 What is your age?
Answered: 292   Skipped: 1

ANSWER CHOICES	RESPONSES	
Under 18	0.68%	2
18–24	3.77%	11
25–34	5.48%	16
35–44	8.22%	24
45–54	24.32%	71
55–64	35.96%	105
65+	21.58%	63
TOTAL		292

Q2 Please check all that apply to you. Do you have/host:

Answered: 148   Skipped: 145

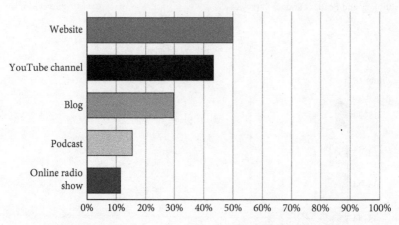

ANSWER CHOICES	RESPONSES	
Website	50.00%	74
YouTube channel	43.24%	64
Blog	29.73%	44
Podcast	15.54%	23
Online radio show	11.49%	17
TOTAL		148

Q3 List of Beatles or solo-themed podcasts and YouTube channels to which you subscribe or at least watch/listen to regularly:

Answered: 184   Skipped: 109

Q4 Where do you usually purchase music, Beatles and otherwise?

Answered: 288   Skipped: 5

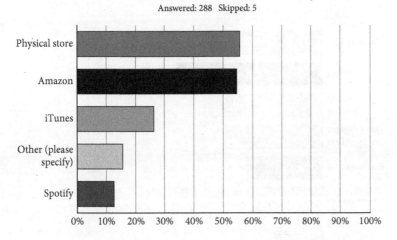

ANSWER CHOICES	RESPONSES	
Physical store	55.56%	160
Amazon	54.51%	157
iTunes	26.39%	76
Other (please specify)	15.63%	45
Spotify	12.85%	37
TOTAL		288

Q5 How do you prefer listening to music (check all that apply)?

Answered: 290   Skipped: 3

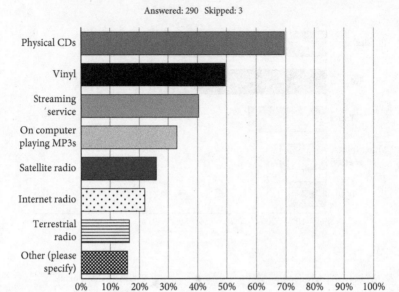

ANSWER CHOICES	RESPONSES	
Physical CDs	69.66%	202
Vinyl	49.66%	144
Streaming service	40.34%	117
On computer playing MP3s	32.76%	95
Satellite radio	25.86%	75
Internet radio	22.07%	64
Terrestrial radio	16.55%	48
Other (please specify)	15.86%	46
TOTAL		290

Q6 What do you use to listen to music most often?

Answered: 289 Skipped: 4

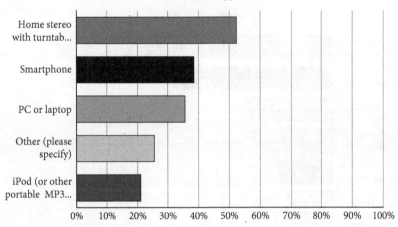

ANSWER CHOICES	RESPONSES	
Home stereo with turntable, CD player, etc.	52.25%	151
Smartphone	38.41%	111
PC or laptop	35.64%	103
Other (please specify)	25.61%	74
iPod (or other portable MP3 device)	21.11%	61
TOTAL		289

Q7 How do you typically receive Beatles or solo-related news (check all that apply)

Answered: 287   Skipped: 6

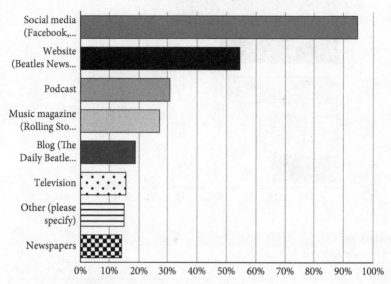

ANSWER CHOICES	RESPONSES	
Social media (Facebook, Twitter, Tumblr)	94.77%	272
Website (Beatles News, official Beatles or solo artist pages)	54.70%	157
Podcast	30.66%	88
Music magazine (Rolling Stone, Billboard, MOJO)	27.18%	78
Blog (The Daily Beatle, Beatles News Insider)	18.82%	54
Television	15.68%	45
Other (please specify)	14.98%	43
Newspapers	14.29%	41
TOTAL		287

Q8 How do you network with fellow Beatles/solo fans most often?

Answered: 283 Skipped: 10

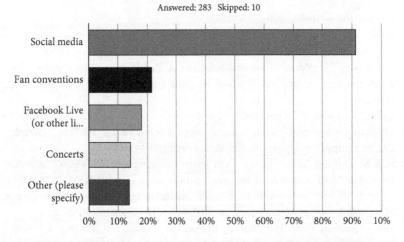

ANSWER CHOICES	RESPONSES	
Social media	91.17%	258
Fan conventions	21.55%	61
Facebook Live (or other live streaming services)	18.02%	51
Concerts	14.13%	40
Other (please specify)	13.78%	39
TOTAL		283

Q9 How do you think technology has impacted how you interact with fans or express your interest in the band (or solo artists)?

Answered: 224 Skipped: 69

Q10 How do you think technological advancements have helped or hurt Beatles and solo fandom (e.g., connecting with fans, personal expression)?

Answered: 223 Skipped: 70

Notes

1. Mark Duffett, "Introduction," in *Popular Music Fandom: Identities, Roles and Practices*, ed. Mark Duffett (London: Routledge, 2014), 7.
2. Henry Jenkins, *Textual Poachers: Television Fans and Participatory Culture* (New York: Routledge, 2013), 278–279.
3. Henry Jenkins et al., *Confronting the Challenges of Participatory Culture: Media Education for the 21st Century* (Cambridge, MA: MIT Press, 2009).

4. John Paul Gee and Elizabeth Hayes, "Public Pedagody," in Handbook of Public Pedagogy, 186.

5. Gee and Hayes, "Public Pedagogy," 186.

6. John Fiske, "The Cultural Economy of Fandom," in *The Adoring Audience: Fan Culture and Popular Media*, ed. Lisa A. Lewis (London: Routledge, 1992), 39.

7. Joli Jensen, "Afterword: Fans and Scholars: A Reassessment," in *Popular Music Fandom: Identities, Roles and Practices*, ed. Mark Duffett (London: Routledge, 2014), 208–209.

8. Fiske, "The Cultural Economy of Fandom."

9. Oh Shari Photography, "Paul McCartney: Appeciate Fan VIdeo," YouTube, November 27, 2013, https://www.youtube.com/watch?v=wkj5OnvOpO4

10. Paul McCartney, "Have You Seen Oh Shari Photography's Fan Video," Facebook, December 10, 2013, www.facebook.com/PaulMcCartney/posts/10152166036203313.

11. Aaron Smith and Monica Anderson, "Social Media Use in 2018," *Pew Research Center*, March 2018, www.pewinternet.org/2018/03/01/social-media-use-in-2018/.

12. Henry Jenkins, "Star Trek Rerun, Reread, Rewritten: Fan Writing as Textual Poaching," in *Gender, Race, and Class in Media: A Critical Reader*, ed. Gail Dines and Jean M. Humez (Thousand Oaks, CA: Sage, 2011), 58–59.

13. Chris Atton, "Popular Music Fanzines: Genre, Aesthetics, and the 'Democratic Conversation,'" *Popular Music and Society* 33, no. 4 (2010): 523.

14. Lynn Van Matre, "Fanzines Keep Alive the Beat of Pop Musicians from Beatles to Brown," *Chicago Tribune*, June 2, 1985, https://www.chicagotribune.com/news/ct-xpm-1985-06-02-8502040396-story.html.

15. Jenkins, *Textual Poachers*, 278–279.

16. Eliot Van Buskirk, "Meet the Beatles Data," *Spotify Insights*, January 22, 2016, https://web.archive.org/web/20160415140616/https://insights.spotify.com/int/2016/01/22/meet-the-beatles-data/.

17. Steve Marinucci, "The Beatles Surpass Two Billion Mark in Music Streaming," *AXS*, December 21, 2016, https://web.archive.org/web/20161222153754/www.axs.com/the-beatles-surpass-2-billion-mark-in-music-streaming-112016.

18. Ed Christman, "Halfway through 2018, Streaming's Continued Growth Defies Mathematical Trends," *Billboard*, July 25, 2018, www.billboard.com/articles/business/8467112/mid-year-2018-streaming-continued-growth-defies-math-trends.

19. Recording Industry Association of America, "Mid-Year 2018 RIAA Music Revenues Report, 2018, www.riaa.com/wp-content/uploads/2018/09/RIAA-Mid-Year-2018-Revenue-Report-News-Notes.pdf.

20. Quoted in Leo Kelion, "Beatles Music Joins Streaming Services," *BBC News*, December 23, 2015, www.bbc.com/news/technology-35166985.

21. Quoted in Kelion, "Beatles Music Joins Streaming Services."

22. Quoted in Kelion, "Beatles Music Joins Streaming Services."

23. International Federation of the Phonographic Industry (IFPI), *Music Consumer Insight Report 2018*. https://www.ifpi.org/resources/

24. IFPI, *Music Consumer Insight Report*.

25. IFPI, *Music Consumer Insight Report*.

26. Smith and Anderson, "Social Media Use."
27. IFPI, *Music Consumer Insight Report.*
28. Sofia Johansson, "Music as Part of Connectivity Culture," in *Streaming Music: Practices, Media, Cultures*, ed. Sofia Johansson et al. (New York: Routledge, 2018).
29. Duffett, "Introduction," 7–8.
30. The Beatles, "Collectors across the Universe—Kristine Summer," YouTube, December 15, 2019, https://www.youtube.com/watch?v=71ni2WGlmLU.
31. Kristine Summer, interviewed by Kit O'Toole, October 23, 2018.
32. Johansson, "Music as Part of Connectivity Culture."
33. Jeffrey Roessner, "Revolution 2.0: Beatles Fan Scholarship in the Digital Age," in *New Critical Perspectives on the Beatles: Things We Said Today*, ed. Kenneth Womack and Katie Kapurch (London: Palgrave Macmillan, 2016), 222.
34. Roessner, "Revolution 2.0," 222–223.
35. Roessner, "Revolution 2.0," 223.
36. Duffett, "Introduction," 7–8.
37. Duffett, "Introduction," 7–8.
38. Duffett, "Introduction," 4.
39. Duffett, "Introduction," 4.
40. Duffett, "Introduction," 4.
41. Duffett, "Introduction," 4.

Bibliography

Atton, Chris. "Popular Music Fanzines: Genre, Aesthetics, and the 'Democratic Conversation.'" *Popular Music and Society* 33, no. 4 (2010): 517–531.

The Beatles. "Collectors across the Universe—Kristine Summer." YouTube, December 15, 2019. https://www.youtube.com/watch?v=71ni2WGlmLU.

Christman, Ed. "Halfway through 2018, Streaming's Continued Growth Defies Mathematical Trends." *Billboard*, July 25, 2018. www.billboard.com/articles/business/8467112/mid-year-2018-streaming-continued-growth-defies-math-trends.

Duffett, Mark. "Introduction." In *Popular Music Fandom: Identities, Roles and Practices*, edited by Mark Duffett, 1–15. London: Routledge, 2014.

Fiske, John. "The Cultural Economy of Fandom." In *The Adoring Audience: Fan Culture and Popular Media*, edited by Lisa A. Lewis, 29–49. London: Routledge, 1992.

Gee, John Paul, and Elizabeth R. Hayes. "Public Pedagogy through Video Games." In *Handbook of Public Pedagogy*, edited by Jennifer A. Sandlin, Brian D. Schultz, and Jake Burdick, 185–193. New York: Routledge, 2010.

International Federation of the Phonographic Industry. *Music Consumer Insight Report 2018.* https://www.ifpi.org/resources/

Jenkins, Henry. "Star Trek Rerun, Reread, Rewritten: Fan Writing as Textual Poaching." In *Gender, Race, and Class in Media: A Critical Reader*, edited by Gail Dines and Jean M. Humez, 57–65. Thousand Oaks, CA: Sage, 2011.

Jenkins, Henry. *Textual Poachers: Television Fans and Participatory Culture.* New York: Routledge, 2013.

Jenkins, Henry, Ravi Purushotma, Margaret Weigel, Katie Clinton, and Alice J. Robison. *Confronting the Challenges of Participatory Culture: Media Education for the 21st Century.* Cambridge, MA: MIT Press, 2009.

Jensen, Joli. "Afterword: Fans and Scholars: A Reassessment." In *Popular Music Fandom: Identities, Roles and Practices,* edited by Mark Duffett, 207–234. London: Routledge, 2014.

Johansson, Sofia. "Music as Part of Connectivity Culture." In *Streaming Music: Practices, Media, Cultures,* edited by Sofia Johansson, Ann Werner, Patrick Åker, and Greg Goldenzwaig, 44–61. New York: Routledge, 2018.

Kelion, Leo. "Beatles Music Joins Streaming Services." *BBC News,* December 23, 2015. www.bbc.com/news/technology-35166985.

Marinucci, Steve. "The Beatles Surpass Two Billion Mark in Music Streaming." *AXS,* December 21, 2016. https://web.archive.org/web/20161222153754/www.axs.com/the-beatles-surpass-2-billion-mark-in-music-streaming-112016

McCartney, Paul. "Have You Seen Oh Shari Photography's Fan Video." Facebook, December 10, 2013. www.facebook.com/PaulMcCartney/posts/10152166036203313.

Oh Shari Photography. "Paul McCartney: Appreciate Fan Video." YouTube, November 27, 2013. https://www.youtube.com/watch?v=wkj5OnvOpO4

Recording Industry Association of America. "Mid-Year 2018 RIAA Music Revenues Report," 2018. www.riaa.com/wp-content/uploads/2018/09/RIAA-Mid-Year-2018-Revenue-Report-News-Notes.pdf.

Roessner, Jeffrey. "Revolution 2.0: Beatles Fan Scholarship in the Digital Age." In *New Critical Perspectives on the Beatles: Things We Said Today,* edited by Kenneth Womack and Katie Kapurch, 221–240. London: Palgrave Macmillan, 2016.

Smith, Aaron, and Monica Anderson. "Social Media Use in 2018." *Pew Research Center,* March 2018. www.pewinternet.org/2018/03/01/social-media-use-in-2018/.

Van Buskirk, Eliot. "Meet the Beatles Data." *Spotify Insights,* January 22, 2016. https://web.archive.org/web/20160415140616/https://insights.spotify.com/int/2016/01/22/meet-the-beatles-data

Van Matre, Lynn. "Fanzines Keep Alive the Beat of Pop Musicians from Beatles to Brown." *Chicago Tribune,* June 2, 1985. https://www.chicagotribune.com/news/ct-xpm-1985-06-02-8502040396-story.html.

"What Girls Want: Seventy Years of Pop Idols and Audiences." *Paley Center for Media,* updated 2009. https://www.paleycenter.org/what-girls-want-seventy-years-of-pop-idols-audiences.

5

The Beatles, Gender, and Sexuality

I Am He as You Are He as You Are Me

Katie Kapurch

Introduction

In the beginning, according to Fab Four lore, girls were the screaming face of Beatles fandom. These Beatlemaniacs are now the touchstone comparison for fandoms of all subsequent boy bands—as well as non-music female-oriented fandoms, such as the *Twilight* literary franchise, which saw girls screaming for sparkly vampires in the 2000s.[1] On the one hand, the visibility of the Beatles' female fans has led to groundbreaking feminist scholarship that celebrates the empowerment behind that iconic scream; critics have also revealed how disparagement of girl audiences reflects broader sexist and ageist attitudes in the culture. On the other hand, the constant association between Beatlemania, girls, and femininity limits the story about Beatles fandom and oversimplifies the gendered and sexual dynamics of the Beatles' popularity. As an example of the latter, take Ron Howard's recent documentary.

The narrative arc of *Eight Days a Week: The Touring Years* (2016) reveals girl fans as the devouring force that drove the band from the stage.[2] But that audience plays two roles in this drama: before their hysteria becomes antagonism, the girl fans are a collective damsel in need of an eight-armed Beatle hero. The "lads" then trade places with their fans, falling victim to their screams (as well as the out-for-blood white Southern evangelical Christians upset by Lennon's Jesus comments). Standing outside this hysteria is the film's director, Howard, the quintessential US baby boomer; he is the intellectual (male) fan, recuperating the story and saving the Beatles from the madness. Howard's film implies that once the Beatles stopped touring, they became free to experiment with studio technology inappropriate for stadium performances. As such, the "true" fans were rewarded. These Howard types, who, like the Beatles themselves, couldn't hear the music over the

Katie Kapurch, *The Beatles, Gender, and Sexuality* In: *Fandom and the Beatles*. Edited by: Kenneth Womack and Kit O'Toole, Oxford University Press (2021). © Oxford University Press. DOI: 10.1093/oso/9780190917852.003.0006 pandemonium, could now finally appreciate the band's innovation without the illegitimate distraction of the girls.

In the mythology of the band and its fans, the story goes on, the liberated post-1966 Beatles stopped writing songs to court girls, whose obsession was deemed less valid because it involved romance rather than serious devotion to musical study. I argue elsewhere that the late-1960s Beatles did not cease in their appeals to girls' and women's experiences.[3] But the gendered split in the band's narrative corresponds with how scholars have theorized sexist attitudes about gendered fan behavior across different fandoms over the last 50 years. Because the obsessive nature of being a fan is already gendered feminine, male fans often seek legitimacy through conventionally masculine pursuits (such as establishing hierarchy through competitive study). In turn, fandoms associated with women and girls are frequently policed for a supposed lack of rigor and belittled for their affective expressions of emotional excess.[4]

The overly simplified narrative about early Beatles fandom ignores the girls who studied and the boys who screamed—and the vast in-between that involves both, neither, or something else. Less attention is paid to boys, who, while not swooning with the visibility of girls, were still present in those famous throngs of screamers. The Beatlemaniac-as-screaming-girl is indeed worthy of consideration, but that singular image ends up limiting the recognition of female musicianship and artistry, as Kit O'Toole observes in her exploration of women's writing about the Beatles.[5] Attention to the screaming girl fan also habitually assumes a heteronormative stance, crowding out the consideration of queer attraction. What is needed is a discussion of the Beatles' complex gendered and sexual appeals to their audiences, as well as attention to the evolution of fan identification processes in the latter part of the 1960s and beyond.

This chapter unites the still-growing body of scholarship that treats various issues of gender and sexuality in relation to the Beatles and their fans. After I consider the theoretical difference between androgyny and gender fluidity, representative Beatles texts are discussed in relation to relevant fan responses. While more focus is given to the early Beatles because of that period's association with Beatlemania, I also survey later periods before turning to a consideration of youth today. Through these examples, I reveal the Beatles' gender fluidity as a key ingredient in their sustained popularity among fans. The band endures because listeners can keep finding themselves—or perhaps the mirrored reflections they seek to find—in the Beatles.

Androgynous or Gender-Fluid?

Many analyses of the early Beatles' popularity among girl fans in America invoke "androgyny" to account for Beatlemania. The oft-cited explanation in the trailblazing reception study by Barbara Ehrenreich, Elizabeth Hess, and Gloria Jacobs announces, "the Beatles' androgyny itself was sexy. . . . Theirs was a vision of sexuality freed from the shadow of gender inequality because the group mocked the gender distinctions that bifurcated the American landscape into 'his' and 'hers.'"[6] Historian Susan Douglas echoes these findings, concluding, "It's not surprising that when four irreverent, androgynous, and irresistible young men came over from England and incited a collective jailbreak, millions of these teens took them up on it."[7] Douglas goes on to provide a memorable comparison: "Without being able to put it into words, but quite able to put it into scream, girls instinctively recognized the Beatles as a Trojan horse, smuggling androgyny, a contempt for middle-class conventionalism, and sexual release into their protected, middle-class world. The Beatles insisted that all kinds of barriers could be finessed."[8] For so many American girls in the early 1960s, the Beatles' vision of gender play meant that sex could be fun; the Beatles were also a vessel for girls to inhabit as they imagined freedom and fun for themselves.

What those American girl fans perceived (or retrospectively understood) as androgyny has specifically British roots. The Beatles' androgyny can be located in an English tradition from Elizabethan cross-dressing ("mumming") to J. M. Barrie's *Peter Pan*, whose forever-a-boy title character is still traditionally played by a female actress onstage.[9] According to Steven D. Stark, "All this emphasis on androgyny was accompanied by a more relaxed attitude toward homosexuality among the English compared to their American—and even Continental—counterparts."[10] In spite of the long, known history of homosexual practices in British boarding schools, homosexuality was still illegal in the United Kingdom in the early 1960s. While forced into the closet in public, gay managers such as the Beatles' own Brian Epstein were prevalent in the bourgeoning rock-and-roll scene, where unconventionality was better tolerated.[11] The latter point is taken up by Jon Savage's contextualization of the Beatles' androgyny in the style of English mods, who, like the dandies (the mods' 19th-century forerunners), were identified by their "narcissistic flamboyance" and whose sexual preference was unclear to outsiders.[12] Like that of the mods, the "Beatles' androgyny" represented "new ways of regarding gender and the self":

> The Beatles began in the showbiz style of a previous generation—homosexual manager, "variety" type packaging, "romantic" lyrics—but quickly expressed a fresh sexuality that supplemented their huge class impact: "neither boys together aggression nor boy-next-door pathos," they challenged pop's previous masculine division between the Stud and passive Boy Slave.[13]

The Beatles diverged from pop music's gendered stereotypes familiar to youth, especially those steeped in American popular culture of the late 1950s and very early 1960s. Elvis Presley's studly virility was also found in tanned, toned beach bodies, since the Southern California aesthetic enjoyed a heyday before the British invaded in 1964. Also sharing the beach towel was the type Savage calls a "Boy Slave," perhaps best embodied by Frankie Avalon. His short physique and dark hair were a twinlike match with his *Beach Party* (1963) costar Annette Funicello. Avalon's nonthreatening, beseeching teen romance was articulated in singles such as "I'll Wait for You" (1958). The Beatles really did offer something new, as one of their American LP titles soon claimed.

The designation of *androgyny* for the Beatles is not necessarily incorrect in all cases, but the problem with that term's persistence is how it suggests intention, as if the Beatles themselves made active, conscious choices to invoke femininity or masculinity at will. Rather, their music, humor, and fashion were responses to rhetorical exigencies at hand, shaped by those around them and changing when needed: they could be this or that or both or neither. After all, they donned tailored suits (abandoning the leather gear) and performance etiquette (eschewing eating, swearing, and smoking onstage); these choices were influenced by Epstein and helped the Beatles break through to a much wider audience.[14] Calling the Beatles androgynous also sometimes assumes that femininity and masculinity are stable and opposing social constructions shared by everyone, but this is wrong for two reasons: first, when we talk about the appeal of androgyny for girl fans, usually we are assuming an American point of view, one that reads elements of British masculinity as femininity. Second, current theoretical conceptions of gender see it as a continuum, not the dueling guns of masculinity and femininity.

This chapter advocates for the use of the more contemporary term *gender fluidity* for the Beatles, especially to explain their popularity among fans.[15] Gender fluidity is a concept that better captures the appeal of the band's gendered spectrum in the early 1960s (and beyond) than androgyny does. Gender fluidity is the slide between masculine and feminine that does not have to occupy either one in the dominant position—but could or could not at any given time. Androgyny, as the aforementioned examples show, connotes outward performance and, as a result, is actually less threatening to cisgender heteronormativity. This is an outcome that gender studies scholars recognized back in the 1970s, when androgyny became more mainstream, the result of the sexual revolution. Daniel Harris termed androgyny a "sexist myth in disguise," pointing to the ways it reinforces "sexist polarizations for the definition of identity."[16] Because androgyny connotes external performance, it is also associated with temporal or whimsical dress-up.

Androgyny frequently refers to feminine play that occurs on top of a (relatively or previously) stable masculine identity: think David Bowie as Ziggy Stardust, for whom Martin King argues the Beatles opened the door.[17] Locating Bowie in the British tradition of pop dandyism, Stan Hawkins identifies Bowie as an icon of "androgyny,"[18] explaining that "his role as a bisexual space alien . . . queered his performance. Positioning himself opposite the conventions of gender representation found in rock, he invented his character through transvestism and theatricality linked up with space travel."[19] In spite of these queer, non-normative displays in the Stardust days, Bowie's later output (for example, *Let's Dance*) affirmed his heterosexual masculinity (albeit still unconventional), which made ironic his 1972 "I'm gay" announcement in *Melody Maker*.

While perhaps oversimplified here, this Bowie counterpoint emphasizes the intentionality of androgyny as queer theatricality associated with stage performance. Bowie's androgyny reads (now, at least) like an undisguised mask: "the look Bowie adopted, with long hair and eyeshadow, bridged the gap between heterosexual and gay culture."[20] Gender fluidity, which does not depend on or dictate sexual preference, can be performed through dress—but it is also associated with self-description that has more implications for situation specificity. The Beatles' gender fluidity accounts for perceptions of their seemingly authentic self-expression, a Romantic rhetoric that ingratiated them to fans even as the band changed throughout the 1960s.

A Girl-Group Boy Band

Beatlemania, the roaring, constant, and seemingly out-of-control emotional expression of Beatles love, was a response to early Beatles' gender fluidity, expressed by their moptops, pointed-toe ankle boots, and tailored suits—and in the songs they were singing. Feminist scholars have demonstrated how the Beatles spoke to girls in their own language, a consequence of the band's familiarity with girl-group music, which they covered in live performance and on the early albums.[21] In those covers and compositions, the Beatles maintain the vocables, call-and-response affirmations, romantic subject matter, and visual intimacy through matching dress and close proxemics that were characteristic of girl groups such as the Shirelles. And the Beatles perform that very girl group's song "Boys" with "a straight face."[22] McCartney's recollection of the song underscores the Beatles' lack of intentionality when it came to queer reversals: "It never occurred to us . . . Ringo used to sing 'Boys' . . . it was so innocent. We just never even thought, why is he singing about boys? We loved the song. We loved the records so much that what it said was irrelevant, it was just the spirit, the sound, the feeling."[23]

The Beatles' cover of "Boys"[24] does include, however, dashes of masculine bravado. Starr's lyrics change the line from "Mama said" to "My girl said" in order to add a brag about his sexual skill; Starr also challenges Harrison ("Come on, George") to show off his comparable skill in the lead guitar break. Meanwhile, McCartney and Lennon confirm the sexual expressions of their boyfriends with ebullient, girlish "bop shoo wop" affirmations.[25] In "Boys," the Beatles illustrate gender fluidity as they slide between conventionally feminine and masculine discourse motivated by an interest in both music and feeling.

In early Lennon-McCartney originals, the Beatles maintain gender-fluid discursive strategies, singing from a gender-ambiguous middle-ground perspective in "She Loves You."[26] The speaker of that song, reflecting the girl-group "advice" tradition, functions as a mediator helping to resolve relationship troubles: "Paul takes a friend aside and passes on vital gossip about the State of his (the friend's) romance, dutifully repeating the message the girl entrusted him with, like a note passed in math class."[27] While speaking from a feminine position, the speaker could be boy or girl, as Warwick recognizes when she proposes that girl groups could cover that song.[28] In fact, the speaker of "She Loves You" could be the "you" addressed in the first track of *Please Please Me* (1963). In "I Saw Her Standing There,"[29] the confidant is a friend to the speaker—the "you" who gets the nudge ("you know what I mean"). Here again is another illustration of gender fluidity whereby "you" are in the intimate position of knowing your friend—regardless of whether you identify as boy or girl, gay or straight.

The Beatles' gender fluidity was not the product of a planned scheme. Rather, their feminine appeals in song lyrics, like their scream-eliciting hair shaking, were rhetorical responses developed largely because of the girl audiences right in front of them. McCartney explains: "We knew that if we wrote a song called 'Thank You Girl' that a lot of the girls who wrote us fan letters would take it as a genuine thank you. So a lot of our songs—'From Me to You' is another—were directly addressed to the fans."[30] As the premise of Rob Sheffield's cultural history of the band goes, the Beatles consistently found "a girl to sing to,"[31] but it was also much more than boy-meets-girl: "For the Beatles, curiosity about girls led to curiosity about the world."[32]

During the raunchy, wild Hamburg days, Warwick surmises, the Beatles sang to "giggling and screaming" girls, who were "delight[ed]" as the Beatles were "musically enacting the subject position of a girl."[33] Back in Liverpool, they further honed their musicianship—both songwriting and performance—in tight spaces such as the Casbah Coffee Club (Pete Best's family home in Hayman's Green) and the Cavern Club on Mathew Street. Cavern Club audiences were largely composed of young working women on their lunch breaks, who formed small groups, giving themselves monikers such as "the Cement Mixers" in order to identify themselves to the band when requesting songs.[34] The Beatles were a gang—singing in front of similar gangs of girls, competing with one another for the band's attention. These girls singled out their favorite Beatle, as Cement Mixer Erika Bale told me (hers was Best).[35] These fan identification processes would end up being replicated on a global level once Beatlemania found footholds all over the world.

The Beatles voiced a first-person assertiveness that both boys and girls wanted to utter. A ready example of gender fluidity in the early Beatles oeuvre can be seen in the pairing of "She Loves You" with its B-side, "I'll Get You." The former is a clear illustration of feminine relationship mediation. But the Beatles did not simply absorb girl-group techniques, which their cover of "Boys" demonstrates. "I'll Get You," with its punctuated and confident "oh yeahs," articulates a conventional masculine pursuit of a love interest. These assertive gender appeals were no doubt informed by the influence of other performers, such as Little Richard, Chuck Berry, and Presley. But perhaps the best example of the early Beatles' masculine appeals is illustrated by another Starr number, "I Wanna Be Your Man."

"I Wanna Be Your Man"[36] is a manifesto of sexual performance, evidenced by Lennon and McCartney giving it to the overtly sexy Rolling Stones (who released it as a single) before handing it off to their drummer. The lyrics include none of the polite requests of "please please me" or "I want to hold your hand" or "I'm happy just to dance with you." Rather, the song, addressed to "baby," is one of explicit desire ("I want to be your lover") and straightforward demands ("tell me that you love me" and "let me understand"). The speaker confidently asserts—without asking—that he, a "man," will love this baby like no one else "can." Starr's vocals on "Boys" also brag about sexual performance, but they are directed to other boys and founded on a girl's testimony. By contrast, "I Wanna Be Your Man" offers no secondhand proof, because the speaker is the authority.

The Beatles answered the questions that girl groups and their girl listeners were asking.[37] For example, the Shirelles sang, "Will you still love me tomorrow?" whose implied coda is *after we have sex tonight*. For girls in the pre-Pill mid-century, premarital sex could have serious consequences, from a ruined reputation to pregnancy, both involving social ostracism, so a boy's response to this question really did matter. Bradby also takes issue with the application of "androgyny," arguing instead that "the Beatles' early hits present a typically masculine answer to the feminine questioning that is forcefully articulated in much girl-group music, and that this answer is requested and almost required by the girls' discourse."[38] At the same time, the song "She Loves You" "represents men as actually saying to each other what women wanted them to."[39] Bradby sees these two outcomes as illustrative of the "dialogue between girl talk and boy talk," leading to the development of the Beatles' "boy-group discourse."[40] I would add to this, however, suggesting that boy-group discourse is gender-fluid: when the Beatles sing first-person songs that sound like their own personal desires, from polite or innocent requests to overt assertions of longing, they present a range of gendered sexual subject-object positions with which both girls and boys could (and still can) identify.

Beatlemania: Screaming and Singing Groups
of Girls and Boys

The Beatles' cheeky confidence, now an expected feature of boy bands, is available in their songs, as well as in their fresh responses to the press, whose questions were answered with what seem like the inside jokes of close friends. Groupness—of both the band and its fans—is, in fact, a key component to the gendered and sexual dynamics of the Beatles' popularity. The Beatles' homosocial group intimacy was partly a product of the rise of working-class Teddy boys in urban England and especially Liverpool, where being without a gang was leaving oneself open to danger as a physical target of roaming, tough Teds.[41] The Beatles' gang followed that tradition, with Lennon as initial leader, cultivating respect through ridicule while valuing wit among those who could stand up to him: "John Lennon liked to be confronted; by his code, if he found you were a pushover he'd push you over."[42] Because of his deep need for attention and constant companionship, Lennon formed multiple gangs of boys throughout his youth, eventually "turn[ing] his gang into his group, the Quarry Men."[43] As McCartney remembers about the early Beatles, "We were all in love with John."[44]

The early Beatles' group dynamics gave the appearance of authenticity while conforming to the logic of male homosociality. These outcomes involve both a cultivation and a policing of a homoerotic gaze. Matthew Bannister explains:

> in order to lead, the leader must become subject to the gaze himself, so that the triangular structure is repeated in an inverted form within the group. Far from being authentically homosocial, the group is riven from the first by a contradictory structure of homoerotic desire. It is a function of the leader to manage these contradictions, thus Lennon's adoption of a Ted persona—simultaneously fascinating and rejecting the gaze. These contradictions ramify as the group performs in public, making them the subject of a gaze which must be managed through various mediators, permitted by the leader, while he himself seems to be aloof from this process. Distinctions between form and substance, image and music, apparently important to homosocial integrity, are negotiated—musical originality becomes part of the group's image. Similarly, the homosocial distinction of male artist and female audience breaks down as the Beatles seek to expand their audience and how to write for/to them. A process of collaboration with audiences evolves, the group changing their repertoire to include more "female-friendly" material, both original and in the form of covers.[45]

Unaware of the complex process that Bannister unravels, fans perceive the band's intimacy and originality, and the Beatles' closeness was mirrored in groups of similarly homosocial fans who bonded in relation to the Beatles as an object of desire. And even though girls were present in larger numbers, the crowds of screaming Beatlemaniacs were heterogeneous in their gendered composition.

The early Beatles' popularity among boys and girls led to a clichéd explanation: "Boys wanted to be them, and girls wanted to be with them." Many girls did play the "Which Beatle would you marry?" game, but feminist scholarship and first-generation fan accounts have also proven the reverse was likewise true: girls also wanted to *be* the fun, free Fabs. Just as the Beatles were free to be girlish and boyish, so were their listeners, as one fan remembers:

> I liked their independence and sexuality and wanted those things for myself. . . . Girls didn't get to be that way when I was a teenager—we got to be the limp, passive object of some guy's fleeting sexual interest. We were so stifled, and they made us meek, giggly creatures think, oh, if only I could act that way and be strong, sexy, and doing what you want.[46]

Additional primary fan accounts echo this theme of the Beatles as fun and freedom, while other firsthand recollections show how girl fans dressed like the Beatles to evidence those feelings.[47]

Girls' desires to be the Beatles are musically communicated in two 1964 Capitol recordings by then-14-year-old Donna Lynn. Her *Billboard*-charting single, "My Boyfriend Got a Beatle Haircut,"[48] suggests that the Beatles encouraged girls' own gender bending, making the outcome obvious (at least to some in the music industry) from the beginning. The lyrics initially bemoan the attention the boyfriend is receiving after he cuts his hair; she "can't chase the girls away," and "his phone is busy." She thus reasons, "to keep him true, I got a Beatle haircut, too." If she means to win back her guy, the logic does not necessarily follow, given the previous details: if a Beatle haircut attracts girls, wouldn't those be the hearts she would now be courting? The song is still about boy-girl romance but with a queer spin, because here is a girl fantasizing about occupying a boy's subject position. Becoming a Beatle— a beloved object for the gaze of others[49]—is similarly expressed in another Lynn song, "I Had a Dream I Was a Beatle."[50] Here Lynn imagines joining the band onstage, singing "upfront with John, George, and Paul," while "the kids would scream and everything." Following the formula of speculation and conclusion in the haircut song, the lyrics have her decide, "The only thing better than having that dream would be to be a Beatle for real."

Of the slew of 1964 Beatles tribute songs (many released by Capitol and Decca in efforts to cash in on what then seemed like a temporary trend),

Lynn's songs are noteworthy for their gender fluidity. Not only are they evidence of what scholars would later theorize about girls wanting to be the Beatles, but they also demonstrate how the Beatles were an avenue for girls' own musical involvement. Lynn did not enjoy major musical success, but other girls who emulated and sang about the Beatles did, such as an early-career Cher, who released "Ringo, I Love You" in 1964 under the pseudonym Bonnie Jo Mason.[51] The track includes a "yeah, yeah, yeah" refrain typical of Beatles tributes and was co-written by Phil Spector (though his Wall of Sound is absent). In spite of its associated talent, Cher's song did not enjoy chart success, because some radio stations refused to play it, mistaking her deep voice for that of a male singer.[52] Those homophobic fears were sidestepped in the Four Preps' 1964 Capitol tune, "A Letter to the Beatles,"[53] which allowed male voices to express Beatles love, under the guise of repeating fan mail written by a girlfriend. In this song, the speaker is essentially cuckolded by the Beatles, who steal the girlfriend away—after she sends multiple letters with monetary payment for returned affection. If, as Eve Kosofsky Sedgwick argues, cuckolding is a "sex act, performed on a man, by another man,"[54] this song can be read as an expression of coded homosexual desire that some male listeners must have also felt for the Beatles.

The music industry sponsored such expressions of fandom in trifling singles, and the early Beatles' live and televised performances also inspired young people to sing and play instruments. We typically think of boys as the Beatles' musical imitators because of males' more visible participation in the rock-music industry. Phil Collins, Elvis Costello, Nile Rodgers, and members of the Byrds, the Monkees, and Crosby, Stills, and Nash (to name a few) are all frequent interview subjects and well-known Beatles devotees, first-generation authorities on the Beatles' influence. Drummer Dave Grohl of Nirvana and the Foo Fighters has tried to establish himself as the ultimate Gen X Beatles fan, collaborating and drumming with McCartney in tribute performances. In a digital liner note for an iTunes compilation, Grohl explains, "If it weren't for the Beatles, I would not be a musician. . . . From a very young age I became fascinated with their songs, and over the years have drowned myself in the depth of their catalogue."[55]

Grohl is not the only Gen X fan-turned-musician inspired by the Beatles. Questlove (Ahmir Khalib Thompson), drummer and joint frontman for the Roots, is also vocal about his admiration for the Beatles, especially Starr's techniques.[56] And Susanna Hoffs of the Bangles describes the Beatles, rarely a point of discussion among 20-somethings in the 1980s, as "the glue between

Vicki [Peterson], Debbi [Peterson] and I on that first night when we met and decided to be a band."[57] Hoffs's Beatles fandom as a Gen Xer suggests that we should think more about women who grew up alongside the Beatles.

While the well-known baby-boomer Beatles devotees are men, that generation did include girls who were serious students of the band's music. Chrissie Hynde of the Pretenders and Ann and Nancy Wilson of Heart all cite the Beatles as the impetus for their musical careers.[58] In addition to imitating the Beatles by covering them and writing songs about them, for Hynde and the Wilson sisters, the Beatles were also a point of connection with their girlfriends. Nancy Wilson, however, recalls being annoyed when the topic of discussion repeatedly turned to the "Which Beatle would you marry?" game:

> It's not that Ann and I didn't imagine romance as part of our future, because we did, but music was more important. To us, the Beatles were deadly serious stuff, something we studied like scholars, looking for meaning and wisdom.
>
> We didn't want to be Beatle girlfriends. We wanted to be the Beatles. All the other girls gushed about wanting to marry a Beatle but we felt that lowered the Beatles to something crass and base. We didn't immediately see ourselves as musicians—that would come soon enough—but it was the music, and not Paul's dimples that had us.[59]

Wilson's recollection is yet another piece of evidence proving that some girls wanted to be the Beatles, so studying the band and its music was the logical outcome.

Despite Wilson's annoyance, for other girls, the marry-a-Beatle game bespoke important expression, because it was a means of articulating one's sexual personality and preference. And the types became part of the "boy-band blueprint" that is now a standard in the pop-music industry: "smart one (John Lennon), cute one (Paul McCartney), quiet one (George Harrison) and funny one (Ringo Starr)."[60] Those personalities were circulated by teen magazines and "concretized" by the 1964 film *A Hard Day's Night*.[61] One first-generation fan recalled: "I remember the girls in my small group, we each had a different favorite Beatle. There could be no sharing, because we each were going to meet our favorite, fall in love, and marry them!"[62] Here is another example of the Beatles as catalyst for homosocial and homoerotic intimacy, whereby girls imagine sex and romance with a boy while they are in the company of other girls. The imaginative play among Beatles' fans was a way of talking about sexual desire, a taboo subject in need of coding in the early 1960s, as girl groups' musical discourse similarly demonstrated.[63]

The freedom from restriction—whether that was sexual or artistic freedom—was what the scream was all about, a predictive inhale before the exhale that was the 1970s women's liberation movement.[64] Beatlemaniacs' screams also brought private-sphere fan behavior, "forged in bedrooms, staring at Beatles posters pasted all over the walls, listening to records, waiting anxiously to hear the Beatles on the radio," into the public domain as mass media distributed their reactions:

> Those girls, seen and heard on streets and in newspapers, magazines, and on television sets, made up an important part of the visual and sonic record of the 1960s. With their screams and shouts, they declared their love for the Beatles, displayed a range of emotions from confusion to elation to exhaustion to exuberance, and trespassed and redrew boundaries governing public behavior, display, and gender.[65]

Nicolette Rohr makes a convincing case for the scream's association with girls in particular, whose rule breaking and decorum shattering "is part of what the screams voice, and that loss of control, both of oneself and of society, held important implications for teenage girls and American culture."[66] Returning to the concept of the scream also brings up questions related to the first part of that being-and-being-with cliché about the Beatles.

Just as girls wanted to be the Beatles, so, too, did boys want to be with them. While not to detract from feminist reclamations of the scream and its important implications for women's liberation, boys did also scream to be with the Beatles, attracted to the band's intimacy. As a British boy situated to recognize the cultural dynamics of the Beatles' British boy gang, Phil Collins is one example of a male fan expressing his admiration and desire to be with the Beatles. In the documentary *You Can't Do That! The Making of "A Hard Day's Night"* (1994), Collins speaks on behalf of fans and his generation, calling the Beatles "our heroes."[67] (Indeed, Collins's boyhood awe may account for the extreme offense he took to a perceived slight by McCartney many decades later.)

Collins saw the Beatles perform live when he was an extra in the audience of the concert scene that concludes *A Hard Day's Night*. Collins, now a pop star in his own right, remembers his participation in the film, describing it as "one of the highlights of my life" in a voiceover that accompanies the documentary's replay of his scene:

> In those days, it really was quite simple: we loved their music and *A Hard Day's Night* was a chance to spend 90 minutes with them at the local cinema. Which is sort of what I was doing. I was in London's old Scala Theater, screaming my head off for the Beatles who were on the stage—in the flesh—singing their latest batch of hit songs, not just for us, but more importantly for the cameras. There! Did you see me? Yes, well I know I wasn't exactly easy to spot, but I am there. Yes, I was an extra in *A Hard Day's Night*. Now trust me, I didn't get the part because of my extraordinary acting ability. Actually, I was there because, like everybody else in the theater, I was crazy about the Beatles. And believe me, we didn't have to do much acting. All we needed was to hear that incredible music.[68]

Collins points to the music as the point of attraction, but he also references the bodily experience of sharing the space with the band. Collins's explanation articulates the appeal of the Beatles as a group for boy fans. In his recollection, Collins does not identify a favorite Beatle, a trend Candy Leonard finds consistent among boy fans in her study. Leonard sees boys' disinclination to choose a favorite Beatle as motivated by their attraction to "camaraderie and groupness," a contrast to girls' competitive claims within their friend groups.[69]

Their strategies may differ, but both boy and girl fans recalled similar underlying feelings that motivated their expressed desires. Like their first-generation female counterparts, male fans of the early Beatles also communicated the desire for intimacy and safety. One first-generation male fan explained, "Each of those guys looked like they were hanging out with the three best friends you could possibly ever have," which is echoed in another male fan's description of the Beatles as "Four very tight, good friends, in their own bubble."[70] These recollections credit exaggerated perceptions of closeness as the defining feature of the band, which is the same kind of attraction articulated by Hynde, whose lifelong ambition was to form a musical group. Seeing the cover of "I Want to Hold Your Hand" was a "huge turning point": "I'd never seen a band that looked like them. In fact, I'd never seen an English band."[71] Hynde explains how her artistry evolved from this moment, as she "put to music a wistful message of love to Paul McCartney and found that singing came naturally when I was strumming my stuff."[72] Hynde's example includes all three rhetorical outcomes shared by boys and girls: attraction to the image of the group itself, affection for a particular Beatle, and musical imitation and inspiration.

The general avoidance of recognizing homoerotic implications of boys' Beatles love shows the effect of that cliché about being the Beatles versus being with the Beatles. The cliché functioned (and still functions) as a heterosexual security blanket: male fans could keep liking the adorable, girlish-boyish Beatles (again, whose early style was largely influenced by their gay manager, Epstein). The cliché shielded against accusations of homosexuality, since boys' attraction was framed as desiring the *life* of a Beatle—a guy who gets the girl (whose heterosexuality is also reaffirmed). Yet Beatles' queer codes were on full display in *A Hard Day's Night* and *Help!*: "Embedded in their films and in their essential identity as four tightly knit men are signals and codes—some overt, some implied— introducing queerness into the cultural icon that is the Beatles, and perhaps reflecting back to the culture at large its own queer concerns."[73] Ignoring the boy-fan screamers who shouted open-mouthed next to their more numerous girl-fan counterparts misses a vital part of the Beatles' appeal.

In the first generation of Beatles fans, boys and girls alike were turned on by the band's range of gendered and sexual possibilities. Boys are not the dominant image of Beatlemania, but they do exist in the footage of screaming audiences and crowds. As the Collins example illustrates, boys are present and screaming alongside the more numerous girls in the concert that concludes *A Hard Day's Night*, whose opening sequence also includes boys in the crowd chasing band members around Liverpool as they make their way to the train.[74] In frequently replayed footage of the Beatles' 1964 JFK Airport landing in New York is more evidence of an American male fan vocalizing possessive desire.[75] A tall, stocky, crew-cut teenager angrily complains to the journalist that the police will not let them get close to the band: "we just want to get a piece of them." He is surrounded by a group of other boys looking to him as he speaks.[76] Clearly, some boys also heard "She Loves You," "Boys," "I'll Get You," and "I Wanna Be Your Man" and imagined themselves as objects in addition to subjects. After all, the Beatles invited boy listeners to join their intimate gang of friends. The members of the Beatles gang could have any girl they wanted, but more often they preferred the company of boys—as both feature films *A Hard Day's Night* and *Help!* would have us believe.

Beatlemania . . . after Beatlemania

The recognition of the early Beatles' gender fluidity leads to other questions: How do the rhetorical effects associated with desires to be and be with the Beatles change as the decade goes along? Do the relationship-jaded day trippers, the psychedelic tourists, and the shaggy-bearded Beatles offer models for both girls and boys to emulate, an "I am he" in which to recognize oneself *and* to imagine as intimate partner? The answer, as Yoko Ono famously printed in tiny letters on a ceiling, is yes. Like Ono's avant-garde art, however, that yes needs a magnifying glass.

First, as the previous examples illustrate, girls were not and are not the only ones who listen to pop music to think about romance. Sheffield, who calls himself a "Paul-girl boy," shares his recollections of hearing certain songs, analyzing their influence on his adolescent understanding of heterosexual dating dynamics and his perceptions of the adult world.[77] His account provides valuable evidence about a Gen X boy's Beatles fandom, proving that girls are not the only ones preoccupied by the window the Beatles open onto relationships and sexuality. About "Ticket to Ride," Sheffield confides:

> I felt wiser after hearing this song—I trusted his voice, because John didn't sound like he was pulling any punches, and neither did the men in his band respectfully hearing him out. Men—not boys in this song. . . . I could identify with the girl's desire to get free—so can John, which is why it's such a powerful song. He's not all unsympathetic to her plight. Why does he bring her down? He just does. She said so.[78]

Sheffield, who articulates a dual identification, evidences the Beatles' gender fluidity as a major point of appeal. In this song, Lennon does not occupy the conventional masculine position, instead relinquishing control to a woman who is more powerful and assertive than he is. Indeed, both "Ticket to Ride" and "Norwegian Wood" seem to accept women's changing cultural roles. In fact, the Beatles' girl-oriented attitude is reflected in Sheffield's own writing in *Dreaming the Beatles*, as well as his previous books, such as *Talking to Girls about Duran Duran* (2010). Sheffield's music criticism is consistently attuned to the preferences and tastes of girls and women, whose ideas he values. "I have a history with George girls," he confesses.[79]

When the Beatles stopped touring in 1966, their styles changed, but they remained gender-fluid in their presentation. In 1967, the *Sgt. Pepper* cover was an attempt to throw off the adorable Fab image, but they actually ended up invoking another mix of boyishness and girlishness—and still as a group: "There is a sense of shared identity: the audience recognise the style and are confident they are in the hands of the Beatles."[80] Ever matching, like their girl-group (and doo-wop) predecessors, each Beatle grew facial hair as a marker of adult masculinity. But in their cute mustachioed sameness, they also read youthful and feminine, playing dress-up in matching military-style Edwardian uniforms made fabulous with individual bright colors, neon pink, orange, yellow, and blue. Surrounding them with flowers and toys and cardboard heroes (the stuff of a childhood bedroom), the whimsical play is another presentation of freedom from the adult world of restrictions, appealing to boys and girls alike, especially while the cohering feminist movement redefines gender roles.[81] One might be apt to term this intentional dress-up "androgyny," but the makeover corresponds to sentiments about how the Beatles wanted to be seen in 1967 as they declared their desire to experiment in their "real" lives, too.

The story of Beatles fandom often assumes that girls turn away from the band as the decade goes along, alienated by the supposed intellectual turn in rock music's shift from "teenage dance music into a mature art form."[82] No longer were the Beatles in a register to which girls could sing along, as Douglas says of early-1960s music.[83] The band's representation of love and romance also evolves as their gendered modes of address change, shifting away from singing as girls or directly to girls. The Beatles may appear to assume more overtly patriarchal, masculine subject positions that are cynical or critical of women ("For No One," "Run for Your Life") or that elevate women when they are maternal ("Julia," "Lady Madonna"), which may have estranged girl and women listeners: "The shift in emphasis is equally matched by a shift in their fan base from that of young females to a more broad-based appeal."[84] Indeed, the rise of the female singer-songwriter in the latter part of the 1960s and the early 1970s offered girl and women listeners other options appropriate to the changing times. The Monkees also filled a void, marketed to younger kids who missed the early Beatles in that heyday.

The supposedly cerebral turn in the Beatles' music did not, however, alienate all girl and women listeners—especially those who would go on to professions in music. Whiteley, a pioneer in the field of feminist musicology, confides, "I recognized myself in the songs of 1966 and beyond. They exerted a fascination and an image to which I subscribed. At that time, I was in my midtwenties and well into psychedelic rock."[85] That sentiment is echoed in recollections of Hynde and the Wilson sisters, who all took the later Beatles up on their invitations to experiment, taking their own drug-induced musical trips in the latter part of the decade and after. Heart's concept album *Dreamboat Annie* (1975)[86] is a perfect illustration of women songwriters inspired by *Sgt. Pepper's Lonely Hearts Club Band* (1967). Heart's title character is a Lucy-type "fantasy child," floating above the action and guiding the speaker. Knowing the importance of the Beatles to the Wilsons, the opening track, "Magic Man," might be read as a continuation of "She's Leaving Home" from the girl's point of view; the song makes an argument for running away in the pursuit and enjoyment of sexual pleasure—an expression of female desire relevant to a decade that saw the sexual revolution unfold.[87] These examples show the theoretical problem of dividing the Beatles periods between early romance (feminine for girls) and late intellectualism (masculine for boys): the songs themselves show how gender and sexuality work on continuums and are not battling opposites.

The Beatles' gender fluidity was still a marker of their groupness even when they began to articulate their supposedly "real" separate identities, which Lennon (during his early-1970s cynical period) claims were hidden by *A Hard Day's Night*. Many late Beatles and solo songs remained highly personal, and they end up corresponding to the types in the early marketing: the cute McCartney falls in love, gets married, and writes more romantic love songs; the smart Lennon falls in love, gets remarried, and uses his platform for political and social critique; the shy Harrison reveals the depth of his inner spiritual life through Krishna devotion; and the everyman Starr proves his lovability by continuing to mock himself in film and staying friends with the other three Fabs. These diverging personalities (albeit oversimplified here) still offer gender-fluid models for fans to emulate and to desire. Taken to an extreme, that was the identification process involved in the Apple Scruffs fandom, a group of mostly girls (but at least one boy, Tommy)[88] who haunted the studios whenever the Beatles were in session from the very late 1960s to the early 1970s.

Waiting for the Beatles, Carol Bedford's 1984 memoir of her Beatles fandom, explains how each Apple Scruff expressed their identity through allegiance to a particular Beatle. Despite the group orientation, a Scruff usually had competitive, sometimes hostile relationships with the Scruffs who had claimed the same band member. Converging in London from countries around the world (Bedford was from Texas), many of them left home without the support of family, so their existence was rather impoverished—especially since keeping a steady job would hinder Beatles watching. In a kind of fitting reversal of those 1964 fan-song tributes to the Beatles, these beyond-devoted fans are immortalized in song. *Abbey Road*'s "She Came in through the Bathroom Window" was inspired by a Scruff break-in at McCartney's Cavendish Avenue residence.[89] Harrison's solo "Apple Scruffs" (1970) details the group's practice of waiting on the steps in order to hand the Beatles flowers regardless of the weather and other personal discomforts; according to Bedford, they would urinate around nearby bushes for fear of missing the Beatles' entrances and exits.[90]

The Scruffs were not a cuddly group of polite girls; they shattered the rules of decorum somewhat like the effect of Beatlemaniacs' screams. And like those early fans, these girls claimed favorites: "They each designated that they were one of the Beatles' property and one Beatle was theirs. If you transgressed the line, claiming their favourite, you had had it."[91] But the Scruffs were also atypical of "groupies" because they were "scruffy," dressed for comfort and mobility rather than to court sexual attention.[92] Scruff goals, according to Bedford, were not to sleep with members of the band but to show loyalty through their steady, faithful presence. As Bedford memorably summarizes, "We waited—our occupation. And waited—our pleasure. And still waited—our choice. 'Everything comes to she who waits' was our motto."[93] The Scruffs were highly secretive, ruthless, and aggressive, stealing film footage during that break-in at McCartney's house and often ridiculing other women. Linda McCartney's breasts were a frequent subject of their verbal abuse and were mocked in caricatures published in *Apple Scruff Monthly Magazine*.[94] Here again, we see the Beatles' gender fluidity mirrored back to them in their fans, a concept that Harrison's tribute song ironically recognizes in the last line: "We're together face to face, my Apple Scruffs."[95]

A New Gender-Fluid Generation

The stereotype of Beatlemaniacs as screaming girls has sometimes led critics to perpetuate the gendered split in the story of Beatles fandom, ignoring the girls who studied, sang, and played, as well as the boys who screamed. Of course, girls' identification with the Beatles based on their feminine sympathies remains valuable to understand. But the critical maintenance of those rigid gendered divisions today is a problem. In a time when there is renewed attention to generational differences and when gender binaries have been rapidly breaking down, we should discuss gender fluidity in order to understand the Beatles' past and ongoing appeal, especially among younger millennials or post-millennials, those dubbed Gen Z and born between 1995 and 2012.

Their gender fluidity makes the Beatles a perfect subject for 21st-century slash, fan fiction that pairs members of the Beatles in romantic relationships. This fan art, often created by teen girls and posted in on-line sharing spaces such as YouTube, shows how youth can playfully re-work the Beatles' narrative. They rewrite the story of the Beatles, often mixing up songs and images from different time periods, because the band offers fungible expressions of gender and sexuality. Indeed, fans pick up the four distinctive types and take them to their logical ends: as the cute one, McCartney is an ideal feminine subject, and Lennon's wit is a way of flirting with the others, whereas sensitive Harrison is love-shy, and Starr is all-around lovable. One popular theme in Lennon-McCartney slash involves McCartney's jealousy about Ono as a romantic rival for Lennon, whose early death dooms McCartney to a lifetime of unrequited love. This sentimentality is, however, frequently accompanied by an ironic wink, discernible in humorous editing or sound-image pairing designed to get laughs. This fan art reveals the very same mixture of feminine and mascu-line communication styles shared by the Beatles.[96]

My recognition of the Beatles as gender-fluid is also motivated by interactions with my students from 2006 to the present. For more than a decade, I have been teaching the Beatles in English courses that range from lower-division rhetoric and composition classes to upper-division literature courses to graduate theory seminars at a large public university in Texas. And during that time, I have noticed increasing favorability to-ward the Beatles based on their gender fluidity. A little more than ten years ago, the students needed more historical context related to the Beatles' style (e.g., why their hair was considered "long"). What I have noticed in the last several years, especially among Gen Z, is that these students are now apt to read the Beatles as gender-fluid to begin with. Regardless of students' level of familiarity with the band, they don't look for the Beatles to be stable cisgender male or masculine subjects—and many find the band appealing for this reason.

More of my undergraduate students now quickly recognize the signs of gender fluidity, proposing the Beatles' presentation of homosocial in-timacy as a reason for their popularity. What director Richard Lester noticed about the Beatles' "freshness"[97] is still applicable, especially after students see footage from the famous 1964 JFK press conference in which the Beatles dole out cheeky responses to the out-of-touch journalists. Of all the examples that I show or play, the banter in that footage seems to be deal-sealing evidence for students unfamiliar with the band. Laughing while Starr mimics Presley and when Lennon dryly explains they "need money first" in order to sing,[98] the students always point to the Beatles' own laughter as the reason the band seems like "real" friends. By and large, in recent years, students are comfortable without assigning a concrete sexual orientation to that intimacy. Overall, this is consistent with observations about young people's attitudes about gender and sex in the 21st century, as numerous journalistic and editorial pieces about Generation Z attest.[99]

Conclusion

This chapter's argument about gender fluidity and fan identification is captured in the logic of a lyric from "I Am the Walrus": "I am he as you are he as you are me." That equation, in a watery song, no less, summarizes the Beatles' gender fluidity and the mirrored process of group and individual identification, which accounts for their popularity among fans and other listeners then and now.

Following the 50th anniversary of their breakup, we should be talking about the Beatles' gender fluidity as attenuation to rhetorical context. They were and remain popular because their images and music were responsive to their time and place; outside of that original context, the sheer range of the Beatles' gendered and sexual performances still communicates. Thus, even though my own previous scholarship has invoked *androgyny* to discuss the Beatles' performance of masculinity and femininity and appeals to fans, in this chapter, I advocate for the concept of *gender fluidity*. I suspect that if some of the aforementioned feminist scholars had been writing in the second decade of the new millennium, many of them would now use *gender fluidity* rather than *androgyny*, given the former's commonness today, evidenced by the accepted use of nongendered *they* as a singular pronoun. Douglas, for example, is talking about gender fluidity when she explains, "the Beatles acknowledged that there was masculinity and femininity in all of us, and that blurring the artificial boundaries between the two might be a big relief."[100] This slipperiness was perceived by fans of the Beatles during Beatlemania—and throughout the decade, even while their music and styles rapidly changed.

Notes

1. Melissa Click, "'Rabid,' 'Obsessed,' and 'Frenzied': Understanding Twilight Fangirls and the Gendered Politics of Fandom," *Flow*, December 18, 2009, http://flowjournal.org/2009.
2. Ron Howard, dir., *The Beatles: Eight Days a Week—The Touring Years*, Capitol, 2016.
3. Katie Kapurch, "The Wretched Life of a Lonely Heart: Sgt. Pepper's Girls, Fandom, the Wilson Sisters, and Chrissie Hynde," in *The Beatles, Sgt. Pepper, and the Summer of Love*, ed. Kenneth Womack and Kathryn B. Cox (Lanham, MD: Lexington, 2017), 145–152.
4. See Kristina Busse, "Geek Hierarchies, Boundary Policing, and the Gendering of the Good Fan," *Participations* 10, no. 1 (2013): 73–91.
5. Kit O'Toole, "'She Said She Said': How Women Have Transformed from Fans to Authors in Beatles History," in *New Critical Perspectives on the Beatles: Things We Said Today*, ed. Kenneth Womack and Katie Kapurch (New York: Palgrave Macmillan, 2016), 180–181.
6. Ehrenreich, Barbara, Elizabeth Hess, and Gloria Jacobs. "Beatlemania: Girls Just Want to Have Fun." In *The Adoring Audience: Fan Culture and Popular Media*, edited by Lisa A. Lewis, 83–106. New York: Routledge, 1992..
7. Susan Douglas, *Where the Girls Are: Growing Up Female with the Mass Media* (New York: Random House, 1994), 98.
8. Douglas, *Where the Girls Are*, 117.
9. Steven Stark, *Meet the Beatles: A Cultural History of the Band That Shook Youth, Gender, and the World* (New York: HarperCollins, 2005), 134.
10. Stark, *Meet the Beatles*, 135.
11. Stark, *Meet the Beatles*, 135; Jonathan Gould, *Can't Buy Me Love: Beatles, Britain and America* (New York: Harmony, 2007), 117. Gould distinguishes Epstein's management style from that of other managers in the immediate area: "Long after any hope of a sexual liaison with one or another of the Beatles had been conclusively laid to rest, Epstein would perfect on their behalf a devotional style of management that bore no resemblance to the predations of gay pop moguls like Larry Parnes."
12. Jon Savage, "Tainted Love: The Influence of Male Homosexuality and Sexual Divergence on Pop Music and Culture since the War," in *Consumption, Identity, and Style: Marketing, Meanings, and the Packaging of Pleasure*, ed. Alan Tomlinson (London: Routledge, 1990), 108.
13. Savage, "Tainted Love," 108.
14. Mark Lewisohn, *Tune In: The Beatles: All These Years* (New York: Crown/Archetype, 2013), 551–552.
15. Martin King, *Men, Masculinity, and the Beatles* (Farnham, UK: Ashgate, 2013). King also favors this word choice, even using *gender fluidity* to paraphrase the work of previously cited scholars who have used the term *androgyny*.
16. Daniel A. Harris, "Androgyny: The Sexist Myth in Disguise." *Women's Studies* 2 (1974): 171.

17. King, *Men, Masculinity, and the Beatles*, 16.
18. Stan Hawkins, *The British Pop Dandy: Masculinity, Popular Music and Culture* (London: Ashgate, 2009), 93.
19. Hawkins, *The British Pop Dandy*, 101.
20. Hawkins, *The British Pop Dandy*, 158. As Hawkins explains, "Representations of masculinity in British Mod culture signified a masking of gender through a process of pluralizing epitomized by pop starts such as Bowie, Bolan, Jagger, Ray Davies, and later Sylvian and Weller."
21. Sheila Whiteley, "'Love, Love, Love': Representations of Gender and Sexuality in Selected Songs by the Beatles," in *Reading the Beatles: Cultural Studies, Literary Criticism, and the Fab Four*, ed. Kenneth Womack and Todd F. Davis (Albany: State University of New York Press), 60–62; Jacqueline Warwick, "You're Going to Lose That Girl: The Beatles and the Girl Groups," in *Beatlestudies 3: Proceedings of the Beatles 2000 Conference at University of Jyväskylä Dept. Music*, ed. Yrjö Heinonen et al. (Jyväskylä, Finland: University of Jyväskylä, 2000), 162–166.
22. Warwick, "You're Going to Lose That Girl," 165.
23. Quoted in Barry Miles, *Paul McCartney Many Years from Now* (New York: Henry Holt, 1997), 82.
24. The Beatles, "Boys," Luther Dixon and Wes Farrell, *Please Please Me*, Parlophone, 1963.
25. Katie Kapurch, "Crying, Waiting, Hoping: The Beatles, Girl Culture, and the Melodramatic Mode," in *New Critical Perspectives on the Beatles: Things We Said Today*, ed. Kenneth Womack and Katie Kapurch (New York: Palgrave Macmillan, 2016), 205–206.
26. The Beatles, "She Loves You" (single), John Lennon and Paul McCartney, Parlophone, 1963.
27. Warwick, "You're Going to Lose That Girl," 165.
28. Warwick, "You're Going to Lose That Girl," 165.
29. The Beatles, "I Saw Her Standing There," John Lennon and Paul McCartney, *Please Please Me*, Parlophone, 1963.
30. Jacqueline Warwick, *Girl Groups, Girl Culture* (New York: Routledge, 2007), 61.
31. Rob Sheffield, *Dreaming the Beatles: The Love Story of One Band and the Whole World* (New York: HarperCollins, 2017), 27.
32. Sheffield, *Dreaming the Beatles*, 14.
33. Warwick, "You're Going to Lose That Girl," 164.
34. Lewisohn, *Tune In*, 785.
35. Erika Bale, personal interview with the author, November 3, 2014.
36. The Beatles, "I Wanna Be Your Man," John Lennon and Paul McCartney, *With the Beatles*, Parlophone, 1963.
37. Barbara Bradby, "She Told Me What to Say: The Beatles and Girl-Group Discourse." *Popular Music and Society* 28, no. 3 (2005): 359–390.
38. Bradby, "She Told Me What to Say," 360.
39. Bradby, "She Told Me What to Say," 361.
40. Bradby, "She Told Me What to Say," 361.

41. Lewisohn, *Tune In*, 61–67, 87.

42. Lewisohn, *Tune In*, 44.

43. Lewisohn, *Tune In*, 7.

44. Lewisohn, *Tune In*, 551.

45. Matthew Bannister, "'Where We Going Johnny?': Homosociality and the Early Beatles." In *The Routledge Research Companion to Popular Music and Gender*, ed. Stan Hawkins (New York: Routledge, 2017), 45.

46. Quoted in Ehrenreich, Hess, and Jacobs, "Beatlemania," 36.

47. O'Toole, "She Said She Said," 184.

48. Donna Lynn, "My Boyfriend Got a Beatle Haircut," Jack Wolf and "Bugs" Bower, Capitol, 1964; *Donna Lynn Meets Robin Clark*, Rare Rockin' Records, 2009.

49. See King, *Men, Masculinity, and the Beatles*, 82. King takes up the issue of the gaze as a multigenerational effect in relation to the Beatles' films: "As texts they also transcend the period in which they were made. Given the popularity of the Beatles in the second and third generation audiences and their continued global fame, the films still provide an opportunity for new audiences to look at the Beatles."

50. Donna Lynn, "I Had a Dream I Was a Beatle," Jack Wolf and "Bugs" Bower, Capitol, 1964; *Donna Lynn Meets Robin Clark*, Rare Rockin' Records, 2009.

51. Bonnie Jo Mason [Cher], "Ringo, I Love You" (single), Phil Spector, Paul Case, Vini Poncia, and Peter Andreoli, Annette Records, 1964.

52. Jennifer Keeley, *Women Pop Stars* (Farmington Hills, MI: Lucent, 2001), 29.

53. The Four Preps, "A Letter to the Beatles" (single), Glen Larson and Bruce Belland, Capitol, 1964.

54. Eve Kosofsky Sedgwick, *Between Men: English Literature and Male Homosocial Desire*. 1985. (New York: Colombia University Press, 2016 [1985]), 49.

55. Quoted in Devon Maloney, "Dave Grohl: Without the Beatles, 'I Would Not Be a Musician,'" *Spin*, July 24, 2012, https://www.spin.com/2012/07/dave-grohl-without-beatles-i-would-not-be-musician/.

56. World's Great Drummers Salute Ringo Starr," YouTube, July 7, 2015, https://youtu.be/wJTjjAXDZSY.

57. Annie Zaleski, "Beatlemania and the Bangles," *Salon*, June 15, 2016, https://www.salon.com/2016/06/15/beatlemania_and_the_bangles_susanna_hoffs_explains_how_our_obsession_with_the_beatles_brought_the_80s_group_together/.

58. Chrissie Hynde, *Reckless: My Life as a Pretender* (New York: Anchor, 2015), 17; Ann Wilson and Nancy Wilson, with Charles R. Cross. *Kicking and Dreaming: A Story of Heart, Soul, and Rock and Roll* (New York: itbooks, 2012), 41–47.

59. Wilson and Wilson, *Kicking and Dreaming*, 43–44.

60. Heather Jones and Emily Maltby, "The Boy-Band Blueprint: From the Beatles to One Direction, All the Young Dudes Are 'N Sync." *Time*, February 17, 2014, http://content.time.com/time/subscriber/article/0,33009,2164808,00.html.

61. Kennneth Womack and Todd F. Davis, "Mythology, Remythology, and Demythology: The Beatles on Film," in *Reading the Beatles: Cultural Studies, Literary Criticism, and the Fab Four*, ed. Kenneth Womack and Todd F. Davis (Albany: State University of New York Press, 2006), 101.

62. Quoted in Candy Leonard, *Beatleness: How the Beatles and Their Fans Remade the World* (New York: Arcade, 2014), 41.

63. Warwick, *Girl Groups, Girl Culture*, 41.

64. Ehrenreich, Hess, and Jacobs, "Beatlemania," 11.

65. Nicolette Rohr, "Yeah Yeah Yeah: The Sixties Screamscape of Beatlemania," *Journal of Popular Music Studies* 29, no. 2 (2017): 3.

66. Rohr, "Yeah Yeah Yeah," 5.

67. David Leaf, writer, *The Making of "A Hard Day's Night,"* MPI Home Video, 1994; *A Hard Day's Night*, Criterion Collection, 2014.

68. *The Making of "A Hard Day's Night."*

69. Leonard, *Beatleness*, 41.

70. Quoted in Leonard, *Beatleness*, 42.

71. Hynde, *Reckless*, 17.

72. Hynde, *Reckless*, 17.

73. Ann Shillinglaw, "'Give Us a Kiss': Queer Codes, Male Partnering, and the Beatles," in *The Queer Sixties*, ed. Patricia Juliana Smith (New York: Routledge, 1999), 127.

74. Richard Lester, dir., *A Hard Day's Night*, United Artists, 1964.

75. "The British Invasion," *The Sixties*, episode 6, CNN, July 10, 2014.

76. "The British Invasion."

77. Sheffield, *Dreaming the Beatles*, 15.

78. Sheffield, *Dreaming the Beatles*, 80.

79. Sheffield, *Dreaming the Beatles*, 15.

80. Sheila Whiteley, *The Space between the Notes: Rock and the Counter-Culture* (New York: Routledge, 1992), 39.

81. Kapurch, "The Wretched Life," 144–146.

82. Elijah Wald, *How the Beatles Destroyed Rock 'n' Roll: An Alternative History of American Popular Music* (New York: Oxford University Press, 2009), 5.

83. Douglas, *Where the Girls Are*, 96.

84. Whiteley, "Love, Love, Love," 68.

85. Whiteley, "Love, Love, Love," 68.

86. Heart, *Dreamboat Annie*, Ann and Nancy Wilson, Mushroom Records, 1975.

87. Kapurch, "The Wretched Life," 153–154.

88. Carol Bedford, *Waiting for the Beatles: An Apple Scruff's Story* (Poole, UK: Blandford, 1984), 72–73.

89. Bedford, *Waiting for the Beatles*, 110.

90. Bedford, *Waiting for the Beatles*, 159.

91. Bedford, *Waiting for the Beatles*, 54.

92. Bedford, *Waiting for the Beatles*, 80.

93. Bedford, *Waiting for the Beatles*, 136.

94. Bedford, *Waiting for the Beatles*, 125.

95. George Harrison, "Apple Scruffs," *All Things Must Pass*, Apple, 1971.

96. Kapurch, "Crying, Waiting, Hoping," 215–218.

97. *The Making of "A Hard Day's Night."*

98. "The British Invasion."

99. Katy Steinmetz, "Beyond 'He' or 'She': The Changing Meaning of Gender and Sexuality," *Time*, March 27, 2017, https://time.com/4703309/gender-sexuality-changing/.
100. Douglas, *Where the Girls Are*, 116.

Bibliography

Bale, Erika. Personal interview with the author, November 3, 2014.

Bannister, Matthew. "'Where We Going Johnny?': Homosociality and the Early Beatles." In *The Routledge Research Companion to Popular Music and Gender*, edited by Stan Hawkins, 35–47. New York: Routledge, 2017.

The Beatles. "Boys," Luther Dixon and Wes Farrell. *Please Please Me*. Parlophone, 1963.

The Beatles. "I Saw Her Standing There," John Lennon and Paul McCartney. *Please Please Me*. Parlophone, 1963.

The Beatles. "I Wanna Be Your Man," John Lennon and Paul McCartney. *With the Beatles*. Parlophone, 1963.

The Beatles. "She Loves You" (single), John Lennon and Paul McCartney. Parlophone, 1963.

Bedford, Carol. *Waiting for the Beatles: An Apple Scruff's Story*. Poole, UK: Blandford, 1984.

Bradby, Barbara. "She Told Me What to Say: The Beatles and Girl-Group Discourse." *Popular Music and Society* 28, no. 3 (2005): 359–390.

"The British Invasion." *The Sixties*, episode 6. CNN, July 10, 1964.

Busse, Kristina. "Geek Hierarchies, Boundary Policing, and the Gendering of the Good Fan." *Participations* 10, no. 1 (2013): 73–91.

Click, Melissa. "'Rabid,' 'Obsessed,' and 'Frenzied': Understanding Twilight Fangirls and the Gendered Politics of Fandom." *Flow*, December 18, 2009. http://flowjournal.org/2009.

Douglas, Susan. *Where the Girls Are: Growing Up Female with the Mass Media*. New York: Random House, 1994.

Ehrenreich, Barbara, Elizabeth Hess, and Gloria Jacobs. "Beatlemania: Girls Just Want to Have Fun." In *The Adoring Audience: Fan Culture and Popular Media*, edited by Lisa A. Lewis, 83–106. New York: Routledge, 1992..

The Four Preps. "A Letter to the Beatles" (single), Glen Larson and Bruce Belland. Capitol, 1964.

Gould, Jonathan. *Can't Buy Me Love: Beatles, Britain and America*. New York: Harmony, 2007.

Harris, Daniel A. "Androgyny: The Sexist Myth in Disguise." *Women's Studies* 2 (1974): 171–184.

Harrison, George. "Apple Scruffs." *All Things Must Pass*. Apple,1971.

Hawkins, Stan. *The British Pop Dandy: Masculinity, Popular Music and Culture*. Farnham, UK: Ashgate, 2009.

Heart. *Dreamboat Annie*, Ann and Nancy Wilson. Mushroom Records, 1975.

Howard, Ron, dir. *The Beatles: Eight Days a Week—The Touring Years*. Capitol, 2016.

Hynde, Chrissie. *Reckless: My Life as a Pretender*. New York: Anchor, 2015.

Jones, Heather, and Emily Maltby. "The Boy-Band Blueprint: From the Beatles to One Direction, All the Young Dudes Are 'N Sync." *Time*, February 17, 2014. http://content.time.com/time/subscriber/article/0,33009,2164808,00.html.

Kapurch, Katie. "Crying, Waiting, Hoping: The Beatles, Girl Culture, and the Melodramatic Mode." In *New Critical Perspectives on the Beatles: Things We Said Today*, edited by Kenneth Womack and Katie Kapurch, 179–198. New York: Palgrave Macmillan, 2016.

Kapurch, Katie. "The Wretched Life of a Lonely Heart: Sgt. Pepper's Girls, Fandom, the Wilson Sisters, and Chrissie Hynde." In *The Beatles, Sgt. Pepper, and the Summer of Love*, edited by Kenneth Womack and Kathryn B. Cox, 137–159. Lanham, MD: Lexington, 2017.

Keeley, Jennifer. *Women Pop Stars*. Farmington Hills, MI: Lucent, 2001.

King, Martin. *Men, Masculinity, and the Beatles*. Farnham, UK: Ashgate, 2013.

Leaf, David, writer. *You Can't Do That! The Making of "A Hard Day's Night."* MPI Home Video, 1994. *A Hard Day's Night*. Criterion Collection, 2014.

Leonard, Candy. *Beatleness: How the Beatles and Their Fans Remade the World*. New York: Arcade, 2014.

Lester, Richard, dir. *A Hard Day's Night*. United Artists, 1964.

Lewisohn, Mark. *Tune In: The Beatles: All These Years*. New York: Crown/Archetype, 2013.

Lynn, Donna. "I Had a Dream I Was a Beatle," Jack Wolf and "Bugs" Bower. Capitol, 1964. *Donna Lynn Meets Robin Clark*. Rare Rockin' Records, 2009.

Lynn, Donna. "My Boyfriend Got a Beatle Haircut," Jack Wolf and "Bugs" Bower. Capitol, 1964. *Donna Lynn Meets Robin Clark*. Rare Rockin' Records, 2009.

Maloney, Devon. "Dave Grohl: Without the Beatles, 'I Would Not Be a Musician.'" *Spin*, July 24, 2012. https://www.spin.com/2012/07/dave-grohl-without-beatles-i-would-not-be-musician/.

Mason, Bonnie Jo [Cher]. "Ringo, I Love You," Phil Spector, Paul Case, Vini Poncia, Peter Andreoli. Annette Records, 1964.

Miles, Barry. *Paul McCartney Many Years from Now*. New York: Henry Holt, 1997.

O'Toole, Kit. "'She Said She Said': How Women Have Transformed from Fans to Authors in Beatles History." In *New Critical Perspectives on the Beatles: Things We Said Today*, edited by Kenneth Womack and Katie Kapurch, 179–198. New York: Palgrave Macmillan, 2016.

Rock & Roll Hall of Fame. "World's Great Drummers Salute Ringo Starr." YouTube. July 7, 2015. https://youtu.be/wJTjjAXDZSY.

Rohr, Nicolette. "Yeah Yeah Yeah: The Sixties Screamscape of Beatlemania." *Journal of Popular Music Studies* 29, no. 2 (2017): 1–13.

Savage, Jon. "Tainted Love: The Influence of Male Homosexuality and Sexual Divergence on Pop Music and Culture since the War." In *Consumption, Identity, and Style: Marketing, Meanings, and the Packaging of Pleasure*, edited by Alan Tomlinson, 103–115. London: Routledge, 1990.

Sedgwick, Eve Kosofsky. *Between Men: English Literature and Male Homosocial Desire*. New York: Colombia University Press, 2016 [1985].

Sheffield, Rob. *Dreaming the Beatles: The Love Story of One Band and the Whole World*. New York: HarperCollins, 2017.

Shillinglaw, Ann. "'Give Us a Kiss': Queer Codes, Male Partnering, and the Beatles." In *The Queer Sixties*, edited by Patricia Juliana Smith, 127–143. New York: Routledge, 1999.

Stark, Steven. *Meet the Beatles: A Cultural History of the Band That Shook Youth, Gender, and the World*. New York: HarperCollins, 2005.

Steinmetz, Katy. "Beyond 'He' or 'She': The Changing Meaning of Gender and Sexuality." *Time*, March 27, 2017. https://time.com/4703309/gender-sexuality-changing/.

Wald, Elijah. *How the Beatles Destroyed Rock 'n' Roll: An Alternative History of American Popular Music*. New York: Oxford University Press, 2009.

Warwick, Jacqueline. *Girl Groups, Girl Culture*. New York: Routledge, 2007.

Warwick, Jacqueline. "You're Going to Lose That Girl: The Beatles and the Girl Groups." In *Beatlestudies 3: Proceedings of the Beatles 2000 Conference at University of Jyväskylä Dept. Music*, edited by Yrjö Heinonen, Markus Heuger, Sheila Whiteley, Terhi Nurmesjärvi, and Jouni Koskimäki, 161–168. Jyväskylä, Finland: University of Jyväskylä, 2000.

Whiteley, Sheila. "'Love, Love, Love': Representations of Gender and Sexuality in Selected Songs by the Beatles." In *Reading the Beatles: Cultural Studies, Literary Criticism, and the Fab Four*, edited by Kenneth Womack and Todd F. Davis, 55–69. Albany: State University of New York Press, 2006.

Whiteley, Sheila. *The Space between the Notes: Rock and the Counter-Culture*. New York: Routledge, 1992.

Wilson, Ann, and Nancy Wilson, with Charles R. Cross. *Kicking and Dreaming: A Story of Heart, Soul, and Rock and Roll*. New York: itbooks, 2012.

Womack, Kenneth, and Todd F. Davis. "Mythology, Remythology, and Demythology: The Beatles on Film." In *Reading the Beatles: Cultural Studies, Literary Criticism, and the Fab Four*, edited by Kenneth Womack and Todd F. Davis, 97–110. Albany: State University of New York Press, 2006.

Zaleski, Annie. "Beatlemania and the Bangles." *Salon*, June 15, 2016, https://www.salon.com/2016/06/15/beatlemania_and_the_bangles_susanna_hoffs_explains_how_our_obsession_with_the_beatles_brought_the_80s_group_together/.

6

How Does It Feel to Be

Beatles Tribute Bands and the Fans Who Dream Them

Aviv Kammay

The four faces on the album cover are staring at us, transcending the darkness that surrounds them. The print above the heads of Lennon and Harrison reads, "With the Beatles." This phrase, first offered on November 22, 1963, is a promise for Beatles fans of all generations. It is an elusive yet irresistible invitation to be *with* this group whose music and charm we so admire. But how? And when? "It won't be long," Lennon's enticing voice tells us. "It won't be long, yeah."

This chapter examines Beatles tribute acts as participatory methods for Beatles fandom, a means for fans to communally achieve that desirable sensation of *with* the Beatles. Georgina Gregory distinguishes live tribute shows from other media of retrospection: "[W]ith the additional quality of embodiment, they provide the valuable live music experience and contact *with* a fellow being in real time—a sensory activity that is sometimes overlooked."[1] This chapter seeks to bring to the surface the key facets of that "sensory activity" experienced by fans on and off the stage at Beatles tribute shows. A context for the evolution of the Beatles tribute phenomenon and several of its characteristics will be addressed, including the caricaturization of the Beatles in the media in the mid-1960s and its influence on impersonation acts; issues related to carrying over the Beatles' concert banter, humor, and self-irreverent attitude into these acts; the scope of fan fantasies in Beatles tribute shows; inclusion and exclusion on the tribute stage; and the pursuit of musical accuracy in live recreations of the Beatles canon.

Aviv Kammay, *How Does It Feel to Be* In: *Fandom and the Beatles*. Edited by: Kenneth Womack and Kit O'Toole, Oxford University Press (2021). © Oxford University Press. DOI: 10.1093/oso/9780190917852.003.0007

"But Which One Are You?": The Beatles
as Dress-Up Characters

Ten days after the release of *With the Beatles*, the Beatles stepped into a London television studio. They played three songs, and then they performed a witty skit alongside the show's hosts, comedians Eric Morecambe and Ernie Wise.[2] The final sequence of the comedic bit placed Lennon, McCartney, and Harrison with Wise, as they all sang a parodic chorus of the 1912 standard "Moonlight Bay," while Starr was drumming in the back. Morecambe entered the frame from the right. Adorned with a "moptop" wig and with his torso squeezed into a dark collarless jacket, he interjected a yell of "twist and shout" into "Moonlight Bay." Morecambe's costume was obvious: he was dressed as a "Beatle." He remained with the Fab Four as all concluded the performance with an exaggerated falsetto "whoo," complete with the head shake that had been particularly effective for McCartney and Harrison in stage performances of "Twist and Shout" and "She Loves You."[3]

The physical accouterments that allowed Morecambe to appear as a "Beatle" were simple: a wig and a jacket. That costume, combined with his falsetto "whoo," situates Morecambe's performance as the prototypical Beatles dress-up act. Decades later, groups and individuals who wish to create an appearance that registers with the viewer as Beatles impersonation still largely count on wigs and token mannerisms such as head shakes. Yet the musicians in these Beatles tribute acts create worlds that offer more than wardrobes and stage quirks. They offer the audience a gateway into the presence of the unreachable, going "beyond the merely real, into the hyperreal realm, bringing the past alive in a single, concise show."[4]

In these scripted dress-up fantasies, the main characters—John, Paul, George, and Ringo—are what Patrick McCarthy calls the "gods" or "divinities and archetypes" of the fans. He defines participants in American Civil War reenactments, the Modern Mountain Man Rendezvous, and Renaissance fairs as "pilgrimaging reenactors." These reenactors face a demand from their "cultural gods [for] perfectionism in relation to iconography (costuming), formalized mannerisms and behaviors, and 'first person' imitation."[5] McCarthy's definition can be applied to Beatles impersonators as well as to their audience in tribute shows. It is that very focus on mimicking the four Beatles' "formalized mannerisms and behaviors" that inevitably leads dress-up performers to turn their main characters—arguably, their "gods"—into pigeonholed caricatures who dress predictably and behave in stereotypical ways.

The origin of the onstage mannerisms and character-specific banter portrayed by Beatles impersonators in tribute shows can be traced back to the stereotypes associated with each member of the Beatles since 1964. Erin Torkelson Weber attributes the manufacturing and spreading of these stereotypes to the Beatles films directed by Richard Lester, *A Hard Day's Night* (1964) and *Help!* (1965). She notes:

> After [*A Hard Day's Night*], the public perception of each Beatle's identity was so influenced by how they were stereotyped in [the movie] that the press took to identifying them by their defining characteristic. Thus Lennon became the smart one, McCartney the cute one, Harrison the quiet one, and Starr the lucky one. Fifty years later, after the deaths of Lennon and Harrison and McCartney's knighthood, the press continues to use these monikers. The Beatles' second film, *Help!*, strengthened these clichés.[6]

A more extreme manifestation of the Beatles' stereotypes was unleashed upon television viewers in the United States between September 1965 and October 1967. The series *The Beatles* was a highly popular show featuring animated versions of the group members offering sing-alongs and stumbling through various cartoonish adventures loosely related to their song lyrics. The show, produced by Al Brodax of *Popeye* fame, presented Beatle characters dubbed by voice actors applying exaggerated and nasal accents.

It is tempting to focus on the artistic shortcomings of the *Beatles* cartoon show and dismiss it as a footnote in the history of the Beatles, representing one of several naive partnership choices by the group's manager, Brian Epstein. However, the cultural effect of the show should not be underestimated. Its 39 episodes, originally broadcast by ABC on Saturday mornings, delivered exaggerated Beatles stereotypes to countless American children and teens. The influence of the series on the young was supposedly significant enough that, according to the show's producer, college sorority "house mothers" in the American Midwest blamed the cartoons when their students chose to stay overnight on Fridays in fraternity houses.[7] The promise of celebrating the morning after by singing along with the animated Beatles was the alleged irresistible culprit.

The nature of the cartoon setting helped amplify each Beatle's already established individual stereotypes into gargantuan proportions: Lennon was the strong, bossy one; McCartney the charming, responsible one; Harrison the cold, sarcastic one; and Starr the goofy, unsophisticated one. These exaggerated characteristics, simple and well defined, have made their way into the onstage banter in dress-up Beatles tribute performances. As the audience lovingly takes in this spectacle of the impossible, the moptopped impersonators artfully immerse themselves in scripted, one-dimensional, thickly accented characters, almost as if personifying a live-action Beatles cartoon sequence. As Mark D. Porcaro points out, the "simulation of the sounds, sights, and atmosphere of a concert by a 'real' band" creates a new reality, in which the tribute musicians "become an image of the original band" in a "Disney-like mixture of reality and fantasy."[8] With each such performance, Beatles fans—both those in the band and those in the audience—contribute to a snowball effect in which the entertainment package they experience is introduced into the cycle of retold mythology, becoming what Peter Doggett identifies as "false memory" of the Beatles story.[9] Thus, in a fate identical to what Gregory Hall found for American Civil War reenactments, Beatles impersonation acts constitute "simulations of simulations" where "the audience may rely on the reenactments as history."[10] When each Beatle character on the stage lives up to its reputation, fulfilling the fans' expectations in its banter and behavior, the performance reinforces the dominant impersonation formula. In Dennis Hall's words, "In reenacting, the imitation of history tends to become the primary reality of history."[11] Ultimately, in their attempt to deliver a recognizable, entertaining Beatles reenactment, the tribute band members stick firmly to the stereotypical traits and mannerisms associated with each Beatle in the new, manufactured reality.

But the inescapable paradox faced by these impersonators is that the greater the effort they put into becoming Beatle characters, the farther they get from actually acting like the Beatles. Throughout the band's career, the Beatles were all but predictable. They defied their own stereotypes, continuously engaging in an ongoing evolution—of their music, their personalities, and their relationship to their art—in which they developed identities worlds away from the simplistic portrayals seen in the cartoon.

One focal point of this evolution was the way in which the Beatles skillfully avoided overcommitting to their own artistic presumptions. When "caught between loyalty to the working class and their position among the elite," they employed musical, lyrical, or visual mechanisms that defused, diluted, or deflated intellectual or pompous statements in their songs.[12]

In their studio recordings, the Beatles applied these mechanisms with varying levels of subtlety. The inclusion of adolescent Liverpool colloquialisms in "Penny Lane" (recorded in late 1966 and early 1967) and "Sun King" (1969) serve to interrupt the songs' otherwise carefree imagery and sounds; Harrison's philosophical "Within You Without You" closes with strategically placed recorded laughter; "It's All Too Much," Harrison's other strong-statement composition of 1967, defuses its own message of psychedelia-enhanced universal love when Lennon dedicates the song to "your mum" as it begins.

The above examples demonstrate the complex identities of the Beatles as seen in their post-touring era, but the seeds of these recorded self-irreverent mechanisms were sown much earlier in the band's career. The Beatles' live performances featured a variety of self-jabs regularly and spontaneously. Moments that were captured on tape include Lennon and Harrison applying a mask of blues rock atop the self-congratulatory "Picardy third" tonic chord that concludes the sentimental "A Taste of Honey" (Hamburg, late 1962);[13] Lennon introducing his vulnerable 1964 ballad as "If I Fell *Over*" in Philadelphia (and also as "If I Fell . . . *Just as If*" in Blackpool);[14] Lennon wisecracking, "Thank you, Ringo, that was wonderful!" after the live debut of McCartney's tender "Yesterday" (Blackpool, 1965);[15] and Lennon using physical or vocal mockery on multiple occasions to offset unchecked self-importance onstage or in the audience.

As we fans encounter these and other quasi-self-sabotaging gestures by the Beatles, we do not always find ourselves on solid ground. The invitation to be *with* the Beatles brings us only as close as a perplexed outsider to an inside joke can be. The Beatles alone forge the path in which they navigate their banter, expression, and attitude. The ability to toggle effortlessly between high art, matter of fact, and tongue in cheek is unscriptable. If dress-up performers repeated any of Lennon's more infamous onstage behaviors, it would not be acceptable. If they reenacted any of the Beatles' documented jokes verbatim, they might artfully tickle the memory muscles of fans but fall short of recreating the singularity and impact of each moment. Beatles impersonators, who are first and foremost musically skilled fans and not necessarily actors, are therefore tasked with what could be appropriately articulated with the help of a most acrobatic Beatles lyrical phrase: they must try to show that they're not trying to pretend.

Interestingly, the Beatles themselves provide us with a demonstration of the perils involved in trying too hard to play "Beatles" as characters. On

January 25, 1968, they were filmed at Twickenham Studios delivering a live-action cameo appearance for the closing of the animated movie *Yellow Submarine*.[16] The short scene begins as the song "It's All Too Much" fades out. The Beatles appear on the screen wearing dark button-down shirts. Their monochromatic uniformity, so symbolic of early periods in their stardom, stands in startling contrast to their 1966–1967 artistic transformation, on which the music and imagery of *Yellow Submarine* are based. McCartney is smiling nervously, bobbing his head in what looks like a genuine attempt to play the stereotypical "Paul." Through their scripted, mechanical dialogue and action, all four Beatles seem to be making an effort to fit into their outdated moptops mold, without a hint of irony. This is perhaps an attempt to present a Beatles model deemed most suitable for a children's film. Coming from the same individuals whose recent creations had been dealing with "areas of social and spiritual significance as never before in the genre," the artifice of this performance, while charming, is palpably awkward.[17]

Similarly, impersonation acts fashion Beatles models of their own. The parade of archetypal traits—strong, cute, quiet, unsophisticated—is not generated as parody. Rather, these scripted Beatles emerge from the decades-old collective psyche of fans, where authenticity of characters plays a secondary role to images, symbols, and affect. The shows are born out of the fans' compelling desire to revel in a romanticized past, revive dead idols, and engage with fame way beyond compare. The dress-up spectacle allows for the audience and musicians alike to sustain the alluring promise of *with* the Beatles. In their collaborative ritual, all participants summon dreamlike Beatles worlds, in which the clichés are true and the myth is reality. What remains is to identify the playground of the dream, and determine whose dreams count.

The World Is at Your Command: Beatles Tribute Shows as Fan Fantasies

Tribute bands allow fans to transport the Beatles and their glorious fame into any setting, regardless of the location's glamor. A Broadway theater, a bar, the children's stage at a music festival, a municipal senior center, and a school gymnasium can all become venues of Beatles magic. The resulting pretend immediacy of the Beatles constitutes the first and most crucial stage in the tribute show experience. It provides the assembled Beatles fans with an initial sense of that impossible *with*. It creates a fictional reality in which the Beatles is a band of the people, unseparated from its fans.

This manufactured sense of intimacy expands when adding to the equation the notion that the musicians performing—the Beatles' avatars in the event—are, undoubtedly, Beatles fans themselves. These performers physically exercise their fan energy through playing and singing the music of the Beatles. In bringing the songs to life, they function as pseudo-mediums, delivering the anticipated musical information from the "real" Beatles to the audience.

Though the music itself is clearly central, it is just one part of the tribute show ritual. The costumes, instruments, and scenarios that accompany the sequence of the songs are also key to the contrived Beatles reality on the stage. In determining the chronological (and sometimes geographical) script of their shows, tribute performers provide their audiences with a roadmap that leads to the specific Beatles reality visited or imagined.[18] As with the characters, the connection between the version of reality presented onstage and the documented historical events may be loose. This reflects what Hall states as a postmodernist view of reenactments: "reenacting is simulation but it need not be strictly representative of history. Selective uses of authentic objects or interactions within the simulation provide links to history, even if it is not the most important aspect of the reenactment."[19] Gregory is more specific in applying this view to the fantasy aspect of tribute shows: "The reconstruction of the past at the live tribute event involves the activation of familiar narratives in the audience's collective remembering, but equally these occasions provide opportunities for the construction of new narratives."[20]

Indeed, Beatles tribute performers generate new narratives leading to otherwise inaccessible Beatles realities. This begins with the very action of producing a live "Beatles" concert when in reality, an actual performance of the Beatles is far beyond reach. By taking matters into their own hands to craft a new reality, tribute performers walk a fandom path somewhat parallel to that of Beatles bootleggers. Members of that mysterious branch of fandom, who, understandably, are mostly anonymous, distribute unreleased Beatles audio or video material without authorization, not always seeking monetary profit. They employ their underground resources to bring to the public concealed, suppressed, half-baked, hypothetical, or not-quite-attained moments and possibilities in Beatles history and introduce them into a new version of Beatles reality. The otherwise unavailable material they release often adds crucial pieces to the puzzle of documented Beatles history.[21] In a similar fashion, tribute performers apply their musical knowledge and skills in ways that can potentially help present that history accurately. However, like bootleggers, they may also manipulate, reshape, or reimagine Beatles reality, sometimes turning it on its head.[22]

Tribute performers' participatory method of fandom—creating rituals of Beatles revival—merely requires live Beatles music and an audience. As no limits for the fantasy are defined, their shows can veer between historical accuracy and fiction, warp the sense of linear time, and casually perform miracles. The various fantasy scenarios created in Beatles tribute shows represent a wide array of dreams and desires of Beatles fans. For baby boomers, the tribute show is a fountain of youth, an opportunity to revisit their younger selves in a state of unsurpassed excitement and awe. According to Gregory, these first-generation fans are the driving force behind the "temporal travel" offered at tribute shows. As "the first generation to experience a youth-oriented popular culture," they are "especially susceptible to nostalgia regarding the cultural pursuits of their youth."[23] In their state of heightened nostalgia, baby boomers may find a sense of kinship with the Beatles, who are practically of the same generation. Watching the act they've known for all these years, boomers can find affirmation in the Beatles' own tendency for nostalgia, demonstrated particularly in the post-touring stage of the band's career.

Kathryn B. Cox points out "a leitmotif of nostalgia that draws inspiration from [the Beatles'] distinctly British youth" in the group's 1967 output: the *Sgt. Pepper's Lonely Hearts Club Band* album, the *Magical Mystery Tour* film and EP, and the accompanying singles of that year.[24] Ripples of that sentiment are present in the Beatles' well-documented 1969 intention to return to their roots—the main concept of the *Get Back/Let It Be* project—which, as Walter Everett articulated, drew from Lennon and McCartney's "[yearning] for the simple innocence of youth."[25] Thus, being in the audience at a Beatles tribute performance is an opportunity for fans of a certain generation not only to hear the music they love but also to mirror a pursuit of the Beatles themselves.

However, a smooth and graceful return to the "innocence of youth" may prove as elusive for the tribute audience as it was for the Beatles through the trials and tribulations of their final years together. Still, the dreams of Beatles fans propel the tribute performers' visions. Among them is the desire to break away from the historical narrative in order to explore otherwise impossible Beatles scenarios. The fact that the Beatles stopped performing live after the summer of 1966 does not prevent dress-up shows from featuring songs from later in the Beatles' career.

As the show moves chronologically to material from 1967, Beatles impersonators may change costumes—almost always to *Sgt. Pepper* suits—sometimes completing their new look with fake facial hair. A historical reality of the Beatles performing live like this does not exist; thus, a manufactured one is essential to maintain the new narrative, in which the Beatles continue touring into 1967 and beyond. Sometimes, for convenience, the *Sgt. Pepper* suits remain even when the music on the stage is from later periods. In this case, the bright-colored suits shift their symbolic role from highlighting a particular event in time—the *Sgt. Pepper* album—to representing a three-year period in history, the entire post-touring chapter of the band's career.

As shifts in the physical appearance of the Beatle characters come with their swift wardrobe changes, the fans experience a show that condenses time itself. In a similar effect to that created by chronologically sequenced Beatles compilation albums, the scope of the entire Beatles recorded career is presented to the fans in a single package of delightful musical nuggets. By progressing chronologically in both song and costume, the show wraps the presented impossible narrative in an appearance of historical authority.

For the performers, the experience in such a show is unavoidably complex. These typically knowledgeable Beatles fans are faced with the task of embodying dramatically different stages of Beatles expression within a short period of real time. In such a show, the same individuals impersonating "John" and "Paul" joyfully riding through 1963's "From Me to You" and "I Want to Hold Your Hand" might be expected to deliver much trickier emotional loads, such as 1969's "I Want You (She's So Heavy)" and "You Never Give Me Your Money" a mere 45 minutes later. Mirroring the trajectory of the Beatles' states of mind—carefree, hopeful, retrospective, desperate, disillusioned—would require the performers to run a gig-long sprint course of expression. Yet the time limit does not actually force them to leap between emotions and stages of maturation. The power of the classic Beatles stereotypes prevails, guiding the delivery of the characters with minimal, or strictly symbolic, regard to which stage in the band's career is being portrayed. In doing so, the reenactment maintains the fan fantasy of the eternally young, uncomplicated, and unified Beatles. In this world, the Beatles never stopped touring, and, more important, they never broke up.

When the Beatles' disbandment became public in 1970, the initial response from fans reflected bereavement. Mark Hertsgaard writes of "a state
of denial" among fans and a demand that "the last act be rewritten and given
a happier ending or, better yet, no ending at all."[26] Torkelson Weber doubles
down on the notion that the impact of the breakup resembled that of a sudden
loss. She writes: "Millions of fans responded to the story with grief, some of
them weeping in public; the same response they had to the news of Lennon's
murder 10 years later."[27] Gregory connects that sense of grief among fans to
the birth of Beatles tribute bands. She notes that the appearance of the first
major commercial Beatles impersonation acts

> can be attributed to an emotional vacuum created by the original band's
> break up in 1970. In terms of its emotional impact, [t]he Beatles' demise
> should not be underestimated—fans reeling from the shock of the split
> continued to hanker for a reunion, but despite rumours, their wishes were
> not fulfilled and no outlet was available for the pent-up emotions.[28]

No outlet was available, of course, except to create new Beatles and new
rituals of remembrance and revival. The Beatles seen on the tribute stage
are a group manually resuscitated with great care and love by dedicated fans
with appropriate musical skills and a fountain of passion for the Fab Four.
Along with the performers, each fan in attendance at a tribute concert assists
in keeping the flame burning by supporting, participating, and seeking that
of *with*. In their combined effort, tribute bands and their audiences work to
erase the breakup and to ensure that their Beatles remains a thriving, living
organism, forever younger than the band's records.

Still, for some fans, erasing the Beatles' breakup does not fully satisfy the
fantasy. These fans demand a staging of what is arguably the ultimate fan
fiction: a happy ending of sorts in the form of a post-breakup Beatles reunion. Indeed, a show called "The Reunion Beatles Fantasy Tribute" features
all four post-breakup Beatle characters onstage. With the relatively mature
"John," "Paul," "George," and "Ringo" delivering their solo and group material as a reunified group, the spectacle goes beyond reenactment and into a
bona fide rewriting of history. Such a faux-reunion show corrects what fans
deem imperfect or unresolved in the story of the Beatles. As impersonators
use the stage language of reenactment to perform events that never actually
happened, they alter the course of documented Beatles history. Their show
offers a dramatized, tangible response to some of the biggest hypotheticals

in Beatles fandom. These are displayed for enhanced promotional effect on the band's website: "What if circumstances had been different? What if [the Beatles] decided to do a reunion concert that featured many of [their] greatest hits . . . plus the best of their solo work too? What would it have looked and sounded like?"[29]

An additional question posted on that web page—"What if all four former Beatles were alive and well?"—touches upon the difficult reality of the deaths of two of the Beatles. In tribute shows, Gregory asserts, "we no longer have to face . . . the murder of John Lennon or the absence of George Harrison," since "[l]ike the aging process, death is similarly dispatched" in these shows.[30] This type of reimagining can be seen in other types of reenactments. In his study of Civil War reenactors, Rory Turner found that they "created a blood-less war, a war within which they can have a good time and learn something about themselves. The pain, violence, and misery of war have been extracted, leaving camaraderie, exhilaration, and a certain beauty."[31] While ignoring Lennon's and Harrison's deaths may not be on par with finding "a certain beauty" in war, as the Civil War reenactors described by Turner do, Beatles impersonators may select which parts of the history of the Beatles to allow in and which to reimagine, gloss over, or disregard.

However, the decision to have "John" and "George" on any tribute stage does not necessarily suggest that the two Beatles' deaths are being overlooked. The presence of these characters can rather serve as a reminder, an homage, and indeed a reality check. "John" and "George" force a limit to the fantasy. Their participation grants self-awareness to the illusion. When the spectators cannot escape the truth that their experience is a dream, the dream's dissolution is only a matter of time. Still, for fans, the image and sounds of four living, performing "Beatles," artificial as they may be, are pow-erful and beautiful and hold a unique sadness. The words of Devin McKinney on the Beatles' own mid-1990s artificial collaborations of the living and the dead—"Free as a Bird" and "Real Love"—aptly fit here: "These Beatles voices, separated by time, acrimony, history, and death, were shadows touching in air. Somehow the touch was felt, and the love felt real."[32] Love, indeed, is what draws fans to the ritual. Love pulls the audience into the dream, and love buoys the performers miles above the stage.

But who are these performers? Who among fans gets to "be" a Beatle? The tribute performers' love for the music of the Beatles is unquestionable, as is their familiarity with it, sometimes to astonishing degrees of nuance. Yet audiences for decades have grown accustomed to expect impersonators to possess specific characteristics beyond Beatles musicianship: that there be four of them, that they be white (in countries with a dominant white culture, at least), and, without a doubt, that they be male.[33] All-female tribute bands break out of this mold, defying "[t]he mythology [that] insists that only men have the ability to become rock gods . . . by demonstrating that they can play the masculine-coded music to an equally high standard."[34] With unambiguous names such as "Penny Ladies," "Beatles by Girls," "The Sheatles," "Magical Mystery Girls," or "Sister Side," all-female Beatles acts claim their part in the Beatles tribute world, expanding the boundaries of the field.

The resulting apparent gender misplacement onstage is an appropriately reciprocal gesture to the Beatles' performance and recordings of African-American girl-group music early in the band's career. Katie Kapurch demonstrates how the Beatles' existence "in an androgynous space between girlishness and boyishness"—most noted in their faithful covers of girl-group songs early in the band's career—also appears in some of their original compositions.[35] By embodying the Beatles, all-female tribute bands occupy the "androgynous space" *with* them. The musicians in these groups present Beatles realities that are at once hyper-gendered and gender-fluid. The formulaic costumes in all-male Beatles acts are given new meanings when displayed by all-female groups: a symbol of masculinity such as the dark necktie may be complemented by a miniskirt, highlighting playful gender fluidity; the flamboyant *Sgt. Pepper* uniforms reclaim their feminine, colorful, demilitarized power. And when "Sister Side" performs with girl-group-styled vocal arrangements, wearing early-1960s dresses, the fans experience the return of the Beatles music to one of its origins.

The musical output of female Beatles fans at the height of Beatlemania was mainly known for novelty fandom songs, such as "We Love You Beatles" by the Carefrees (1964), "We Love the Beatles" by the Vernon Girls (1964), or "I Want to Kiss Ringo Goodbye" by Penny Valentine (1965). The trajectory leading from releasing songs *about* the Beatles to taking the stage and commandeering performances of the Beatles music itself is akin to the evolution Kit O'Toole identifies in female fans' authorship that expanded from "establishing the Beatles as legends" to "creating new [Beatles] knowledge" and legacy.[36]

Still, the dominant tribute-act model features four men, in costume and in character. And on top of the expectation that these performers dress in "Beatles" code, the ritual also demands that their instruments match or symbolize the Beatles period depicted.[37] The use of Beatles-related guitars supports the visual believability of the fantasy, preventing potential contamination of the dream (imagine character "John" in a reenacted *Ed Sullivan Show* exuberantly strumming chords in "All My Loving" on, say, a fluorescent green Ibanez). The Beatles tribute fantasy, therefore, demands a specific mixture of reality and non-reality: the impersonators must display meticulous accuracy in the visual realm (guitars, costumes), while presenting Beatle characters with exaggerated, myth-based behaviors, often performing fictional show scenarios that defy documented historical records and events.

What remains tangible is the music. The tribute ritual must connect Beatles fans *with* Beatles music. It is what allows any Beatles fantasy, however imaginative, to take shape on the stage. That music—the Beatles' body of work, a significant portion of which requires more than four musicians to recreate live—is the nexus that branches out to various performance paths. Traditional Beatles tribute acts restrict themselves to four "Beatles" on the stage, whatever the musical implications may be. Other acts maintain the four characters but may add prerecorded audio to their live show. Some acts bring in extra musicians to play along with the "Beatles," sometimes excusing their presence by referring in publicity material to one or all of them as the "George Martin" of the band. There are also Beatles tribute bands that completely do away with impersonation. Some of them rearrange the musical material, often presenting it in a specific style (e.g., jazz, heavy metal, soul, bluegrass). Others focus solely on the source text—the recorded Beatles corpus—and painstakingly transcribe and prepare it for live performances, aiming to stay true to the original recordings.

In this latter branch of Beatles recreation, the performers labor to make every sound from the original recordings materialize live onstage, unwilling to compromise musical accuracy. These productions are dreamed up by Beatles fans who care profoundly about what they perceive as the integrity of the music and insist on performing the songs with utter faithfulness to the original material. In seeking a "faithful reproduction in order to recover the reality of originary performances," the musicians involved create a new kind of reality: a live unraveling of all the audio layers that were captured on record.[38] But what are the limitations of such an endeavor? How "true" is true enough?

They Just Wrote It Like That: Purity and Compromise in Note-for-Note Beatles Tribute Concerts

When the Beatles opened their first world tour in Copenhagen on June 4, 1964, the foursome consisted of Lennon, McCartney, Harrison, and Jimmie

Nicol.[39] Starr had been diagnosed with tonsillitis and pharyngitis one day before the tour commenced, and Nicol was quickly recruited to sit in for him. One of the factors making Nicol a fitting candidate for the task was his experience recreating Starr's drum parts for budget Top Six EPs (and one LP, titled *Beatlemania*).[40] These affordable records contained current chart-toppers performed by studio musicians, imitating the hit versions, note for note. Since the days of Top Six, the aim of true-to-the-source Beatles recreations has shifted from selling records to performing live concerts. While the musicians in these shows do not end up touring with the Beatles as Nicol did, they do fulfill a different fan fantasy: they get to be *inside* the music. By looking deeply at a song, they have the opportunity to physically and mentally experience the humanity of the Beatles (technical errors and fortunate accidents included) as they retrace each thread in sometimes highly complex tapestries of audio.

In order to recreate the exact arrangement of a given song, musicians in note-for-note ensembles must identify every vocal and instrumental component, assign each part within the personnel of their group (recruiting additional musicians if needed), and prepare the song for performance. The most immediate resources for aurally identifying the musical parts are the official Beatles recordings. However, specific intricacies are occasionally better heard in early takes or isolated tracks, sometimes available only on bootleg releases.[41] Still, generating a flawless onstage reenactment of an original Beatles recording is not always possible, especially with real-life budgetary or logistical limitations in play. Challenges vary when tackling material from different Beatles recording periods, and compromise and ingenuity are practical necessities. The following is a collection of considerations potentially faced by note-for-note Beatles tribute acts when producing their shows. It is not a complete list, by any means, but rather a series of examples meant to highlight key challenges in translating Beatles music into a live concert setting, sorted by recording period.

1962–1964: While on the surface much of the material from this period feels "live" in the recordings, there are early Beatles songs that do not easily lend themselves to a straightforward live recreation, certainly not by a four-person group. Additional personnel are most clearly needed in songs with a keyboard part (e.g., "Baby It's You," "A Hard Day's Night," "What You're Doing") or overdubbed harmonica (e.g., "I'll Get You," "Little Child"). But more subtle musical components need to be considered as well. Should double-tracked vocals (e.g., "Don't Bother Me," "Can't Buy Me Love") be performed by two singers? Is it essential to bring in musicians to perform handclaps, or should handclaps be an opportunity for guided audience participation (e.g., "I Saw Her Standing There," "I Want to Hold Your Hand")? How should songs that fade out on the record end onstage (e.g., "Love Me Do," "I Should Have Known Better")? Other song-specific decisions include whether to designate a 12-string electric guitar only to play in the introduction and closing of "Eight Days a Week" and whether timpani should be brought in and tuned for (the appropriately titled in this case) "Every Little Thing."

1965–1966: In addition to the challenges presented in earlier recordings, songs from this period pose their own set of considerations. How crucial is it to include all six distinct vocal parts (some of which are quite hidden in the mix) in "I'm Down"? Should "What Goes On" end as it does in the original mono mix or stereo mix? Is there a way to accurately mimic the timbre of the "wound-up" piano in "In My Life" other than with a digital sample? How precisely must each effect be recreated and timed in "Yellow Submarine"? Is it important to tune all the guitars down a semitone to match the original key of "I'm Only Sleeping"? In the same song, is it best to play the reversed guitar parts as heard, or should they be prerecorded? Since the Beatles used prerecorded loops in "Tomorrow Never Knows" and faded them in and out "live" in the studio, is it important to repeat that method on the stage (perhaps with digital recordings, if not tape)? How should the band approach instrumental or vocal parts that were recorded in a certain key and then slowed down or sped up (e.g., "Rain," "For No One")?

1967: Productions such as *Sgt. Pepper's Lonely Hearts Club Band* and *Magical Mystery Tour* were created without any regard to potential live performances of songs. Preparing true-to-the-source material from this period for a live concert requires the gathering and redistribution of countless musical details. In addition to challenges caused by the inclusion of prerecorded or "found" audio material (also present in some recordings from 1966), two new questions arise when working on Beatles music from 1967: how critical is it for orchestral sections to match in size those recorded, and how to recreate chaotic, loosely metered music?[42] Of particular note are the difficulties posed by "Strawberry Fields Forever," "A Day in the Life," "Being for the Benefit of Mr. Kite," "Only A Northern Song," the coda of "Flying," and the outro of "It's All Too Much."

1968–1970: Alongside songs characterized by a straightforward rock arrangement, this final batch of Beatles music contains some of the hardest-to-replicate moments and sounds in the Fab Four's output. For example, "Revolution 9" brings back and multiplies manifold the loops question posed by "Tomorrow Never Knows"; the coda of "Hey Jude," with its constant lead-vocal ad-libbing, may lose much of its spirit if mechanically (or "too accurately") resung; the staging (and therefore the type of intimacy) of "Julia" can be significantly altered if multiple singers deliver the double-and-triple-tracked vocals; large and small differences between mono and stereo mixes are present in much of the *White Album* material; "I Want You (She's So Heavy)" ends with an abrupt tape cut; some of the background vocals in "Octopus's Garden" are processed in a way that mimics underwater sounds; handclaps in "Come Together" and some of the hi-hat cymbal part in "Let It Be" (album version) feature tape delay. Other relevant points to consider may be: Should the Spanish guitar introduction in "The Continuing Story of Bungalow Bill" be played live even though it is originally an audio sample? How can the "scratchy record" voice in "Honey Pie" be recreated? Is stereo panning crucial in songs whose original recordings feature it prominently (e.g., "Sun King," "Her Majesty")? Is it important to replicate unusually soft levels of lead vocals (in relation to instruments) heard in some original mixes (e.g., "Old Brown Shoe," parts of "Let It Be")?

Unquestionably, the amount and variety of musical details to consider in the entire recorded Beatles corpus is practically infinite. Note-for-note performers may spend long hours perfecting a single element that will last mere seconds on the stage, possibly going unnoticed by most members of the audience. Yet these musicians are not only performing for the spectators. The additional force in play is their drive to *be* in Beatles history. Taking immense pride in their familiarity with the nuts and bolts of each song, they express their fandom by presenting onstage every sound left by the Beatles in the studio as if it were an archeological find. As they perform the music, they turn the tribute show into an athletics-event-like spectacle in which members of the audience (especially detail-oriented Beatles fans), as well as the musicians themselves, are implicitly invited to judge the accuracy level of the performance. Did the tambourine switch to 16th notes two beats before the first "middle eight" in "Ticket to Ride"? Was the singer clearly stifling laughter when singing "writing 50 times" in "Maxwell's Silver Hammer"? Is the band attentive enough, smart enough, or fast enough to pull off the enormous feat of completely accurate reproduction?

By dismantling each song and then carefully reassembling it, note-for-note Beatles tribute performers take musical reenactment to such an extreme that costumes and characters are rendered unnecessary or distracting. But, like characters in dress-up shows, note-for-note Beatles musicians—while in layperson attire—are leaders in the tribute ritual. However, since they do not need to stay "in character," there is no "fourth wall" in their show. Band-audience communication may be open and two-sided, with the musicians discussing the band's working process, including how they deal with obstacles posed by the music.

McCarthy finds that reenactors of historical periods or events engage in "[t]elling and retelling stories about every part of the reenactment experience," including "about how icons . . . are made."[43] In Beatles tribute shows, the songs being rehearsed and performed constitute these "icons" being created. When band members share stories about their experience preparing the music for the concert, they engage with the audience as their peers in Beatles fandom. When it is clear that everybody, on and off the stage, has gathered to celebrate the same love for the Beatles, that love is affirmed and protected.

Conclusion

Beatles fans create and nurture fandom spaces in festivals, conferences, literature, and online. The tribute show fandom space is unique in how it involves simulation. It is a space where fans not only engage *about* the Beatles but also practice *being* in Beatles history, whether a mythological, fictional, or evidence-based version. Beatles tribute shows are physical, visceral manifestations of Beatles fandom. Yet they are also potent platforms for participatory, analytical, and playful engagement with Beatles music. They stage fantasies and dreams, manipulate histories and narrative, and create moments of bliss and wonder. They are arenas of artifice but overflowing with real love. Tribute shows allow the performers and audiences to be immersed in the music and memory of the Beatles. As the music starts, we sing. We sing together as fans. We sing because the tribute show is our space to be ourselves, *with* one another.

Notes

1. Georgina Gregory, "Days of Future Past: Temporal Travel in the World of Tribute Entertainment," *Journal of European Popular Culture* 6, no. 2 (2015): 124.

2. *The Morecambe and Wise Show* information is in Mark Lewisohn, *The Complete Beatles Chronicle* (London: Octopus, 1992), 131.

3. A video clip of the skit appears in "Early Television Appearances," *The Beatles Anthology*, dir. Kevin Godley, Bob Smeaton, and Geoff Wonfor, ITV and ABC, 1995; EMI, 2003 (DVD).

4. Mark D. Porcaro, "Hyperreality in Cyberspace: Web Sites of Three American Beatles Tribute Bands," *American Music* 26, no. 1 (2008): 133.

5. Patrick McCarthy, "'Living History' as the 'Real Thing': A Comparative Analysis of the Modern Mountain Man Rendezvous, Renaissance Fairs, and Civil War Reenactments," *ETC* 71, no. 2 (2014): 115–116.

6. Erin Torkelson Weber, *The Beatles and the Historians: An Analysis of Writings about the Fab Four* (Jefferson, NC: McFarland, 2016), 31.

7. Al Brodax, *Up Periscope Yellow: The Making of the Beatles Yellow Submarine* (New York: Proscenium, 2004), 39.

8. Porcaro, "Hyperreality in Cyberspace," 133–134.

9. Peter Doggett, *You Never Give Me Your Money: The Beatles after the Breakup*. New York: HarperCollins, 2009, 165.

10. Gregory Hall, "Selective Authenticity: Civil War Reenactors and Credible Reenactments," *Journal of Historical Sociology* 29, no. 3 (2016): 419. Both Hall in his discussion of Civil War reenactments and Porcaro in his analysis of three websites of Beatles tribute bands mention the "hyperreality" created in these simulation performances.

11. Dennis Hall, "Civil War Reenactors and the Postmodern Sense of History," *Journal of American Culture* 17, no. 3 (1994): 10.

12. William M. Northcutt, "The Spectacle of Alienation: Death, Loss, and the Crowd in Sgt. Pepper's Lonely Hearts Club Band," in *Reading the Beatles: Cultural Studies, Literary Criticism, and the Fab Four*, ed. Kenneth Womack and Todd F. Davis (Albany: State University of New York, 2006), 132.

13. Heard in two different performances of the song at the Star Club, both available on *The Beatles Live Volume One*. The Beatles, "A Taste of Honey," Bobby Scott and Ric Marlow, recorded December 1962, *The Beatles Live Volume One*, Purple Chick, 2008.

14. The Beatles, "If I Fell," John Lennon and Paul McCartney, recorded September 1964, *The Beatles: Convention Hall Wisdom*, Purple Chick, 2008; and the Beatles, "If I Fell," John Lennon and Paul McCartney, recorded July 1964, *The Beatles: Seattle Down*, Purple Chick, 2008.

15. The Beatles, "Yesterday," John Lennon and Paul McCartney, recorded August 1965, *The Beatles Anthology 2*, Apple, 2008.

16. *Yellow Submarine*, directed by George Dunning (1968; London: Apple Corps, 2012), DVD.

17. Walter Everett, *The Beatles as Musicians: Revolver through the Anthology* (New York: Oxford University Press, 1999), 89.

18. The February 1964 *Ed Sullivan Show* studio and the January 1969 Apple headquarters rooftop are popular choices.

19. Hall, "Selective Authenticity," 423.

20. Gregory, "Days of Future Past," 118.
21. The most comprehensive and significant musical analysis of the Beatles corpus, Walter Everett's two-volume *The Beatles as Musicians*, relies on bootlegged demonstration tapes and studio session recordings to relay to readers the most complete possible picture of a number of Beatles compositions.
22. It is incumbent upon the listener or viewer to vet bootlegged material for possible mislabeling. Some audio or video may be deliberately fake or artificially reconstructed. The latter type includes playful Beatles music mash-ups that serve to realize fantasies similar to those of some Beatles tribute shows' imaginative scenarios.
23. Gregory, "Days of Future Past," 124.
24. Kathryn B. Cox, "Mystery Trips, English Gardens, and Songs Your Mother Should Know: The Beatles and British Nostalgia in 1967," in *New Critical Perspectives on the Beatles: Things We Said Today*, ed. Kenneth Womack and Katie Kapurch (London: Macmillan, 2016), 41.
25. Everett, *The Beatles as Musicians*, 213.
26. Mark Hertsgaard, *A Day in the Life: The Music and Artistry of the Beatles* (New York: Delacorte, 1995), 278.
27. Torkelson Weber, *The Beatles and the Historians*, 64.
28. Georgina Gregory, *Send in the Clones: A Cultural Study of the Tribute Band* (Bristol, CT: Equinox, 2012), 41.
29. The Reunion, "About Us," https://www.reunionbeatles.com/about-us.
30. Gregory, "Days of Future Past," 126.
31. Rory Turner, "Bloodless Battles: The Civil War Reenacted," *Drama Review* 34, no. 4 (1990): 134.
32. Devin McKinney, *Magic Circles: The Beatles in Dream and History* (Cambridge, MA: Harvard University Press, 2003), 359.
33. Not only has this traditional formula excluded women musicians and musicians of color, but it has also favored dress-up optics over full musical recreations requiring more than four musicians. Expectations regarding the impersonators' ages or body types do not seem to be of critical importance. Nor does left-handedness for "Paul," but if a dress-up act's bassist does play left-handed, this will prominently appear in promotional material. While Starr is also left-handed, that is not a relevant criterion for authenticity of impersonation, since he has always played his kit in its right-handed configuration.
34. Georgina Gregory, "Transgender Tribute Bands and the Subversion of Male Rites of Passage through the Performance of Heavy Metal Music," *Journal for Cultural Research* 17, no. 1 (2013): 32.
35. Katie Kapurch, "Crying, Waiting, Hoping: The Beatles, Girl Culture, and the Melodramatic Mode," in *New Critical Perspectives on the Beatles: Things We Said Today*, ed. Kenneth Womack and Katie Kapurch (London: Macmillan, 2016), 204.
36. Kit O'Toole, "'She Said She Said': How Women Have Transformed from Fans to Authors in Beatles History," in *New Critical Perspectives on the Beatles: Things We Said Today*, ed. Kenneth Womack and Katie Kapurch (London: Macmillan, 2016), 180–195.

37. Some guitar models seem to be of greater importance onstage than others, simply due to their prominence in Beatles iconography, regardless of the song being performed. For "John," the black Rickenbacker 325 and the "natural" Epiphone Casino; for "Paul," the Höfner "violin" bass (much more than the Rickenbacker 4001 bass); for "George," the Gretsch Country Gentleman, the Rickenbacker 360/12 (either the prototype or the "rounded" design), and the painted Fender Stratocaster ("Rocky").

38. Allan Moore, "Authenticity as Authentication," *Popular Music* 21, no. 2 (2002): 217.

39. Concert date in Lewisohn, *The Complete Beatles Chronicle*, 161.

40. *Top Six* and *Beatlemania* information in Jim Berkenstaadt, *The Beatle Who Vanished* (Madison, WI: Rock and Roll Detective, 2013), 45–48.

41. Complementing the audio sources are written musical and technical analyses such as Everett, *The Beatles as Musicians*, and Hammack, *Beatles Recording Reference Manual*, as well as Fujta, *The Beatles: Complete Scores*. The latter, while unquestionably thorough in scope, leaves some details out and cannot be used as a definite note-for-note transcription.

42. "Found" audio examples from 1967 include the animal sounds in "Good Morning Good Morning" and the radio material in "I Am the Walrus."

43. McCarthy, "Living History," 111.

Bibliography

The Beatles. "If I Fell," John Lennon and Paul McCartney. Recorded July 1964. *The Beatles: Seattle Down*. Purple Chick, 2008.

The Beatles. If I Fell," John Lennon and Paul McCartney. Recorded September 1964. *The Beatles: Convention Hall Wisdom*. Purple Chick, 2008.

The Beatles. "A Taste of Honey," Bobby Scott and Ric Marlow. Recorded December 1962. *The Beatles Live Volume One*. Purple Chick, 2008.

The Beatles. "Yesterday," John Lennon and Paul McCartney. Recorded August 1965. *The Beatles Anthology 2*. Apple, 1996.

Berkenstaadt, Jim. *The Beatle Who Vanished*. Madison, WI: Rock and Roll Detective, 2013.

Brodax, Al. *Up Periscope Yellow: The Making of the Beatles Yellow Submarine*. New York: Proscenium, 2004.

Cox, Kathryn B. "Mystery Trips, English Gardens, and Songs Your Mother Should Know: The Beatles and British Nostalgia in 1967." In *New Critical Perspectives on the Beatles: Things We Said Today*, edited by Kenneth Womack and Katie Kapurch, 31–50. London: Macmillan, 2016.

Doggett, Peter. *You Never Give Me Your Money: The Beatles after the Breakup*. New York: HarperCollins, 2009.

Dunning, George, dir. *Yellow Submarine*, 1968; London: Apple Corps, 2012, DVD.

Everett, Walter. *The Beatles as Musicians: Revolver through the Anthology*. New York: Oxford University Press, 1999.

Fujita, Tetsuya, ed. The Beatles: Complete Scores. Milwaukee, WI: Hal Leonard, 1993.

Godley, Kevin, Bob Smeaton, and Geoff Wonfor, dirs. *The Beatles Anthology*. ITV and ABC, 1995; EMI, 2003 (DVD).

Gregory, Georgina. "Days of Futures Past: Temporal Travel in the World of Tribute Entertainment." *Journal of European Popular Culture* 6, no. 2 (2015): 117–128.

Gregory, Georgina. *Send in the Clones: A Cultural Study of the Tribute Band.* Bristol, CT: Equinox, 2012.

Gregory, Georgina. "Transgender Tribute Bands and the Subversion of Male Rites of Passage through the Performance of Heavy Metal Music." *Journal for Cultural Research* 17, no. 1 (2013): 21–36.

Hall, Dennis. "Civil War Reenactors and the Postmodern Sense of History." *Journal of American Culture* 17, no. 3 (1994): 7–11.

Hall, Gregory. "Selective Authenticity: Civil War Reenactors and Credible Reenactments." *Journal of Historical Sociology* 29, no. 3 (2016): 413–436.

Hammack, Jerry. *The Beatles Recording Reference Manual Volume 1.* Toronto: Gearfab Books, 2017.

Hertsgaard, Mark. *A Day in the Life: The Music and Artistry of the Beatles.* New York: Delacorte, 1995.

Kapurch, Katie. "Crying, Waiting, Hoping: The Beatles, Girl Culture, and the Melodramatic Mode." In *New Critical Perspectives on the Beatles: Things We Said Today,* edited by Kenneth Womack and Katie Kapurch, 199–220. London: Macmillan, 2016.

Lewisohn, Mark. *The Complete Beatles Chronicle.* London: Octopus, 1992.

McCarthy, Patrick. "'Living History' as the 'Real Thing': A Comparative Analysis of the Modern Mountain Man Rendezvous, Renaissance Fairs, and Civil War Reenactments." *ETC* 71, no. 2 (2014): 106–123.

McKinney, Devin. *Magic Circles: The Beatles in Dream and History.* Cambridge, MA: Harvard University Press, 2003.

Moore, Allan. "Authenticity as Authentication." *Popular Music* 21, no. 2 (2002): 209–223.

Northcutt, William M. "The Spectacle of Alienation: Death, Loss, and the Crowd in Sgt. Pepper's Lonely Hearts Club Band." In *Reading the Beatles: Cultural Studies, Literary Criticism, and the Fab Four,* edited by Kenneth Womack and Todd F. Davis, 129–146. Albany: State University of New York Press, 2006.

O'Toole, Kit. "'She Said She Said': How Women Have Transformed from Fans to Authors in Beatles History." In *New Critical Perspectives on the Beatles: Things We Said Today,* edited by Kenneth Womack and Katie Kapurch, 179–198. London: Macmillan, 2016.

Porcaro, Mark D. "Hyperreality in Cyberspace: Web Sites of Three American Beatles Tribute Bands." *American Music* 26, no. 1 (2008): 133–136.

The Reunion. "About Us." https://www.reunionbeatles.com/about-us.

Torkelson Weber, Erin. *The Beatles and the Historians: An Analysis of Writings about the Fab Four.* Jefferson, NC: McFarland, 2016.

Turner, Rory. "Bloodless Battles: The Civil War Reenacted." *Drama Review* 34, no. 4 (1990): 123–136.

7

A Hard Day's Write

Beatles Fanfic and the Quantum of Creativity

Mark Duffett

One typical Beatles fan fiction story on Archive of Our Own, is listed as male-to-male romance between John Lennon and Paul McCartney and tagged with the terms *angst, love confessions, rejection, unrequited love,* and *period-typical homophobia.*[1] Its author notes, "I'm not super amazing with dates and I ask that you take the timelines/events with a grain of salt. I didn't do an amazing amount of research. Just what I needed. Either way its [*sic*] fiction." Such examples of fanfic can arouse a range of responses from intrigue to disapproval. Fan fiction is, ordinarily, nonprofessional writing—fiction premised thematically, to some degree, on media texts, celebrities, or their artistic creations. Beyond stories based on fictional source texts, some fanfic uses public figures as the basis for characters and is called real person fiction (RPF). Bandfic is a subgenre of RPF involving rock musicians as central characters. Slash fiction, meanwhile, is a subset of fanfic with narratives involving same-sex intimacy between pairs of central characters. Real person slash (RPS) is a fanfic subgenre that hybridizes the approach of RPF with the form of slash, and it can involve pairs of musicians. In academia, a diverse range of discussions about fanfic in recent years has covered questions of copyright, fan labor or play, fan literacy and reading practice, community-created archives, world building, identity politics, or subversion and censorship. My aim in this chapter is to consider a less-discussed question: how does RPF relate to celebrity fandom? At first sight, this might seem an odd question. After all, surely, you have to know about the Beatles to write about them. That is partly true, but, do you also have to *love* them, in any dedicated sense, to pursue such literary activity? How might we discern a more nuanced picture? We tend to assume that fanfic is either a logical extension of celebrity fandom or its own category of communal activity. How might we

Mark Duffett, *A Hard Day's Write* In: *Fandom and the Beatles.* Edited by: Kenneth Womack and Kit O'Toole, Oxford University Press (2021). © Oxford University Press. DOI: 10.1093/oso/9780190917852.003.0008 understand fanfic in ways that do not necessarily alienate it from other fan practices, while still recognizing its specificity?

Fanfic has become a more popular activity due to convergence cultures forming on the internet.[2] For the generation that has grown up with it, the internet is treated as an environment rather than a tool. Many young people produce content daily on social media. Fanfic reading and writing have increasingly become normal practice. Even allowing for a dedicated subculture of older fanfic writers, in this circumstance, we might expect contemporary bands to inspire the most stories and past acts to be forgotten. Relatively speaking, however, the Beatles appear to be an exception to this equation. In relation to fan fiction, a first thing to say is that stories about the group are disproportionately common compared with other acts from their era. For example, a cursory search in one prominent online fan fiction archive (one so large it features thousands of communities of fanfic enthusiasts) shows around 1,500 stories about the Beatles.[3] In comparison, One Direction has 4,500 stories. The discrepancy is magnified when we consider that the Beatles began just less than six decades ago, whereas One Direction started in 2010. Nevertheless, Beatles stories are much more prominent than those about other acts from the 1960s. Consider, for example, the Rolling Stones— a group that never split up and whose members are (as of this writing) still alive. They have about 200 stories, not much more than 10% of the Beatles total. Lagging behind are Bob Dylan with 55 and the Grateful Dead with a total of only 39. The largest category of Beatles stories on the site is labeled "Across the Universe"; there are more than 300 stories in the category, meaning that it represents more than 20% of the total. In 2007, a colorful, Anglo-American feature film titles *Across the Universe*, directed by Julie Taymor, featured more than 30 Beatles numbers. There is a sense in which such a project was arguably equivalent to professionally made fanfic, in a similar way to Danny Boyle's 2019 film, *Yesterday*. The "Across the Universe" category, however, contains a wide variety of Beatles stories, only some of which refer to the 2007 jukebox musical. This may be because "across the universe" sounds similar to "alternative universe" (AU), a fannish term for stories set in parallel worlds where canonical characters are explored in non-canonical ways. One poster complained about the confusion and admonished Beatles fanfic and slash writers to post elsewhere, on sites dedicated to RPF, because she found it hard to find any actual stories about the *Across the Universe* film. The world of Beatles fanfic is diverse.

Using the Beatles as a case study, this chapter will discuss fanfic's social and academic positioning, the unstable boundary between celebrity following and fanfic authorship, and the generative possibilities of the celebrity image. Until we do further empirical work, carefully examining when and how celebrity-following fans adopt the craft of fanfic writing, our working models will be based on little more than speculation. However, even with such empirical work, discerning any firm relationship between fan identity, celebrity following, and fanfic will be difficult for at least two reasons. First, as Kristina Busse notes, in fanfic, "Discourses about fans—where real-life identity is partially hidden and where online identities are partially performed—allow fans to engage in one another's personas, which are understood to not fully coincide with the actual person."[4] Even using techniques like email interviewing, it can be hard to know just who is who. Second, bandfic is variable in both its form and the reasons for its existence. Abigail De Kosnik says that "Internet fan fiction archives serve as queer spaces" and also cites survey figures suggesting that anywhere between 15% and 56% of fanfic writers do not identify as queer in their gender or sexual identities.[5] Even with the caveats she carefully notes, the figures at least imply that a range of things might be going on. Besides slash, fanfic sites also contain general fiction ("genfic") stories, for instance, some of which explore grief—a universal social process that, though it may be experienced differently, is hard to directly tie to an identity held by any one group of writers. Such variation also complicates fanfic writing in relation to celebrity fandom. Not only is celebrity following itself complex—a composite of a whole range of possible affective intensities, identifications, and practices—but it also could be argued that fanfic writing is a specific form of craft practice that becomes acceptable within certain cultures at certain times. Just as celebrity followers can enter such cultures, those who are already part of them can also turn to well-known musicians as productive vehicles for their writing practice. It is important to remember here that the Beatles was not simply a popular group but one that went stratospheric in terms of sales and recognition, in effect becoming a "supergroup" of four icons, not through amalgamation but through collaboration. That makes it easy to casually write about. Hence, just as not all Beatles fans are fanfic writers, it also appears that not all Beatles fanfic writers may actually be Beatles fans. By definition, however, fanfic can never be about absolute transformation; it has to have some relationship to the original text. According to Sheenagh Pugh in her study of the literary aspects of the form, "No fanfic reader I know likes or approves of fiction in which the canon characters are made substantially different from their originals, doing things that seem out of character for them ('character rape,' as the term is)."[6] In this ambiguous territory, is the Beatles' own story inviolable when it comes to fanfic or merely a platform for departure? It can be either, depending on the subset of fanfic narratives (and, thus, communities of writers) that one examines. My argument in what follows is that although the question of whether celebrity following and fanfic writing have an *innate* relationship depends on the particular fanfic culture examined, what, at least notionally, distinguishes Beatles fanfic writing from celebrity-following Beatles fandom is the adoption of a "quantum of creativity" on the writer's part.

In a Private Moment? Impregnating Paul McCartney

In the late 1990s, an online poster uploaded a fan fiction story about McCartney named after a Beatles song. The RPF story was reproduced, sometimes being featured in online categories tagged "SBIH" (so bad it's horrible). In it, a female narrator had sex with McCartney and accidentally impregnated him. Male pregnancy, of course, has happened in reality, through a combination of artificial insemination and growing the baby in the male stomach cavity lining. In the story concerned, however, the male pregnancy was a natural one, an example of the convention known in fanfic communities as "mpreg"—a subgenre of fantasy storytelling that places men in vulnerable bodily predicaments in order to expose new aspects of their character.[7] In August 2011, an online poster I will call *Culturalcritic_ continued her own vlogging series with a two-part, 85-minute YouTube review of the story in question. *Culturalcritic_ had already gathered a small following by releasing more than 100 videos in which she gleefully performed evaluations exploring the low aesthetic value of fanfic stories. Since its release, her two-part critique of the McCartney mpreg story has collectively attracted 11,000 views (though the total number of viewers is likely to be smaller due to many watching both halves). The McCartney mpreg story provided a prime opportunity for *Culturalcritic_ to gleefully dissect a notorious example of poor-quality fanfic. She ended the second part of her review with a summary, sung to the tune of "Hey Jude," in which she explained, "And, as for this fan fiction having a real person, that is completely wrong, you Moron. And it was really creepy, because your character fucks the real person that's in this fanfic. Oh, you have issues! You have issues!" Such responses demonstrate that fanfic writing has been stigmatized and that its participants often operate in the context of such social shaming."[8] After coming across the review by *Culturalcritic_ online, the story's author uploaded her own YouTube response. Instead of angrily defending her writing, she explained that she had created the story in school when she was 14, adding, "It was a dare from a couple of boys." The author expressed a mixture of contrition at her youthful folly and reluctant pride for inspiring a whole internet culture based on a worst-case example: "It's immortalized on quite a few Beatles fan fiction sites as . . . one of the worst fan fictions in general ever written." Directly addressing *Culturalcritic_, she also added a qualifier:

> I realize you yourself are not a Beatles fan; you aren't versed in what the Beatles fan fiction community is like. There's many facets of it. There's just about anything under the sun you can imagine exists. At one point, there was an entire community just for "Paul in pain" fan fictions; some of the people who wrote these actually were into it in that way, whereas, I just—I don't know—the first Beatles fan fictions I ever read were in that category, so then I was just trying to keep up, I suppose I wrote a few of those. This was one of them. But then there were also the gutter communities. Some of them are still around, which basically offer glorified Beatles sex stories. And one can imagine there's also slash ones too, and those seem to be an overabundance nowadays. I'm not quite sure how or why that is, but . . . I'm just pointing out that this was not some whacked-out, creeptastic, sex fantasy fetish type thing.

The author's claim was that community norms—however supposedly "whacked-out"—had become subgenre conventions that lifted such stories beyond being case examples of personal psychological quirks. Some senior fanfic scholars have recognized such a community-based reading and writing strategy in other contexts. Busse, for instance, has argued that fanfic should be distinguished from other forms of transformative work. She explains that fanfic "challenges many attempts at traditional aesthetic evaluation, because critics who ignore the guiding frameworks of how, when, and where a fan text was created can easily misread and misjudge."[9] In the case of the Beatles story in question, one thing that *Culturalcritic_ commented on was the use of sighing in parentheses, something the author defended as a naive but communal decision:

The sighing in parentheses thing wasn't lack of knowledge on my part, so much as it was a lack of knowledge on a lot of people's parts at that time. Because almost any Beatles fan fiction you would read around the time that I wrote this—back in like 1999—would have things such as sighing written in parentheses. Since that's how I saw it done, that is how I wrote it. Because it was what I saw: this is how I thought was the correct way of doing it.

Busse explains what some of the frameworks guiding fanfic might be. One is a concern for a full expression of the writer's self, especially in fantasy, that transcends the need to please any wider audience. Busse calls this "pleasing the Id Vortex" and says that fanfic "often caters to highly individualized reading desires."[10] Another is simply the immediate audience for the story:

> Moreover, there tend to be specific and limited audiences for every story— sometimes the recipient of a gift exchange, other times all fans of a particular pairing—and these particular audiences often share a sizable number of assumptions with the writer that won't be spelled out and are thus invisible to outsiders.[11]

Such observations distance fanfic from some other kinds of archived, transformative work (such as fan art emblazoned across social media) and position it more as a kind of locally performed event, a writerly act pursued in a semiprivate space, inhabited by only certain members of the fanfic community. Fanfic is presented in this scenario as a cultural practice that can only be properly understood by those who study or are in the community translating its specificities to a lay audience. In other words, the analysis is premised on an assumption of cultural distance in which the academic expert is either already an "insider" or has—through immersion—acquired a sufficient degree of "insider" knowledge to be able to explain the form. While there are merits to this position, it locates fanfic writing in particular as a remote form of fan practice and maintains an absolute separation that can hide certain nuances. Specifically, for instance, some fanfic writers *are* fans of the artist concerned who write as an extension of their interest as celebrity followers, while other participants in the fanfic community are primarily writers who use the object concerned as an inspirational vehicle for their authorial practices, and yet others may belong to other fandoms and be attracted to uniting diverse sets of characters. While acknowledging the specificity of fanfic as a practice that can directly or indirectly express particular identities and experiences, rather than ghettoizing it as a unique form, my own aim here is to begin exploring fanfic's conceptual alignment with other fannish identities and practices.

Is Affirmational Fandom the Shadow Side
of Transformation?

We can date a key distinction made in the fan studies discussion back to a 2009 post by obsession_inc on the website dreamwidth.org.[12] Primarily, it centered upon whether fan practices and identities (there is a slippage from one to the other) aimed to transform the text or perpetuate the authorial intent collectively perceived to be behind it. Transformational fans were those who used the text as a premise for transformative activity, perhaps writing poetry or fanfic or otherwise reworking the text. For obsession_inc, it was "all about laying hands upon the source and twisting it to the fans' own purposes"—a process that could "fix a disappointing issue (a distinct lack of sex-having between two characters, of course, is a favorite issue to fix) in the source material, or using the source material to illustrate a point, or just to have a whale of a good time." The crucial thing was that "everyone has their own shot at declaring what the source material means, and at radically re-interpreting it." In contrast, "In 'affirmational' fandom, the source material is re-stated, the author's purpose divined to the community's satisfaction, rules established on how the characters are and how the universe works, and cosplay etc. occur." Here "it's all about nailing down the details." Obsession_inc did not simply venture a distinction between two types of fan practice or two types of fan. She also loaded or superimposed other distinctions on this binary. First, the majority of fans attracted to pursuing transformational practices are female, while most of those who "trend strongly toward" affirmational practices are male. Second, since transformational fans change the text, they are "non-sanctioned" and may use pseudonyms, unlike their "sanctioned" affirmational counterparts. Just as obsession_inc had already begun to do, scholars further loaded the transformational/affirmational binary with significant cultural distinctions by talking about a kind of tension between transformative and affirmational fandom, which in turn mapped onto a number of other binary opposites: support for creative freedom versus a concern to maintain intellectual property (fans against the industry), female literary productivity and male attempts to police it (female against male fans), queer activity against a heteronormative backlash, and identity politics itself against straight, white, male hegemony.[13] Affirmational fandom, in particular, however, deserves more sustained attention. Celebrity following requires agency but is itself neither affirmational nor transformational. There are, meanwhile, affirmational protests, strategies, or stances and perhaps, in consequence, spaces or communities of practice that manifest to promote them. While there may also be writers who *only* pursue transformational practices, at least in the sphere of fans who follow music celebrities, are there *actually* "affirmational fans"—individuals whose central raison d'être as fans is asserting authorial intent?

What divided conceptions of media fandom neglect is the extent to which affirmational fandom is the *product* of the transformational argument. On closer inspection, it is itself something of a phantom category. The concept upon which affirmational fandom depends, that of fidelity to the source text, is itself debatable, because of the "neutrosemic" dimension of reception. In saying this, I am drawing on Cornel Sandvoss's notion of "neutrosemic" meaning—asking "whether, in the practice of fan consumption, texts are emptied of meaning and take on a mirror-like function."[14] Do fans simply draw what they want from the text, reading it in a way that is shaped by their own filters and concerns? Fandom, some argue, is a case of celebrities having images that are "blank slates" upon which each member of the audience reads whatever he or she likes, but celebrity images are, nevertheless, intertextual, malleable, and ambiguous, so readings made by individual fans are likely to be diverse. Totemic engagement does not depend on one form of identification, because it "houses" a variety of actual identifications that are subjective and based on various thoughts or emotions, which—at the level of the individual fan—does not preclude elements of fantasy as an aspect of engagement. For this reason, even though the affirmational protest can express anger or disappointment at the transformations made in fanfic, when we look at the original text, its contours and boundaries may not be quite as expected. For a start, it is hard to valorize one focus or fan practice, such as listening to the music, as primary and affirmational, because of the variety of "hooks" through which people encounter their bands. The Beatles, in particular, for instance, have been enjoyed by deaf fans. It is true that deafness is often partial and that almost all fans hear the music in some form, but it is possible that *watching* a band can play a major and perhaps decisive or primary role for some fans. Such routes to attachment should not be ignored.

Theorizing Celebrity Followers' Motives
for Writing Fanfic

At the heart of the issue of affirmational versus transformative fandom stands the question of how celebrity-following caterpillars morph into transformational butterflies. One problem is that there is not an adequate theoretical model to explain this transition. Two theories will be discussed in this section: the notion that fans are necessarily unhappy with the text as it exists and the opposite idea, that fans are staying in the frame of their interest for an extended period. Neither seems quite adequate to understand the appeal of fanfic writing.

In his 1992 book *Textual Poachers*, Henry Jenkins argued, "I am not claiming that there is anything particularly empowering about the texts that fans embrace. I am, however, claiming that there is something empowering about what fans do with those texts in the process of assimilating them to the particulars of their lives."[15] While he was evidently a dedicated fan of the telefantasy franchises at the center of the fan cultures he investigated, Jenkins's statement could also be read as a kind of academic dismissal: if it is academically useful at all, the content of popular culture is useful only insofar as fans do things with it. For Jenkins, this fan productivity was diverse and included the making of new meanings and new conversations, as well as objects or texts. Nevertheless, his claim marks a moment when transformational fandom was prioritized. This raises the question: should other fans be ignored because what they "do with those texts" is not transformative?

Jenkins's statement was associated with a hypothesis that he offered to describe fans' motivations for transformational practice. More specifically, for Jenkins, media fandom is generally about fascination and frustration: "As I have already suggested, fan culture reflects both the audience's fascination with programs and fans' frustration over the refusal/inability of producers to tell the kinds of stories viewers want to see."[16] In other words, because the texts of popular culture do not quite measure up as satisfactory in the lives of dedicated fans, they remake them in their own image (for obsession_inc, "twisting it to the fans' own purposes"), for example, telling slash stories that transformed the masculinities of key characters by portraying unexpected intimacy between them. Jenkins reformulated his ideas for his book *Fans, Bloggers, Gamers* in 2006:

> [The metaphor of poaching] masked or distorted some significant aspects
> of the phenomenon, focusing on the frustration more than the fascination,

encouraging academics to read fan fiction primarily in political terms, and constructing a world in which producers and consumers remain locked in permanent opposition. My more recent work has been more focused on negotiations or collaboration as media industries embrace some still ill-formulated and often contradictory notion of audience participation.[17]

Both Jenkins's earlier formulations and his later ones posit transformative fan productivity as a natural and normal but distanced extension of engaging with the text. In other words, while critics practice a sufficient level of disinterested engagement to give them enough distance to stand in aesthetic judgment, fans embrace their texts on a more intimate level and naturally reach a point where their fascination meets frustration at the fact that the text does not quite suit. They complement it, in consequence, by creating various transformative works, which can be read, in effect, as evidence of their dedication. Beatles fanfic, however, does not necessarily emerge from frustration as a very specific form of affect. Neither is it necessarily an attempt to strictly maintain pleasures that emerge from fascination. To rephrase, it does not at least *read* like a series of reworkings of the Beatles story that *take issue* with the group as a source text. Instead, it often *plays* with the band members as established characters or further *extends* existing tendencies within the Beatles' celebrity images.

An alternative hypothesis to the frustration-motivation idea is that fanfic allows fans of celebrities to immerse themselves in the worlds of the objects they follow. In her study of fanfic writers who used Audrey Niffenegger's 2003 novel *The Time Traveler's Wife* and its 2009 movie adaption as their source of inspiration, Angela Lee found that, in addition to self-enrichment and escapism, fanfic writers cited motivations including personalization and celebration of media content, plus a desire to "stay a little longer" in the text. Some of these suggest transformation as a consequence of celebrity following: for fans who *also* pursue their fandom through practices related to it—watching, listening, collecting, discussing—writing fanfic may be a way to stay in the frame. As one fan explained:

> Writing and reading fanfiction is . . . a way to stay with a favourite story after it's over. Everyone knows what it's like to read a book and wish there were more of it. Fanfiction is a way to stay immersed in the story and character. Some good fanfiction is actually like reading a continuation of the story.[18]

This reading chimes with Kurt Lancaster's work on media fandom as the pursuit of immersion in a mythology or meaningful story universe.[19] In relation to music fandom, it reflects Dan Cavicchi's claim, "I've come to see fandom as a means of approaching consumption of the arts that involves obstinately remaining in the performance frame when it is no longer there."[20]. Where it loses some force, I think, is that there are *all sorts of other possible ways* to maintain immersion, including repeated consumption of the text, fan tourism, and simply being sociable with other fans. In other words, immersion does not account for the *specificity* of fanfic.

For a moment, let's entertain the idea that Beatles RPF and RPS are attempts by their music fans to "stay in the frame" of their performance and continually inhabit the mythology centered on the group. What is this mythology? *Help!* and *A Hard Day's Night* contributed to the band's cheery, moptop image. Creative albums (notably *Sgt. Pepper*) and films (such as *Yellow Submarine*) immersed fans in the group's colorful imaginative world. The story of the Beatles' public and private lives was well known, from Beatlemania and the Shea Stadium concert to Lennon's "bigger than Jesus" PR catastrophe and ongoing passion for Yoko Ono. Audiences also explored their own perspectives, one example of which was the persistent "Paul is Dead" rumor,[21] which was arguably a way to explore whether McCartney's musical talents mattered to the band. Given all these reference points, one might expect fanfic writers to have easy pickings, but this raises the issue of what they *do* with such narrative elements. In fact, excavation of the fanfic archive mentioned previously reveals that *Sgt. Pepper* is the basis for only four fanfic stories, and none of them is actually about the Beatles; instead, they use *Sgt. Pepper* as a creative template to write lyrics or otherwise shape prose forms that are about characters from other media products, such as the *Harry Potter* film series. Similar results were found by looking at uses of "Yellow Submarine" in fan stories—most of the 14 entries found were songs spoofing or parodying the Beatles' song but pertaining to other phenomena, from *Star Trek* to *SpongeBob SquarePants*. What this suggests, first, is that a proportion of the 1,500 "Beatles" fanfic stories on the site may have less to do with the Beatles, and, second, when writers do write about the Beatles, they are not necessarily using the material most obviously given to them by the band as an inspiration or creative resource.

Fanfic and the Quantum of Creativity

Returning to the territory of Jenkins's claims about fascination and frustra-tion, there seems something suspect about denying that there is a distinct-ness or specificity to the practice of fanfic writing. Distinctness is there, but rather than considering it an unproblematic expression of the personal and collective identities of the authors, my argument is that this difference is overridingly *formal*, something differently written into different narratives. Instead of a dichotomy separating transformational from affirmational fandom, perhaps we should be thinking carefully about the quantum of cre-ativity that transformational fandom necessarily entails. This quantum, in my view, is a central element that separates transformational practices from other types. It necessarily changes the meaning of the text, sometimes in ways that are controversial, especially in RPF. Attention to it, however, offers a different perspective on fanfic, because it helps us to see different kinds of fic as commensurate and—particularly for those who are less familiar with the form—helps to dispel the sensation of otherness that functions only to marginalize fanfic's more controversial subgenres.

In some types of fanfic, the quantum of creativity is built into the conventions of the story. This is the case, for example, in some Beatles fanfic stories that involve "time traveler" narratives. One of the interesting things about such stories is the way they comment on the predicament of contem-porary popular-music culture. Music critic Simon Reynolds has described this as an era of "retromania" in which commercially successful cultural forms from decades past are constantly repackaged.[22] Other critics such as Mark Fisher have more squarely rejected this situation. In his book *Capitalist Realism* (2009), Fisher suggested that the hyper-commodification of popular culture was responsible for its artistic stagnation. The glamor of each new phase of digital delivery masked an ongoing moment of creative stasis—a process typified in popular music by the constant reselling of back catalogs at the expense of promoting new artists. Fisher lamented, "Tradition counts for nothing when it is no longer contested and modified. A culture that is merely preserved is no culture at all."[23] While there is some merit in his cri-tique, it ignores how the audience uses recycled culture. Young audiences, in particular, are invited to do cultural work in embracing the present ubiq-uity of stars from past decades. For them, the process of reselling these stars effectively queers nostalgia, because it asks them to yearn for moments they could never have experienced. Borrowing a term from Reynolds, for example, Nuné Nikoghosyan posits a case of "nostalgia without nostalgia" in a study of young Beatles fans.[24] I have analyzed this circumstance using the idea of "imagined memories" in my own work. Here a moment of memory that young fans could never, by definition, have experienced becomes highly valued as the unobtainable basis for their desire. So, for example, due to their "imagined memories" of what it was like to be at the Cavern Club when the Beatles held court in the 1960s, vast numbers of younger fans desired to see McCartney play there again in 1999.[25] In Beatles fanfic, the ontological question of imagined memories is worked through in a subset of stories based on time-traveler narratives. The plot of one story is summarized as "Courtney suddenly finds herself to have time traveled to London in 1963, when she is from 49 years in the future, 2012. She encounters the Beatles, and they're kind enough to take her in, and she quickly makes friendships with them and one special bond. Will she want to go back to her home in the next century once she has an unforgettable relationship with one Beatle?" Such stories, which are a specific subset of "insertion fantasies"—stories in which fans meet their heroes[26]—do the cultural work of associating the popularity of the Beatles in the present with past experiences to which younger fans, by definition, could never have had access. We could read these stories as fantasies—wish-fulfillment dreams, in a Freudian sense—and to some extent, they are that. Considering them only as personal fancies, however, would be to ignore their function as logical responses to the broader cultural environment. In other words, time traveling becomes the quantum of creativity here precisely because, in a context of pervasive "retromania," a time bridge is necessary to address an acute experience of time out of joint. Nowadays, what immersion in Beatles music, videos, websites, CDs, or DVDs fulfills in one way increasingly common transformation practices fulfill in another.

"McLennon": (Ab)using an Aspect of the Celebrity Image

In slash, the quantum of creativity operates by positing a variety of often ambiguous homosocial or homosexual intimacies in male pairings. Given their close camaraderie, one might expect the Beatles to be prominent candidates for slash. Fanfic writers have played with a number of pairings based on amalgamations of the names of different members of the band. These include "McHarrison," "Lennison," "Lennstarr," "Starrison," and "John/Paul/George" (apparently, Beatles foursomes or threesomes featuring Starr are very rare). The most prominent Beatles slash pairing unites the two most prominent band members, however. This imagined relationship between McCartney and Lennon is known as "McLennon." One of the most famous stories about them is an epic with more than 40 chapters. In the "About Me" section of her own website, the author offers a time-traveler motive for her fanfic writing:

> I would so build a time machine so I could see them perform in concert, or so I could steal a kiss from Paul McCartney. Also so I could save George from lung cancer, save John from being shot, & make sure John & Yoko never ever meet each other.

By positing celebrity following as a premise for fanfic writing, this statement arguably appears to somewhat erode the distinction between celebrity following and transformational fandom, in effect positing one as a motive for the other. It also fails to exactly fit the idea of either expressing frustration at the text or desiring to stay within its frame. Embracing the quantum of creativity here allows the fan-author not so much to fix frustrations (although, I admit, it looks like that) but rather to *perfect* history in relation to her fannish desires. The difference is a subtle one; it rests on exactly what the fan wants to do. For example, seeing the Beatles in concert or kissing McCartney is not so much a matter of staying in the frame of performance as of enhancing its intimacy (i.e., creating an "insertion fantasy"). Saving Harrison and Lennon and scuppering Lennon's marriage are not so much about bemoaning what happened as inappropriate as about offering a kind of divine intervention, redemptive assistance that pushes history toward outcomes that other Beatles fans may well approve (in effect, in quite a similar way to obsession_inc's affirmational fandom, reinstating the source material to the fan community's satisfaction).

The background of the author's website contains a relatively tasteful cartoon picture of Lennon and McCartney having sex. There are also links to photographs of the writer and another female cosplayer playing at being Lennon and McCartney, coming together in a romantic embrace. What is interesting about the site is the way it raises the issue of queerness, not just in relation to sexuality but also in relation to the two types of fandom. That queerness is also reflected in the site's "About Me" section:

I live and breathe The Beatles, they've made me happier. I pretty much changed my whole image and appearance to look like a '64 version of Paul McCartney, moptop era bitches! . . . I'M A BEATLEMANIAC FOR LIFE!! So I think it's safe to say that I'm madly in love with The Beatles & everything about them; from their sexy suits, to their adorable smiles, down to their amazing voices. . . . I really love John/Paul. I absolutely adore this couple. So fricken much. There's just something about them that makes me smile, as much as when I listen to any song from The Beatles.

If the quantum of creativity in such Beatles slash pushes the intimacy between band members beyond homosocial camaraderie, who is responsible? On one level, it is easy to dismiss slash on textual grounds. Fans interested in fidelity might protest that Lennon and McCartney were straight and never had erotic moments with each other, but slash writers' passions and desires are not quite as inventive as one might suggest. Claims about a breach of textual fidelity ignore a certain tendency, particularly in the moptop-era image. Like other fans, the fanfic author is "madly in love" with the Beatles and finds McCartney, especially, adorable. Her interest in Lennon and McCartney playing music together references a close male camaraderie. Various products in the Beatles' heyday, such as the Richard Lester films *Help!* and *A Hard Day's Night*, deliberately cultivated their image as cheeky, accessible lads from Liverpool enjoying a close friendship in the heart of swinging London. As Martin King has noted, the group offered a softer, new, 1960s form of masculinity to female fans:

The discussion presented so far is built on the premise that "The Beatles" can be read as the representation of an alternative version of masculinity . . . one which values creativity and the intellectual above the mundane and the physical, one which involves colour and an "outrageous" appearance as a contrast to smart sobriety, with long hair as a symbol of defiance. It is a version of masculinity, which values the child-like above the norms of adult society and values fun and exuberance over the serious. . . . The Beatles' engagement with the female and the "feminized" became part of their appeal, part of their representation of alternative masculinities, and, thus, the female/feminine became a positive rather than a negative concept within "The Beatles" as text. As one interviewee in the author's PhD study remarked, at the beginning of the film *A Hard Day's Night* (1964) they are "running like big daft girls," away from female fans rather than chasing after women.

King adds:

> The dressed-by-Brian look of *A Hard Day's Night* (1964) combined with the queer codes at work in this film and *Help!* (1965) . . . and their general "to-be-looked-at-ness" . . ., at work in all of the films, add weight to the arguments about alternative versions of masculinity. Authors . . . have emphasised that it is hard to understand, in retrospect, just how shocking and subversive this actually seemed and what an impact it had on "establishment" values in the 1960s.[27]

In other words, a central part of the Beatles' appeal was that they rejected established masculinity in favor of a softer, more feminized look, which had its counterpart in them being actively objectified by their female followers.

On a site dedicated to McLennon, one visitor wrote that their dad was a huge Beatles fan but thought McLennon "the most idiotic thing to come from the Beatles fandom." The site owner replied, "I'm not sure if you view McLennon as a RELATIONSHIP or just a friendship with deeper connection. . . . But talk about how they're the greatest writers in history and how they truly were so powerful around each other." This slippage between "just a friendship" and an erotic relationship suggests that the variety of slash can be placed on a spectrum that effectively queers the Beatles' famous camaraderie. At this point, it may be worth drawing a parallel. Discussing the cinema of Pedro Almodóvar for *Senses of Cinema*, Steven Marsh has explained:

> His obsessive concern with the fluidity of genders, the interchangeability of sexual tastes and orientations, his constant interrogation of discrete sexual identities has disappointed certain militant gay activists who, for political reasons, evidently would prefer a clearer—and less ambiguous—definition of sexual identity (and would also like to have seen Almodóvar take a stance in favour of gay rights). The point is an important one, Almodóvar's characters are never exclusively heterosexual or homosexual, instead they perform their identities and thus are identifiable by what they choose to be at any particular moment.[28]

I include this because I think that perhaps we can talk about a kind of "Almodovarian Beatles" consisting of musicians who are "never exclusively heterosexual or homosexual, [but] instead they perform their identities" primarily to evoke the erotic curiosity of a female audience. This formulation of the Beatles' celebrity image raises questions of authorship. One gets the impression that the band was packaged to tease, but the Beatles' degree of complicity remains open to question: although they appeared conveniently hapless at the time, they later rebelled against such packaging, with Lennon famously singing that he did not "believe in Beatles" in his 1970 song "God." Whoever co-created the Almodovarian Beatles, their packaging in the 1960s struck a nerve just as raw as Elvis Presley's hip movements had done in the 1950s. Barbara Ehrenreich, Elizabeth Hess, and Gloria Jacobs, however, discussed these fans' responses:

> For the girls who participated in Beatlemania, sex was an obvious part of the excitement. One of the most common responses to reporters' queries on the sources of Beatlemania was, "Because they're sexy." And this explanation was itself a small act of defiance. It was rebellious (especially for the very young fans) to lay claim to sexual feelings. It was even more rebellious to lay claim to the active, desiring side of sexual attraction: the Beatles were objects; the girls were pursuers.[29]

These authors emphasized, "The Beatles were sexy; the girls were the ones who perceived them as sexy and acknowledged the force of an ungovernable, if somewhat disembodied, lust. To assert an active, powerful sexuality . . . was, in its own, unformulated, dizzy way, revolutionary."[30] Ehrenreich and her coauthors' work rests on a generalization, that primarily it was girls who liked the band and that their expressed interest was primary lustful, and on an interpretation, that this collectively expressed lust was rebellious and therefore progressive in a feminist sense. If we accept those things, what it shows is that the erotic performances and fannish counter-performances evoked by the band were there well before contemporary fanfic writers used them. The irony is that if many of the original 1960s Beatles fans were female, comparatively few of *their* practices at the time were transformational in any obvious sense. By considering the McLennon slash pairing, I have suggested that when the quantum of creativity is added to the Beatles' moptop image, it pushes a tendency already in the celebrity image a step further along its existing trajectory. In other words, the queering of the band's image was not simply a fannish construct but was instead a tendency in the group's moptop-era styling, pushed further by those who embraced the quantum of creativity.

McLennon writers have sometimes publicized their identities as celebrity-following Beatles fans. Hence, another blog, on Tumblr, begins by explaining that the author is a female Beatles fan who, like "every girl," has her own sexual needs. Equally, though it could have been a move motivated to defuse criticism, a site previously mentioned includes links to Beatles music, suggesting, again, that she is a celebrity-following fan *as well as* a transformative one, and in her mind there is no difference. These performances of celebrity fandom are interesting because—whether such fans are "genuine" celebrity followers or not—the idea that they feel the need to *perform* their celebrity following suggests that it functions as a kind of authenticating device, perhaps in the face of disapproval from outsiders. It implies that one can be a casual Beatles fanfic writer without doing much celebrity following, but perhaps a performance of celebrity following can signify the passion and research necessary to be recognized as a dedicated Beatles fanfic specialist.

McCartney announced in an interview for *GQ* magazine in September 2018 that he and fellow Beatles had been casually involved in a lights-out session of collective fantasizing and group masturbation. Participants shouted, "Brigitte Bardot!" for inspiration, until Lennon spoiled the mood by proclaiming, "Winston Churchill!"[31] Winston was Lennon's middle name; it was as if by bringing the fantasy so close to home, he was extinguishing the flame of sexual intimacy. This apparently true story suggests that the Beatles *were* close enough to share a sexual moment, just not one in which they were thinking about one another. On the surface, the scenario sounds tailor-made for a slash story, but as of 2018, there is none evident in the archive. It would require fanfic writers to add something extra to make it work: the quantum of creativity. In this chapter, I have argued against fully separating fanfic writing as a unique practice, making a strict division between transformational and affirmational fan identities, or assuming that frustration or "staying in frame" are obvious motivations for all fanfic writing. Instead, I have argued for much greater specificity in describing the overlapping roles of celebrity following and fanfic writing, suggesting that celebrity following is an independent activity that *can* act as a premise for transformational activity depending on immediate cultural circumstances. Finally, I have introduced the idea that fanfic writing is actually about accepting the need to use a quantum of creativity to make the partial but necessary departure from textual fidelity that allows the form to actually exist. Each shared quantum of creativity can be productively examined on a case-by-case basis, in terms of what shape it takes, what affordances it produces for particular communities, and what it might say about the cultural work pursued by fanfic writers, in some instances in relation to their celebrity-following practices.

Notes

1. In service of fanfic writers' general preferences to maintain low visibility, following researchers such as Catherine Hoad, I have withheld story titles and authors' names to protect their privacy. Catherine Hoad, "Slashing through the Boundaries: Heavy Metal Fandom, Fan Fiction and Girl Cultures," *Metal Music Studies* 3, no. 1 (2017): 12.
2. Henry Jenkins, *Convergence Culture: Where Old and New Media Collide* (New York: New York University Press, 2006), 2.
3. I have made the site anonymous here; my interest is in the general pattern of the data, not in contravening copyright or reproducing site content.
4. Kristina Busse, "My Life Is a WP on My LJ: Slashing the Slasher and the Reality of Celebrity and Internet Performances," in *Fan Fiction and Fan Communities in the Age of the Internet: New Essays*, ed. Karen Hellekson and Kristina Busse (Jefferson, NC: McFarland, 2006), 207.
5. Abigail De Kosnik, *Rogue Archives: Digital Cultural Memory and Media Fandom* (Cambridge, MA: MIT Press, 2016), 148.
6. Sheenagh Pugh, *The Democratic Genre: Fan Fiction in Literary Context* (Bridgend, UK: Seren, 2005), 36.
7. Kristina Busse, "'I'm Jealous of the Fake Me': Postmodern Subjectivity and Identity Construction in Boy Band Fan Fiction," in *Framing Celebrity: New Directions in Celebrity Culture*, ed. Su Holmes and Sean Redmond (New York: Routledge, 2006), 263.
8. Kristina Busse, "Intimate Intertextualities and Performative Fragments in Media Fan Fiction," in *Fandom: Identities and Communities in a Mediated World*, 2nd ed., ed. Johnathan Gray, Cornel Sandvoss, and C. Lee Harrington (New York: New York University Press, 2017), 55.
9. Busse, "Intimate Intertextualities," 53.
10. Busse, "Intimate Intertextualities," 55, 57.
11. Busse, "Intimate Intertextualities," 52.
12. Obsession_inc, "Affirmational Fandom vs Transformational Fandom," June 1, 2009, http://obsession-inc.dreamwidth.org/82589.html.
13. See, for example, Kristina Busse, "Geek Hierarchies, Boundary Policing and the Gendering of the Good Fan," *Participations* 10, no. 1 (2013): 82.

14. Cornel Sandvoss, *Fans: The Mirror of Consumption* (Cambridge: Polity, 2005), 127.
15. Henry Jenkins, *Textual Poachers: Television Fans and Participatory Culture* (New York: Routledge, 1992), 284.
16. Jenkins, *Textual Poachers*, 162.
17. Henry Jenkins, *Fans, Bloggers, Gamers: Exploring Participatory Culture* (New York: New York University Press, 2006), 37.
18. Quoted in Angela Lee, "Time Traveling with Fanfic Writers: Understanding Fan Culture through Repeated Online Interviews," *Participations* 8, no. 1 (2011): 254.
19. Kurt Lancaster, *Interacting with Babylon 5: Performance in a Media Universe* (Austin: University of Texas Press, 2001).
20. In Nancy Baym, Daniel Cavicchi, and Norma Coates, "Music Fandom in a Digital Age: A Conversation," in *The Routledge Companion to Media Fandom*, ed. Melissa Click and Susanne Scott (New York: Routledge, 2018), 142.
21. Devin McKinney, *Magic Circles: The Beatles in Dream and History* (Cambridge, MA: Harvard University Press, 2003), 273.
22. Simon Reynolds, *Retromania: Pop Culture's Addiction to Its Own Past*. London: Faber and Faber, 2012.
23. Mark Fisher, *Capitalist Realism: Is There No Alternative?* (Ropley, UK: Zer0, 2009), 3.
24. Nuné Nikoghosyan, "'But Who Doesn't Know the Beatles Anyway?': Young Fans of New Beatlemania Today," in *Keep It Simple, Make It Fast: An Approach to Underground Music Scenes*, Vol. 1, ed. Paula Guerra and Tânia Moreira (Porto, Portugal: University of Porto, 2015), 581.
25. Mark Duffett, "Imagined Memories: Webcasting as a 'Live' Technology and the Case of Little Big Gig," *Information, Communication and Society* 6, no. 3 (2003): 307–325, https://doi.org/10.1080/1369118032000155267.
26. Busse, "'I'm Jealous of the Feke Me,'" 256.
27. Martin King, "It Was 50 Years Ago Today: Reading the Beatles as a Challenge to Discourses of Hegemonic Masculinity," *Sociology Study* 4, no. 1 (2014): 48–49 (source citations omitted).
28. Steven Marsh, "Great Directors: Pedro Almodóvar," *Senses of Cinema* 40, July 2006, http://sensesofcinema.com/2006/great-directors/almodovar/.
29. Barbara Ehrenreich, Elizabeth Hess, and Gloria Jacobs, "Beatlemania: Girls Just Want to Have Fun," in *The Adoring Audience*, ed. Lisa Lewis (London: Routledge, 1992), 90.
30. Ehrenreich, Hess, and Jacobs, "Beatlemania," 90.
31. Chris Heath, "The Untold Stories of Paul McCartney," *GQ*, September 11, 2018, XX, https://www.gq.com/story/the-untold-stories-of-paul-mccartney.

Bibliography

Baym, Nancy, Daniel Cavicchi, and Norma Coates. "Music Fandom in a Digital Age: A Conversation." In *The Routledge Companion to Media Fandom*, edited by Melissa Click and Susanne Scott, 141–152. New York: Routledge, 2018.

Busse. Kristina. "Geek Hierarchies, Boundary Policing and the Gendering of the Good Fan." Participations 10, no. 1 (2013): 73–91.

Busse, Kristina. "'I'm Jealous of the Fake Me': Postmodern Subjectivity and Identity Construction in Boy Band Fan Fiction." In Framing Celebrity: New Directions in Celebrity Culture, edited by Su Holmes and Sean Redmond, 253–268. New York: Routledge, 2006.

Busse, Kristina. "Intimate Intertextualities and Performative Fragments in Media Fan Fiction." In Fandom: Identities and Communities in a Mediated World, 2nd ed., edited by Johnathan Gray, Cornel Sandvoss, and C. Lee Harrington, 45–59. New York: New York University Press, 2017.

Busse, Kristina. "My Life Is a WP on My LJ: Slashing the Slasher and the Reality of Celebrity and Internet Performances." In Fan Fiction and Fan Communities in the Age of the Internet: New Essays, edited by Karen Hellekson and Kristina Busse, 207–224. Jefferson, NC: McFarland, 2006.

De Kosnik, Abigail. Rogue Archives: Digital Cultural Memory and Media Fandom. Cambridge, MA: MIT Press, 2016.

Duffett, Mark. "Imagined Memories: Webcasting as a 'Live' Technology and the Case of Little Big Gig." Information, Communication and Society 6, no. 3 (2003): 307–325. https://doi.org/10.1080/1369118032000155267.

Ehrenreich, Barbara, Elizabeth Hess, and Gloria Jacobs. "Beatlemania: Girls Just Want to Have Fun." In The Adoring Audience, edited by Lisa Lewis, 84–106. London: Routledge, 1992.

Fisher, Mark. Capitalist Realism: Is There No Alternative? Ropley: Zer0, 2009.

Heath, Chris. "The Untold Stories of Paul McCartney." GQ, September 11, 2018. https://www.gq.com/story/the-untold-stories-of-paul-mccartney.

Hoad, Catherine. "Slashing through the Boundaries: Heavy Metal Fandom, Fan Fiction and Girl Cultures." Metal Music Studies 3, no. 1 (2017): 5–22. https://doi.org/10.1386/mms.3.1.5_1.

Jenkins, Henry. Convergence Culture: Where Old and New Media Collide. New York: New York University Press, 2006.

Jenkins, Henry. Fans, Bloggers, Gamers: Exploring Participatory Culture. New York: New York University Press, 2006.

Jenkins, Henry. Textual Poachers: Television Fans and Participatory Culture. New York: Routledge, 1992.

King, Martin. "It Was 50 Years Ago Today: Reading the Beatles as a Challenge to Discourses of Hegemonic Masculinity." Sociology Study 4, no. 1 (2014): 44–51.

Lancaster, Kurt. Interacting with Babylon 5: Performance in a Media Universe. Austin: University of Texas Press, 2001.

Lee, Angela. "Time Traveling with Fanfic Writers: Understanding Fan Culture through Repeated Online Interviews." Participations 8, no. 1 (2011): 246–269.

Marsh, Steven. "Great Directors: Pedro Almodóvar." Senses of Cinema 40, July 2006. http://sensesofcinema.com/2006/great-directors/almodovar/.

McKinney, Devin. Magic Circles: The Beatles in Dream and History. Cambridge, MA: Harvard University Press, 2003.

Nikoghosyan, Nuné. "'But Who Doesn't Know the Beatles Anyway?': Young Fans of New Beatlemania Today." In Keep It Simple, Make It Fast: An Approach to Underground Music Scenes, Vol. 1, edited by Paula Guerra and Tânia Moreira, 573–584. Porto, Portugal: University of Porto, 2015.

Obsession_inc. "Affirmational Fandom vs Transformational Fandom." June 1, 2009. http://obsession-inc.dreamwidth.org/82589.html.

Pugh, Sheenagh. *The Democratic Genre: Fan Fiction in Literary Context*. Bridgend, UK: Seren, 2005.

Reynolds, Simon. *Retromania: Pop Culture's Addiction to Its Own Past*. London: Faber and Faber, 2012.

Sandvoss, Cornel. *Fans: The Mirror of Consumption*. Cambridge: Polity, 2005.

PART III
TOMORROW

8

The Beatles

Today . . . and Tomorrow

Kenneth L. Campbell

One Christmas morning, a young boy named Austin Staulcup woke up to find, as many young boys and girls did that Christmas, that one of his presents was an interactive electronic game called "Beatles Rock Band." Staulcup is currently a student in a Monmouth University course I teach on the Beatles, and he recently wrote in an essay that for months thereafter, he devoted all his free time "playing that game, learning every song beat by beat in order for the controls to hit on time with each song." He continued, "Playing every aspect of the songs, from the perspective of all of the different instruments, really engrained every beat of the songs in my mind through the muscle memory of tapping the controls." However, Staulcup admitted that it was not only because he liked playing the Beatles' music on Rock Band that made the group and its music so special to him; it was also "the nostalgia of enjoying the music with my grandparents [that] really inspired my love for the group's music, and has contributed to that remaining the case today."[1]

I have taught a course on the Beatles to first-year students at Monmouth for the past decade and have come to realize that the Beatles are not just part of the past to the students who take my course; the Beatles are part of *their* past. They are just as capable of feeling nostalgic for the role the Beatles played in their childhood as baby boomers have always been regarding the Beatles since the early 1970s. For instance, Abby Moskow wrote:

> My parents introducing me to the Beatles as a child gave me a taste of quality music and may have been the very start of my ever-developing music taste. I still listen to songs like "Let It Be" and "Here Comes the Sun" when I miss my family and my childhood. They make me feel nostalgic and feel like I'm back in my old house with my whole family.[2]

Kenneth L. Campbell, *The Beatles* In: *Fandom and the Beatles*. Edited by: Kenneth Womack and Kit O'Toole, Oxford University Press (2021). © Oxford University Press. DOI: 10.1093/oso/9780190917852.003.0009

Bryan Derr explained that although his favorite songs are Leonard Cohen's "Hallelujah" and Pink Floyd's "Wish You Were Here," the only other songs capable of evoking similar feelings for him are the Beatles' "Yesterday" and "Let It Be," both of which his parents introduced to him at a young age. However, he also remembered hearing *Rubber Soul* constantly playing in his fourth-grade art class and still knew all the lyrics to each song on the album. Both Moskow and Derr had just started college in September 2019. Another student, Julian Rebelo, like many first-generation Beatles fans, said he found the Beatles' later work, beginning with *Rubber Soul*, more meaningful than their earlier work. He attached special significance to "Michelle," which he remembered his mother singing in the car, and *Abbey Road*, which "would become the soundtrack to my summers; my window open, a cool breeze flowing in, the beautiful lyricism of [the album] pouring out into the great beyond, me not having a care to who could hear it."[3] Natalie Lopez said she had trouble bonding with her father when she was younger, until they took a road trip together, listened to Beatles songs, and discovered suddenly that they actually shared a common taste in music. She wrote, "I was able to develop such a love for this music in a measly few days and experienced a completely changed mindset. I felt like a new person, because only a few days earlier, I had been renouncing music not created during the 2000s."[4] Ruth Mandel, who grew up in the late 1950s and 1960s, told me a similar story of long car rides when her now-23-year-old daughter was still a child. She said that when they started listening to the Beatles, her daughter "was enraptured, and it got to the point where she knew every song on every album and which number it was on the tape deck."[5] For 18-year-old Sofia Cassese, it was not a relative but her boyfriend who convinced her that the Beatles had more to offer than just the few of their well-known songs such as "Yesterday," "Hey Jude," and "I Want to Hold Your Hand," with which she was familiar. She had fond memories of dancing in her kitchen with her boyfriend to "All My Loving," which she now considered their song.[6]

Mine is hardly the only Beatles course offered at colleges and universities. Students can take courses on the Beatles at Duke University, Texas Christian University, the University of Vermont, Ohio State University, and the University of Southern California, among a multitude of others.[7] For students enrolled in those courses, the Beatles will always carry an association with their college years. Even students who did not have strong memories of the Beatles before taking my course discover something new that will now stay with them for the rest of their lives. For example, Gabriella Herbert related the following incident that occurred during the fall 2019 semester:

> One morning, I was commuting to school, and I began listening to the Beatles' first album, *Please Please Me*, as it was an assignment. I was driving on my usual route when I suddenly realized my exit was closed. In a situation like this, I would usually panic. However, having the Beatles' music playing calmed me down and allowed me to find my way to class with ease. Ever since this event, I have used the Beatles' music as a way to lower my anxiety. Through using the Beatles this way, I have come upon truly amazing and influential songs.[8]

Noel Gᴇasser, in his 2019 book *Why You Like It: The Science and Culture of Musical Taste*, notes that "musical engagement helps heal and succor the body when something goes wrong."[9] He cites a number of research studies to support this assertion, but this reality is something that people seem instinctively to learn from an early age, especially when they discover particular examples of music that have this effect. At the age of 18, Catherine Melman-Kenny had already realized the beneficial effects of certain Beatles songs in this regard. She wrote:

> Songs like "Here Comes the Sun" and "Hey Jude" have always struck me as wonderful. I had always recognized the simple genius of [the former], how it would make one's problems feel like they were slipping away along with the winter George Harrison sings about. With such a simple song, a perfect image of light returning to one's life is made. "Hey Jude" was always one of the most perfect songs to play when feeling down. The harmonies at the ending "na-na-nas" give the feeling that a group of people is supporting you, that you are not alone, and [that] can fix a bad day for me.[10]

In a similar vein, Jordan Bachman wrote:

> whenever I am down, I can just put on some Beatles tunes and instantly feel better. [When listening to] songs like "Lady Madonna" or "Good Day Sunshine," I feel instantly better, because the music is bright, and the lyrics are upbeat and make you smile and want to sing along with them. . . . Songs like "Let It Be" and "Yesterday" put a deep notion about things going on in your life, and you can feel that.[11]

One of the points I have stressed in these classes, especially with first-year college students, is how many valuable life lessons they can learn from the experiences and music of the Beatles. Lennon, McCartney, Harrison, and Starr experienced the same struggles, difficulties, growing pains, and personal decisions about love, marriage, career, success, lifestyle choices, and personal identity that everyone does in their late teens and 20s, even if they did so while playing in the most famous rock band in the world. Herbert especially took to heart Lennon's song "I'm a Loser," which, she wrote, helped her "to realize many people in society put on a front. They hide who they truly are and attempt to appear to be better. Although this song is highly pessimistic, John is accepting who he thinks he is, which goes against the norm of society." In today's performance-oriented culture, in which young people in particular feel pressure always to present their best selves on social media and pretend everything is perfect in their lives, this strikes me as a particularly powerful realization. To Herbert, Lennon's willingness to give fans insight into how he might really feel constitutes "the appealing nature of the Beatles."[12] Lopez wrote, "Hardship and challenges are still experienced in life by nearly all, and the Beatles experienced their fair share of challenges and reflected on these difficulties through their songs. Many listen to their songs in order to feel comfort and to feel that they are not alone."[13]

For those born shortly before or after the turn of the 21st century, the Beatles have come to them not only through introduction by parents or older relatives but also through the Beatles' continued presence in contemporary popular culture. One could argue that the Beatles now belong as much to the popular culture of 2021 as they did to that of their own decade of the '60s. In recent years, I had a wave of students who said they became interested in the Beatles because of the 2007 film *Across the Universe*. Ten years from now, I can imagine students enrolling in courses on the Beatles when they get to college because the 2019 film *Yesterday* had inspired their interest in the group and its music. Current students, as part of the YouTube generation, have also taken special note of James Corden's episode of *Carpool Karaoke* filmed with McCartney in Liverpool.

In *Yesterday*, screenwriter Richard Curtis and director Danny Boyle combined to present a vision of what the contemporary world might be like if no one had ever heard of the Beatles. Why exactly this alternative reality had occurred Curtis and Boyle leave largely to the viewer's imagination, but the film nonetheless becomes a vehicle for imagining how people would respond if they heard the Beatles' music for the first time in 2019. In the film, a bus strikes the main character, Jack Malik (played by Himesh Patel) at the exact moment when some kind of electrical surge causes a power failure that ends up altering reality. In this parallel universe, almost no one knows about the existence of the Beatles—except for Jack, who decides to pass off some of their most popular songs as his own. The concept of the film provides the backdrop for a belated and apparently long-overdue romance between Jack and his childhood friend and current manager (played by Lily James). Plausibility and realism are neither the film's strengths nor its intended goals. It asks the viewer to accept a number of premises that it does not bother to explain and relies on the romantic plot line and the strength of the acting to keep viewers' minds from wandering down any of the rabbit holes in which they might feel abandoned. However, other problems exist with the concept of the film itself that have much to do with the topic of this chapter.

First, it ignores the fact that many young Beatles fans will, in fact, hear or discover the Beatles and their music for the first time in 2019, as has happened in every year since the band burst onto the music scene in 1963 in Britain and 1964 in the United States. This will no doubt continue to be the case for the indefinite future. How is the reaction of young people in the film to hearing Beatles' songs for the first time, then, different from what already happens on a daily basis, without having to resort to such a fanciful construct? The obvious answer is that in the film, the Beatles do not perform their own songs, yet we are led to believe that the contemporary response to the songs would be just as enthusiastic if performed by a sincere but obscure second-rate singer-songwriter. Thus, the film implies that the Beatles' songs would be popular in any era simply because they are great songs and would succeed no matter who sang them (provided the singer has at least a modicum of talent) or the context in which listeners hear them. In other words, it ignores the question of whether young people today continue to respond to the Beatles because of the songs themselves or because of the way the Beatles sang and performed them.

Furthermore, these questions themselves raise an even more serious problem with the main concept of the film, in that while it removes the Beatles' entire catalog from the popular-music lexicon, it does not remove all of those groups that were influenced by the Beatles, without whom the entire history of popular music would have unfolded quite differently. As music historian and cultural critic Chuck Klosterman has put it, "The Beatles defined the concept of what a 'rock group' was supposed to be, and all subsequent rock groups are (consciously or unconsciously) modeled upon the template they naturally embodied."[14] Thus, when teenagers today hear the Beatles, they recognize the style of music and certain things about it, especially if they are musicians or play an instrument, as many of my students do. If they were to hear, as happens in the film, a solo artist playing "I Want to Hold Your Hand" on an acoustic guitar, they might like it, but they would not hear the song as the one into which the Beatles poured their energies, transforming it into an electrifying musical experience. Similarly, when I play the two versions of "While My Guitar Gently Weeps" on *The Beatles* (the *White Album*) and from *The Beatles Anthology*, most students like the *White Album* version better, even though, to my ears, the acoustic version is more hauntingly beautiful in and of itself. I think they prefer the former because it has a familiarity with which they are comfortable, whether they had previously heard the song or not. In short, while the original Beatles fans loved their music because they had never heard anything like it before, third- and fourth-generation fans like it because it somehow sounds familiar to them, even if they listen to individual Beatles songs for the first time. "Eleanor Rigby," such a departure from anything the Beatles had done before their 1966 album *Revolver*, fits well with any number of contemporary folk-rock artists who do not shy away from emotional and meaningful lyrical content.

The film ignores one other issue with importance for an exploration of the relationship between the Beatles' past and their present and future: the cover songs performed and recorded by the Beatles early in their career. For example, to take the premise of the film more seriously than perhaps the writer and the director intended it should be, the Isley Brothers' "Twist and Shout" would have still existed without the Beatles, but would the song still be as widely known without the Beatles' cover version? I would suggest not, based on the numbers of times in my life I have heard the Beatles' version on the radio or at sports venues compared to the numbers of times I have heard the Isley Brothers' version, which I find myself having to make a conscious decision to play if I ever want to hear the original. Most of my students, when I ask them to identify the cover songs and the original songs on the album *Please Please Me*, are shocked to hear that "Twist and Shout" was a cover song and not a Beatles original. This fact alone suggests that the appeal of the Beatles went beyond the appeal of their songs but depended on the way they performed them in particular, however many admirable cover versions of Beatles songs there might be.

This is not to say that *Yesterday* will not serve a useful function of introducing a new generation to the music of the Beatles, particularly very young viewers of the film. It has demonstrated the continued relevance and appeal of the Beatles today, even if it has proven a qualified disappointment to critics and audiences alike. It is an enjoyable enough film, but most of the college students I have asked about it have told me that they did not particularly care for it.

Corden's video of *Carpool Karaoke* with McCartney is a different matter. So many people, of all ages, have asked me if I have seen the video, and they all are enthusiastic about it. More than 30 million people have watched the video on YouTube. It seems to appeal to young viewers with limited knowledge about or interest in the Beatles as much as it does to lifelong Beatle fans. In the video, Corden and McCartney visit sites around Liverpool associated with McCartney's life and music, such as Penny Lane and the home where he grew up, ending with a surprise live musical appearance by McCartney at a pub, where he performs some of the Beatles' best-known songs. After watching the video and noting the joy on the faces of people of vastly differing ages, my student Marissa Berkowitz wrote, "There is something about their music that is revolutionary and that creates a connection between all generations. Nowadays, I feel as though older adults and today's teenagers may not understand each other, but we can all agree on how revolutionary The Beatles are."[15] When the episode first appeared, television critic David Bianculli wrote, "Few things on TV or the Internet can generate as much pure joy as a solid Carpool Karaoke segment. But even by those standards, a new one showcasing Sir Paul McCartney stands above all others."[16] James Parker wrote in the *Atlantic*, "If you watched McCartney recently on James Corden's 'Carpool Karaoke,' doing a nostalgia tour of Liverpool with his host blushing and chirping at the wheel, you'll have seen how people—young, old, of every shape and color—respond to him."[17] Bianculli compared the episode to the rooftop concert at Savile Row at the end of the *Let It Be* sessions and to the Beatles' first appearance on the *Ed Sullivan Show*, commenting that 54 years after that cultural milestone, "Paul McCartney is still making exciting, unforgettable television."

In recent years, the Beatles' legacy has also continued to thrive because of intelligent and strategic marketing that has offered new ways to experience the Beatles, even for their longtime fans. The Beatles entered the 21st century with a compilation CD of their number one hits, appropriately titled *1*, which sold more than 31 million copies worldwide. It outsold every other CD in the first decade of the century and in 2015 was still selling 1,000 copies a week.[18] In 2010, after a long delay in making the Beatles' catalog available in digitized form, Apple relented and gave its subscribers full access. In just one week, listeners purchased 450,000 albums and more than 2 million individual songs, sales worth about $800,000.[19] In 2015, Apple released a DVD, also called *1*, which contains original video footage of the Beatles performing or set to many of their hits. Kenneth Womack has attributed part of the Beatles' enduring appeal to the way they "have branded themselves extremely well, establishing their name as representative of a blue-chip musical corpus waiting to be discovered by new legions of listeners with each passing year."[20]

Yet, as Womack indicates, merchandising and marketing can only go so far to explain the Beatles' continuing appeal. For without the strength of the original material, fans simply would not buy the new products. Even more astonishing and promising for the future of the Beatles and their continuing cultural presence is how well the old products still sell. By 2014, the Beatles had sold an astonishing 1.6 billion singles just in the United States.[21] Before 2019, had even ended, listeners had streamed 1.7 billion Beatles songs on Spotify, 30% of them by subscribers between the ages of 18 and 24.[22] The past five years have witnessed a number of anniversary releases and celebrations 50 years after the height of the Beatles' fame and popularity, including an expanded, deluxe version of 1969's *Abbey Road* in 2019. Yet it was the original *Abbey Road* album that reached number one on the *Billboard* charts for the week of October 12.[23] In doing so, the album broke a Guinness World Record for longest time before returning to the top of the charts, its return coming 49 years and 252 days after it dropped from the number one slot.[24]

At the same time, the super-deluxe edition allows listeners to experience the music from *Abbey Road* in new ways, helping to keep the music fresh while simultaneously expanding an appreciation for the original. As rock critic Rob Sheffield wrote in his engaging book *Dreaming the Beatles*, "There's no sense they belong to the past, because they don't. The Beatles sell a million albums a year—the closest rock band is Led Zeppelin, at 800,000, then Pink Floyd and Fleetwood Mac at about half that."[25]

When I asked people from the baby boom generation about the continuing relevance of the Beatles, many of them expressed doubt and uncertainty. Stanton Green, a professor of anthropology at Monmouth University, for example, told me that in his experience talking with students, he did not think the Beatles were "on their radar."[26] The evidence presented in this chapter, however, would seem to bear out better the assumption of Tom Noce (a fan who has followed the Beatles since the 1960s) who told me he thought the Beatles remained relevant "because of their messages of harmony and peace," continuing, "I think they are getting played more than we think they are."[27] Wade Lawrence, the director and senior curator at the Museum at Bethel Woods, the site of 1969's Woodstock festival, expressed some reservations about the appeal of some of the Beatles' music to young people but also said "most of their music is timeless." He thought Lennon's experimental songs might resonate particularly well, along with some of the music of Harrison, which "has that complexity and has that grit that young people can get their hands around."[28] Robin Levine, who attended Woodstock, cited "While My Guitar Gently Weeps" and "Blackbird" as examples of songs "that if you just listen to the words, you are given something to think about, while the musicality, the harmonies, the musicianship [are] still magnificent to listen to."[29] Nick Ercoline, who, along with his soon-to-be-wife, Bobbi, appeared as the famous "couple in the blanket" on the original *Woodstock* album cover, observed that "if you can take music at the time when it was created and if you can apply it toward what is going on today it certainly is relevant. I actually think that a lot of the stuff that the Beatles did is relevant—absolutely."[30] David Scher, a retired financial adviser in Baltimore who also attended Woodstock in 1969, professed curiosity about so many young people being aware of the Beatles 50 years later.[31] Jane Barnes said, "As a college professor, I mention the Beatles once in a while, and everybody seemed to know their songs and they just seemed to be timeless."[32] Marbie Foster, another Woodstock attendee with whom I spoke, pointed to the continued popularity of McCartney today, while also observing that anyone interested in the history of rock and roll of whatever age had to take account of the Beatles, who "changed rock and roll music" and "changed the way young people think."[33] Tom Blazucki called attention to the immediate availability of the Beatles to young people through YouTube and their phones, access that the baby boom generation did not have to past artists when they grew up from the 1950s through the 1970s.[34] Rebecca Duncan simply stated, "If you are serious about music, the Beatles will always be relevant."[35] As she wrote in an op-ed piece on the influence of the Fab Four, "The Beatles expressed many creative impulses, and their combined work lifts them beyond the extremes of any single jag that they chose to explore."[36]

Many members of Generation Z have echoed the sentiments of the baby boomers about the continued relevance of the Beatles. Lopez wrote she believes that "the fundamental core values or life experiences people shared during that time are still being experienced by today's generations. For example, people still value love, and many spend their entire lives searching for it. The Beatles tend to preach love in their music."[37] In 2018, I organized a session for several students to speak at a conference commemorating the 50th anniversary of the *White Album*. Katherine Fernandez, a junior music industry major at Monmouth at the time who described herself as "a Beatles fanatic practically since birth," said, "the attack on greed and materialism [in the song 'Piggies'] still applies just as much (if not more) in today's society." She thought young people today could relate to "Happiness Is a Warm Gun" because of their current concerns with school shootings in the United States.[38]

Raymond Laux, a multi-instrumentalist who performs in the band Malibu and another music industry major at Monmouth, performed a hauntingly beautiful solo acoustic rendition of that song. It sounded as if he could have written it in 2018, because of his investment in the song and topicality of the lyrics. Justin Szuba, a student-athlete majoring in history and secondary education at Monmouth, opined, "For the most part, the Beatles break free from their time and culture. The Beatles tackled topics and issues that transcended the confines of the 1960s and appealed to universal facets of humanity." Beyond that, he continued:

> They were also so ahead of their time in terms of musical ability and even production that listening to the Beatles doesn't feel like listening to a 50-year-old band. Especially in their latter albums, which sound like they could have been recorded within the last five years. This makes it easy to listen for the universal messages of the band, for their music and presentation is anything but archaic.[39]

Cassese wrote, "Despite the disbandment of the group and the passing of two members, the Beatles are still a part of everyone's lives. . . . People of this generation have over 200 songs, five movies, and dozens of documentaries and books to explore a band that broke up 30 years before most of them were born."[40]

The Beatles, indeed, continue to enter the culture in new and varied ways that reveal their continued relevance in the 21st century. Malcolm Gladwell cites them as a leading example in understanding what makes people successful in his 2008 book, *Outliers*, while Joshua Wolf Shenk uses the example of Lennon and McCartney in his 2014 study of creative partnerships, *Powers of Two*.[41] Gladwell refocuses attention on the Beatles' formative years in Hamburg, a subject popularized by the 1994 film *Backbeat*, and how long the Beatles had played together before they hit it big in 1963 and 1964. Shenk makes an interesting point about creative partnerships and about another possible reason for the enduring appeal of the Beatles when he suggests, provocatively, that the Beatles never really broke up. He writes, "The reason we can't assign a date to when John and Paul definitely split is that it never definitely happened. . . . One reason it's so murky is that there's no final way out of [that] kind of creative partnership."[42]

Writing about the future of the Beatles in 2016, Jeffrey Roessner argued that the Beatles were still "a dominant historical and musical force—and the most compelling rock and roll band we're ever likely to see." He attributed this to "the vitality and ingenuity of their fans," who continue to treat the band as a subject for debate, controversy, and current interest instead of listening to them merely for the purposes of nostalgia or historical curiosity.[43] In 2014, Marco della Cava wrote a column in *USA Today* titled "The Beatles: Will We Still Need Them in 2064?" Della Cava thought, on balance, that the answer would be yes, but no doubt, in 2064, someone will write a column asking whether the Beatles will still be relevant in 2114. As a historian, I am reluctant to predict the future, because I know how many times the very unexpected has happened and how many times people have failed to anticipate what would occur even in the near future. We can only rely on the information we have available to us in the present, along with whatever insights we can draw from the past. In the case of the Beatles, both the present and the past would indicate their continued importance far into the future, a legacy we can now anticipate Generation Z handing down to their children and them handing down to their children into the indefinite future. In this way, each generation will recall the Beatles as a part of their childhood experience. Each of us retains echoes from the past as part of our childhood, whether through popular reimaging of 18th-century fairy tales, ancient and medieval mythologies, or 20th-century superheroes, even as new creative musical and cultural forces add something new to each generation's experience. It seems that the Beatles have already become that kind of cultural staple.

The Beatles, I suggest, will continue to live on in the culture, the popular imagination, and people's private lives in important and minor ways, as they have done for the first 50 years since the band broke up in 1970. Visitors to London from all over the world will continue to make pilgrimages to the Abbey Road studio in St. John's Wood. They will invariably have their photos taken reenacting Lennon, McCartney, Harrison, and Starr crossing the street as they did for the cover photo for *Abbey Road* in front of the studio at the most famous crosswalk in the world. Visiting the site for the 50th anniversary of the album, 22-year-old Peter McCoid, a musician from Oregon, said, "We are all here because they crossed a sidewalk and made it look cool."[44] A life-size sculpture of that same album cover welcomes visitors to the town of Walnut Creek, Arkansas, where the Beatles once made a brief stopover on a flight during their US tour in 1964. The town now hosts an annual festival to commemorate that visit.[45] Hundreds, if not thousands, of tribute bands, from the Liverpool Legends of Branson, Missouri, to the Shouts of Buenos Aires, Argentina,[46] will continue to perform the Beatles oeuvre to the delight of fans of all ages and all nationalities. These shows do not just capitalize on a market demand for nostalgia among the baby boomers; they capture the imagination of the current generation as well. One of my young students, Dylan Welsh, revealed to me that only the Red Hot Chili Peppers had more songs on his own personal playlist of his 593 favorite songs than the Beatles did. Furthermore, those visits to Abbey Road, those concerts by Beatles tribute bands, and, as we have seen, the extent to which the Beatles' music has become a part of the listening experience of members of a new generation will themselves become sources of nostalgia that will fuel interest in the Beatles for years to come.

Klosterman has written, "There are still things about the Beatles that can't be explained, almost to the point of the supernatural: the way their music resonates with toddlers, for example, or the way it resonated with Charles Manson."[47] However, there do exist myriad explanations for the continuing appeal of Beatles music to young people as we are now well into the 21st century. Sarah Curtis, another first-year college student in my 2019 class, set out to answer that question in a paper in which she wrote:

So, why are we, or those who were not even alive while the Beatles were an active band, still listening to the Beatles today? Because the Beatles give us a taste of the '60s, a time of peace, love, and happiness, that we have disconnected from by connecting with electronics in the 21st century. Because the Beatles have many, many songs that we like to stream and play on these electronics, and we could not continue on into the 21st century without bringing them with us. This is because we relate to these songs; we understand what John and Paul, George, and scarcely Ringo, were feeling when they wrote them. Because John said he is right and will be proved right [when he predicted that Christianity would eventually fade but the Beatles would last forever]. And the list of answers goes on. I would say the best response to this question, however, is simple: because it's the Beatles. There is no band like them and there never was and never will be. If I could give the young Paul in "When I'm Sixty-Four" advice, I would tell him not to worry. He, and the other Beatles, are not going to be wasting away anytime soon, as long as their music is available on iTunes or Spotify, at least.[48]

On her debut album, *The Captain*, released in 1999, country/folk singer Kasey Chambers opens with a song called "Cry Like a Baby," in which she sings the lines "Well I'm not much like my generation / Their music only hurts my ears." This chapter has not argued that the Beatles will appeal to everyone today or tomorrow, any more than they have in the past. However, there will always be people who discover the Beatles simply because the music is so good and so timeless, as many of the voices quoted here have articulated. Like Chambers, there will be those with whom the experiences and music of the past resonates much more than those that enjoy a contemporary but perhaps more ephemeral popularity. One of the great things about music and its easy accessibility today is that we all have access to listen to whatever we want—we get to choose what we like. It is the one area of our lives in which we have—not total freedom, given the bombardment of sounds emanating from television commercials, public venues like malls and grocery stores, and sporting arenas—but perhaps more latitude than in any other area. It helps us to define who we are, what we think, and what we value and to discover what sounds heal us, soothe us, inspire us, calm us, and excite us.

Given that the Beatles recorded music that blended and covered so many genres—rock and roll, rhythm and blues, country, country-rock, pop, hard rock, soft rock, folk, folk-rock, ballads, lullabies, music hall, ska, Indian, show tunes, and more—one need not even like all of the Beatles' music to like some, or much, of it. Their versatility and creativity continue to impress, inspire, and make them impossible to ignore. Barring some kind of inexplicable spasm in the cosmos or a weird warping of the time-space continuum, such as occurs in the film *Yesterday*, none of that is going to change. The Beatles are here today . . . and they will be here tomorrow.

Notes

1. Austin Staulcup, "What the Beatles Mean to Me," student paper, Department of History and Anthropology, Monmouth University, 2019, 2.

2. Abby Moskow, "Personal Essay," student paper, Department of History and Anthropology, Monmouth University, 2019, 5.

3. Julian Rebelo, "The Evolution of My Musical Taste: With the Beatles," student paper, Department of History and Anthropology, Monmouth University, 2019, 3.

4. Natalie Lopez, "How the Beatles Have Had a Personal Effect on My Life," student paper, Department of History and Anthropology, Monmouth University, 2019, 5.

5. Ruth Mandel, personal phone interview, March 28, 2019.

6. Sofia Cassese, "Personal Experience with the Beatles," student paper, Department of History and Anthropology, Monmouth University, 2019, 3.

7. For additional examples, see Punch Shaw, "The Beatles in the Classroom: John, Paul, George, and Ringo Go to College," in *New Critical Perspectives on the Beatles: Things We Said Today*, ed. Kenneth Womack and Katie Kapurch (London: Palgrave Macmillan, 2016), 246.

8. Gabriella Herbert, "The Beatles: Personal Essay," student paper, Department of History and Anthropology, Monmouth University, 2019, 3.

9. Nolan Gasser, *Why You Like It* (New York: Flatiron, 2019), 640.

10. Catherine Melman-Kenny, "My Experience with the Beatles," student paper, Department of History and Anthropology, Monmouth University, 2019, 3.

11. Jordan Bachman, "The Beatles in My Life and in Class," student paper, Department of History and Anthropology, Monmouth University, 2019, 3.

12. Herbert, "The Beatles," 3.

13. Lopez, "How the Beatles Have Had a Personal Effect," 5.

14. Chuck Klosterman, "Which Rock Star Will Historians of the Future Remember?" *New York Times Magazine*, May 23, 2016, https://www.nytimes.com/2016/05/29/magazine/which-rock-star-will-historians-of-the-future-remember.html.

15. Marissa Berkowitz, "The Beatles: A Personal Essay," student paper, Department of History and Anthropology, Monmouth University, 2019, 4.

16. David Bianculli, "Beep Beep, Yeah! Paul McCartney on Corden's 'Carpool Karaoke' Is TV at Its Best," *NPR*, 2018, https://www.npr.org/2018/06/25/623165594/beep-beep-yeah-paul-mccartney-on-cordens-carpool-karaoke-is-tv-at-its-best.

17. James Parker, "The Eternal Sunshine of Paul McCartney," *Atlantic* 322, no. 4 (2018): 34–36.

18. Alan Light, "The Beatles' Video Collection '1': Baby, You Can Film My Song," *New York Times*, November 4, 2015. http://nytl.ms/1kaPKUo.

19. Randy Lewis, "Beatles' Sales Strong," *Los Angeles Times*, November 24, 2010. I am thankful to Sarah Curtis for this reference.

20. Kenneth Womack, "Introduction: Keeping It New with the Beatles," in *New Critical Perspectives on the Beatles: Things We Said Today*, ed. Kenneth Womack and Katie Kapurch (London: Palgrave Macmillan, 2016), 3.

21. "The Beatles, by the Numbers," *CBS News*, 2014. https://www.cbsnews.com/news/the-beatles-by-the-numbers/. I am thankful to Julian Rebelo for this reference.

22. Martin Kielty, "Thirty Percent of Spotify Beatles Streams Are by 18–24 Year Olds," Ultimate Classic Rock, Oct. 2, 2019, https://ultimateclassicrock.com/spotify-beatles-streams. Again, thanks to Julian Rebelo for this reference.

23. Keith Caulfield, "The Beatles' Road Returns," *Billboard*, October 12, 2019, 94.

24. Sammy Lloyd, "The Beatles Set Another Record as Abbey Road Returns to the Top of the UK Charts," *GuinnessWorldRecords.com*, October 9, 2019, https://guinnessworldrecords.com/news/2019/10/the-beatles-set-another-record-as-abbey-road-returns-to-the-top-of-the-uk-charts-594219/.

25. Rob Sheffield, *Dreaming the Beatles; The Love Story of One Band and the Whole World* (New York: HarperCollins, 2017), 315.

26. Stanton Green, personal interview, January 30, 2019.

27. Tom Noce, personal phone interview, March 26, 2019.

28. Wade Lawrence, personal interview, April 4, 2019.

29. Robin Levine, personal interview, March 5, 2019.

30. Nick Ercoline, personal interview, February 7, 2019.

31. David Scher, personal interview, March 7, 2019.

32. Jane Barnes, personal interview, January 18. 2019.

33. Marbie Foster, personal interview, February 5, 2019.

34. Tom Blazucki, personal interview, March 30, 2019.

35. Rebecca Duncan, personal interview, January 21, 2019.

36. Rebecca Duncan, "Fifty Years Later, the Enduring Electricity of the Beatles (Yeah, Yeah, Yeah)," *News and Observer* (Raleigh, NC), February 7, 2014.

37. Lopez, "How the Beatles Have Had a Personal Effect," 5.

38. Katherine Fernandez, "The *White Album*: A Student's Perspective," The Beatles' *The White Album*: An International Symposium, Monmouth University, November 2018.

39. Justin Szuba, "The *White Album*," The Beatles' *The White Album*: An International Symposium, Monmouth University, November 2018.

40. Sofia Cassese, "The Beatles in America," student paper, Department of History and Anthropology, Monmouth University, 2019, 7.

41. Malcolm Gladwell, *Outliers: The Story of Success* (New York: Little, Brown, 2008); Joshua Wolf Shenk, *Powers of Two: Finding the Essence of Innovation in Creative Pairs* (Boston: Houghton Mifflin, 2014).

42. Shenk, *Powers of Two*, 226.

43. Jeffrey Roessner, "Revolution 2.0: Beatles Fan Scholarship in the Digital Age," in *New Critical Perspectives on the Beatles: Things We Said Today*, ed. Kenneth Womack and Katie Kapurch (London: Palgrave Macmillan, 2016), 222.

44. Quoted in Iliana Magra, "Beatles Fans Come Together on Abbey Road for a 50-Year Anniversary," *New York Times*, August 8, 2019, https://www.nytimes.com/2019/08/08/world/europe/beatles-abbey-road-crossing-anniversary.html.

45. Michael Bowman, "Liverpool, Abbey Road, and Walnut Ridge: How a Small, Southern Town in Northeast Arkansas Became a Destination for Beatles Fans," *Arkansas Review* 46, no. 2 (2015): 114–120.

46. John Paul Meyers, "The Beatles in Buenos Aires, Muse in Mexico City: Tribute Bands and the Global Consumption of Rock Music," *Ethnomusicology Forum* 24, no. 3 (2015): 329–348.

47. Klosterman, "Which Rock Star Will Historians of the Future Remember?"

48. Sarah Curtis, "Because It's the Beatles: Why We Still Love a '60s Rock-and-Roll Band," student paper, Department of History and Anthropology, Monmouth University, 2019, 5–6.

Bibliography

Bachman, Jordan. "The Beatles in My Life and in Class." Student paper, Department of History and Anthropology, Monmouth University, 2019.

Barnes, Jane. Personal phone interview, January 18, 2019.

Berkowitz, Marissa. "The Beatles: A Personal Essay." Student paper, Department of History and Anthropology, Monmouth University, 2019.

Bianculli, David. "Beep Beep, Yeah! Paul McCartney on Corden's 'Carpool Karaoke' Is TV at Its Best," *NPR*, 2018. https://www.npr.org/2018/06/25/623165594/beep-beep-yeah-paul-mccartney-on-cordens-carpool-karaoke-is-tv-at-its-best.

Blazucki, Tom. Personal interview, March 30, 2019.

Bowman, Michael. "Liverpool, Abbey Road, and Walnut Ridge: How a Small, Southern Town in Northeast Arkansas Became a Destination for Beatles Fans." *Arkansas Review* 46, no. 2 (2015): 114–120.

Cassese, Sofia. "The Beatles in America." Student paper, Department of History and Anthropology, Monmouth University, 2019.

Cassese, Sofia. "Personal Experience with the Beatles." Student paper, Department of History and Anthropology, Monmouth University, 2019.

Caulfield, Keith. "The Beatles' Road Returns." *Billboard*, October 12, 2019, 94.

CBS News. "The Beatles, by the Numbers," February 2, 2014, https://www.cbsnews.com/news/the-beatles-by-the-numbers/.

Curtis, Sarah. "Because It's the Beatles: Why We Still Love a '60s Rock-and-Roll Band." Student paper, Department of History and Anthropology, Monmouth University, 2019.

Duncan, Rebecca. "Fifty Years Later, the Enduring Electricity of the Beatles (Yeah, Yeah, Yeah)." *News and Observer* (Raleigh, NC), February 7, 2014.

Duncan, Rebecca. Personal phone interview, January 21, 2019.

Ercoline, Nick. Personal phone interview, February 7, 2019.

Fernandez, Katherine. "The *White Album*: A Student's Perspective." The Beatles' *The White Album*: An International Symposium, Monmouth University, November 2018.

Foster, Marbie. Personal phone interview, February 5, 2019.

Gasser, Nolan. *Why You Like It: The Science and Culture of Musical Taste.* New York: Flatiron, 2019.

Gladwell, Malcolm. *Outliers: The Story of Success.* New York: Little, Brown, 2008.

Green, Stanton. Personal interview, January 30, 2019.

Herbert, Gabriella. "The Beatles: Personal Essay." Student paper, Department of History and Anthropology, Monmouth University, 2019.

Kielty, Martin. "Thirty Percent of Spotify Beatles Streams Are by 18–24 Year Olds," October 2, 2019. https://ultimateclassicrock.com/spotify-beatles-streams/.

Klosterman, Chuck. "Which Rock Star Will Historians of the Future Remember?" *New York Times Magazine*, May 23, 2016. https://www.nytimes.com/2016/05/29/magazine/which-rock-star-will-historians-of-the-future-remember.html.

Lawrence, Wade. Personal interview, April 4, 2019.

Levine, Robin. Personal phone interview, March 5, 2019.

Lewis, Randy. "Beatles' Sales Strong," *Los Angeles Times*, November 24, 2010.

Light, Alan. "The Beatles' Video Collection '1': Baby, You Can Film My Song." *New York Times*, November 4, 2015. https://www.nytimes.com/2015/11/08/arts/music/the-beatles-video-collection-1-baby-you-can-film-my-song.html.

Lloyd, Sammy. "The Beatles Set Another Record as *Abbey Road* Returns to the Top of the UK Charts." *GuinnessWorldRecords.com*, October 9, 2019. https://guinnessworldrecords.com/news/2019/10/the-beatles-set-another-record-as-abbey-road-returns-to-the-top-of-the-uk-charts-594219/.

Lopez, Natalie. "How the Beatles Have Had a Personal Effect on My Life." Student paper, Department of History and Anthropology, Monmouth University, 2019.

Magra, Iliana. "Beatles Fans Come Together on Abbey Road for a 50-Year Anniversary." *New York Times*, August 8, 2019, https://www.nytimes.com/2019/08/08/world/europe/beatles-abbey-road-crossing-anniversary.html.

Mandel, Ruth. Personal phone interview, March 28, 2019.

Melman-Kenny, Catherine. "My Experience with the Beatles." Student paper, Department of History and Anthropology, Monmouth University, 2019.

Meyers, John Paul. "The Beatles in Buenos Aires, Muse in Mexico City: Tribute Bands and the Global Consumption of Rock Music." *Ethnomusicology Forum* 24, no. 3 (2015): 329–348.

Moskow, Abby. "Personal Essay." Student paper, Department of History and Anthropology, Monmouth University, 2019.

Noce, Tom. Personal phone interview, March 26, 2019.

Parker, James. "The Eternal Sunshine of Paul McCartney." *Atlantic* 322, no. 4 (2018): 34–36. https://searchebscohostcom.ezproxy.monmouth.edu/login.aspx?direct=true&db=a9h&AN=132171202&site=ehost-live&scope=site.

Rebelo, Julian. "The Evolution of My Musical Taste: With the Beatles." Student paper, Department of History and Anthropology, Monmouth University, 2019.

Roessner, Jeffrey. "Revolution 2.0: Beatles Fan Scholarship in the Digital Age." In *New Critical Perspectives on the Beatles: Things We Said Today*, edited by Kenneth Womack and Katie Kapurch, 221–240. London: Palgrave Macmillan, 2016.

Scher, David. Personal interview, March 7, 2019.

Shaw, Punch. "The Beatles in the Classroom: John, Paul, George, and Ringo Go to College." In *New Critical Perspectives on the Beatles: Things We Said Today*, edited by Kenneth Womack and Katie Kapurch, 243–263. London: Palgrave Macmillan, 2016.

Sheffield, Rob. *Dreaming the Beatles; The Love Story of One Band and the Whole World.* New York: HarperCollins, 2017.

Shenk, Joshua Wolf. *Powers of Two: Finding the Essence of Innovation in Creative Pairs.* Boston: Houghton Mifflin, 2014.

Staulcup, Austin. "What the Beatles Mean to Me." Student paper, Department of History and Anthropology, Monmouth University, 2019.

Szuba, Justin. "*The White Album*." The Beatles' *The White Album*: An International Symposium, Monmouth University, November 2018.

Womack, Kenneth. "Introduction: Making It New with the Beatles." In *New Critical Perspectives on the Beatles: Things We Said Today*, edited by Kenneth Womack and Katie Kapurch, 1–10. London: Palgrave Macmillan, 2016.

9

Anthems of Whose Generation?

The Beatles and the Millennials

Richard Mills

Millennials Rising

Millennial Beatles fandom is a cultural space where fans merge online with the Beatles. Millennial fans want to be involved instead of passively wallowing in nostalgic fandom; they want to unnostalgize. Millennial fans (born between 1982 and 2004) are a generation who mine Beatles history to appropriate the Beatles' art into their lives. They want to inhabit fandom, to get inside and be involved. As we shall see, they do this in many diverse, eccentric, innovative, and creative ways: through tribute bands, such as such as the 20-something Funkles, who reinterpret Beatles songs in a soul and funk style, reinvent the Beatles' music and fashion into a forward-facing hybrid of new and old; transgressive and carnivalesque slash fiction imagines the Beatles in dreamlike erotic scenarios; on YouTube, millennial fans mash Beatles videos into new bricolage texts made up of the old and the new; and conventions and heritage culture are two spheres where millennial Beatles fans can read new meanings into Beatles text through memorabilia at conventions and the psychogeography of Beatles walks in London and Liverpool.

I use two case studies of millennial Beatles fandom in this chapter: Polish Beatles fan Joanna Kozlowska and Mexican-American Beatles fan Stephanie Hernandez. I chose them because they typify millennial fans who keep Beatles fandom fresh and vital with their "fascination and mastery of new technologies."[1]

Kozlowska and Hernandez responded to a questionnaire I gave to Beatles fans at Liverpool's Beatleweek in August 2017. Of the total of 30 respondents, thirteen were in the 40–49 age group, six were 50–59,; three were 30–39, three were 60–69, two were 16–21, and one was in the 22–29 age group. These findings show that the majority of the Beatleweek demographic are baby

Richard Mills, *Anthems of Whose Generation?* In: *Fandom and the Beatles.* Edited by: Kenneth Womack and Kit O'Toole, Oxford University Press (2021). © Oxford University Press. DOI: 10.1093/oso/9780190917852.003.0010 boomers and Gen Xers, so I wanted to use two examples of young Beatles fans to demonstrate the diverse age range of fans (I once interviewed a 7-year-old at a Beatles convention in Chicago). Also, the millennial fans may be a minority, but they are always a significant presence at conventions, at the Abbey Road site in London, and the Beatles Story museum in Liverpool. My discussion of millennials is predicated on a group who grew up with and are comfortable with technology and who want to interact with physical space and at every opportunity post about walks, Beatles museums, and conventions online. These millennial fans digitize physical space, which transforms the physical world into an interactive and transgressive cyberspace. Henry Jenkins calls this "textual poaching," where fans become artists themselves, changing the meaning of Beatles texts by posting videos. Hernandez and Kozlowska are typical millennial poachers, as they circulate videos of Beatles shrines online and have appropriated Beatles texts into the web and weft of their lives, and this activity also gives other fans the freedom to comment and instantly criticize these FB, Instagram, slash, Tumblr, and YouTube posts. Jenkins calls this "fan art," and for fans, it is a "form of cultural creation with its own aesthetic principles and traditions."[2] Hernandez is also an example of a late-millennial fan; born in 1996, she is on the cusp of Gen Z, which makes her an example of a very young fan who appropriates the Beatles into digital spheres that are often transgressive and carnivalesque.

Both Hernandez and Kozlowska embody two distinct traits of millennial Beatles fans. First, their fandom is an example of progressive nostalgia, by which I mean that they look far backward in order to look far forward. Both take the Beatles' songs, lyrics, and image and make them relevant to their own lives; they appropriate 1960s Beatles culture and refashion it into the web and weft of their own lives—recasting Beatles texts to give them a 21st-century spin, which I call unnostalgizing. Second, they exhibit a typical millennial trait of wanting to be involved; they are examples of active fans who mash fan vids, set up Facebook groups, bring personalized signs to McCartney concerts, which often elicit a response from the performer himself, and collect '60s memorabilia. Unlike boomer Beatles fans, they are not content to be passive: millennial tribute bands, slash fiction, YouTube videos, Beatles conventions, and heritage culture are inhabited to make Beatles culture fresh, new, and exciting. Millennials form Beatles tribute bands to reimagine the songs, to make them anthems for a new generation. Millennials write pornographic fiction that transgresses and reinterprets the Beatles as fictional characters. YouTube is galvanized to mash Beatles songs and to make new visual collages of old Beatles footage. Conventions are spaces where millennial fans sell memorabilia and use online culture to breathe life into buying and selling: "Fans of popular culture such as Star Wars or the Beatles . . . share the desire both to know as much as they can about a subject and collect as much physical material as they can."[3] Besides using the physical space of Beatles conventions to actively buy and sell, they use cyberspace to sell their memorabilia, changing the meaning and value of these old Beatles artifacts. Beatles museums and Beatles walks are spaces from which millennial fans upload their psychogeographic experiences online. Boomers nostalgically experience walks and museums, whereas millennials inhabit these spaces and morph the experience of physical space into an online simulacrum.

Millennial Beatles fans want to appropriate the Beatles into their lives and make the band relevant to the here and now. I spoke to Kozlowska at a Beatleweek in Liverpool in 2017. She was 32 years old, a millennial Beatles fan who wanted to interact with the Beatles and inhabit their world. She told me of fans:

Many of them [young teenage girls] are drawn to the retro forms of communication and devices—so acquiring an LP player is a goal for many. I remember a whole wave, a trend to get the awesome-looking Crosley turntable. I actually was affected, too, and am also planning on buying it, although it is a very bad LP player, but it looks very '60s and is cheap for a turntable—one after another posts around Christmastime showed these young people who asked their parents to get a Crosley.[4]

I interviewed Hernandez, a 21-year-old Beatles fan from Houston who lives in the United Kingdom and works at the Beatles Story museum in Liverpool. Her job in the Beatles industry is an example of 21st-century Beatles fandom; her collections of '60s vinyl, candy-store jewelry, and badges is a psychological romanticizing of the 1960s but also a progressive nostalgia of a 21-year-old fan who couches her fandom in the present tense when she tells me that "the human race is a Beatles fan."[5]

Her stories from Beatleweek unnostalgize Beatles cultural tourism; she relates one story in which a bus full of 10-year-old Italian children arrived at the museum looking bored and travel-weary, but after the visit, they had morphed into energized fans who were begging their parents to buy them every conceivable kind of Beatles merchandise in the shop. Her job at the Beatles Story museum and her fandom epitomize progressive nostalgia or unnostalgizing of the Beatles cultural phenomenon as young fans interact with cultural space and memorabilia to create new meanings that take the old and reboot it for the present.

Millennial Beatles Tribute Bands

This Lazarus desire to reform the Beatles is at its most performative in Beatles tribute acts. Andy Bennett's description of the tribute-band phenomenon expresses this Lazarus effect and retrospective urge as "a postmodern landscape in which real and the hyperreal blur into one. An oft cited explanation for the origin of the tribute band phenomenon is that it began as a response to the perpetual unavailability of original acts."[6] However, this resurrection of the dead bands is creative, as the live simulation is new and fresh, depending on the interaction between band and performer on any given night. The key to understanding tribute acts, according to Bennett, is that tribute bands add a new dimension as they appropriate the image, history, and style of the original band into a new live context and add a new forward-looking perspective to the retro:

> In the course of tribute band performances, dead rock stars are brought back to life, defunct bands are reassembled, and classic live performances of yesteryear are accurately reproduced.... Moreover, in revisiting a tribute group or artist's recording and performing history, tribute bands are in the privileged position of being able to creatively play around with that history.[7]

A discussion of Beatles tribute bands is based on the fact that the Beatles are unavailable, so the corpse has to be reanimated, and the audience gets to enjoy an eerie and haunting simulation of the Beatles, and the added value of experiencing a unique and singular performance based on the specific live context. In short, a tribute band produces a creative copy of the original by adding new stagecraft, songs never performed live by the band (that's almost everything from *Revolver* to *Abbey Road*), and unrehearsed rapport between audience and band, in a sense, just like recorded music and image, with tribute bands as the "singing dead."[8] It is important to acknowledge, however, that a band being unavailable is not the sole motivation for seeing a tribute act; bands that are still playing also have tribute bands now and problematize this thesis, such as Coldplace for Coldplay and Mused for Muse.

The Funkles use funk and soul to completely reimagine the Beatles' texts; they are millennial Beatles fans who reinterpret Beatles songs into contemporary new sounds. When I watched them perform live, classic Beatles songs were unrecognizable at first, as the band reimagined the familiar songs into George Clinton/Funkadelic/Motown-style grooves.

As the Funkles demonstrate, tribute acts are not ventriloquists, and they are not reducible to the status of mimetic karaoke; they change the performance every night because of the live context (the audience and the venues) and the human element of performance. As Georgina Gregory argues:

> rather than judging a tribute as failed execution of a text, it is more constructive to appreciate the individuality of single performances, the responses of the audience and the diversity of approaches within the process. The human component and real-time setting ensure that each act and each event is unique, and in this sense, the performance contains an element of the aura ... ascribed to original artwork untainted by mass production.[9]

My experience of Beatles tribute bands at Beatleweek in Liverpool bears out this thesis of performative uniqueness. The tribute act lineup in August 2017 included bands whose performances were different in their performative context and that also mashed Beatles songs into their own eccentric bricolage.

The performance of the Beatles' *White Album* by Dutch tribute band the Analogues can be understood in the context of Beatles tribute acts and millennial fandom in three ways: first, the extent to which film augments the stagecraft of the Analogues act; second, the millennial fans at the Analogues shows who are engaged in unnostalgizing the Beatles; and third, the Analogues inexact fidelity to the Beatles' music on the *White Album*.

Tribute performances of the *White Album* use film, art installation, video, and Richard Hamilton's design to put the album into the artistic, cultural, and political context of 1968. The Analogues put this performance style to good effect in their shows by using commentary by Beatles historian Mark Lewisohn and film accompaniment for their visual realization of "Revolution 9."

The demographic at concerts by Beatles tribute acts such as the Analogues is an age range from millennials to first-generation fans. The millennials in the audience unnostalgize the Beatles' image and music; to them, the Beatles are not retrogressive nostalgia, but they fans encounter the Beatles 35 years after Beatlemania, and they make the Beatles relevant to their childhoods and their lives. This unnostalgizing or progressive nostalgia unanchors the Beatles from their '60s context, and so the songs are enjoyed in a contemporary cultural setting that is different in every performance.

Musically, Beatles tribute acts play a part in fans' desire to keep the past alive, but a tribute act is much more complicated than that. The Analogues appeal to millennial fans because of their unnostalgizing. Millennials want to be involved in cosplay, slash fiction, remixing Beatles songs. Millennial fandom is about looking backward in order to look far forward. Kozlowska and Hernandez belong to an atypical Beatles demographic, but the fact remains that millennials are an important unnostalgizing fan element who gave a standing ovation to the Analogues' version of "While My Guitar Gently Weeps" at the Liverpool Philharmonic on August 27, 2018. The Analogues' shows are a space where boomer, Gen X, and millennial fans connect to create unique performative events.

Tony Giangreco (age 26), a millennial Beatles fan who plays Starr in the Meet the Beatles tribute band, is typical of a fan who inhabits the Beatles' cultural phenomenon. Giangreco said he "built an exact replica of the drum kit Ringo used on the *Ed Sullivan Show*.[10] The emphasis here is on the verb *built*. He wanted to create and interact with a physical Beatles object in a similar manner to Kozlowska's fetishization of the Crosley record players. He elaborated about the stagecraft of Meet the Beatles: "It's the thrill of walking onstage and seeing the audience. Making everybody there feel as if they are in the '60s.[11] Giangreco said he listens almost exclusively to '60s music: "I mainly listen to Beatles and classic rock. It feels new every show. I remember when I first saw the *Beatlemania* show, I realized I wanted to impersonate Ringo."[12] However, this is not retrospective nostalgia or what Jacques Derrida called *mal d'archive* (an unhealthy fixation with the past). It is a progressive instinct, a living millennial culture that makes Giangreco want to physically interact with the Beatles and embody the performance in an unnostalgizing manner. Millennials look backward in order to look far forward, and in fact, each tribute band influences others in a creative way; as Giangreco suggests, tribute bands are not simply nostalgia, because they are constantly learning from one another: "We all learn from other tribute bands. We learn from each other. American English. British Export. Liverpool Legends."[13]

Beatles authority and co-editor of this book Ken Womack agrees that millennials are concerned not with nostalgia but with inhabiting and interacting with the Beatles phenomenon to make it new. When I interviewed him in August 2017, he said he discerned

> "a shift away from nostalgia. Almost everyone who is loving the Beatles now is not a first-generation fan. They are not a second-generation fans. They discovered the Beatles fully formed. They can buy everything, or download everything in mass, in minutes. They are not necessarily going to discover them chronologically—they probably won't! So nostalgia will be increasingly less interesting, but what will be interesting is being able to put themselves in the time, not for nostalgic purposes but for entertainment.[14]

To Womack, millennial Beatles fans are

> "increasingly moving toward the interactive. Kids today want to be in-volved. They don't want to sit on the sidelines. When they have a class, they don't want to be sat and lectured to. . . . At the *White Album* conference, we are going to have a room where the recordings are made . . . where you can mix a track and take away the MP3.[15]

Womack told me about seeing a millennial fan at St. Peter's Church Hall, Woolton, in Liverpool, where Lennon met McCartney on July 6, 1957. The millennial fan took a video because she wanted to be "in the space" and "to be interactive," whereas a first-generation fan would feel nostalgia for the past: "Millennials want to be involved."[16] We discussed museum spaces and the extent to which millennials want to interact with the displays: "At the British Music Experience in Liverpool, people will not be at the cos-tume displays but at the end [the interactive part of the museum], where they can touch something."[17] The assistant curator of the "David Bowie Is" exhibition at the Victoria and Albert Museum in 2013, Kathryn Johnson, affirmed that exhibitions should be predicated on the interactive experience and the dynamism of fan interpretation. To Johnson, this type of fandom "is innately polysemic and open-ended. While curatorial text can carry a particular, carefully considered and researched story, it is a fact that only a small proportion of visitors will read it—however well written. The majority are drawing their own conclusions from primarily visual stimuli."[18] And we can extend this further: millennials will appropriate meaning from a visual text, but they want to inhabit exhibits as well. At "David Bowie Is," I saw that millennials were crowded at the video installations, where they could wear headphones and sing along passionately to "Life on Mars." Millennial Beatles fans read their own transgressive and creative meanings into the visual, and they are happier when they enter the performance through singing along in a museum, playing in a tribute band, mashing Beatles songs on YouTube, or writing carnivalesque slash fiction.

This tendency for millennial fans to appropriate what they want from the Beatles' canon is typified on Spotify, where a Harrison song, "Here Comes the Sun," is the most streamed. According to US pollsters Statista, 55% of Spotify users are millennials, and it is significant that the most popular Beatles song is not "Yesterday" or "Something" but a less popular and lesser-known piece for first- and second-generation Beatles fans. It is also in the present tense and available through interactive technology, which highlights two aspects of millennial Beatles fandom: interactivity and unnostalgizing.

Millennial Slash Fiction

The interactive element of slash fiction is vitally important to an appreciation of millennial Beatles fandom. Every slash website is overflowing with bespoke sexual choice. The prosumer can choose any configuration of Beatles group sex. Here young millennial fans display the minutiae of their Beatles knowledge. Storylines about aspects of the band's career are available online. Not only is there every configuration of Beatles sex—Lennon with McCartney and so on—but also sex involving every player in Beatles history: Brian Epstein, Pete Best, Stu Sutcliffe. For instance, a fan fiction guide on "Beatles Sex" has recommendations for all four Beatles and a section on "Others" such as Sutcliffe.[19] Beatles slash is very explicit, it is hastily written, and the sexual dream scenarios are an aspect of fandom in which sexual identity is fluid and malleable. For instance, we often don't know the gender of the author or the author's sexual orientation. The ambiguity of this writing is immersed in the changing state of things. Sexual identity, gender, and authorship are all subsumed to the act of reading. It is an I. A. Richards[20] reading exercise where the text is a self-contained aesthetic object. Beatles characters are unmoored into a realm of personal fantasy, a self-contained imaginative world where fixity is rejected. For example, the story "Who Knows How Long I've Loved You" by sherlocked221 shifts Lennon into a performative personal fantasy that transgresses any sense of control from the machinery of the music industry:

This morning, I wake up naked. It's a little more surprising than it probably should be, but I haven't slept in the nude for quite a while. Moreover, I haven't slept beside John in about a week. His naked body is draped over mine. I feel his breath curling against the back of my neck. Maybe he thinks my back is an extension of the mattress, judging by the way he practically has me pinned by the shoulders. I nuzzle the back of my head into his mess of fair hair.[21]

Predictably, the story develops into a graphic pornographic fantasy that is highly personal; it is an "oppositional subculture" that is not deliberately setting out to be oppositional, as Matt Hills suggests attempting to be subversive "restricts possibilities for expressing personal significance."[22] In fact, what we have here is "nomadic writing," which is a site of play in which identities are unmoored (Lennon, author, reader) into a sphere of writing where identities blur into a fluid Rabelaisian orgy of words that express fan emotions in an indeterminate space of play. Slash fiction is "play that is not always caught up in a pre-established 'boundedness' or set of cultural boundaries, but may instead imaginatively create its own set of boundaries and its own auto-'context.' "[23] It is also significant that interactive technology is remote from being couched in a paperback, giving slash writers much more agency to annotate and comment on stories.

In reading thousands of Beatles slash stories, recurrent leitmotifs begin to become apparent. Taking another example, , "Evasion" by quietprofanity ticks many of the slash fiction boxes. Each story often has a detailed home page, which has a guide, in this instance "Rating: Explicit. Category: M/M. Fandom: The Beatles. Relationships: Paul McCartney/George Harrison, John Lennon /Brian Epstein/George Harrison, John Lennon/Ringo Starr. Characters: George Harrison, John Lennon, Brian Epstein, Paul McCartney, Ringo Starr, Bob Wooler, Billy J. Kramer, Pete Shotton, Cynthia Lennon, Gerry Marsden." There is also a statistics section: "Stats: Words: 20808. Chapters: 3/3. Comments: 25. Kudos: 90. Bookmarks: 17. Hits: 2971."[24] The stories are very well written, character and dialogue are convincing, and the detail about Beatles history is scrupulously researched. "Evasion" is set at McCartney's 21st birthday party at his Auntie Jin's, a real event where Lennon in a violent rage beat up the Cavern Club disc jockey, Bob Wooler, after Wooler had insinuated that Lennon had had an affair with Epstein while they were on holiday together in Barcelona. After the party, and Lennon disgracing himself, the Beatles make up in the usual predictable manner for this type of fiction. Nearly all these stories end in an in orgy, in this case a foursome:

> George wiped his mouth, trying to clean it, although the taste of Paul's come lingered in his mouth despite his efforts. He raised his head to look at the others. Paul had collapsed back in the chair, his trousers tangled about his ankles and his cock mostly limp in his lap. Ringo looked back at him, his eyes wide and confused. George had no idea what was going through his mind, wasn't sure if it was arousal or pity. Then there was John, smiling triumphant John. His eyes made George want to sink into the floor. George was still incredibly horny, his cock fully erect inside his clothes, and even though he was on his hands and knees on the floor, crouched so John probably couldn't see him well, it seemed like John nevertheless knew everything he felt.[25]

Slash fiction is written by young girls in the 14–18 age bracket and epitomizes millennials' desire to create new transgressive fan art out of the Beatles' image.

Millennial Beatles Fans and YouTube

Vidders on YouTube are remixing and mashing the Beatles video archive; *archive* comes from *archon*, Greek for "ruler," and with YouTube, the archive is untethered from the Apple CEO or *archon* and released into a digital space where old videos become transformed into hybrid texts, living cultures, progressive bricolage, where the past and the future collide and mingle in a confusion of strains that look backward in order to progress forward. YouTube is a fan community that is shifting, progressing, and transforming. YouTube is a transgressive and messy space where videos, carnivalesque comment, and surreal, often absurd debates coexist in a strange palette of the old and the new. Paul Booth's words about Tumblr are also relevant to YouTube; Booth calls the radical mimicking and alloying of the old and the new "transformative fandom," and this appellation is a synonym of progressive fandom: "Whereas affirmative fandom tends to uphold the text and its creator, transformative fandom tends to take the text and mold it, to create something new with it."[26] The vidders on YouTube remold the Beatles video archive and in so doing are creating messy spaces of hybrid fan visual art. It is important to note, however, that YouTube is the second-biggest website in the world and is a subsidiary of Google, so the playfulness of vidding and comment is couched in the machinery of a multi-billion-dollar company that relies on advertisement revenue to pay creators, although its subversive nature remains extant as the company relies on crowdsourcing and fans to monitor controversial content by clicking the Report button. However, the primary concern of Beatles fans on YouTube is to take pleasure in the of act fandom, engaging with the Beatles phenomenon for enjoyment. Or, as Mark Duffett contends:

> Evidently, as fans, we are not stooges. We are human beings with the full range of human capabilities. This does not mean, however, that our primary aim is *always* political in the traditional sense: to poach, subvert or negate corporate culture or intellectual property. In reality, fandom is inspired by media output but not restricted to it. Its concerns escape the matrix of corporate production by raising more humanist issues: seeking pleasure, exploring creativity and making social connections.[27]

Baby boomers and millennial Beatles fans engage with Twitter accounts or Facebook groups as well as on YouTube. Fandom has moved into the era of Web 2.0, and aging fans have connected. This is also empirically and theoretically interesting as YouTube and Tumblr allow Beatles fans from boomers to millennials to "curate their own personal journey through fandoms."[28] Twitter, Facebook, YouTube, and Tumblr offer "multiple interdisciplinary conversations with other academic areas and developing connections with areas that might appear disparate; for instance, links between fan studies and political science might reveal civic commonalities, or between fan studies and history could help nuance discussions of fans through time."[29] As I have argued, millennials fans are more likely to interface with technology at every opportunity, but given the historical context of millennial fandom, they fetishize the '60s by interacting with physical space (pen-pal letters, vinyl, Crosley record players), but concurrently they are active with technology and have a tendency to digitalize these '60s pop artifacts. Boomers are becoming increasingly adept at interacting with technology, but boomer fans are less likely to want to digitize museum spaces and walks. When I went on Richard Porter's London Beatles walks, boomer parents were content to listen to the tour guide and wistfully enjoy Abbey Road Studios, the zebra crossing, Savile Row, and Trident Studios, whereas their 20-year-old children were constantly making videos of these physical spaces and actively inhabiting them. There is a caveat about this boomer/millennial binary, however: physical space and the activity of being a first-generation fan were also emancipatory; lining up for concerts, going to record shops, and writing letters to *Beatles Monthly* were imaginative, creative acts with agency. The only difference here between boomers and millennials is historical context: millennials were born into an era when technology was ubiquitous in the first world; therefore, millennial fandom is more technologically advanced than boomers.

We now have emancipatory spaces where individuals and communities are creating remixed and mashed content that moves Beatles art into a new realm of bricolage and citizen art, but concurrently, a practical engagement with politics and society has become severed. Sara Linden and Henrik Linden posit that "in the Web 2.0 era bands and artists are increasingly expected to market themselves via Twitter and Facebook,"[30] and for younger-generation musicians, this is seen a natural component of being an artist.[31] Also, fans are incorporated into high consumerism:

> for brands, it is important to keep track of fan communities and learn about their consumer behaviour. . . . The recommending function is a central part of what businesses such as Amazon are doing, and through increasingly sophisticated software, online companies are able to steer potential customers in a certain direction. Consumers seem to like this, as they do not mind buying what others have bought. Perhaps, rather than convergence culture, we are increasingly being "spoon-fed" by the company trying to sell us products.[32]

So YouTube is an innovation that offers a certain agency and autonomy for the individual, but praxis or practical uses of knowledge (political application, for example) are coached in YouTube's capitalist/corporate framework.

In fact, Guy Debord's words on the deconstruction of art are germane to YouTube; it is a cultural form that takes fragments and reconstructs the old Beatles art into bricolage of past and present:

> When art, which was the common language of social inaction, develops into independent art in the modern sense, emerging from its original religious universe and becoming individual production of separate works, it too becomes subject to the movements governing history of all separate culture. Its declaration of independence is the beginning of its end.[33]

YouTube is a technological fragmentary bricolage art form that makes the old new, but its transgressive play is couched in individualistic consumerism, and the YouTube company is part of a web or paradigm of profit making. For this writer, YouTube is obviously a multi-billion-dollar business concern, but it is also a dazzling people's guerrilla art, and its brilliance lies in the fact that it is a collage and bricolage form that remixes, mashes, reimagines, reboots, and appropriates the Beatles archive into a new expression of old and new technological strains; it takes the canon of "great" Beatles art and shifts it into texts of forward motion that are affirmed on looking backward.

Millennials, Heritage Culture, and Beatles Walks

Beatles heritage culture is concerned with a new empirical and immersive experience, new social spheres for fan interaction. For instance, Richard Porter's London Beatles Walks are an opportunity for fan interaction and fresh "meaning-making,"[34] Speaking to Porter and the fans who go on his walks, we find that fans are a heterogeneous mass of divisive and contradictory impulses and that cultural tourism adds something new to enjoying and understanding music in a fresh context: "Popular music is not a national industry. It comes from cities, but negotiates with myths and narratives of the urban and pastoral past. Through popular music, new groups and communities negotiate the meaning of city to find an identity."[35]

Nostalgic memories of the past, on which cultural tourism is predicated, are wedded to digital memory, and the result is a physical walk that stimulates a cognitive experience of progressive and forward-looking thoughts that are then spread communally via the internet. My findings from the questionnaire I used in London and Liverpool reach a similar conclusion, with the participants suggesting that Beatles tourism made them feel "optimistic." Karen Worcman and Joanne Garde-Hansen call this "social memory technology" and express memory as a creative reworking of past memories:

It is from the past that we take the "meaning" that we give to our present. This same logic is reproduced in the sphere of the collective. Yet, even though we have the "sensation" that the past we remember is exactly the same as what actually happened, we cannot fail to highlight that our memories are dynamic and the narratives we construct come from our present moment as a story we tell ourselves and others. They are creative choices, and, as the historian Peter Burke confirms, memory is much more about what we forget than what we remember: "the process of 're-remembering' is influenced by changing situations in which are recalled. . . . What is recorded in our memory is that which . . . is important at that time and will change from moment to moment. Moreover, we cannot assume that producing a history of a group's mental process will inextricably produce a 'collective.' to focus on collective mentalities is to forget that individuals do not think exactly alike." . . . This is a constant and dynamic process of recording and constructing narratives on behalf of the self or the group's members, and sharing those selves amongst the group and beyond.[36]

Consequently, the experience on a Beatles walk is a transformative one, millennial Beatles fans changing a *mal d'archive* into a forward-looking, progressive, living culture that is not anchored to the here and now of the walking tour or the museum.

Millennials at Beatles Conventions

When I spoke to Kozlowska at the 2017 Liverpool Beatleweek convention, she told me that Beatles fans come to conventions "because they have a certain sense of identity as a true fan." These fans use conventions as vehicles for meeting other obsessives and creating "a sense of community."[37] Kozlowska also saw similarities between conventions and YouTube: both keep fandom fresh and vital, and YouTube is "more about the account; it is coming from the people who regularly visit it [subscribers] and maybe post a video themselves." To Kozlowska, conventions and YouTube were "about the movement and flow of expression."[38] By this, I think she meant that community interaction and group behavior keep the Beatles canon fresh and burgeoning. She used the word *community* when she described how fanzines such as *Beatles Monthly* have been replaced by Facebook groups, the extent to which such networks have taken over from fan clubs, and how Facebook groups impact physical communal gatherings such as conventions and McCartney concerts:

Also, the communities like Facebook groups or message boards took over the relevance that fan clubs once had, also typical for these times where people prefer informal gatherings. I belong to Facebook group Beatles På Svenska [Kozlowska is Polish but lives in Sweden], and we even organized a meeting before a Macca concert in Stockholm where anybody could perform, and we had crisps, cola, a mini market for exchanging Beatles merch we didn't need. And we even designed T-shirts for that Facebook group.[39]

My interview with Kozlowska provided a counterargument to the findings of the questionnaire I distributed at the 2017 Beatleweek that the majority of Beatles fans had been attending conventions for 20-plus years. Kozlowska told me that Beatles fandom is a very wide demographic and that an online survey would provide a very different indication of fans' age groups from what would be seen at a convention or a concert. She said, "Another interesting thing I thought about when it comes to Beatles online communities like Tumblr or Instagram is that a huge percent is made up of the youngest generation of fans, of teenagers, especially girls."[40] It was fascinating to hear that young teenagers who were obsessed with the Beatles also had retro mania for something they were too young to have experienced—neophiliac retro mania! Kozlowska was very expansive on the fetishization of the '60s:

A typing machine was a thing, and of course, many of the young fans want to have actual old-fashioned pen pals from around the world. When I was growing up, I had pen pals, people whom I contacted through notification in magazines like *Mojo*, as that was just before the internet became a thing. But nowadays, this is more interesting, because young people who are "fed" on the internet and all modern ways of communication do recognize the value of writing by hand, of making one's message more personal, being able to attach a gift or maybe draw something, etc. And the joy of receiving a real letter. But my guess is that the inspiration comes from letter writing coming from the "older times," so it's reliving the older ways, making them relevant today. It's like nostalgia, but none of those people *lived* through those times, so it's nostalgia in another sense of the word, and also—it's bringing *back* that way of listening to music, communicating to the present, so it is kind of "un-nostalgia-ing" in a way.[41]

After Liverpool's Beatleweek, the Fest for Beatles Fans is the biggest Beatles convention in the world, and the attendance of a diverse demographic of fans is very revealing about millennial fans. The online *Rebeat* magazine makes two very important points about "new" Beatles fans. First, millennial fans have the distinction that their fandom is always tainted with the deaths of Lennon and Harrison. One of the spokes on the wheel of conventions is grief:

If you became a fan after 1980, the Beatles' story inevitably included John Lennon's horrific murder. Kids learn about it as soon [as] they start asking adults about the Beatles ("Can we see them live?" "What are they doing now?"). It was heartbreaking to learn that the cheeky Beatle standing stage left at *The Ed Sullivan Show* is not only gone but met such a gruesome end.

For me, a new fan at eight years old, it was the first time I learned about such a tragic event happening anywhere to anyone. As the years have gone on, more events have compounded this sadness for fans of all ages. Perhaps we're lucky to have never felt the innocence-shattering sorrow that so many first-generationers describe on that tragic day. But we didn't know that innocent time either.[42]

This piece of writing contextualizes Beatles fandom in 2017, a phenomenon that grows exponentially year by year; this is one of the most fascinating aspects of Beatle fandom, that it is constantly reimagined into something fresh:

The way fans express Beatlemania has changed with the time and the power of global communication, and many second- and third-gen fans now consider themselves part of a fandom, much like those who are devoted to *Doctor Who* or *Harry Potter*. Creative extensions of the Beatles, like cover bands, original music, visual art, and even fan fiction (go on, search "McLennon" . . . I dare you) aren't relegated to someone's garage or journal.

They're shared with the world through social media, Tumblr, SoundCloud, and so many other outlets. Beatles-themed music and art are appearing more and more at Comic Cons alongside traditional "nerd" culture—check out Vivek Tiwary's *Fifth Beatle* graphic novel about Brian Epstein for one—and with the Fest and similar gatherings, Beatles fans have their own dedicated cons.[43]

The fact that Beatles fandom is mentioned alongside that of *Harry Potter* indicates the former's mass-market appeal.

As of August 2017, the Fest for Beatles Fans had continued to grow exponentially. Fans gathered in Chicago's Hyatt Regency O'Hare Hotel to create enterprising new types of fandom. The Fest had a "Fabatory" that invited fans to appropriate and transgress the Beatles phenomenon and "invent the future of being a Beatles fan."[44] The Fest for Beatles Fans looks far backward in order to look far forward. Conventions are cultural industries that continue to attract new fans who demand fresh and innovative approaches to the Fabs.

Beatles conventions are an arena where fantasy brings the band back together; conventions represent magical thinking or creative fantasies of fans:

> Where do all these fictional Beatles fantasies come from? Just off the top of my head, there's the musical *Beatlemania*, the Seventies TV movie *The Birth of the Beatles*, the early Robert Zemeckis film *I Wanna Hold Your Hand*, recent films like *The Hours and Times* and *Backbeat*, Beatle fan-fiction Web sites, and *Austin Powers*, which goofs on the Beatles even more than it goofs on Bond. Nobody makes movies about Dylan or the Stones or Zeppelin. And if memory serves, none of these Beatles fantasies is entirely rubbish, either—not even Beatlemania, which rocked me and my little sisters just fine in fourth grade. I guess the dream of a Beatles reunion dies hard, even twenty years after tragedy settled that question. There's a bond we hear in the Beatles' music, as the lads start off celebrating their friendship (the joy of "Boys") and end up remembering it mournfully (the ache of "Two of Us"). Movies like Two of Us tap into a fantasy that we Beatles fans have shared since long before John died: Because the Beatles can't bring themselves back together, the job falls to us. In our dreams, John and Paul are still on their way back home.[45]

LeakyCon, Potterverse, and Millennial Beatles Fans

As Womack states, millennial Beatles fans want to be involved, and they want to inhabit fan spaces, as opposed to boomers, who are often nostalgic spectators of culture. Louisa Ellen Stein writes, "In its diverse fannish energy, LeakyCon encapsulates millennial fan cultures and values in all their complexity and contradiction."[46] LeakyCon involves millennial fans who engage with various aspects of fandom; these "congoers" are "an intersection of largely female, queer-friendly youth cultures who use media around them for their own (not necessarily normative) ends and who move freely from media, digital interface to digital interface, and most especially from role of audience, reader, and viewer to (transmedia) producer."[47] LeakyCon is a postmodernist mélange of fandoms. For example, Siriusly Hazza P's guide to LeakyCon in London in 2013 had a top 10 of fandom attractions.

Number 1 was the center of the *Harry Potter* universe, platform 9¾ at King's Cross Station; number 2 was shared between Sherlock Holmes's house on Baker Street and the Beatles Shop; and number 3 was the Abbey Road zebra crossing in St John's Wood. The *Harry Potter* fans at LeakyCon performed as Sgt. Potter's Lonely Horcrux Band, which is an example of unnostalgizing Beatles fandom, weaving Beatles fandom and *Harry Potter* fandom together to create a new hybrid form of entertainment. This type of millennial fan activity again expresses the desire to inhabit Beatles fandom, to create a performative act inspired from the Beatles canon. Often, millennial tribute acts are no respecters of the tradition, and they appropriate Beatles culture into contemporary forms.

Millennials Making the Past Current

Hernandez, a Mexican-American who divides her time between London and Liverpool, was very revealing about the heterogeneity of Beatles fans who, like herself, are employed in Beatles cultural tourism and those who participate in it. Her personal fandom narrative illustrates three very important points about fandom. First is her unnostalgizing or progressive fandom, in that she first became a fan in 2008, when she was 9 years old, her choir was singing "I Want To Hold Your Hand," her teacher give her a picture of the Beatles, and she immediately developed a "crush" on Lennon. However, although this anecdote is illuminating regarding the Beatles' appeal with image and music, it is more important for the fact that the Beatles' image and music are not retrogressive nostalgia. Here is a fan who encountered the Beatles 35 years after Beatlemania, the band is relevant to her childhood, and her reaction is unnostalgizing or progressive as the Beatles are unanchored from their '60s context and enjoyed in a contemporary cultural setting. Second, Hernandez's job at the Beatle Story museum gave her access and unique insight into an incredibly diverse demographic of fans. While working in the shop and as a Spanish speaker, she talked to fans who spoke very little English; she found out that "one of the most common nationalities of fans was Argentinian."[48] She characterized the age group at the museum as ranging from "10 to 80," and said that the psychological motivation for these fans visiting Abbey Road, the Beatles' homes in Liverpool, and every other site that had any conceivable connection to the Beatles was "taking things from the past and making them present to them now." One of the ways they did this was by collecting items from the shop. Hernandenz said they buy "one of everything, key rings, dolls, bottle openers, they make a point of buying a record."[49] Not only do fans have a contemporaneous experience of walking around old Beatles haunts, but they also furnish their lives with merchandise that seems to bring them a sense of security and comfort; Hernandez adheres to this theory, describing her own room in London as a "shrine" to the Beatles. Third, her age links to the previous two points; she is young, and the Beatles phenomenon for her is present and progressive, so working in Beatles cultural tourism is engaging with fans in the here and now and looking forward.

Hernandez's fan narrative is a fascinating case study. When she first arrived in London from the United States, she took a taxi straight to Abbey Road (before seeing Shakespeare's Globe and Buckingham Palace) and from there went to the main cultural Beatles sites in Liverpool (the National Trust Houses and the Beatles Story museum). She said that "when visiting these places, it's not 1962, and you can't possibly know how it was then, so you make it up in your head."[50] In a sense, this is active cultural tourism in the moment. Hernandez exemplifies the millennial Beatles fandom that is making the past current.

"All You Need Is Love": Global Millennial Fandom

Millennial Beatles fans were born circa 1982 and graduated from college around 2000. They are a generation of Beatles fans who are remaking the Beatles phenomenon with a millennial spin. That spin is a global international identity predicated on technology. What this means is that Beatles tribute bands, millennial Analogues fans, Beatles slash fiction writers, Beatles fans on YouTube, Beatles fan conventions, and Beatles English heritage culture have been energized by technology into creating an international Beatles millennial identity. This is evidenced by tribute bands at conventions that spring from a dizzying proliferation of countries all over the world. This is true of all the aspects of millennial Beatles fandom that I have mentioned in this chapter; the Beatles' music and image are transgressed, and these "new" bricolage art forms (tribute bands, mash-ups, pornographic stories) are disseminated globally. This multicultural Beatles fandom is "part Harry Potter, part Lego [Lego Beatles], part Kwanzaa, and part Pokemon."[51] Millennial Beatles fans are putting into effect a bricolage art that is not only

a complicated weave of the old and the new, Beatles art enhanced by technology and millennial creativity, but also a more international Beatles fan
identity, the possibility of which was augured in *Our World*, the first live international satellite show, broadcast on June 25, 1967. Artists, including the
Beatles, opera singer Maria Callas, and painter Pablo Picasso, represented 19
nations. The two-and-a-half-hour event had the largest television audience
ever up to that date: an estimated 400 million to 700 million people around
the globe watched the broadcast. The broadcast is most famous for the segment from the United Kingdom starring the Beatles. Millennial Beatles fans
have grown up with the technology to spread this quixotic multicultural uto-
pianism. As Neil Howe and William Strauss contend:

> The world's Boomers grew up with domestically produced movie and TV
> shows. Gen Xers grew up with VCRs and the rise of personal computers.
> The idea of worldwide linkages dawned while they were still children.
> Millennials are growing up after this already happened. . . . Where global
> Gen Xers feel they are pioneering a new high-tech frontier, Millennials are
> growing up as the frontier is being settled—and, in time, will adapt the new
> technologies to suit themselves.[52]

Stein, in her book *Millennial Fandom*, echoes Howe and Strauss's definition
of millennials:

> the millennial generation purportedly spans across two decades,
> encompassing those born between 1982 and 2004. This wide age range merges
> two desirable markets, teens and young adults, both of whom are thought to
> have significant disposable income. This compounded demographic positions
> millennials as a highly desirable target audience for advertisers and TV
> networks alike.[53]

Although they are a target audience—Google owns YouTube, for
example—millennial Beatles fans subvert Beatles product in a transgressive manner; millennial fans have agency despite being part of a capitalist
electronic envelope. An integral aspect of millennial Beatles fandom is using
technology to appropriate new meanings from the cultural Beatles phenomenon through YouTube, online slash fiction, and videos from Beatles walks,
museums, and conventions.

Millennial Beatles fans are recasting Beatles art by inhabiting Beatles culture, whether that is dressing as the band members, writing erotic stories about the band, mashing the canon to add beats and raps to old songs, and posting videos of fans at shrines such as Lennon's and McCartney's childhood homes, the church where Lennon and McCartney met, and Abbey Road Studios during Beatles walks. The tendency to mash and reimagine Beatles songs is most subversive when it comes to the peerless canon of Beatles songs. For example, in 1968, the Beatles released the *White Album*; in 2003, Jay-Z released the *Black Album*; and in 2004, Danger Mouse mashed both to create the *Grey Album*. This intersection of musical genres demonstrates how art is changed by new generations into an updated song. Jay-Z was born in 1969 and is a boomer, Danger Mouse (Brian Burton) was born in 1977 and is a Gen-Xer, but they breathe new life into old songs by musical bricolage of the old and the new. Millennials are continuing Danger Mouse's iconoclastic tendency by either mashing Beatles songs or adapting the Beatles' lyrics into their work. Rae Sremmurd (Ear Drummers) is made up of two millennial Beatles fans, Swae Lee and Slim Jxmmi, an American hip-hop duo from Tupelo, Mississippi, who have appropriated Beatles lyrics for their US number one hit, "Black Beatles." *Rolling Stone*'s Rob Sheffield chose it as one of his top 25 songs of 2016, and his review of the song demonstrates that Beatles songs are anthems of a millennial generation who want to inhabit Beatles art and twist the music and lyrics into new cultural forms:

> Money, hoes and clothes, all a Beatle knows. I love how this crowd-pleaser gets the flex zone of the Fabs so bizarrely yet beautifully right—a utopian rap party where everybody's rich, everybody's high, everybody's famous. It's a hit that forces you to sing along even if you have to keep making up new verses ("That girl she's a real crowd-pleaser / Hold you in her armchair you can feel her diseases") to up the Beatle ante ("A broke ho can only point me to a rich ho / She came in through the bathroom window / Like Chapo serving yayo to the gringo / You a Pete Best bitch, she a Ringo"). After all, the Beatles wrote "Can't Buy Me Love" in the haze of a nine-day orgy with Miami's finest groupies—as Paul McCartney said, "It should have been 'Can Buy Me Love,' actually." So no wonder Paul loves this song as much as the rest of us do.[54]

Rae Sremmurd epitomize the millennial desire to adapt and change Beatles art; in this example, Swae Lee and Slim Jxmmi are millennial fans who rework the Beatles' lyrics into new intertextual pieces that become anthems for a postmillennial generation.

Christopher Shaw and Malcolm Chase describe how the "inventor" of English folk song, Cecil Sharpe, used "unscholarly interference" to create a canon of English music. Shaw and Chase contend that

> Far from being half remembered, quaint, and archaic, tradition may be selective, with the past actively organized to speak to current anxieties and tensions. Such structures do not erect themselves. We should look carefully at the process of cultural construction to see how, when, and by whom they become articulated, and look carefully at their intentions and effects.[55]

In a sense, millennial Beatles fans embody "unscholarly interference"; fans want to be playful with canons and reimagine Beatles songs and films. Millennials' digital "cultural construction" and their remix bricolage texts epitomize a desire to reorganize anthems of the past to make them relevant to "current anxieties," as millennials give way to postmillennials or Gen Zers. (There is much contemporary debate on postmillennial identity. Are they called Gen Z? Was 1998 or 2004 the cutoff point for millennials?) These historical and semantic discussions emphasize that it is anybody's guess into what new directions Gen Zers or postmillennials will warp Beatles art.

Notes

1. N. Howe and W. Strauss, *Millennials Rising: The Next Great Generation* (New York: Vintage, 2000), 10.
2. H. Jenkins, *Textual Poachers: Television Fans and Participatory Culture* (New York: Routledge, 1992), 248.
3. L. Geraghty, *Cult Collectors: Nostalgia, Fandom and Collecting Popular Culture* (London: Routledge, 2014), 128.
4. Joanna Kozlowska, personal interview, 2017.
5. Stephanie Hernandez, personal interview, 2017.
6. A. Bennett, "Even Better Than the Real Thing? Understanding the Tribute Band Phenomenon," in *Access All Eras: Tribute Bands and Global Pop Culture*, ed. Shane Homan (London: Open University Press, 2006), 23.
7. Bennett, "Even Better Than the Real Thing?" 23.
8. R. Ellis, *The Singing Dead* (Skipton, UK: Magna Large Print, 2002).
9. G. Gregory, *Send in the Clones: A Cultural Study of the Tribute Band* (Sheffield, UK: Equinox 2012), 128.

10. Tony Giangreco, personal interview, 2018.
11. Giangreco, interview.
12. Giangreco, interview.
13. Giangreco, interview.
14. Ken Womack, personal interview, 2018.
15. Womack, interview. He was referring to The Beatles' *The White Album*: An International Symposium, Monmouth University, November 2018.
16. Womack, interview.
17. Womack, interview.
18. K. Johnson, "David Bowie Is," in *David Bowie: Critical Perspectives*, ed. E. Devereux, A. Dillane, and M. J. Power (New York: Routledge, 2015), 14.
19. https://missmcharrison.tumblr.com/fanfiction.
20. Rhetorician and literary critic, co-author of *The Meaning of Meaning: A Study of the Influence of Language upon Thought and of the Science of Symbolism* (1923).
21. Sherlocked221, "Who Knows How Long I've Loved You," https://archiveofourown.org/works/11600004.
22. M. Hills, *Fan Cultures* (London: Routledge, 2002), 93.
23. Hills, *Fan Cultures*, 112.
24. Quietprofanity, "Evasion," https://thebeatlesfanfiction.tumblr.com/post/99655322369/evasion.
25. Quietprofanity, "Evasion."
26. P. Booth, *Digital Fandom 2.0: New Media Studies* (New York: Peter Lang, 2017), 238–239.
27. M. Duffett, *Understanding Fandom: An Introduction to the Study of Media Fan Culture* (London: Bloomsbury, 2013), 285.
28. Booth, *Digital Fandom 2.0*, 236.
29. Linden and Linden, *Fans and Fan Cultures*, 72.
30. Linden and Linden, *Fans and Fan Cultures*, 72.
31. Liden and Linden, *Fans and Fan Cultures*, 72.
32. Linden and Linden, *Fans and Fan Cultures*, 72.
33. G. Debord, *Society of the Spectacle* (London: Rebel, 2002), 103
34. S. Fremaux and M. Fremaux, "Remembering the Beatles' Legacy in Hamburg's Problematic Tourism Strategy," *Journal of Heritage Tourism* 8, no. 4 (2013): 303–319.
35. T. Brabazon, *Popular Music: Topics, Trends and Trajectories* (London: Sage, 2012), 54.
36. K. Worcman and J. Garde-Hansen, *Social Memory Technology: Theory, Practice, Action* (New York: Routledge, 2016), 54 (source citations omitted).
37. Kozlowska, interview.
38. Kozlowska, interview.
39. Kozlowska, interview.
40. Kozlowska, interview.
41. Kozlowska, interview.
42. Erika White, "10 Reasons Why the Second- and Third-Gen Beatles Fan Experience Is Unlike Any Other," *Rebeat*, August 6, 2017, http://www.rebeatmag.com/10-reasons-second-third-gen-beatles-fan-experience-unlike/.

43. White, "10 Reasons."
44. The Fest for Beatles Fans, "Propose a FABoratory session for #FESTCHESTER here,": Facebook, https://www.facebook.com/beatlesfest/photos/a.68630068175/10152692520178176
45. R. Sheffield, "VH1's Beatles Fantasy (and Ours)," *Rolling Stone*, March 2, 2000.. http://web.b.ebscohost.com/ehost/detail/detail?vid=1&sid=f095dbb8-0edb-4d54-a242-7cfa66e389a4%40pdc-v-sessmgr01&bdata=JnNpdGU9ZWhvc3QtbGl2ZQ%3d%3d#AN=2854215&db=aph
46. L. Stein, *Millennial Fandom: Television Audiences in the Transmedia Age* (Iowa City: University of Iowa Press, 2015), 171.
47. Stein, *Millennial Fandom*, 172.
48. Hernandez, interview.
49. Hernandez, interview.
50. Hernandez, interview.
51. Howe and Strauss, *Millennials Rising*, 298–299.
52. Howe and Strauss, *Millennials Rising*, 297.
53. Stein, *Millennial Fandom*, 7.
54. R. Sheffield, "Rob Sheffield's Top Twenty Five Songs of 2016," *Rolling Stone,* December 22, 2016, https://www.rollingstone.com/music/music-lists/rob-sheffields-top-25-songs-of-2016-191110/david-bowie-i-cant-give-everything-away-191133/.
55. C. Shaw and M. Chase, eds., *The Imagined Past: History and Nostalgia* (Manchester: Manchester University Press, 1989), 14.

Bibliography

"Beatles Sex." https://missmcharrison.tumblr.com/fanfiction.
Bennett, Andy. "Even Better Than the Real Thing? Understanding the Tribute Band Phenomenon." In *Access All Eras: Tribute Bands and Global Pop Culture*, edited by Shane Homan, 19–31. London: Open University Press, 2006.
Brabazon, Tara. *Popular Music: Topics, Trends and Trajectories*. London: Sage, 2012.
Booth, Paul. *Digital Fandom 2.0: New Media Studies*. New York: Peter Lang, 2017.
Debord, Guy. *Society of the Spectacle*. London: Aldgate, 1992.
Duffett, Mark. *Understanding Fandom: An Introduction to the Study of Media Fan Culture*. London: Bloomsbury, 2013.
Ellis, Ron. *The Singing Dead*. Skipton, UK: Magna Large Print, 2002.
The Fest for Beatles Fans, "Propose a FABoratory session for #FESTCHESTER here," Facebook, February 28, 2015. https://www.facebook.com/beatlesfest/photos/a.68630068175/10152692520178176.
Fremaux, Stephanie, and Mark Fremaux. "Remembering the Beatles' Legacy in Hamburg's Problematic Tourism Strategy." *Journal of Heritage Tourism* 8, no. 4 (2013): 303–319.
Funkles. *The Black Album: The Beatles on Funk* (2017), https://thefunkles.bandcamp.com/releases.
Geraghty, Lincoln. *Cult Collectors: Nostalgia, Fandom and Collecting Popular Culture*. London: Routledge, 2014.

Gregory, Georgina. *Send in the Clones: A Cultural Study of the Tribute Band*. Sheffield, UK: Equinox, 2012.

Hills, Matt. *Fan Cultures* London: Routledge, 2002.

Howe, Neil, and William Strauss. *Millennials Rising: The Next Great Generation*. New York: Vintage, 2000.

Jenkins, Henry. *Textual Poachers: Television Fans and Participatory Culture*. New York: Routledge, 1992.

Johnson, Kathryn. "David Bowie Is." In *David Bowie: Critical Perspectives*, edited by E. Devereux, A. Dillane, and M. J. Power, 1–18. New York: Routledge, 2015.

Linden, Sara, and Henrik Linden. *Fans and Fan Cultures: Tourism, Consumerism and Social Media*. London: Palgrave McMillan, 2017.

Quietprofanity. "Evasion." https://thebeatlesfanfiction.tumblr.com/post/99655322369/evasion.

Shaw, Christopher, and Malcolm Chase, eds. *The Imagined Past: History and Nostalgia*. Manchester: Manchester University Press, 1989.

Sheffield, Rob. *Dreaming the Beatles: The Love Story of One Band and the Whole World*. New York: HarperCollins, 2017.

Sheffield, Rob. "Rob Sheffield's Top Twenty Five Songs of 2016." *Rolling Stone*, December 22, 2016. https://www.rollingstone.com/music/music-lists/rob-sheffields-top-25-songs-of-2016-191110/david-bowie-i-cant-give-everything-away-191133/.

Sheffield, Rob. "VH1's Beatles Fantasy (and Ours)." *Rolling Stone*, March 2, 2000. http://web.b.ebscohost.com/ehost/detail/detail?vid=1&sid=f095dbb8-0edb-4d54-a242-7cfa66e389a4%40pdc-v-sessmgr01&bdata=JnNpdGU9ZWhvc3QtbGl2ZQ%3d%3d#AN=2854215&db=aph.

Sherlocked221. "Who Knows How Long I've Loved You." https://archiveofourown.org/works/11600004

Stein, Louisa Ellen. *Millennial Fandom: Television Audiences in the Transmedia Age*. Iowa City: University of Iowa Press, 2015.

White, Erika. "10 Reasons Why the Second- and Third-Gen Beatles Fan Experience Is Unlike Any Other." *Rebeat*, August 6, 2017. http://www.rebeatmag.com/10-reasons-second-third-gen-beatles-fan-experience-unlike/.

Worcman, Karen, and Joanne Garde-Hansen. *Social Memory Technology: Theory, Practice, Action*. New York: Routledge, 2016.

10

Beatles Heritage Tourism in Liverpool

Standing at the Crossroads?

Michael Brocken

> People have just lived off the fact that if you've got The Beatles, the football and Scouse then that's enough to bring people here. To a certain extent that's true, but once they get here what they really like about Liverpool is its sense of place and that sense of place comes from its incredible built environment. What I can't understand about Liverpool is why there is this polarised opposition between heritage and development—they're not in conflict.[1]

During the summer months of 2017, several celebrations in Liverpool revolved around the 50th anniversary of the release of the Beatles' seminal *Sgt. Pepper* album and the opening of the city's Metropolitan Cathedral. Rather curiously, both sets of events were somewhat nostalgically and inaccurately linked via that rather hackneyed 1967 Summer of Love cliché (from personal memory, there wasn't much to "love" about Liverpool in 1967). While it was apposite for local marketing consultants to attempt to connect the city with both the year and the album in any way possible (although arguably, *Sgt. Pepper* is perhaps one of the Beatles' least Liverpool-informed albums), the relationship between the mythologized Summer of Love and the Roman Catholic authorities in the city appeared historically thin, to say the least. Alongside popular music luminaries Spencer Leigh and Ron Ellis, I was involved in the "Summer of Love" project. My conversations with several local oral-history scholars induced feelings within me of great discomfort; in truth, I felt like a fraud, so strong were

Michael Brocken, *Beatles Heritage Tourism in Liverpool* In: *Fandom and the Beatles.* Edited by: Kenneth Womack and Kit O'Toole, Oxford University Press (2021). © Oxford University Press. DOI: 10.1093/oso/9780190917852.003.0011 the strains of mythology and indigenous chauvinism emanating from the researchers.

Such parody historicity has always been intrinsic to the fascinating shadow play taking place between the Beatles and the city of their birth, with both imagery and imagination conjuring up compelling beliefs that, in turn, command narratives of authority. However, more recently, such heritage strategies have smacked a little of desperation, perhaps masking a growing reality that the relationship between surviving Beatles fragments in Liverpool and the development of popular-music heritage tourism across the globe has irrevocably changed. Indeed, the very passage of time between "then" and "now" informs us that the rhetoric concerning the Beatles, Liverpool, and "the '60s, man"—employed over the years by local entrepreneurs with great approbation and at times even a touch of bravado—is beginning to wear at the edges and represents little more than a rather outdated, white, gendered, anglophone rock meta-narrative in what has now become a truly multifaceted global popular-music (tourism) marketplace.

Arguably, this is at least partially because Liverpool's position as both *the* authentic site for Beatles and Merseybeat tourism and a World Heritage Site of great significance has never been more precarious. As Beatles fans age and pass away, making the need for those "I was there, so I know" tellings intrinsic to most Beatles tourism offerings somewhat redundant, and as citizens of previously socially restricted nations (in the capitalist sense) emerge into a heritage tourism environment, the next decade of popular-music tourism in Liverpool is clearly up for grabs. For me, one major question keeps recurring: how can the city continue to attract Beatles tourists en masse as the time period represented (the '60s) inexorably slips away into the annals of popular-music historiography? Linked to this significant question is an additional one of how the legacy of the group might be explained to visitors with little to no knowledge of the Beatles as a global popular-music phenomenon (in any case, the culturally imperialist term *global* as it might have been coined in the 1960s no longer means *global* in the 21st-century sense). These are without doubt serious economic issues, for if Liverpool also has to weather its possible removal from UNESCO's prestigious World Heritage Site list,[2] what kind of commercial tourist-based future awaits the city? For at least the past 25 years, the communication of heritage has been a vital component of the new ways of doing business in Liverpool (in practical terms, rescuing the city from economic oblivion).

Rhetoric

The passage of time has a large role to play in changing rhetorical evaluations of place significance in relation to popular music. Forever kinetic, popular music never stands still and constantly (re)invents new traditions "on the hoof"—hence the great difficulty in representing anything to do with popular music "historically" (where does one begin?). In the case of popular-music historicization, ever since the demise of the Beatle City attraction in Liverpool more than 30 years ago, the very lack of success across the United Kingdom in "museumifying" popular music (e.g., the failure of the popular-music museum in Sheffield and the British Music Experience in London, the boredom induced by the "Beat Goes On" exhibition in Liverpool, and the confusion for non-Bristolians about "Bristol Music: Seven Decades of Sound" in 2018, etc.) has been all too evident, suggesting that popular-music activities cannot simply be preserved and/or presented in a glass case.

Further, even though the Royal Albert Dock (and the Beatles Story museum housed within) is testament to the potential of vast historic buildings to deliver representations of the popular in inventive ways (fortunately, it is a building to which people are almost "naturally" drawn), the housing of historical and/or experiential representations of popular music within such architectural virtuosity remain somewhat problematic for local Liverpudlians, who are drawn neither to a 1980s Conservative government initiative nor to a pop group that effectively "deserted the city."[3] One local popular-music guide even remarked to me despondently about the arrival of the British Music Experience at the Cunard Building (one of Liverpool's "Three Graces") on the waterfront: "Here we go again—more guitars in glass cases, and this time in a building that might have more sensibly been reverted back to its original purpose."[4]

The annual cruise-liner market is now worth an astonishing £28 billion a year worldwide but, according to Tom Barber, carries with it severe drawbacks for riverine cities:

> If you've ever been in a harbour when a cruise liner hoves into view, you'll understand the full horror of what happens next. These leviathans, sometimes 18 storeys tall, disgorge their thousands of wobbly, sunburnt inmates into the port where they swarm around shops selling tat—never venturing even a yard off the tourist drags to bother finding out what exists beyond. And then, as quickly as they appeared, they're gone, sailing off, belching

noxious fumes, to swamp the next poor coastal town that's got itself hooked on the easy dollars such cruises provide.[5]

Should we inform these visitors that they have somehow missed out on the "greatness" of the Beatles? Do they need a popular-music re-education program concerning this 20th-century historical phenomenon? (Like Barber above, I'm being somewhat ironic here.) And what kind of histories do we present? Historical continuity or discontinuity? Diachronic or synchronic historical models? Do we rhetorically represent "our" version of Beatles history as a dialectic challenge and engage in a plurality of versions, or do we just stick with the hagiography? After all, cruise ship tourists are only with us long enough to purchase two T-shirts and a key ring and quite literally have no time for complexities (should they even be bothered at all). Such questions also invite us to interrogate our cultural periodizations and popular-music ownership (e.g., what is a popular-music "era," and to whom does a period "belong"—the Beatles? their fans?). We should also seriously contemplate the fact that all history tellings are, to some extent, apprehensions of change—yet times *are* undoubtedly changing.

Thus far, what appears to have been put over to the Beatles fan and tourist alike has been a narrative of absolute Beatles reality, insisting that what is subjectively real and important to the fan must also be essentially real and important in the objective world of fact. In the present scheme of things in Liverpool, a "Beatles reality" is not supposed to be relative, open to interpretation, or dependent upon changing factors of time and space. Instead, it is sold to the fan as a narrative of absolute truth and value and something against which all other popular-music values should be measured. It is, in fact, a classic example of a function myth. Although function myths are truly fascinating, we all appreciate—do we not?—that they are almost entirely rhetorical.

Perhaps if we disengage our representations from the absolutism of myth and consider other ways of acknowledging the important legacy of the Beatles, a few positives might emerge from the approaching dilemma; for example, Ernesto Laclau informs us that

The relationship between a foundation and what it founds is quite different from a symbol representation and that which is symbolized. In foundational logic there is a necessary, determining relation between the founding agency and the founded entity; in symbolic representation, on the other hand, no such internal motivation exists and the chain of equivalent signifieds can be extended indefinitely. The former is a relation of delimitation and determination, i.e. fixation. The latter is an open-ended horizon.[6]

An "open-ended horizon" sounds fantastic; nevertheless, in practical terms, how do we go about implementing such indeterminacy across Beatles tourism strategies of the future? In purely practical terms, and in spite of great progress being made by this relatively new business sector in Liverpool (particularly on its beautiful waterfront), real problems still persist across the city. For example, the city still has only a 64% employment rate, while nationally this figure is nearer to 74%. The arterial districts of Kirkdale and Kensington are among some of the most deprived in the United Kingdom, never mind Merseyside. Popular-music tourism's past has partly helped to address this by bringing new revenue streams into the city, but, as I have written elsewhere,[7] certain Beatles-related sites remain off the Beatles track because they are situated, in a tourist sense, in "unpresentable" districts.

If Beatles tourism is more than merely an entrepreneurial tendency (I think it is) and if it is truly capable of being a historical-cum-cultural phenomenon in its own right (I also think this is possible), perhaps in the future, Beatles tourism might begin to revolve around and cultivate resistant and identity-awarding contemporary cultures, while at the same time referring backward toward popular music's historical and creative strengths and weakness, resynthesizing elements drawn from diverse origins along the way—just as rock and roll and skiffle did, in the first place. After all, any city as a living and breathing organism, and any genre of popular music as a living and breathing craft, holds potential for imaginative (re-)encounters, from which all kinds of disparate activities and representations might emerge. We already know (do we not?) that popular-music histories on their own develop in ways *not* just on their own. Each and every popular-music history informs us of pop's coexistence with variable social mores, recycled built environments, and the variegated habitus of those both for and against it; pop creativity thrives by and through such encounters. If the Beatles' legacy cannot be subject to mutations, compromises, or challenges, how on earth are we going to invite and then inspire younger, less absolutist popular-music visitors to the city?

Liverpool's built environment actually has a long history of colluding with popular music in a creative yet also critical stance. Coffee bars encouraged creativity, warehouses were recycled into nightclubs, and boxing, football, and speedway stadiums, together with open spaces, were turned into venues and festival sites. Entire city streets (such as Whitechapel) became "musical." Such activities did not encourage historical conformism but instead tempered and mediated creativity according to the specifics of place. They advanced the possibilities of heterogeneous activities and traditions thereby representing a zeitgeist, the very spirit of creativity, and the significance of place in their time. Edward Lefebvre posits three types of space: perceived, conceived, and lived. Edward Soja later "re-described" this "spatial triad" with perhaps more straightforward terms: "firstspace," "secondspace," and "thirdspace." In the case of Lefebvre's first two spaces, perceived and conceived (both of which concern infrastructure and the enhancement of everyday activities), Soja states:

> two terms (and the oppositions and antinomies built around them) *are never enough* [my emphasis]. *Il y a toujours l'Autre*, there is always an-Other term, with *Autre*/Other capitalized to emphasize its critical importance. When faced with a choice confined to the either/or, Lefebvre creatively resisted by choosing instead an-Other alternative, marked by the openness of the both/and also . . ., with the "also" reverberating back to disrupt the categorical closures implicit in the either/or logic.[8]

For Soja, "thirdspace" adds an imagined dimension to our interpretations of the value of space and asks us to consider the spaces that, once they have been encountered, generate real meaning as part of the very experience of living; Liverpool's urban built environment is full of such spaces.

I have stated elsewhere that "the illumination of disparate popular music discourses has been overshadowed by an over concentration on selected genres, idealised images, and the creation of a popular music 'universal standpoint' concerning meaning and value where no such universality actually exists."[9] This perspective was drawn from my studies concerning how significant local practices and networks, together with their associated authenticities, are frequently overlooked and disregarded as popular-music discourses, when more commercially successful homilies are rhetorically acknowledged as the only or, at the very least, "central" focus. If popular music is indeed a "lived experience," then local practices surrounding other forms of popular music—from country music to "Scouse house"—should not be systematically downgraded by a static historical/spatial hyperreality of the Beatles. Doing so takes us into a space that gives us no sense of popular-music

historical reality and is merely a shadowy resemblance of something else created for the purpose of exclusion and exclusivity. The increased empowerment behind such hyperreal places and spaces has certainly generated new
ways of doing business, with communication-intensive economies and technological innovations. Yet in Liverpool, this has supported rather than led to
a questioning of the totalizing, essentialist meta-narratives surrounding the
Beatles and place.

Green Badge guide Charlotte Martin informed me:

> You can't help but wonder where new, more interesting initiatives are going
> to come from—especially in the light of there being more guides in the city
> than are needed. But also for me, one of the real partly hidden problems
> lies in the fact that although this summer [2018] over 60 cruise liners are
> visiting the city—which has to be very encouraging, of course—most of
> them, I think, are only stopping overnight, which means that there's barely
> any time left for passengers to spend money, never mind go on a tour, and
> of course, how many of these people are actually interested in the Beatles?
> There are other issues, too; for example, my complaints about the state of
> Mathew Street became front-page news in the *Liverpool Echo* a few months
> ago. It's like walking along the boardwalk in Tenerife, you are hassled by
> guys trying to drag you in for a drink; at times, the atmosphere's not great.
> More thought is needed; in fact, more creative future planning is now
> essential.[10]

In November 2015, Liverpool City Council published a strategic report concerning Beatles tourism titled "Beatles Heritage in Liverpool and
Its Economic and Cultural Sector Impact: A Report for Liverpool City
Council." The document (hereafter "the strategic report") was produced by
the University of Liverpool and Liverpool John Moores University on behalf
of the city council and, it should be stated, was by no means the kind of "future planning"-style document suggested by Martin. In fact, it was largely restricted by its own purpose and its methods and approaches—those being to
statistically analyze tourism in a quantifiable and politicized way. Arguably,
nothing could be more removed from the essence of a city as a popular-
music "creatopolis" than the institutionalization of the popular via statistics
and politics.

The Strategic Report: Missing the Point?

It would be entirely wrong for me to condemn this diminutive report out of hand, for it contains several important cultural observations that do need our careful consideration regarding the future of Beatles heritage tourism. For example, the report correctly considers how the Beatles' "brand" is of great significance and that Liverpool's associations with that brand require quality delivery programs. Also, training within specific sectors of the industry need to be taken more seriously (both are discussed on p. 3 of the report). The document also suggests (more broadly via its tone) that definitions of what constitutes or defines the Beatles' legacy (p. 7) need to be expanded by encompassing issues related to music activities, quality offerings to visitors, heritage, industry, and so on. What is offered to visitors via tourism in the city of Liverpool has created a variety of services, and these are described as an "industry." Yet this term appears dated and politically hidebound. The Beatles "sector" (a word that allows a far better grasp of what's goes on) evidently requires more integration with the creative and performing arts; however. little discussion takes place in the report concerning coordinating and integrating with other sectors. The fact that the creative and performing arts might even come to more authentically represent the Beatles' performative heritage to younger visitors (inspired not only by the Beatles' music but also by their collective messages of peace and love) is neither proposed nor discussed, creating a significant lacuna. The Beatles' menagerie of intertextualities is vital to any understanding of their history—arguably far more so than the historical-cum-mythological tellings involved in certain Beatles tourism initiatives ("John Lennon said to me . . .").

The strategic report also makes an astounding claim by suggesting that groups and subgroups of people (one presumes committees) should strategically "control" the tellings, outputs, branding, and market availability of Beatles tourism. It also suggests that there should be long-term monitoring and evaluation of activities, together with the creation of one single major heritage resource in the city. While I have written elsewhere[11] that the concept of a resources repository and research center is an excellent one, the report's proposal of a kind of "civil service" or "local government" bureau of Beatles intervention officials appears ludicrous and extremely outmoded (an echo of the 1970s, if ever there was one). Such a suggestion has more to do with how a political space develops and consolidates itself as a recognizable entity in a city than anything to do with heritage tourism surrounding the creative arts per se.

It is illogical to suggest that every "teller" in Liverpool should be "telling" the same story. If we cannot distinguish between one narrative and another, how can we formulate historical and contextual differentiations? In any case, there already exists in Liverpool an entire body of informing conventions concerning how each "teller" paraphrases Beatles images and imaginings. The report correctly states that investment and reinvestment in the industry are patchy, with some players having failed to invest in either the mainte-nance or the organization of the products on offer, but it does not discuss fully enough the growing investment in the Beatles by the education sector (pp. 18–19). In any case, I discussed the majority of the above points in 2015.[12]

The strategic report's analysis of direct employment appears sound enough; visitor numbers are based on previously recognized analysis (such as the UK Music document published in 2014);[13] however, curiously, the sig-nificant Locum document from 2005 is not cited.[14] Discussions concerning the "youthfulness" of the brand (p. 23 of the strategic report) appear to be little more than rhetoric exchanged between interviewers and those with a direct interest perhaps based on press reports about the growing potential of Chinese and Brazilian tourist markets (in the case of Brazil, this is now out of date). So, although "the youthfulness of some of those engaging with the Beatles was emphasised by core stakeholders" (see also p. 23), the report only addresses a little of its writing to the fact that stakeholders urgently need to consider transitioning to new perceptions about the next step: *who* the next Beatles visitors are actually going to be and (more important) *how* they will be accommodated via different, perhaps more inspirational provision.

The strategic report, therefore, dated itself almost from the moment it appeared; written to sustain an "approved" Beatles meta-narrative at a given moment in time, it merely confirms, rather than projects, and sits far too comfortably with that ever-growing pile of documents concerning Beatles tourism that go back more than 30 years. It ignores the potential of a trans-actional tapestry where new development space in the city might be linked to the Beatles in many different and exciting ways—what Hannah Arendt has termed "the space of human experience."[15] It also neglects the role of creativity in existing "thirdspaces" within Liverpool's built environment; for example, it does not discuss the potential for youth arts and education, surely the most creative, inspiring, dynamic, and powerful way of making a difference socially and structurally. Indeed, perhaps the creative and performing arts are seen as existing in conflict with what might be described as the strategic report's dominant dialectic. Of course, popular culture is always anachronistic, for it does not necessarily engage in the dialectical process of struggles between classes and capital; instead, it usually has more to do with the historical impulses to attack and defend. Yet there is no excuse for ignoring how important imaginative motifs might be further developed by and through the aforementioned (scenic) "creatopolis."

Sites of Creativity: Where Are They?

I have personally witnessed the prospect of a visit to a gallery filling a young student with trepidation. Such spaces can be considered alien to young students, and I have also witnessed staff being at times elitist and uncaring and carrying overintellectualizing tendencies to the level of the excruciatingly boring. Nicola Sim's research investigated an interesting partnership between galleries and youth organizations that were using a four-year program called Circuit:

> Circuit is led by Tate galleries and is funded by the Paul Hamlyn Foundation. It involves organisations in eight towns and cities around England and Wales: Cambridge, Colchester, Liverpool, Llandudno, London, Manchester, Nottingham and St Ives. The chief goal of the programme is to connect 15–25 year olds to the arts in galleries and museums, through working together with the youth and cultural sector.[16]

Taking a multi-site, ethnographic approach, Sim followed the development of these cross-sector relationships between 2013 and 2015.

> Circuit is one example of a number of large-scale initiatives running concurrently in the UK, which have sought to foster sustainable partnerships between arts and youth organisations. While there is a long history of work in this field, gallery education and youth work are arguably less familiar to one another than the performing arts and youth work, where there are more embedded traditions of practice.[17]

According to Sim, for many young people, the creative and performing arts are far preferable to conventional gallery education, and perhaps the latter also needs to recontextualize, in order to embrace young people's needs. The education department at the Beatles Story realized this many years ago, and its Discovery Zone has been so successful via its interactive and integrated work with young visitors that it has recently been redesigned. Proprietors Merseytravel are soon to invest in an expansion of the Zone, truly an investment for the future.

The almost daily sessions with visiting schoolchildren already contribute a great deal to the economy of the attraction, while creating "informal" educational spaces to accommodate formal curriculum topics in user-friendly ways—in other words, giving expression to education's function in an informal and nonelitist setting (using "the popular" as a matrix). Here young people can express themselves individually and collectively in relation to (for example) the Beatles' legacy of music and peace, but this is not an exclusive requirement, for the young people might just as easily create their own authenticities from the Discovery Zone, thereby expressing the legacy of the Beatles in perhaps the truest sense: "being oneself."

I was monitoring a third-year undergraduate on work-based learning in the Discovery Zone in 2017. The student was teaching in the "1960s record shop zone," where children are invited to change into '60s clothing and wigs and dance the Twist after placing vinyl records on the record player. I was simply entranced by one small British Asian boy trying to get into an Elvis Presley jumpsuit (hardly the 1960s, but there we are); he struggled and struggled until he achieved his goal, just before the bell rang for the young people to move into the next "zone." His arms were raised as if he had scored a goal in the World Cup final, so delighted was he to have squeezed his small frame into the white polyester suit. My thoughts were that he would probably remember that particular "struggle" for the rest of his life.

In July 2018, there was a teachers' open day at the Beatles Story. Education officer Shelley Ruck informed me:

> Future teachers were invited to come along and see what is on offer, how can the exhibition and the Discovery Zone help in their teaching, encouraging that understanding and intrigue in Liverpool's place in history from their children, helping to understand the music it produced and the society that helped to form what the city has become today. Liverpool John Moores University also sent over 200 of their postgraduate trainee teachers along

to the Beatles Story over a two-day period so that they could understand what is on offer, how it will fit into their future teaching—this will potentially provide some financial return to the Beatles Story once those teachers have qualified and gone out into the world of teaching, when they look for a school trip that will "bring *that* topic to life."

There is so much for the next generation to absorb, and without a doubt, tourism and the financial benefit this has brought to the city is colossal—the City of Culture, the Royal Albert Dock and moving towards the "Northern Powerhouse." But education is also *essential*: involving future generations by sharing and explaining the past and helping them to understand heritage and what it means by whatever means.[18]

Something good is evidently starting to happen.

The creative and financial legacy of the Liverpool Institute for Performing Arts (LIPA) is now also an extremely powerful brand in its own right and, owing to McCartney's interest and financial investment, one that is authentically associated with the Beatles. LIPA has provided a significant space not only in the city of Liverpool but also in students' minds, where the legacy of both the Beatles and all popular-music creativity can be brought into focus—an excellent example of creative "thirdspace" where a dialectical relationship can be enacted between space, place, and history to bring about positive effects via contemplation of the ways experiences are recorded and represented. However, LIPA has also at times in its history appeared to some extent disconnected from both Liverpool and the legacy of the Beatles. Its impressive buildings appear akin to a fortress behind which are activities related to whatever current machinations of the performing-arts industries dictate. Via its community arts and drama program, we do see an example of the potential of creative interaction with the local community, and its musicians do integrate with the local music economy in several different ways; yet more might be done.

Years ago, as a freelance lecturer, I taught for a short time at LIPA, but was invited back in July 2018. I immediately received the impression of not feeling part of a community. Instead, I was required to understand just where I was—not so much in an intellectual way but by making me feel that I had entered an inner sanctum of a hallowed sect. A deeper connection through the framework of architecture—place and space—and the communication of creative and performing arts within was, for me, effectively lost, for the sake of projecting a kind of gnostic performance-based shrine (rather than "workshop"). After my brief visit, which lasted for perhaps two hours at most, I was left wondering, how in the future can this place possibly work *for* Liverpool in a broader sense? Indeed, how can it adequately relate in the present to the cityscape from which it was recycled (and to which it still belongs) and open itself up to a more undetermined and metrics-free creative consciousness? I was reminded of composer Michael Nyman's comments way back in 1970 (just as the Beatles were splitting up):

> I think that this whole question of art is a question of changing our minds and that the function of the artist is not self-expression but rather self-alteration . . . [I]f we have the view we used to have, that there was only one right way of observing the relationship of things, then we have a situation that really doesn't appeal to me. We have, in other words, one thing that's right and all the rest are wrong. I would like to have a multiplicity of rights.[19]

Liverpool deserves a "multiplicity of rights" without "wrongs" (not a Beatles police or a performance redoubt). Bricolage and the recycling of existing structures were to begin with at the very heart of the LIPA experiment, and the reuse of leftover buildings allowed those in charge to go exploring through and salvage them, finding inventive ways of transforming what was actually physically falling apart into what might "become."

My own Beatles master's program at Liverpool Hope University is discussed a bit in the strategic report. This program produced more than 70 MA graduates, some of whom have also gone on to achieve doctorates and/or work-related advancement. The master's program also enjoys a work-based learning partnership with the Beatles Story, which has meant that in exchange for undergraduates enjoying work-based experiences in the Discovery Zone as part of their degree, several members of the Beatles Story staff have been able to study in the master/s program, making not only the Beatles Story staff but also several other Blue and Green Badge guides working in Liverpool's popular-music heritage tourism industry among the most highly qualified in the country. Further, the master's degree has brought to Liverpool Hope University approximately £1 million in fees alone and has also contributed far more than this to Liverpool's economy via students embracing the cultural life of the city. Yet the future of the Beatles MA was, of course, like any postgraduate program in the United Kingdom in 2018, in some doubt, as fees increased and the time between the Beatles and younger popular-music

academics grew away from each other. So what happens in the future in relation to this unique master's program is anybody's guess.

The MA is facing an uncertain future as it is anchored to the fixity of academic rules, regulations, a frustratingly slow admissions system, and the
control of dreaded "metrics." Difference and nonconformity in creative
rearticulation should be encouraged in both tourist and academic sectors.
Beatles heritage tourism came from nothing and will survive as long as it
recognizes itself as a multifunctional set of communities, ready to change in
an ever-changing world. Academic initiatives in the city such as those mentioned above have also helped to reinvent Liverpool, not simply via financial
inputs (although this has been important) but also in ways that ask us to rethink apparent certainties. This needs to continue.

The Absolute versus the Ambiguous

Perhaps all mythologies, if they do not pass away altogether, eventually express ambiguities in some way, shape, or form. Usually, a difference comes
to play a part between the instigators of the development of the myth and
the factual existence of the systems promulgated to express and capitalize
on the myth. Time, of course, plays its part in all of this, for although most
popular-music mythologies emphasize the fact that the absolute is still per-
ceivable, although, say, Presley will always be the mythological king of rock
and roll, we also appreciate that the "Elvis" we imagine was not the "real"
Presley. The myth will always be placed under pressure by temporal and spatial erosion, and while the "timelessness" of the auteur is a good cliché, it is
less credible in a changing world where absolute reality will always be sullied
by time, place transformation, and relativity. Green Badge guide Martin further informed me:

> In terms of Liverpool and popular-music histories, errors are being made.
> I've learned over time that the myths surrounding the Beatles and Liverpool
> have turned into concrete statements without proper research to back them
> up. For example, the Cunard Yanks are real enough, but, you know, where
> are the records? Also, time changes everything. I was studiously watching a
> large group of Chinese tourists at the Beatles Story last month [May 2018].
> They were in and out of the exhibition in about 15 minutes. It left me won-
> dering whether they were at all interested in the Beatles or indeed whether

they had the slightest idea of what they were looking at. They didn't even last long in the Beatles Shop—very interesting, I thought. Was the Beatles Story just part of an itinerary of things to do? Let's have more research, both in terms of histories and myths and also the future of tourism.[20]

Following the advent of the Beatles in 1963, Liverpool came to be regarded as a prescribed "special" place; after all, the Beatles were, it seems, self-evidently "special," having supposedly risen above the ranks of post–World War II British urban decline and mediocrity. This was explained to the British public mostly via the audiovisual contract (radio, TV, film, etc.), and Liverpool was designated an "edgy" place. For example, Daniel Farson in his 1963 documentary *Beat City* described Liverpool as a "hard drinking, hard fighting and hardly pleasant" place.[21] Within this audiovisual "reality," and according to the matrix of the audiovisual contract, a presumed continuum between place and auteur was presented as "self-evident." It then came to be sold to the world as "authentic" experience.

Thus, simulacrum emerged, and the "history of the Beatles" came to be oddly sustained by the city of Liverpool. But were these really the Beatles, and was this really the city? Are we quite sure we are not replicating an audiovisual contract of both the Beatles and Liverpool *as* history? The inarticulate stereotype is clear: across local guiding mono-narratives, Liverpool is a city that stretches people's imaginations and critical sensibilities and creates space for those who feel that they must express themselves past the point of toleration. Liverpool is a place, it seems, where new tactics and strategies have come into being that draw upon not only a radical tradition but also new ways of transmitting ideology. But is it? One wonders these days whether any of the surviving Beatles, or indeed the many thousands of Liverpudlians supposedly "left behind," actually recognize themselves in such mono-representations.

So, for me, it has become increasingly evident that the Beatles tourism sector (a better word than *industry*, I feel) needs to be more open to change and willing to work in partnership with other sectors such as the creative and performing arts, rather than merely resort to income generation via a tourist-inclined, ill-researched historiography. The creative legacy of the Beatles is undeniable. Therefore, the key to future expansion of the sector lies within a youthful enlargement of their true legacy across the creative and performing arts. There needs to be far more "creativity" in the way that legacy is sustained. What the Beatles actually stood for, rather than perhaps who people think they were and are, might just provide young people of the future with an *entitlement* to creative opportunities by and through the legacy of the Beatles. Although the heritage tourism industry in Liverpool emerged in times of great economic difficulties and should be commended for its stubbornness and determination, perhaps the legacy of the Beatles should now more fully embrace what they actually did; their creativity should inspire others and should not be seen as something that sits in a glass case to be "appreciated."

The great pleasure we enjoy in visiting new places with important creative- and performing-arts legacies should not be used as a way of simply "commemorating" the past. Commemorations turn the creative and performing arts into closed spaces. The tactile resilience of the place-form and the capacity of our minds to read the environment in terms other than historical instruction actually suggest to us new ways for the imagination to move away from dominant discourses. Visiting the excellent John and Yoko exhibition in Liverpool in 2018, I was reminded of just how important Yoko Ono has been as a creative and performing artist. It is the artist, not the archaeologist, who is the best reinterpreter of the past. The creative and performing arts of the present support and express further creativity. Younger people are free to explore and to realize their own potential by extending relationships between different aspects of disparate narratives. Such expressions are actually fundamental to the histories of popular music, where a single unitary idea of value and meaning has never really existed. We should all work toward creating a new objectivity for Beatles-related tourism, where the abandonment of the myth of foundation leads to myriad discourses about meaning and value, with open-ended inventiveness "in the name of the Beatles" at the center of the creativity.

In the summer of 2018, another museum opened its doors in Liverpool, called the Magical Beatles Museum (now the Liverpool Beatles Museum). It belonged to Roag Best, brother of Pete Best and the son of Mona Best and Neil Aspinall. Mona Best was the Anglo-Indian woman who effectively handled most of the Beatles' business dealings prior to the arrival of Brian Epstein. The museum houses many artifacts collected by Aspinall and by Roag, Rory, and Pete Best over the decades, but it ostensibly concerns itself with the long-neglected exclusion of Mona Best by the Beatles and Merseybeat narrative. One hopes that its presence creates an ongoing debate surrounding a more culturally heterogeneous and pluralistic Beatles history and historiography. However, what is also at stake is the further canonization of the past via artifacts within Liverpool's built environment. Liverpool must take care that it does not turn itself *into* a museum. The spaces occupied by Roag Best's museum (on Mathew Street) could form a critical and physical resistance, a stance adversarial to the overarching Beatles narrative on the rest of that street, avoiding the usual auterist myth and retaining a sense of the possibilities of heterogeneous traditions by a focus on Roag Best's mum.

I was encouraged by the plan announced in 2018 by the Salvation Army for Strawberry Field, the former children's home in Woolton. This is the building that Lennon could see from the rear of "Mendips"; memories of looking at it as a youngster were an inspiration for his song "Strawberry Fields Forever," which was concerned with how recalling looking at places can create a mental space in which one might perhaps even create a moment of "thirdspace" while contemplating one's own sense of reality. Strawberry Field was turned into not only a visitors' center but also a training center for young people with learning disabilities plus a spiritual place of meditation. Launched with the assistance of Julia Baird and opened to the public in 2019, perhaps an enterprise such as this relates more to the use of memory as a creative rather than mythological process. As a place, Strawberry Field might adhere more to tactile and spiritual possibilities, rather than merely supporting a singular set of values.

In 2006, the Arts Council England produced an interesting document discussing its agenda for the arts in the northwest of England. In the document, "new ways to participate" and "collaborative working among arts organisations" were discussed. The writers pointed out the significance of "building young people's self-confidence and positive life skills" and ways of acknowledging the "diversity of young people's artistic output."[22]

There has never been a better time to consider the creative and performing arts as part of Liverpool's visitor strategy. Liverpool is a wonderful city to visit, but it is also an amazing place in which to learn and create and have one's creativity accredited. Enshrined within an exciting future for Beatles visitors might be a "splendid time guaranteed for all," creatively complementing, rather than replacing, the T-shirts and providing perhaps a little more *un*certainty rather than the usual affirmative absolute convictions. It might even define the legacy of the Beatles as a motivational force by placing young people at the very center of the Beatles' legacy. Who knows, it might just open doors to all kinds of creative rearticulations and performing-arts augmentations. Soja's "thirdspace" "can be described as a creative recombination and extension, one that builds on a Firstspace perspective that is focused on the 'real' material world and a Secondspace perspective that interprets this reality through 'imagined' representations of spatiality."[23]

I have written elsewhere that Liverpool's "built environment presents our bodily sense with historical discourses and reverberating homologies."[24] The built environment of this "Beat City" resonates with immensely complex meanings and echoes derived from important symbolisms and explicit associations. Although in terms of the legacy of the Beatles the orchestration of messages and connotations do need to reflect past associations, they are also required to contribute to the present and, by doing so, stimulate the future.

Notes

1. John Belchem, quoted in Lawrence Saunders, "Worth Fighting For?" *Your Move*, July 16, 2017, 35, https://ymliverpool.com/liverpools-world-heritage-site-status/27523.
2. "Alongside medieval monuments in Kosovo, Liverpool is the only other European site on UNESCO's 'in danger' list. It's a list it was added to in 2012, with the granting of planning permission for the £5.5 billion Liverpool Waters project cited as the main reason." Saunders, "Worth Fighting For?" 34.
3. Michael Brocken, *The 21st Century Legacy of the Beatles* (Farnham, UK: Ashgate, 2015).
4. The Cunard Building was designated to be the new liner terminal (its original function), but the project was shelved.
5. Tom Barber, "Decks Appeal: Cruise Liners Are Revolting, but a New Breed of Boutique Ships Is Making Floating Holiday Hip," *Esquire*, July/August 2018, 29–30.
6. Ernesto Laclau, "Politics and the Limits of Modernity," in *Postmodernism: A Reader*, ed. Thomas Docherty (New York: Columbia University, 1993), 342.
7. Michael Brocken, "Phillips' Sound Recording Services: The Studio That Tourism Forgot," in *Routledge Companion to Popular Music History and Heritage*, ed. Sarah Baker et al. (London: Routledge, 2018), 388–397.
8. Edward Soja, *Thirdspace: Journeys to Los Angeles and Other Real-and-Imagined Places* (Oxford: Blackwell, 1996), 7.
9. Michael Brocken, *Other Voices: Hidden Histories of Liverpool's Popular Music Scenes, 1930s–1970s* (Farnham, UK: Ashgate, 2010), 10.
10. Charlotte Martin, phone interview, July 14, 2018.
11. Brocken, *The 21st Century Legacy*, final chapter.
12. Brocken, *The 21st Century Legacy*, final chapter.
13. UK Music, "Imagine the Value of Music Heritage Tourism in the UK," 2014.
14. Locum Destination Consulting, "Music and Beatles Tourism in the City of Liverpool," report for Liverpool Culture Company and Beatles Industry Group, Haywards Heath, April 2005.
15. Hannah Arendt, *The Human Condition* (Chicago: University of Chicago Press, 1958), 201.

16. Howard, Frances, Steph Brocken, and Nicola Sim. "Youth Work, Arts Practice, and Transdisciplinary Space." *In The Sage Handbook of Youth Work Practice,* eds. Pam Alldred, Fin Cullen, Kathy Edwards, and Dana Fusco (London: Sage, 2018), 274.
17. Howard et al., "Youth Work," 274.
18. Shelley Ruck, email, September 2018.
19. Interviewed by Frank Kermode, "Is an Elite Necessary?" BBC Radio, November 5, 1970.
20. Martin, personal interview, May 21, 2018.
21. Daniel Farson, *Beat City*, TV documentary, Associated Rediffusion, December 24, 1963.
22. Arts Council England, "Our Agenda for the Arts in the North West," Manchester, 1–4.
23. Soja, *Thirdspace*, 6.
24. Brocken, "Phillips' Sound Recording Services, 396.

Bibliography

Arendt, Hannah. *The Human Condition*. Chicago: University of Chicago Press, 1958.

Arts Council England. "Our Agenda for the Arts in the North West." Manchester, 2006.

Barber, Tom. "Decks Appeal: Cruise Liners Are Revolting, but a New Breed of Boutique Ships Is Making Floating Holiday Hip." *Esquire*, July/August 2018, 29–30.

Brocken, Michael. *Other Voices: Hidden Histories of Liverpool's Popular Music Scenes, 1930s–1970s*. Farnham, UK: Ashgate, 2010.

Brocken, Michael. "Phillips' Sound Recording Services: The Studio That Tourism Forgot." In *The Routledge Companion to Popular Music History and Heritage*, edited by Sarah Baker, Catherine Strong, Lauren Istvandity, and Zelmarie Cantillon, 388–397. London: Routledge, 2018.

Brocken, Michael. *The 21st Century Legacy of the Beatles*. Farnham, UK: Ashgate, 2015.

Farson, Daniel. *Beat City*. TV documentary, Associated Rediffusion, December 24, 1963.

Kermode, Frank. Interview of Michael Nyman. "Is an Elite Necessary?" BBC Radio, November 5, 1970.

Laclau, Ernesto. "Politics and the Limits of Modernity." In *Postmodernism: A Reader*, ed. Thomas Docherty, 329–343. New York: Columbia University, 1993.

Locum Destination Consulting. "Music and Beatles Tourism in the City of Liverpool." Report for Liverpool Culture Company and Beatles Industry Group, Haywards Heath, April 2005.

Saunders, Lawrence. "Worth Fighting For?" *Your Move*, July 16, 2017, 34–35, https://ymliverpool.com/liverpools-world-heritage-site-status/27523.

Soja, Edward. *Thirdspace: Journeys to Los Angeles and Other Real-and-Imagined Places*. Oxford: Blackwell, 1996.

UK Music. "Wish You Were Here (Music Tourism Report)," 2013.

Yates, Simeon; Evans, Richard; and Jones, Mike. *Beatles Heritage in Liverpool and Its Economic and Cultural Sector Impact: A Report for Liverpool City Council*. Liverpool: University of Liverpool, 2015.

Biographical Notes

About the Editors

Kenneth Womack is Professor of English and Popular Music at Monmouth University. He is the author or editor of numerous works of nonfiction, including *Reading the Beatles: Cultural Studies, Literary Criticism, and the Fab Four* (2006), *Long and Winding Roads: The Evolving Artistry of the Beatles* (2007), and *The Cambridge Companion to the Beatles* (2009), which was named *The Independent*'s "Music Book of the Year." His award-winning two-volume compendium *The Beatles Encyclopedia: Everything Fab Four* was published in 2014 in celebration of the 50th anniversary of the Beatles' legendary appearance on the *Ed Sullivan Show*. He is the author of a two-volume study of the life and work of Beatles producer George Martin. His most recent books include *Solid State: The Story of Abbey Road and the End of the Beatles* (2019) and *John Lennon 1980: The Last Days in the Life* (2020). Womack is Editor of *Interdisciplinary Literary Studies: A Journal of Criticism and Theory*, published by Penn State University Press, and Co-Editor of the English Association's prodigious *Year's Work in English Studies*, published by Oxford University Press.

Kit O'Toole is a Chicago-based independent scholar who has written about rock, jazz, and soul for more than 25 years. She is the author of *Michael Jackson FAQ* (2015) and *Songs We Were Singing: Guided Tours through the Beatles' Lesser-Known Tracks* (2015). O'Toole is a contributor to the anthologies *Interdisciplinary Essays on Environment and Culture: One Planet, One Humanity, and the Media* (2016), *New Critical Perspectives on the Beatles: Things We Said Today* (2016), and *The Beatles, Sgt. Pepper, and the Summer of Love* (2017). Her work has appeared in such print publications as *Showcase Chicago* and *Goldmine*. She is a longtime contributing editor for *Beatlefan* magazine. As a blogger, O'Toole writes for *Something Else Reviews*, *Blinded by Sound*, and *Cinema Sentries*, and she cohosts the biweekly program *Talk More Talk: A Solo Beatles Videocast*. She received her EdD in Instructional Technology from Northern Illinois University.

About the Contributors

Michael Brocken is an independent scholar. He was formerly Senior Lecturer in Popular Music Studies at Liverpool Hope University, where he founded the world's only master's degree in Beatles-related studies. He has written and broadcast on a wide variety of topics, including the Beatles and Merseybeat, Green Day, Burt Bacharach, British folk music and industry, and rugby league football. In addition to hosting Great Britain's longest-running specialist music radio program, *BBC Radio Merseyside's Folk Scene*, he is the author of *The Twenty-First-Century Legacy of the Beatles: Liverpool and Popular Music Heritage Tourism* (2015).

Kenneth L. Campbell is Professor of History at Monmouth University. He is the author of *A History of the British Isles: Prehistory to the Present* (2017), named by the American Library Association as a Choice Outstanding Academic title. Campbell's other books include *Ireland's History: Prehistory to the Present* (2014), *Windows into Men's Souls: Religious Nonconformity in Tudor and Early Stuart England* (2012), *Western Civilization: A Global and Comparative Approach*, Vol. 1, *To 1715*, and Vol. 2, *Since 1600* (2012), and *The Intellectual Struggle of the English Papists in the Seventeenth Century* (1986). His next book, *The Beatles and the 1960s: Reception, Revolution, and Social Change*, is forthcoming in 2021.

Mark Duffett is Reader in Media and Cultural Studies at the University of Chester. He is widely recognized as an expert on popular music and media fandom, a role cemented by the publication of his book *Understanding Fandom* (2013). He has edited two books and various journal special issues in his research area and has published many academic chapters and articles. His expert comments have been featured in *Rolling Stone*, the *New York Times*, TalkSport Radio, and the BBC World Service.

Michael Frontani is an independent writer and scholar and the author of The Beatles: Image and the Media (2007) [CHOICE Outstanding Academic Title, 2008] and several book chapters and journal articles on Beatles-related topics, as well as numerous publications concerning mass media and mass culture.

Aviv Kammay is a music educator at Wingra School in Madison, Wisconsin. He has presented work at key Beatles symposia at universities around the United States, focusing on self-irreverence and humor in the music of the Beatles. A Beatles performer since childhood, Kammay played "John" and "George" as a preteen, and currently leads an ensemble dedicated to accurate live recreations of the entire Beatles core catalog.

Katie Kapurch is Associate Professor of English at Texas State University. Her publications address the intersections of youth, gender, sexuality, and race in pop culture and have appeared in numerous edited collections and journals. Kapurch is the author of *Victorian Melodrama in the Twenty-First Century* (2016) and co-editor of *New Critical Perspectives on the Beatles: Things We Said Today* (2016, with Kenneth Womack). Kapurch's forthcoming books include *Blackbird Singing: Black America Remixes the Beatles*, which is supported by a grant from the National Endowment for the Humanities, and *Sex and Gender in Rock and Pop: From the Beatles to Beyoncé* (with Walter Everett).

Mark Lapidos founded the Fest for Beatles Fans in 1974. During the April 1974 March of Dimes Walkathon in New York City, he met with John Lennon at the Pierre Hotel and pitched the idea of a Beatles fan-related event. "I'm all for it! I'm a Beatles fan too!" Lennon responded. That September, Lapidos held the inaugural Fest, attracting more than 8,000 Beatles devotees. In the intervening years, Lapidos has hosted annual events in New York and Chicago.

Candy Leonard is the author of *Beatleness: How the Beatles and Their Fans Remade the World* (2014), as well as a sociologist, first-generation Beatles fan, and Beatles scholar. She has spent her career studying the effects of popular culture on human development, gender relations, and family life, and she is a qualitative research consultant to the healthcare and entertainment industries, with a focus on baby boomer issues. She lives in Cambridge, Massachusetts.

Richard Mills is a Senior Lecturer at St. Mary's University, where his research interests include Irish literature and popular culture. He served as Program Director for Cultural Studies at St. Mary's from 2006 to 2012 and Program Director for Screen Media in 2013. In 2019, he published *The Beatles and Fandom: Sex, Death, and Progressive Nostalgia.*

Punch Shaw is a journalist and educator from Fort Worth, Texas, who began his career as a music critic with a review of a George Harrison concert in 1974. For the past 25 years, he has been a frequent contributor to the arts pages of the *Fort Worth Star-Telegram*, writing a wide range of performing-arts reviews and features. He has also taught a variety of courses for various departments at Texas Christian University, on topics that have included film history, basic journalism, and the Beatles and the 1960s.

Index

For the benefit of digital users, indexed terms that span two pages (e.g., 52–53) may, on occasion, appear on only one of those pages.